Y0-BPW-424

SCHOLASTIC

LITERACY PLACE

IT WORKS...AND KIDS LIKE IT!

SCHOLASTIC

SCHOLASTIC

LITERACY PLACE

IT WORKS...AND KIDS LIKE IT!

Manageable Instructional Plans

Literacy Place follows a clear, consistent pattern of instruction and provides support for all learners. The Teacher's Edition includes explicit skills instruction and integrates the language arts.

The Strongest System for Beginning Readers

Literacy Place provides direct instruction in phonics and phonological awareness and fully reflects current and confirmed research.

Assessment Tools to Monitor and Modify Instruction

Literacy Place features focused assessment that informs instruction and measures progress. The program offers strategies targeting students who need skills intervention, language-development support, and enrichment.

Power and Confidence for the Information Age

Literacy Place uses technology as an integral part of learning while connecting the classroom to the real world.

The Matrix

	PERSONAL LITERACY **Personal Voice** We communicate in our unique voices as we grow and learn.	INTELLECTUAL LITERACY **Problem Solving** People have the power to solve problems.	SOCIAL LITERACY **Teamwork** Successful teams depend on the collaboration of individuals.
K	**Stories About Us** **Big Idea** We listen to, tell, and create stories. **Mentor** Grandmother: *Honey Wada* **Place** Storytelling Corner **Project** "All About Me" Class Book	**See It, Solve It** **Big Idea** We see problems and find solutions. **Mentor** Clay Animator: *Becky Wible* **Place** Claymator's Studio **Project** Dramatization	**All Together Now!** **Big Idea** We share and help each other. **Mentor** Pizza Maker: *Kwaku Twumasi* **Place** Restaurant **Project** Big Book of Menus
1	**Hello!** **Big Idea** We share what we like. **Mentor** Author: *Donald Crews* **Place** Writer's Home **Project** Scrapbook	**Problem Patrol** **Big Idea** There are many kinds of problems. **Mentor** Veterinarian: *Fay Vittetoe* **Place** Veterinarian's Office **Project** Pet Care Guide	**Team Spirit** **Big Idea** It's fun to do things together. **Mentor** Soccer Coach: *Danny Prenat* **Place** Soccer Stadium **Project** Game Rule Book
2	**Snapshots** **Big Idea** Our actions tell about us. **Mentor** Photographer: *Bruce Thorson* **Place** Sports Arena **Project** Exhibit	**Super Solvers** **Big Idea** There may be more than one way to solve a problem. **Mentor** Toy Designer: *Mary Rodas* **Place** Toy Company **Project** Safety Poster Campaign	**Lights! Camera! Action!** **Big Idea** Creative teams produce great performances. **Mentor** Theater Director: *Judith Martin* **Place** Children's Theater **Project** Play Production
3	**What's New?** **Big Idea** We learn about our world through new experiences. **Mentor** Wilderness Guide: *Keith Jardine* **Place** Wilderness School **Project** Anecdote	**Big Plans** **Big Idea** Making and using plans can help us solve problems. **Mentor** Architect: *Jack Catlin* **Place** Construction Site **Project** Floor Plan	**On the Job** **Big Idea** Teams work best when they use each member's strengths to get the job done. **Mentor** Art Director: *Max Jerome* **Place** Ad Agency **Project** Ad Campaign
4	**Chapter by Chapter** **Big Idea** We are always adding to our life story. **Mentor** Author: *Jerry Spinelli* **Place** Bookstore **Project** Personal Narrative	**What an Idea!** **Big Idea** People solve problems by inventing new things. **Mentor** Inventor: *Julie Lewis* **Place** Inventor's Office **Project** Invention Marketing Plan	**Discovery Teams** **Big Idea** When we work as a team, we learn new things about our world. **Mentor** Astronaut: *Dr. Mae Jemison* **Place** Space Center **Project** Multimedia Presentation
5	**Making a Difference** **Big Idea** Each of us is inspired by the lives of others. **Mentor** Musician: *Joseph Shabalala* **Place** Concert Hall **Project** Tribute	**It's a Mystery** **Big Idea** We can solve mysteries using reason, logic, and intuition. **Mentor** Forensic Chemist: *Lilly Gallman* **Place** Detective Headquarters **Project** Investigative Report	**Voyagers** **Big Idea** We depend on a network of people when we explore. **Mentor** Travel Agent: *Marie French* **Place** Travel Agency **Project** Travel Magazine

scholastic.com
Look for the Unit-by-Unit Extensions in the Literacy Place area.

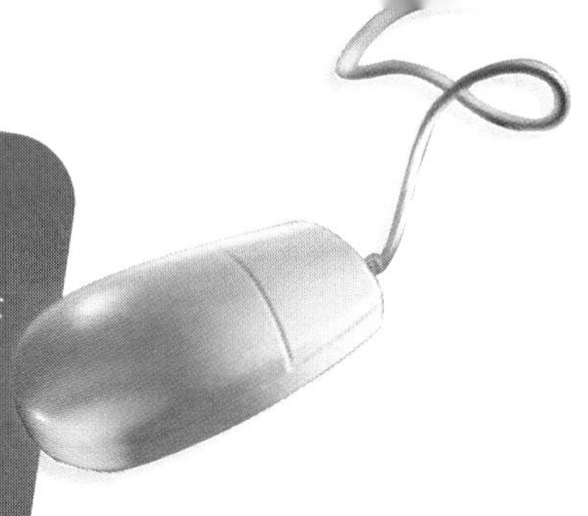

PERSONAL LITERACY

Creative Expression

People express themselves in many creative ways.

Express Yourself

Big Idea We express ourselves through songs, sounds, stories, dance, and art.
Mentor Author: *Pat Mora*
Place Author's Studio
Project Storybook

Imagine That!

Big Idea Imagination lets us look at things in new ways.
Mentor Muralist: *William Walsh*
Place Artist's Studio
Project Story Mural

Story Studio

Big Idea People express themselves through stories and pictures.
Mentor Author & Artist: *Tomie dePaola*
Place Author's Studio
Project Picture Book

Hit Series

Big Idea A creative idea can grow into a series.
Mentor Author & Illustrator: *Joanna Cole & Bruce Degen*
Place Publishing Company
Project New Episode

The Funny Side

Big Idea Sometimes humor is the best way to communicate.
Mentor Cartoonist: *Robb Armstrong*
Place Cartoonist's Studio
Project Comic Strip

In the Spotlight

Big Idea We use our creativity to reach an audience.
Mentor Drama Coach: *José García*
Place Actor's Workshop
Project Stage Presentation

INTELLECTUAL LITERACY

Managing Information

Finding and using information helps us live in our world.

I Spy!

Big Idea Information is all around us.
Mentor Farmer: *Steven Powell*
Place Gardening Center
Project Garden Journal

Information Finders

Big Idea Information comes from many sources.
Mentor Marine Biologist: *Laela Sayigh*
Place Aquarium
Project Big Book of Information

Animal World

Big Idea We use information to understand the interdependence of people and animals.
Mentor Zoo Curator: *Lisa Stevens*
Place Zoo
Project Zoo Brochure

Time Detectives

Big Idea Finding information in stories and artifacts brings the past to life.
Mentor Archaeologist: *Dr. Ruben Mendoza*
Place Archaeological Site
Project Time Capsule

Nature Guides

Big Idea Gathering and using information help us understand and describe the natural world.
Mentor Park Ranger: *Veronica Gonzales-Vest*
Place National Park Headquarters
Project Field Guide

America's Journal

Big Idea Considering different points of view gives us a fuller understanding of history.
Mentor Historian/Author: *Russell Freedman*
Place Historical Museum
Project Historical Account

SOCIAL LITERACY

Community Involvement

Communities are built on the contributions of the people who live there.

Join In!

Big Idea We help our community.
Mentor Singer/Songwriter: *Tom Chapin*
Place Performance Stage
Project Community Sing

Home Towns

Big Idea We are all members of a community.
Mentor Mayor: *Steve Yamashiro*
Place Mayor's Office
Project Visitor's Map

Lend a Hand

Big Idea People can make a difference in their communities.
Mentor Police Officer: *Nadine Jojola*
Place Police Station
Project Community Expo

Community Quilt

Big Idea In a community, some things continue and some things change.
Mentor Community Garden Director: *Lorka Muñoz*
Place Community Garden
Project Community Quilt

It Takes a Leader

Big Idea In every community there are people who inspire others to take action.
Mentor Editor: *Suki Cheong*
Place Newspaper Office
Project Op-Ed Page

Cityscapes

Big Idea Cities depend on the strengths and skills of the people who live and work there.
Mentor Urban Planner: *Karen Heit*
Place Urban Planner's Office
Project Action Plan

Components

Pupil's Editions & Teacher's Editions

Kindergarten Place
Kindergarten Place
SCHOLASTIC
Tell a story about what is happening in each picture.

K

Literacy Place Kindergarten

provides a rich learning environment including Big Books, Read Alouds, Sentence Strips, Audiocassettes, Phonics Manipulatives, Workbooks, Teacher Editions, and much more.

1

SCHOLASTIC
LITERACY PLACE

TEACHER'S EDITION
LITERACY PLACE

Grades 1-5

- Literacy Place brings you what you would expect from Scholastic—authentic, award-winning children's literature.
- Our Teacher's Editions are easy to use, and provide explicit skills instruction.
- You'll also find a management CD-ROM to help you customize instruction to state and district standards.

2

SCHOLASTIC
LITERACY PLACE

TEACHER'S EDITION
LITERACY PLACE

3

SCHOLASTIC
LITERACY PLACE

TEACHER'S EDITION
LITERACY PLACE

scholastic.com
Check it out! You'll find a wealth of professional support resources, plus a lot of great stuff for kids and parents.

4

SCHOLASTIC
LITERACY PLACE

TEACHER'S EDITION
LITERACY PLACE

5

SCHOLASTIC
LITERACY PLACE

TEACHER'S EDITION
LITERACY PLACE

Pupil's Editions | **Teacher's Editions**

Support Materials

SCHOLASTIC LITERACY PLACE
SCHOLASTIC LITERACY PLACE
LITERACY PLACE
LITERACY PLACE
ESL/E
gate
late
bake
rake

Practice Literacy Place includes comprehensive practice resources.

- ✔ My Reading Workbook (1)
- ✔ Workshop and Project Cards (K-2)
- ✔ Practice Books (1-5)
- ✔ Spelling Resource Book (1-5)
- ✔ Grammar Resource Book (1-5)
- ✔ Handwriting Practice Book (K-3)
- ✔ ESL/ELD Resource Book (K-5)
- ✔ Skills Overhead Transparencies (2-5)
- ✔ Vocabulary Overhead Transparencies (2-5)
- ✔ Place Cards (3-5)

Assessment Literacy Place provides a wide range of assessment and evaluation options. (K-5)

- ✔ Placement Tests
- ✔ Assessment Handbook
- ✔ Classroom Management Forms
- ✔ Selection Tests (for every story!)
- ✔ Unit Tests (Forms A and B)
- ✔ Oral Reading Assessment
- ✔ Scholastic Reading Inventory
- ✔ TAAS Preparation and Practice Book
- ✔ Assessment System CD-ROM

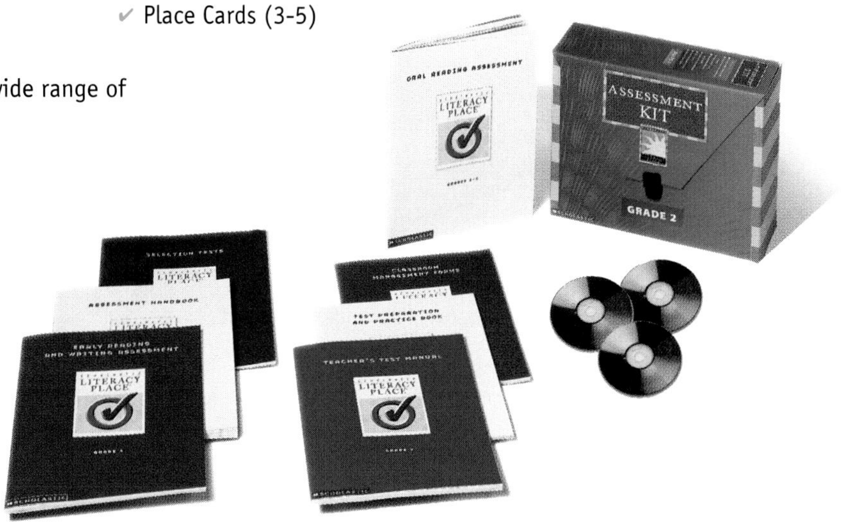
ASSESSMENT KIT
GRADE 2
LITERACY PLACE

MENTOR VIDEO
THE BEGINNING READER
SMART PLACE
Cityscapes

Technology We set the industry standard.

- ✔ Phonics Practice CD-ROM (K-2)
- ✔ WiggleWorks Plus CD-ROM (K-2)
- ✔ Smart Place CD-ROM (3-5)
- ✔ Scholastic Management Suite (K-5)
- ✔ Staff Development Videos (K-5)
- ✔ Meet the Mentor Videos (K-5)
- ✔ Scholastic Network (K-5)
- ✔ Selection Audiocassettes (1-5)
- ✔ Classroom Resources CD-ROM (K-5)

Scholastic Solutions Only Scholastic can offer you the diverse range of materials you need for your classroom. Please call 1-800-Scholastic for a catalog. Ask about these exciting products:

- ✔ High-Frequency Readers (K-1)
- ✔ Sound and Letter Books (K-1)
- ✔ Big Books/Little Books (K-2)
- ✔ Phonemic Awareness Kit (K-2)
- ✔ Phonics Readers (K-3)
- ✔ Phonics Chapter Books (1-3)
- ✔ Phonics Workbooks (K-2)
- ✔ Guided Reading Program (K-5)
- ✔ Bilingual Support (K-5)
- ✔ Solares (K-5)
- ✔ Transition Program (3-6)
- ✔ Sprint Plus Intervention (3-6)
- ✔ READ 180 (4-8)
- ✔ Reading Counts! (K-8)

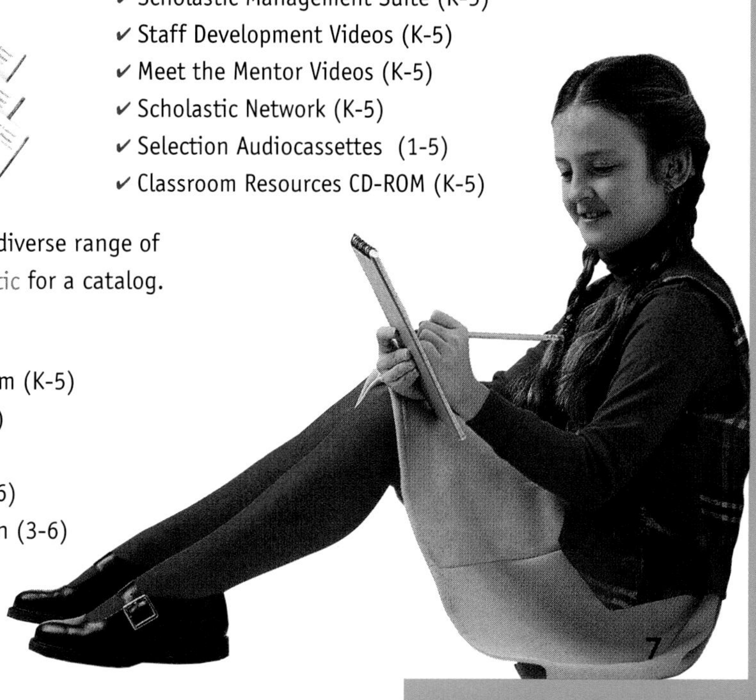

Advisors

Program Consultants

SKILLS, STRATEGIES, INSTRUCTION
James Bauman
Professor, University of Georgia,
Athens, Georgia

PHONICS AND EARLY READING
Wiley Blevins
Consultant and Educational Writer
New York, New York

ESL/ELD
Jacqueline Kiraithe-Cordova
Professor, California State, California

STAFF DEVELOPMENT
Nancy Cummings
Western Director of Implementation
Success For All School Restructuring
Phoenix, Arizona

BILINGUAL EDUCATION
James Cummins
Professor, Ontario Institute for
Studies in Education
Ontario, Canada

EARLY LITERACY DEVELOPMENT
Nell K. Duke
Michigan State University

ASSESSMENT/WRITING
Adele Fiderer
Consultant and Educational Writer
Scarsdale, New York

HANDWRITING
Steve Graham
Professor, University of Maryland
College Park, Maryland

WRITING
Shelley Harwayne
Director of Manhattan New School
New York, New York

SPELLING
Richard E. Hodges
Professor, University of Puget Sound
Tacoma, Washington

SPELLING
Louisa Moats
County Office of Education
Sacramento, California

VOCABULARY
William E. Nagy
Assistant Professor, University of Illinois
Champaign-Urbana, Illinois

FLEXIBLE GROUPING
Michael Opitz
Professor, University of Colorado
Boulder, Colorado

ESL/ELD
Robert Parker
Consultant, Brown University
Providence, Rhode Island

ESL/ELD
Cao Anh Quan
ESOL Program Specialist
Tallahassee, Florida

ESL/ELD
Kim Quan Nguyen-Lam
California State University
Long Beach, California

WRITING
Michael Strickland
Author, Consultant
Orange, New Jersey

Teacher Reviewers

Kim Andrews
Fourth Grade Reviewer
Baltimore, Maryland

Shirley Beard
Fourth Grade Reviewer
El Paso, Texas

Barbara Bloom
Fifth Grade Reviewer
Wall Lake, Iowa

Sherry Brown
Third Grade Reviewer
Georgetown, Texas

Lisa Buchholz
First Grade Reviewer
Wheaton, Illinois

Kathy Burdick
Fifth Grade Reviewer
Austin, Texas

Marianne Chorba
Fourth Grade Reviewer
Baltimore, Maryland

Peggy Colley
Third Grade Reviewer
Rocky Face, Georgia

Carol Curry
Third Grade Reviewer
Tallahassee, Florida

Claire Dale
First Grade Reviewer
National City, California

Mildred DeStefano
First Grade Reviewer
Brooklyn, New York

Doris Dillan
Grade Two Reviewer
San Jose, California

Oneaster Drummer
First Grade Reviewer
Cincinnati, Ohio

Ethel Durham
Third Grade Reviewer
Grand Rapids, Michigan

Patty Ernst
Second Grade Reviewer
Naples, New York

Alzada Fowler
First Grade Reviewer
Lake Helen, Florida

Jane Ginn
First Grade Reviewer
Rohnert Park, California

Amy Gordon
Third Grade Reviewer
New City, New York

Janet Gray
Fourth Grade Reviewer
Lake Helen, Florida

Velma Gunn
Fourth Grade Reviewer
New Rochelle, New York

Annie Ruth Harris
Third Grade Reviewer
Decatur, Alabama

Barbara Ann Hawkins
Second Grade Reviewer
Hamer, South Carolina

Amy Hom
Second Grade Reviewer
New York, New York

Min Hong
First Grade Reviewer
Brooklyn, New York

Susan Howe
Third Grade Reviewer
Ellicott City, Maryland

Barbara Jansz
First Grade Reviewer
Naperville, Illinois

Michele Jessen
First Grade Reviewer
El Paso, Texas

Ellen W. Johnson
Second Grade Reviewer
Chalfont, Pennsylvania

Vera Johnson
First Grade Reviewer
Uniondale, New York

Carol Kaiser
Third Grade Reviewer
Los Angeles, California

Karen Kolsky
Third Grade Reviewer
Philadelphia, Pennsylvania

Judy Keyak
Second Grade Reviewer
St. Petersburg, Florida

Jacqueline Krass
Second Grade Reviewer
Gulfport, Mississippi

Warren Livesley
Fourth Grade Reviewer
New York, New York

Libby Lesley
First Grade Reviewer
San Angelo, Texas

Dora I. Magana
Fourth Grade Reviewer
El Paso, Texas

Tim Mason
Second Grade Reviewer
Willington Florida

Carol Mercer
Fourth Grade Reviewer
National City, California

Betty Milburn
Third Grade Reviewer
Grand Prairie, Texas

Jane Moore
Third Grade Reviewer
Dallas, Texas

Sandy Nolan
Third Grade Reviewer
Salem, Wisconsin

Carol Ochs
Fifth Grade Reviewer
Noble, Oklahoma

Lynn Olson
Fifth Grade Reviewer
Omaha, Nebraska

Cynthia Orange
Second Grade Reviewer
Bronx, New York

Sue Panek
Fourth Grade Reviewer
Hawthorne, New Jersey

Deborah Peale
Fourth Grade Reviewer
Miami, Florida

Arturo Perez
Second Grade Reviewer
Ventura, California

Jeanette Reber
First Grade Reviewer
Rock Hill, South Carolina

Charlene Richardson
Fourth Grade Reviewer
Everett, Washington

Daria Rigney
Fifth Grade Reviewer
Brooklyn, New York

Andrea Ruff
First Grade Reviewer
Brooklyn, New York

Carol Shirmang
First Grade Reviewer
Palatine, Illinois

Wendy Smiley
Fourth Grade Reviewer
Syracuse, New York

Barbara Solomon
Second Grade Reviewer
Hempstead, New York

Alicia Sparkman
First Grade Reviewer
Plant City, Florida

Elaine Steinberg
Third Grade Reviewer
Fresh Meadows, New York

Bobby Stern
Third Grade Reviewer
Winston-Salem, North Carolina

Laura Stewart
First Grade Reviewer

Kate Taylor
Fifth Grade Reviewer
Baltimore, Maryland

Vasilika Terss
Second Grade Reviewer
St. Louis, Missouri

Linda Thorn
Fifth Grade Reviewer
Cranford, New Jersey

Gayle Thurn
Second Grade Reviewer
Piedmont, South Carolina

Jerry Trotter
Fifth Grade Reviewer
Chicago, Illinois

Julia Tucker
First Grade Reviewer
Hampton, Virginia

Patricia Viales
First Grade Reviewer
Salinas, California

Janielle Wagstaff
Second Grade Reviewer
Salt Lake City, Utah

Gail Weber
Fourth Grade Reviewer
Sherman Oaks, California

Elizabeth White
First Grade Reviewer
Bronx, New York

Karla Hawkins-Windeline
Second Grade Reviewer
Hickman, Nebraska

National Advisory Council

Barbara R. Foorman, Ph. D.
Professor of Pediatrics
Director of the Center for
Academic and Reading Skills
Houston, TX

Dr. Wilmer Cody
Commissioner of Education
Kentucky State Department
of Education
Frankfort, KY

Ms. Judy Mountjoy
Vice President
The National PTA
Chicago, IL

Ms. Anne Bryant
Executive Director
National School Boards
Association
Alexandria, VA

Dr. Anthony Alvarado
Chancellor for Instruction
San Diego City Schools
San Diego, CA

TEACHER'S EDITION

SCHOLASTIC

LITERACY PLACE®

UNIT 4

Imagine That!

Literacy Place Authors

Cathy Collins Block
Professor, Curriculum and Instruction, Texas Christian University

Linda B. Gambrell
Professor, Education, University of Maryland at College Park

Virginia Hamilton
Children's Author; Winner of the Newbery Medal, the Coretta Scott King Award and the Laura Ingalls Wilder Lifetime Achievement Award

Douglas K. Hartman
Associate Professor of Language and Literacy, University of Pittsburgh

Ted S. Hasselbring
Co-Director of the Learning Technology Center and Professor in the Department of Special Education at Peabody College, Vanderbilt University

Adria Klein
Professor, Reading and Teacher Education, California State University at San Bernardino

Hilda Medrano
Dean, College of Education, University of Texas-Pan American

Gay Su Pinnell
Professor, School of Teaching and Learning, College of Education, Ohio State University

D. Ray Reutzel
Provost/Academic Vice President, Southern Utah University

David Rose
Founder and Executive Director of the Center for Applied Special Technology (CAST); Lecturer, Harvard University Graduate School of Education

Alfredo Schifini
Professor, School of Education, Division of Curriculum Instruction, California State University, Los Angeles

Delores Stubblefield Seamster
Principal, N.W. Harllee Elementary, Dallas, Texas; Consultant on Effective Programs for Urban Inner City Schools

Quality Quinn Sharp
Author and Teacher-Educator, Austin, Texas

John Shefelbine
Professor, Language and Literacy Education, California State University at Sacramento

Gwendolyn Y. Turner
Associate Professor of Literacy Education, University of Missouri at St. Louis

No part of this publication may be reproduced in whole or in part, or stored in a retrieval system, or transmitted in any form or by any means, electronic, mechanical, photocopying, recording, or otherwise, without written permission of the publisher. For information regarding permission, write to Scholastic Inc., Education Group, 555 Broadway, New York, NY 10012. Scholastic Inc. grants teachers who have purchased *Scholastic Literacy Place* permission to reproduce from this book those pages intended for use in their classrooms. Notice of copyright must appear on all copies of copyrighted materials.

Acknowledgments and credits appear on pages R123–R124, which constitute an extension of this copyright page.

Copyright © 2000 by Scholastic Inc. All rights reserved.

Published by Scholastic Inc. Printed in the U.S.A.

ISBN 0-439-07886-5 (National)

SCHOLASTIC, SCHOLASTIC LITERACY PLACE, and associated logos and designs are trademarks and/or registered trademarks of Scholastic Inc.

3 4 5 6 7 8 9 10 14 07 06 05 04 03 02 01 00

TABLE OF CONTENTS

Imagine That!

THEME
Imagination lets us look at things in new ways.

Chicken Pedro and the Falling Sky

The Night Sky

IN THE Attic

Starring First Grade

THE THREE BILLY GOATS GRUFF

GOING HOME
PIERRE
A cautionary tale IN FIVE CHAPTERS AND A PROLOGUE
MAURICE SENDAK
JENNY'S JOURNEY

Trade Book Library

UNIT AT A GLANCE
READ

LITERATURE	PHONICS	COMPREHENSION	VOCABULARY	LISTENING/ SPEAKING/ VIEWING
WEEK 1 *Chicken Pedro and the Falling Sky* pp. T24–T39	☑ **FINAL** *e (a-e)*, p. T22 ☑ **INFLECTIONAL ENDING** -*ing*, p. T46	☑ **MAKE INFERENCES,** p. T44	☑ **HIGH-FREQUENCY:** *soon, went,* p. T20 • **STORY WORDS:** *lemon, sky, sun, king, cave, cake,* p. T21	• **MAKE UP A CONVERSATION,** p. T59 • **RADIO NEWS BROADCAST,** p. T59 • **MAKE A CLASS BOOK,** p. T60 • **MAKE UP A SCENE,** p. T60
WEEK 2 *The Night Sky* pp. T72–T85	☑ **FINAL** *e (e-e, i-e, o-e, u-e)*, p. T70 ☑ **VOWEL** /ē/*ea, ee*, p. T92	**CATEGORIZE INFORMATION,** p. T90	☑ **HIGH-FREQUENCY:** *some, many,* p. T68 • **STORY WORDS:** *stars, planets, night, shine, moon, light,* p. T69	• **WRITE ABOUT THE DAY SKY,** p. T105 • **WRITE A POSTCARD,** p. T105 • **MAKE A MOBILE,** p. T106 • **WRITE DIRECTIONS,** p. T106
WEEK 3 *In the Attic* pp. T122–T146	☑ *l*-**BLENDS,** p. T120 ☑ *r*-**BLENDS,** p. T152	**PLOT,** p. T150	☑ **HIGH-FREQUENCY:** *look, about,* p. T118 • **STORY WORDS:** *bored, attic, toys, game, talk, ladder,* p. T119	• **IMAGINE YOUR OWN STORY,** p. T165 • **MAKE A RHYMING CHAIN,** p. T165 • **RETELL THE STORY,** p. T166 • **WRITE DIALOGUE,** p. T166
WEEK 4 *Starring First Grade* pp. T178–T205	☑ *s*-**BLENDS,** p. T176 ☑ **DIGRAPHS** /ch/*ch*, /hw/*wh*, p. T212	☑ **SEQUENCE,** p. T210	☑ **HIGH-FREQUENCY:** *which, make,* p. T174 • **STORY WORDS:** *actors, first, story, play, troll, goat,* p. T175	• **ADD TO THE STORY,** p. T225 • **ACT OUT A PLAY,** p. T225 • **BE A REPORTER,** p. T226 • **INTERVIEW A CHARACTER,** p. T226
WEEK 5 *The Three Billy Goats Gruff* pp. T242–T257	☑ **CONTRACTIONS,** p. T240 ☑ **PLURALS,** p. T262	**DRAW CONCLUSIONS,** p. T260	☑ **HIGH-FREQUENCY:** *were, way,* p. T238 • **STORY WORDS:** *problem, lunch, bridge, booth, dime, nickel,* p. T239	• **RETELL THE STORY,** p. T275 • **ACT OUT THE PLAY,** p. T275 • **DRAW A COMIC STRIP,** p. T276 • **CREATE A NEW STORY,** p. T276

WEEK 6

Unit Wrap-Up
pp. T277–T293

TRADE BOOK LIBRARY

• *Pierre*, by Maurice Sendak
  AVERAGE

• *Jenny's Journey*, by Sheila White Samton
  EASY

• *Going Home*, by Margaret Wild
  CHALLENGE

✓ = TESTED SKILL ✓= TESTED WORD

WRITE		EXTEND SKILLS		
SPELLING/ GRAMMAR, USAGE, MECHANICS	**WRITING**	**INTEGRATED CURRICULUM**	**REAL WORLD SKILLS/ STUDY SKILLS**	**LEVELED RESOURCES**
✓ **SPELLING:** Words With Final *e (a-e)*, pp. R4–R5 ✓ **GRAMMAR, USAGE, MECHANICS:** Word Order, pp. R6–R7	✓ **SHARED WRITING:** Stories with Animal Characters, p. T50 • **JOURNAL,** p. T24	• **MATH:** Math, p. R8 • **SCIENCE:** Find Out About the Sun, p. R8 • **SOCIAL STUDIES:** Spreading the News, p. R9 • **THE ARTS:** Make Paintings of the Sky, p. R9	• **MEET THE MENTOR VIDEO,** p. T9 • **READ ALOUD:** *Curious George Rides a Bike*, p. T54 • **TECHNOLOGY:** pp. T20, T22, T31, T37, T43, T46, T48, T51, T55, T60	• **PHONICS READERS:** *The Big Race* *The Pancake Man* • **PHONICS CHAPTER BOOK:** *The Puppet Club* • **MY BOOKS:** *Make a Face* • **GUIDED READING PROGRAM**
✓ **SPELLING:** Words With Final *e (i-e, o-e)*, pp. R12–R13 ✓ **GRAMMAR, USAGE, MECHANICS:** Capitalizing Titles, pp. R14–R15	✓ **SHARED WRITING:** List of Tips, p. T96 • **JOURNAL,** p. T72	• **MATH:** Count the Days, p. R16 • **SCIENCE:** Model Sun, Earth, and Moon, p. R16 • **SOCIAL STUDIES:** Retell Moon Tale, p. R17 • **THE ARTS:** Make a Space Mobile, p. R17	• **WORKSHOP 1:** How to Make a Story Plan, p. T107 ✓ **STUDY SKILLS:** Sort/Organize Information, p. T101 • **TECHNOLOGY:** pp. T68, T70, T77, T85, T89, T92, T94, T97, T99, T101, T106	• **PHONICS READERS:** *Lime Ice Is Nice, Hen Pen's Joke, The Three Little Pigs, The Street Band* • **PHONICS CHAPTER BOOK:** *The Puppet Club* • **MY BOOKS:** *Alone* *What Did You See?* • **GUIDED READING PROGRAM**
✓ **SPELLING:** Words With *l*-Blends, pp. R20–R21 ✓ **GRAMMAR, USAGE, MECHANICS:** Irregular Verbs, pp. R22–R23	✓ **SHARED WRITING:** Fantasy Story, p. T156 • **JOURNAL,** p. T122	• **MATH:** Solve Picture Problems, p. R24 • **SCIENCE:** Explore Structures, p. R24 • **SOCIAL STUDIES:** What's Real and What's Not?, p. R25 • **THE ARTS:** What Do You Get When..., p. R25	✓ **STUDY SKILLS:** Graphic Aids: Pictures, p. T160 • **TECHNOLOGY:** pp. T118, T120, T127, T143, T149, T152, T154, T157, T159, T161, T166	• **PHONICS READERS:** *Play the Animal Game! Troll Tricks* • **PHONICS CHAPTER BOOK:** *The Puppet Club* • **MY BOOKS:** *Maggie Bloom's Messy Room* *Grandpa Gray* • **GUIDED READING PROGRAM**
✓ **SPELLING:** Words With *s*-Blends, pp. R28–R29 ✓ **GRAMMAR, USAGE, MECHANICS:** Describing Words, pp. R30–R31	✓ **SHARED WRITING:** Description, p. T216 • **JOURNAL,** p. T178	• **MATH:** Count Characters, p. R32 • **SCIENCE:** Build Model Bridges, p. R33 • **SOCIAL STUDIES:** Cooperation!, p. R33 • **THE ARTS:** Design a Set, p. R33	• **WORKSHOP 2:** How to Sketch, p. T227 **STUDY SKILLS:** Test-Taking Strategies, p. T220 • **TECHNOLOGY:** pp. T174, T176, T187, T193, T209, T212, T221, T226	• **PHONICS READERS:** *Slip Slide Baseball Jokes, Say It and Smile!, Chuck's Lunch, Whale of a Joke!* • **PHONICS CHAPTER BOOK:** *The Puppet Club* • **MY BOOKS:** *Still Snoring, Where Is My Chick?* • **GUIDED READING PROGRAM**
✓ **SPELLING:** Contractions, pp. R36–R37 ✓ **GRAMMAR, USAGE, MECHANICS:** Capitalizing Names and First Words, pp. R38–R39	✓ **SHARED WRITING:** Dialogue, p. T266 • **JOURNAL,** p. T242	• **MATH:** Solve Money Problems, p. R40 • **SCIENCE:** Learn About Goats, p. R40 • **SOCIAL STUDIES:** Map the Play, p. R41 • **THE ARTS:** Make Troll and Goat Masks, p. R41	• **READ ALOUD:** *The Three Billy-Goats Gruff*, p. T270 • **TECHNOLOGY:** pp. T238, T240, T245, T257, T259, T262, T264, T271, T276	• **PHONICS READERS:** *Slip Slide Baseball Jokes, Say It and Smile* • **PHONICS CHAPTER BOOK:** *The Puppet Club* • **MY BOOKS:** *Don't Be Afraid, Lots of Oranges* • **GUIDED READING PROGRAM**

✓ **WRITING PROCESS:** Write a Story With Dialogue

PROJECT: Make a Story Mural

✓ **PRESENTATION SKILL:** Make an Oral Presentation

TECHNOLOGY: WiggleWorks Plus

LAUNCH THE UNIT

UNIT TRADE BOOK LIBRARY

PIERRE
A cautionary tale
IN FIVE CHAPTERS
AND A PROLOGUE
MAURICE SENDAK

Pierre by Maurice Sendak

Challenge
▶ Average
Easy

JENNY'S JOURNEY

Jenny's Journey by Sheila White Samton

Challenge
Average
▶ Easy

GOING HOME
by Margaret Wild
illustrated by Wayne Harris

Going Home by Margaret Wild

▶ Challenge
Average
Easy

KEY

■ Cultural Connections
▲ Kid Picks
✹ Science
★ Social Studies
◆ Math
✚ The Arts

Books for Independent Reading

EASY

Lily Takes a Walk
by Satoshi Kitamura
Puffin, 1991 ▲ ■
Lily enjoys sightseeing with Nicky, her watchdog.

My Daddy and I
by Eloise Greenfield
Writers and Readers, 1991 ■ ★
An African-American child enjoys playing with Daddy.

One Monday Morning
by Uri Shulevitz
Scholastic, 1994 ▲ ◆
In this cumulative tale, a boy dreams up some imaginary playmates.

Together
by George Ellan Lyon
Orchard Books, 1989 ▲ ■
Two girls have fun doing all kinds of things together.

When Sheep Cannot Sleep
by Satoshi Kitamura
Farrar, Straus & Giroux, 1989 ✹ ▲
This funny tale imagines what sheep do at night.

AVERAGE

Harold and the Purple Crayon
by Crockett Johnson
Scholastic, 1993 ▲ ✚
The inimitable Harold gets into and out of exciting situations with the help of his purple crayon.

Henny Penny
by H. W. Zimmerman
Scholastic, 1993 ▲ ■
Henny Penny sets out to tell the king that the sky is falling.

How the Stars Fell Into the Sky
by Jerry Oughton
Illustrated by Lisa Desimini
Houghton Mifflin, 1992 ■ ✹
This simple retelling of a Native American legend explains the origin of the stars.

Ned and the Joybaloo
by Hiawyn Oram
Illustrated by Satoshi Kitamura
Farrar, Straus & Giroux, 1989 ▲ ■
Ned finds a playmate in his closet and his imagination soars.

Three by the Sea
by James Marshall
Puffin, 1994 ▲ ✚
Three friends have a contest to see who can tell the best story.

CHALLENGE

A Boy Wants a Dinosaur
by Hiawyn Oram
Illustrated by Satoshi Kitamura
Farrar, Straus & Giroux, 1991 ✹ ■
Alex convinces his grandfather to buy a dinosaur for a pet.

First Grade Takes a Test
by Miriam Cohen
Dell, 1983 ▲ ■ ★
Anna Marie does so well on a test that she may go to a new class.

Leo and Emily's Big Ideas
by Frank Brandenburg
Illustrated by Aliki
Greenwillow, 1982 ▲ ★
In this chapter book two friends share lots of fun.

What the Moon Is Like
by Franklin M. Branley
Crowell, 1986 ✹ ◆
An introductory book about the moon.

BOOKS WITH PHONIC ELEMENTS

Chicken Soup With Rice
by Maurice Sendak
Scholastic, 1990
(final *e*)

Max's Chocolate Chicken
by Rosemary Wells
Dial, 1989
(final *e, ch*)

Sheep in a Shop
by Nancy Shaw
Houghton Mifflin, 1991
(*sh*)

The Snail's Spell
by Joanne Ryder
Scholastic, 1993
(*sp, sn*)

This Is the Place for Me
by Joanna Cole
Scholastic, 1990
(*pl*)

Trees
by Harry Behn
Holt, 1993
(*gr, tr*)

When Crocodiles Clean Up
by Ronni Schotter
Illustrated by Thor Wickstrom
Macmillan, 1993
(*wh*)

Books in Other Languages

SPANISH

Cuando los borregos no pueden dormir
by Satoshi Kitamura
Lectorum, AT, 1986 ✸ ▲
This funny tale imagines what sheep do at night.

Harold y el lapiz color morado
by Crockett Johnson
Harper Arco Iris, 1995 ▲ ✚
The inimitable Harold gets himself into and out of exciting situations with the help of his purple crayon.

Pollita chiquita
by H. W. Zimmerman
Scholastic, 1993 ▲ ■
Henny Penny sets out to tell the king that the sky is falling.

Silba por Willie
by Ezra Jack Keats
Scholastic, 1994 ▲ ■ ✸
Peter is excited to learn how to whistle—now he can call his dog.

Un dia de nieve
by Ezra Jack Keats
Scholastic, 1994 ✸ ▲ ■
A small boy delights in a city snowfall in this Caldecott winner.

CHINESE

Harold and the Purple Crayon
by Crockett Johnson
Multicultural Distributing Center ▲ ✚
The inimitable Harold gets himself into and out of exciting situations with the help of his purple crayon.

JAPANESE

Three Billy Goats Gruff
by Marcia Brown
Multicultural Distributing Center ▲ ■
A noted artist created the illustrations for this version of the well-known tale.

Technology

You'll find this Scholastic technology referenced in the Literacy Place Teacher's Editions.

AUDIO

Literacy Place Listening Library
Selections from the student anthology as well as every Big Book in grades K–2 are available on audiocassette.

VIDEO

Literacy Place Meet the Mentor
One Meet-the-Mentor video per unit gives children an opportunity to meet a real-life professional who models ways in which literacy is used in his or her career.

SOFTWARE

WiggleWorks Plus
Scholastic (Win/Mac)
This CD-ROM component for Kindergarten through Grade 2 of Literacy Place supports children's language development. These activities integrate reading, writing, listening, and speaking.

Scholastic Reading Counts!
Formerly known as The Electronic Bookshelf, this interactive reading motivation and management program is for students at all reading levels.

I Spy
Scholastic (Win/Mac)
These scavenger-hunt games build reading, math, problem-solving, and logic skills.

Usborne's Animated First Thousand Words
Usborne/Scholastic (Win/Mac)
This fun-to-use vocabulary tool introduces pre- and beginning readers to 1,000 common English and Spanish words.

INTERNET

www.scholasticnetwork.com
This comprehensive online curriculum service for grades K–8 features unit-by-unit extensions for Literacy Place.

www.scholastic.com
Scholastic's corporate web site includes Literacy Place resources and unit-related Internet links.

Other Sites
The Internet is growing and changing every day, so be sure to preview all sites before your students visit them.

For more information about Scholastic's technology, please call 1-800-SCHOLASTIC.

LAUNCH THE UNIT

BASELINE ASSESSMENT

The Baseline Assessment activity helps you determine the conceptual level at which each child starts the unit. Repeat the task at the end of the unit.

Have children use their imagination to think up stories. Invite children to draw pictures that represent parts of their stories. Children can tell their stories and show their pictures. Save these pictures to use for comparison at the end of the unit.

K-W-L

Start a K-W-L chart for *Imagine That!* that you will return to at the end of the unit. Ask children the following questions:

- What is the most interesting story you know?
- Why do you think people make up stories to tell?

What do we know?	What do we want to know?	How do we find out?

Set Up the Place: Artist Studio

Opportunities for hands-on learning activities abound in an artist's studio. Transform your classroom into a workplace model where children can explore the visual arts through direct experience with materials and techniques. An artist's studio learning center can also provide a format for integrating other content areas and introducing and reinforcing literacy skills.

Idea File: Artist's Studio

- Create a display area for sculptures and constructions. Also, set aside a studio table for individual and group projects.
- Articles and pictures cut from newspapers, magazines, and art supply catalogs can be the basis of a new archive.
- Set up a mural center.
- Create a list of "Art Words."
- Use **WiggleWorks Plus** PlaceMaker to make banners, posters, and calendars to help organize the learning center.
- Post Literacy Place Cards in the learning center as options for independent activities.

"A mural is one way to express your imagination. Children share their ideas and then get together to paint their story."

—WILLIAM WALSH

Meet the Mentor: William Walsh

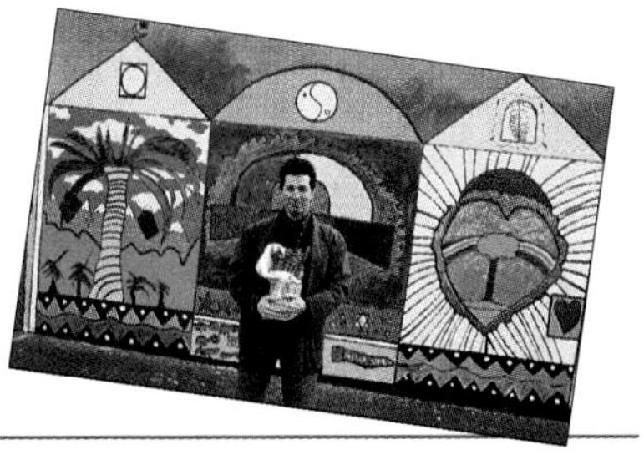

View the Video

Before viewing the mentor video, explain that William Walsh is a muralist—a person who paints very big pictures, often on walls or ceilings. Point out that he and some friends decided to make a mural about friendship.

- Invite children to look for ways that William Walsh and the other artists in the video show friendship.

Think About the Video

After viewing, give children time to discuss their thoughts and opinions about the video with questions such as:

> **Why do you think William Walsh shares his secrets?**

> **How would you teach someone to read the pictures in one of the finished murals in the video?**

Invite children to think about a place in their neighborhood that could be improved by having a mural painted there.

Have them suggest themes and big ideas that they think would be appropriate for these places.

Invite children to use the computer to create their own murals about friendship.

Viewing as a Learning Tool

Teach/Model Share with children that they can learn a lot by looking at pictures such as murals. Freeze-frame on the first mural in the video and model "picture-reading."

Think Aloud *In this mural I see a new city, and in the background I see trees and a mountain. In the sky, it looks like another painting is being shown—an older city. I think this mural is about change, or about how people change the world around them.*

Practice/Apply Freeze-frame on the next mural and have children talk about the picture and the ideas they think are expressed in it.

Real-World Skills

- Organize the basic elements of a story.
- Identify and write rhymes.
- Use clues to make inferences.
- Assess a problem and devise a solution.
- Write descriptions of oneself and others.
- Create lively, realistic dialogues.
- Use images to tell a story.

Preview of Workshops and Project

The Workshops and Project will give children an opportunity to apply to hands-on activities what they have learned about the mentor and place.

Workshop 1
How to Make a Story Plan
(T107–T110)
Children will detail a plan for an original story. The plan will include characters, settings, and plot.

Workshop 2
How to Sketch
(T227–T230)
Children will learn to sketch by practicing on their original story setting and story character ideas.

Project
How to Make a Mural
(T284–T287)
Children work together to plan and make a storytelling mural.

Mama, Do You Love Me?
by Barbara M. Joosse illustrated by Barbara Lavallee
SCHOLASTIC

Big Book

Share the Big Book

THEME CONNECTION In this story, children find out the many ways a little girl uses her imagination to discover how much her mother loves her.

Preview and Predict

USE PICTURE CLUES Read aloud the title and the names of the author and illustrator. Give children time to preview the story and respond to the illustrations before they read.

> **Where does the story take place?**

Explain that the story takes place in Alaska, near the North Pole where it is very cold and snowy. Show children Alaska on a map and explain that the characters in the story belong to a group of people called the Inuit.

MAKE PREDICTIONS Encourage children to predict what the story will be about.

> **Who do you think the story will be about?**

Write children's predictions on the chalkboard or on chart paper.

Read the Big Book

CHECK COMPREHENSION As you read the Big Book with children, track the print. You may want to use a different tone to say the words of the mother and the girl. After reading aloud the first six pages, pause to discuss the structure of the story.

> **Who is asking the questions? Who is answering them?**

> **What do you think will happen next?**

DISCUSS VOCABULARY As you continue reading, discuss the meanings of unfamiliar words as they come up. After reading, ask children if the story turned out to be the way they predicted.

Respond to the Big Book

Personal Response

SHARE OPINIONS

Give children an opportunity to share their thoughts and opinions about the story. You may wish to prompt discussion with questions such as:

> **Did you like the story? What was your favorite part?**

> **Why do you think the girl asked so many questions?**

> **What do you think about the way the mother answered these questions?**

> **How did the girl feel at the end of the story?**

> **What did you learn about Inuit life from the story?**

THEME CONNECTIONS

Point out to children that—just like the girl in the story—everyone can use their imagination to express themselves in a new way. Ask:

> **Have you ever gotten carried away asking questions like the girl in the story does?**

> **What kinds of questions did you ask? Who were you talking to?**

Draw Special Greeting Cards

DRAWING YOUR FEELINGS

Have children make greeting cards for people who are special to them.

- Distribute sheets of large drawing paper. Have children draw pictures that show how they feel about the people.
- Before they begin drawing, ask children to close their eyes and imagine the people to whom they are sending their greetings and why the people are important.
- Then, after children complete their greeting cards, suggest that they write greetings at the top of their cards or questions they might like to ask.
- Have volunteers share their "special greeting" drawings and then, if possible, "deliver" them to the special people.

LAUNCH THE UNIT

FAMILY LITERACY NIGHT

Involve families every step of the way and close the unit with a Family Literacy Night. See page T290 for details.

HOME INVOLVEMENT

TAKE HOME

Families who are active in supporting literacy in the school may increase children's motivation to learn. Distribute the following items for children to take home and read with their families:

- *Family Letter* in the **Literacy-at-Home Kit**
- *Family Literacy Newsletter* on **pages T3–T4** of the **Practice Book**
- *Family Newsletter* on **page 170** of the **Literacy Place Spelling Teacher's Resource Book**
- **My Books** and **Phonics Readers**

Family Literacy Tips

TEACHER'S EDITION

In the Teacher's Edition you'll find these valuable tips at point of use.

- **FAMILY TIME** The role-play activity on page T35 involves families in meaningful interactions that can motivate learning.
- **HOME-SCHOOL CONNECTION** Children take selected books home to read to a family member in the activities on pages T48, T53, T100, T105, T160, T165, T220, and T225.
- **FAMILY TALK** Children's school performance benefits from talking about school events at home. See the 15-minute activity on page T131.
- **FAMILY LITERACY** Reading together is most effective if family members use a specific reading strategy. See the 10-minute activity on page T211 for echo reading.
- **FAMILY LITERACY RESOURCES** The ALA web site in the tip on page T257 provides families with hints for promoting reading, as well as booklists for children.

Internet

SCHOLASTIC
Enter the Dear Big Bill Sweepstakes
in school
at home
around the world
Scholastic India
CHANGE IS COMING
NEW ANIMORPHS TV TIME!

Suggest that parents visit the Scholastic web site at **www.scholastic.com** for links to valuable resources. Parents can learn all about their children's favorite books, authors, and characters.

Chicken Pedro and the Falling Sky

AWARD WINNER
Chicken Pedro and the Falling Sky
By Alma Flor Ada and F. Isabel Campoy
Illustrated by Loretta Lopez

Main Selection
Genre: Folk Tale
Award-winning author

Lemonade Recipe

Paired Selection
Genre: Recipe

WEEK 1 TESTED SKILLS

- **Key Comprehension Skill: Make Inferences**
- **Daily Phonics: Final *e* (a-e); words with *-ing***
- **Vocabulary**
- **Spelling: Words With Final *e* (a-e)**
- **Grammar, Usage, Mechanics: Word Order in Complete Sentences**

Technology Connection

BUILD BACKGROUND
Children will be learning about food and recipes later in this story. Discuss the common elements of all recipes. Mention the ingredients list and the sequential steps of a recipe. Guide children to **www.whatscooking.com** where they can browse through some kid-tested and kid-approved recipes.

Selection Summary

Chicken Pedro is hit by a lemon that falls from a tree. Believing that the lemon is the sun, Chicken Pedro concludes that the sky is falling. He decides to tell the King about this. Along the way to the King's palace, Chicken Pedro meets friends who join him. When they reach the palace, the Queen explains that the sun is actually a lemon. Everyone celebrates by making lemonade and cake.

PAIRED SELECTION Children can make and enjoy their own lemonade.

Author

Born in Cuba, **ALMA FLOR ADA** studied first in Spain and Peru before moving to the United States to continue her studies. Her storybooks are published in both Spanish and English so that readers can appreciate both languages.

Weekly Organizer

Visit Our Web Site
www.scholastic.com

Chicken Pedro and the Falling Sky	DAY 1	DAY 2
READ and Introduce Skills • VOCABULARY • PHONICS • COMPREHENSION • LISTENING • SPEAKING • VIEWING Chicken Pedro and the Falling Sky	**BUILD BACKGROUND,** p. T19▲ **VOCABULARY,** p. T20 ▲ ✸ Practice Book, p. 5 **DAILY PHONICS:** ▲ ✸ Final *e (a-e)*, pp. T22–T23 Practice Book, pp. 6, 7 **PREVIEW AND PREDICT,** p. T24 **READ:** ▲ ✸ ■ *Chicken Pedro and the Falling Sky*, pp. T24–T31 **COMPREHENSION:** Make Inferences, p. T27	**READ:** ▲ ■ ✸ *Chicken Pedro and the Falling Sky*, pp. T32–T39 **DAILY PHONICS:** Words With *-ing*, p. T33 Practice Book, p. 11, 12 **GENRE:** Folk Tale, p. T37
WRITE and Respond • GRAMMAR • USAGE • MECHANICS • SPELLING • WRITING	**SHARED WRITING,** p. T19 **JOURNAL: High-Frequency Words,** p. T21 **QUICKWRITE: Predict,** p. T31 **SPELLING:** Pretest: Words With Final *e (a-e)*, p. R4 Spelling Resource Book, p. 84 **GRAMMAR, USAGE, MECHANICS:** Teach/Model: Word Order in Complete Sentences, p. R6 **ORAL LANGUAGE,** p. T31	**SHARED WRITING:** Prewrite, p. T39 **SPELLING:** Vocabulary Practice, p. R4 Spelling Resource Book, pp. 85–87 **GRAMMAR, USAGE, MECHANICS:** Practice, p. R6 **ORAL LANGUAGE,** p. T39
EXTEND SKILLS and Apply to Literature • SKILLS • INTEGRATED LANGUAGE ARTS • INTEGRATED CURRICULUM • GUIDED READING • INDEPENDENT READING	**READ ALOUD,** p. T31 **GUIDED READING,** pp. R2–R3 **INTEGRATED CURRICULUM:** Science, p. R8 **TRADE BOOKS** • *Pierre* • *Jenny's Journey* • *Going Home* PIERRE MAURICE SENDAK GOING HOME JENNY'S JOURNEY	**READ ALOUD,** p. T39 **GUIDED READING,** pp. R2–R3 **INTEGRATED CURRICULUM:** Math, p. R8 The Arts, p. R9 Social Studies, p. R9
TECHNOLOGY and **REAL-WORLD SKILLS**	**WIGGLEWORKS PLUS CD-ROM** Magnet Board, T20, T22 **FIRST THOUSAND WORDS CD-ROM** Expanding Vocabulary, T31	**AUDIO** Listening Skills, T37 **WORKSHOP 1,** pp. T107–T110

MODIFY INSTRUCTION

● INTERVENTION ▲ ESL/ELD ■ EXTRA HELP
✳ GIFTED & TALENTED ✓ = TESTED SKILL

DAY 3	DAY 4	DAY 5
READ: ▲ ■ "Lemonade Recipe," pp. T40–T41 ✓ **COMPREHENSION:** ▲ ■ Make Inferences, pp. T44–T45 Practice Book, pp. 9, 10 ✓ **DAILY PHONICS:** ▲ ■ Words With *-ing*, pp. T46–T47 Practice Book, pp. 11, 12 **BUILDING FLUENCY,** p. T48 **FOCUS ON HIGH-FREQUENCY WORDS,** p. T49 **FOCUS ON PHONICS,** p. T49	✓ **VOCABULARY REVIEW,** p. T52 ✓ **DAILY PHONICS:** Final *e (a-e)*, p. T53	**READING ASSESSMENT,** p. T56 Selection Test Conference Decoding Test
RESPOND: ▲ ■ Think About Reading, p. T42 Practice Book, p. 8 **WRITE A RECIPE,** p. T43 ✓ **SPELLING:** Write/Proofread, p. R5 Spelling Resource Book, p. 88 ✓ **GRAMMAR, USAGE, MECHANICS:** Practice, p. R7 **ORAL LANGUAGE,** p. T43	**SHARED WRITING:** ▲ ■ Writing Stories With Animal Characters, p. T50 Practice Book, p. 13 ✓ **SPELLING:** Study/Review, p. R5 Spelling Resource Book, p. 161 ✓ **GRAMMAR, USAGE, MECHANICS:** Apply, p. R7 **ORAL LANGUAGE,** p. T51	**WRITING ASSESSMENT,** p. T58 Child Model Children's Writing Rubic ✓ **SPELLING:** Posttest, p. R5 Spelling Resource Book, p. 163 ✓ **GRAMMAR, USAGE, MECHANICS:** Assess, p. R7 **ORAL LANGUAGE,** p. T58
READ ALOUD, p. T49 **GUIDED READING,** pp. R2–R3 **OPTIONAL MATERIALS,** p. T48 Phonics Reader #37: *The Big Race*	**READ ALOUD,** p. T55 **GUIDED READING,** pp. R2–R3 **EXTEND VOCABULARY:** Review High-Frequency Words, p. T52 Review Story Words, p. T52 **OPTIONAL MATERIALS,** p. T53 Phonics Reader #38: *The Pancake Man* **READ ALOUD:** *Curious George Rides a Bike*, T54–T55	**READ ALOUD,** p. T60 **GUIDED READING,** pp. R2–R3 **INTEGRATED LANGUAGE ARTS:** Make Up a Conversation, p. T59 Radio News Broadcast, p. T59 Make a Class Book, p. T60 Make Up a Scene, p. T60
SCHOLASTIC NETWORK Finding the Facts, T43 **WORKSHOP 1,** pp. T107–T110	**WIGGLEWORKS PLUS CD-ROM** Writing Skills, T51 **AUDIO** Speaking Skills, T55 **WORKSHOP 1,** pp. T107–T110	**WIGGLEWORKS PLUS CD-ROM** Language Development, T60 **WORKSHOP 1,** pp. T107–T110

Weekly Assessment

ASSESSMENT PLANNING

USE THIS CHART TO PLAN YOUR ASSESSMENT OF THE WEEKLY READING OBJECTIVES.

- **Informal Assessment is ongoing and should be used before, during, and after reading.**
- **Formal assessment occurs at the end of the week on the selection test.**
- **Note that intervention activies occur throughout the lesson to support students who need extra help with skills.**

ASSESSMENT
ASSESSMENT HANDBOOK
SCHOLASTIC

YOU MAY CHOOSE AMONG THE FOLLOWING PAGES IN THE ASSESSMENT HANDBOOK.

- **Informal Assessment**
- **Anecdotal Record**
- **Portfolio Checklist and Evaluation Forms**
- **Self-Assessment**
- **Second-Language Learners**
- **Using Technology to Assess**
- **Test Preparation**

SKILLS AND STRATEGIES	Informal Assessment
COMPREHENSION Make Inferences	**OBSERVATION p. T27** • Did children use story and picture clues to make inferences? **QUICKCHECK p. T44** • Can children use picture and word clues to make inferences? **CHECK PRACTICE BOOK p. 9** **CONFERENCE p. T56**
PHONICS Final *e (a-e)* Words With *-ing*	**OBSERVATION pp. T29, T33** • Did children recognize words with final *e* (*a-e*)? • Did children recognize words with *-ing*? **CHECK PRACTICE BOOK pp. 6, 11** **DICTATION pp. T23, T47**
VOCABULARY Story Words **lemon king sky cave sun cake** High-Frequency **went soon**	**OBSERVATION p. T52** • Did children identify story words? • Did children identify high-frequency words? **CHECK PRACTICE BOOK p. 5**

Formal Assessment	INTERVENTION and Instructional Alternatives	Planning Notes
SELECTION TEST • Questions 1–3 check children's mastery of the key strategy, make inferences. UNIT TEST	If chidren need help with make inferences, then go to: • **Instructional Alternatives, p. T45** • **Review, p. R43** • **Reteach, p. R56**	
DECODING TEST • See p. T57 SELECTION TEST • Questions 4–7 check children's ability to recognize words with final *e (a-e)* and words with *-ing*. UNIT TEST	If children need help identifying words with final *e (a-e)*, then go to: • **Intervention Activity, p. T49** • **Review, p. R47** • **Reteach, p. R57** If children need help identifying words with *-ing*, then go to: • **Review, p. R48** • **Reteach, p. R58**	
SELECTION TEST • Questions 8–10 check children's recall of high-frequency words and story words. UNIT TEST	If children need additional practice with the vocabulary words, then go to: • **Intervention Activity, p. T49** • **Extend Vocabulary, p. T52** • **Integrated Language Arts Activity, p. T59**	

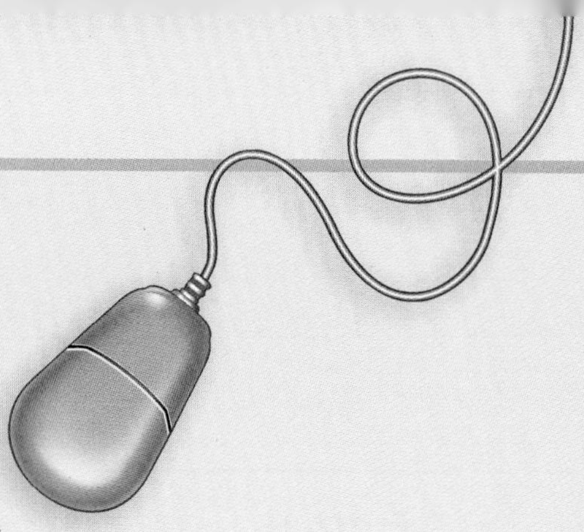

Technology

The technology in this lesson helps teachers and children develop the skills they need for the 21st century. Look for integrated technology activities on every day of instruction.

DAY 1 Expanding Vocabulary	• Children use Usborne's Animated **First Thousand Words** CD-ROM to learn the Spanish translations for animal words.
DAY 2 Listening Skills	• Children listen to the story and identify what is predictable.
DAY 3 Finding the Facts	• Children explore other food-oriented folk tales at **Scholastic Network.**
DAY 4 Speaking Skills	• Children record their oral presentations of story parts that are predictable and repetitive.
DAY 5 Language Development	• Children use **WiggleWorks Plus** Unit Writer to innovate on the Chicken Pedro story.

la vaca

First Thousand Words CD-ROM

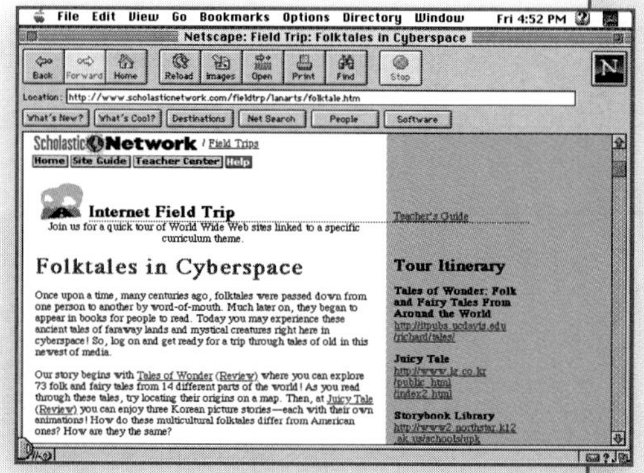
File Edit View Go Bookmarks Options Directory Window
Netscape: Field Trip: Folktales in Cyberspace
Internet Field Trip
Folktales in Cyberspace
Tour Itinerary

www.scholasticnetwork.com

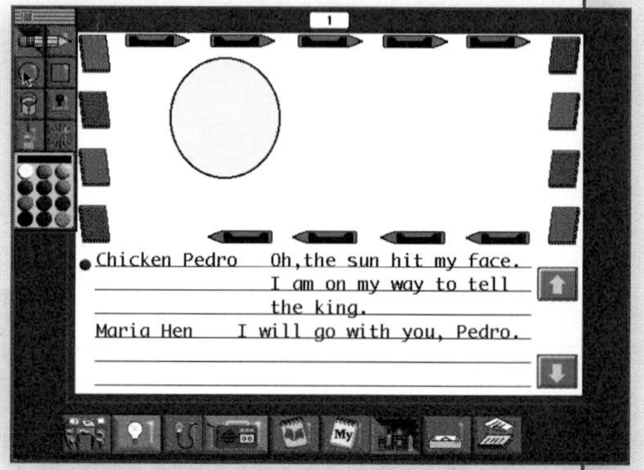
Chicken Pedro
Oh, the sun hit my face. I am on my way to tell the king.
Maria Hen
I will go with you, Pedro.

WiggleWorks Plus Unit Writer

Build Background

Some stories are passed along from country to country. Imagine how the story of Chicken Licken *would be different if some of the details were changed.*

Activate Prior Knowledge

DISCUSS FOLK TALES Remind children that folk tales are stories that used to be told out loud and passed down from generation to generation. As the stories were retold, they were often changed by the storytellers. Have children tell stories that their parents have told them about their family traditions, cultures, or places they've lived. Have children compare other cultures, regions, and customs. Have them retell the stories they have heard.

RETELL THE STORY Ask how many children have heard or read a story called *Chicken Licken.* Encourage volunteers to briefly retell the story.

> **Who are the characters in *Chicken Licken*?**

SHARED WRITING *Stories With Animal Characters*

INTRODUCE Build background for writing stories with animal characters by having children name characters from cartoons, movies, or books that are animals. Have children write a sentence or two about an animal character. Explain that in the story they are going to read, most of the characters are animals.

DAY 1 OBJECTIVES

CHILDREN WILL:

READ 35 MINUTES

- **Build Background**
- **Vocabulary**
- **Daily Phonics: Words With Final *e* (*a-e*)**
- ***Chicken Pedro and the Falling Sky*, pp. 9–15**
- **Key Comprehension Skill: Make Inferences**

WRITE 25 MINUTES

- **Shared Writing: Introduce Stories With Animal Characters**
- **Quickwrite: Predict**
- **Spelling: Words With Final *e* (*a-e*)**
- **Grammar, Usage, Mechanics: Word Order in Complete Sentences**
- **Oral Language**

EXTEND SKILLS 30 MINUTES

- **Integrated Curriculum**
- **Read Aloud**
- **Guided Reading**

RESOURCES

- **Practice Book, pp. 5–7**
- **Spelling Resource Book, p. 84**

MODIFY Instruction

ESL/ELD

▲ Collect visuals of the animals represented by the characters. Help children say the animal names. Let them give each one a name, such as Chicken Charlie, and make animal sounds. As they read, children can compare the names they gave the animals with the story names. **(MULTISENSORY)**

VOCABULARY

High-Frequency Words

VOCABULARY

HIGH-FREQUENCY

went soon

STORY WORDS

lemon sky

sun king

cave cake

Ⓐ TEACH/MODEL

INTRODUCE HIGH-FREQUENCY WORDS Write the high-frequency words ***soon*** and ***went*** in sentences on the chalkboard. Read the sentences aloud, underline the high-frequency words, and ask children if they recognize them. You may wish to use the above sentences.

He went to see the king.
He soon met Daniel Duck.

Ask volunteers to dictate sentences using the high-frequency words. Add these to the chalkboard.

Ⓑ PRACTICE/APPLY

FOCUS ON SPELLING Write each high-frequency word on a note card. Read each aloud. Then do the following:

ROUTINE

1. **Display one card at a time, and ask children to state each word aloud.**
2. **Have children spell each word aloud.**
3. **Ask children to write each word in the air as they state aloud each letter. Then have them write each word on a sheet of paper or in their Journals.**

went

soon

MAINTAIN VOCABULARY Add the note cards to the **Word Wall.** Then review the following words on the wall: ***over, from, came, through.***

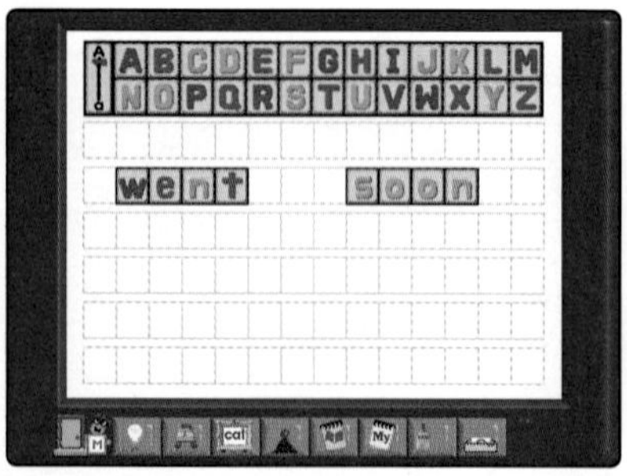
ABCDEFGHIJKLM
NOPQRSTUVWXYZ
went
soon

TECHNOLOGY

For children needing additional practice with high-frequency words prior to reading the story, have them build, explode, and rebuild each high-frequency word on the **WiggleWorks Plus** Magnet Board.

MODIFY Instruction

ESL/ELD

▲ Establish the story words with visual clues, such as picture cards or pictures from magazines. Have children draw a picture as you say, for example: *Draw the sky...; Draw the sun in the sky...;* Children can add details and describe their completed pictures aloud. **(TOTAL PHYSICAL RESPONSE)**

GIFTED & TALENTED

✷ Have children write incomplete sentences for a partner. The missing word in each sentence should be a high-frequency word: *went* or *soon*. Partners exchange sentences and fill in the missing words. **(WORK IN PAIRS)**

Story Words

A TEACH/MODEL

INTRODUCE STORY WORDS

The story also contains the following Story Words — ***lemon, sky, sun, king, cave, cake.***

- Write these words on the chalkboard, read them aloud, and discuss their meanings if necessary.
- Point out previously taught sound-spelling correspondences, such as ***/k/c, k*** and ***/u/u.***
- If possible, provide a visual clue for each. For example, let children pass around a real lemon or show a picture of a cave.

B PRACTICE/APPLY

BUILD STORY BACKGROUND

Discuss the sky with children.

- Have children describe what they usually see in the sky.
- If possible, take children outside or have them look through a window. Ask them to name the things they see in the sky and write a message about it.
- Then have children draw or paint sky pictures. Have them include things they see in the sky such as clouds, the sun, airplanes, birds, and kites.

WRITE TO READ

When completed, have children write a sentence about their picture using one or more of the story words.

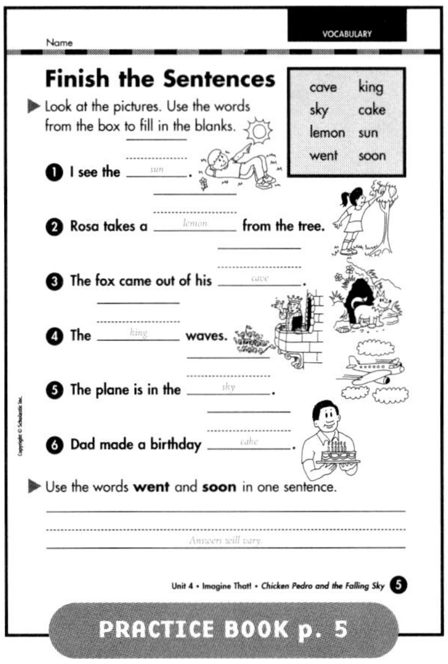

Name VOCABULARY

Finish the Sentences

▶ Look at the pictures. Use the words from the box to fill in the blanks.

cave king
sky cake
lemon sun
went soon

1. I see the sun.
2. Rosa takes a lemon from the tree.
3. The fox came out of his cave.
4. The king waves.
5. The plane is in the sky.
6. Dad made a birthday cake.

▶ Use the words **went** and **soon** in one sentence.

Answers will vary.

Unit 4 • Imagine That! • Chicken Pedro and the Falling Sky 5

PRACTICE BOOK p. 5

I see the sun in the sky.

BINGO

Make and distribute Bingo cards. Use the game board template on page R87 (Teamwork, Unit 3).

- Have children write the story and high-frequency words in the Bingo squares in random order. If necessary, children can repeat words to fill in the squares.
- As you call out the words, have children cover them with tokens. Children should try to complete either a horizontal or a vertical row.

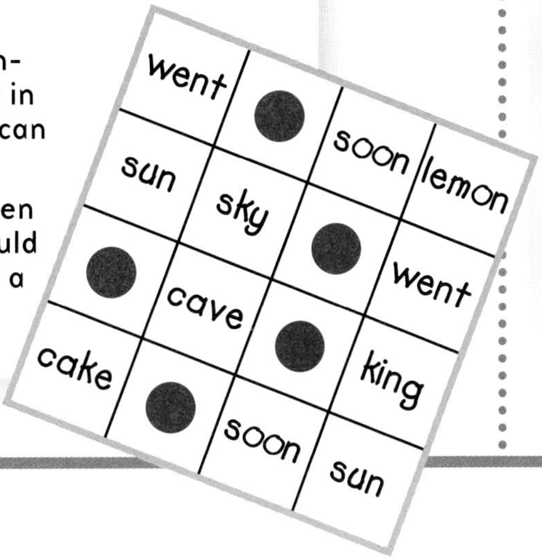
went
soon
lemon
sun
sky
went
cave
king
cake
soon
sun

JOURNAL

Ask children to write a sentence using each **high-frequency word** in their Journals. You might suggest the following sentence starters:

We went _____.

We will soon _____ .

Chicken Pedro and the Falling Sky

SELECTION WORDS With Final *e* (*a-e*)

bake	face
cake	lake
cave	shade

SKILLS TRACE

Words With Final *e* (*a-e*) TESTED

Introduce . . .p. T22, –T23
Practice . . . .pp. T29, T48, T49, T131
Review . . . . .p. R47
Reteach . . . . .p. R57

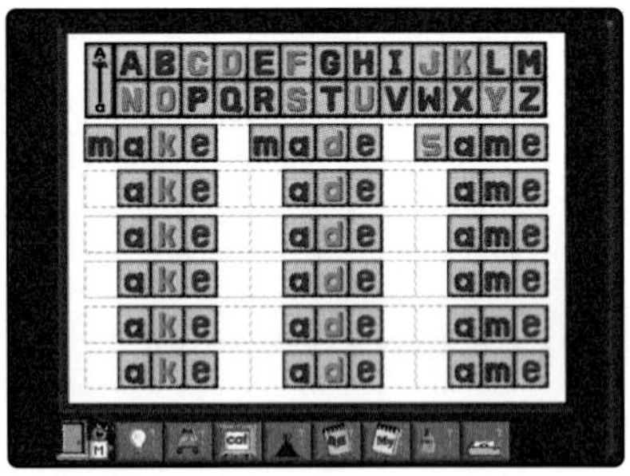

TECHNOLOGY

Have children build words with /ā/ spelled **a-e** on the Magnet Board.

- Begin with the word *make* or write rows of **a-e** patterns *(-ake, -ade, -ame)* to which children will add initial consonants.
- Have children search for **a-e** pattern words in classroom books to add to the list.

DAILY PHONICS

Final *e* (*a-e*)

A PHONOLOGICAL AWARENESS

RHYME Read aloud "Down by the Bay" from the *Big Book of Rhymes and Rhythms 1B*, page 4. As you read, stress the words that contain /ā/ spelled with ***a-e***, such as ***whale.***

- Have children read the rhyme along with you.
- Isolate the words ***tale*** and ***whale*** and have children repeat them. Point out the /ā/ sound in each.

Down by the Bay
Down by the bay,
Where the watermelons grow,
Back to my home I dare not go.
For if I do,
My mother will say,
"Did you ever hear a whale
Tell a silly tale?"
Down by the bay.
whale

***Big Book of Rhymes, 1B,* p. 4**

ORAL BLENDING Say the following word parts and ask children to blend them. Provide corrective feedback and modeling as needed.

/m/ . . . ake	/g/ . . . ame	/g/ . . . ate
/r/ . . . ake	/n/ . . . ame	/l/ . . . ate

B CONNECT SOUND-SPELLING

INTRODUCE FINAL *e* (a-e). Write the words ***tap*** and ***tape*** on the chalkboard as you read each aloud. Ask children what vowel sound they hear in each word. Point out that the long ***a*** sound in ***tape*** is made by adding ***e***. Write ***_a_e*** on the chalkboard.

THINK ALOUD *If I put **m** in the first blank, and **k** in the second blank, I can make a new word. Let's say the word slowly as I move my finger under the letters. Listen as I blend the sounds in this word. What's the word? (Make)*

MODIFY Instruction

ESL/ELD

▲ Help children read words with long *a*, such as *gate*, *lane*, and *lake*. List these words on the chalkboard. Use colored chalk to write over or underline the long *a* and the silent *e* in each of the words. Ask children to find other words to add to the list. Say each word aloud. **(COLOR CODE)**

GIFTED & TALENTED

✱ Have children assemble flip books. The top word should be *made*. Under the *m*, have children write *w*, *b*, and *f*, one letter per page. Under the *d*, have children write *t*, *k*, and *n*, one letter per page. The *a* and the *e* remain constant. Children can take turns reading flip books. **(HANDS-ON LEARNING)**

- Ask children to suggest other /ā/ words spelled ***-ake, -ame, -ate,*** and ***-ade.*** List these in separate columns on a chart.

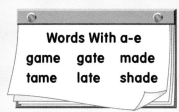

Words With a-e		
game	gate	made
tame	late	shade

PHONICS MAINTENANCE Review the following sound-spellings: */ā/a-e, /u/u, /e/e, /sh/sh, /th/th, /z/s.* Say one of these sounds. Have a volunteer write on the chalkboard the spelling that stands for the sound. Continue with all the sounds.

C PRACTICE/APPLY

BLEND WORDS To practice and review sound-spellings, list the following words and sentences on the chalkboard. Have children read each chorally. Model blending as needed.

mad	made	can
cane	bake	cake

We will bake a cake.

The King made lemonade.

DICTATION Dictate the following words: ***make, gate, shut, quick, van.***

BUILD WORDS Distribute the following letter cards, or have children use their own sets: ***a, e, g, m, d, t, k, s.*** Allow children time to build as many words as possible using the letter cards. Children can write their words on a separate sheet of paper. **(INDEPENDENT WORK)**

t
a
k
e

MAKE A CAKE

Have children draw and cut out cake shapes, at least one cake per child. Then have children decorate their cakes by writing **/ā/a-e** words with different colored crayons or markers. Ask children to display their cakes and read aloud their words.

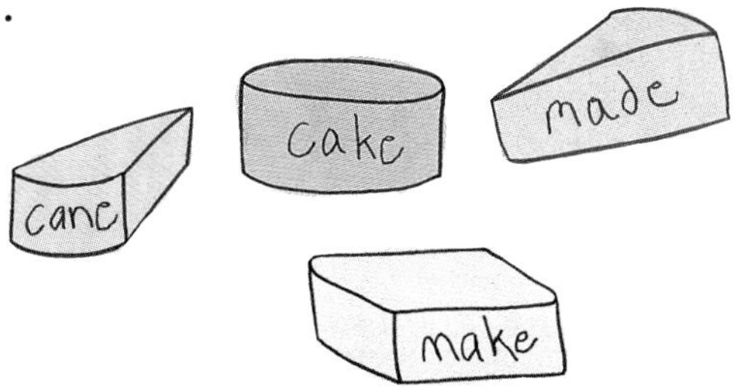
cane
cake
made
make

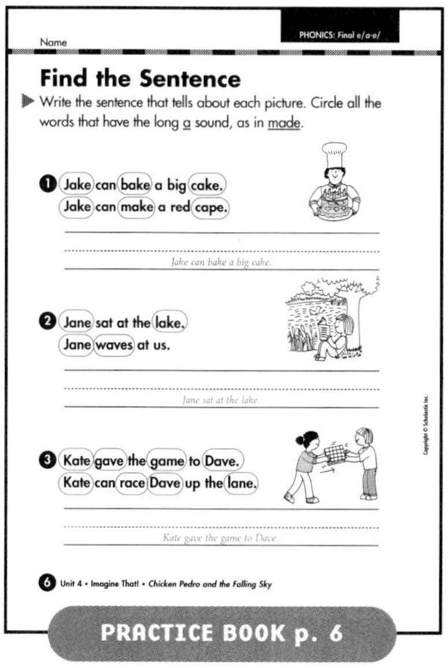

Name PHONICS: Final e/a-e/

Find the Sentence

Write the sentence that tells about each picture. Circle all the words that have the long a sound, as in made.

1. Jake can bake a big cake.
   Jake can make a red cape.
   Jake can bake a big cake.
2. Jane sat at the lake.
   Jane waves at us.
   Jane sat at the lake.
3. Kate gave the game to Dave.
   Kate can race Dave up the lane.
   Kate gave the game to Dave.

Copyright © Scholastic Inc.

6 Unit 4 • Imagine That! • *Chicken Pedro and the Falling Sky*

PRACTICE BOOK p. 6

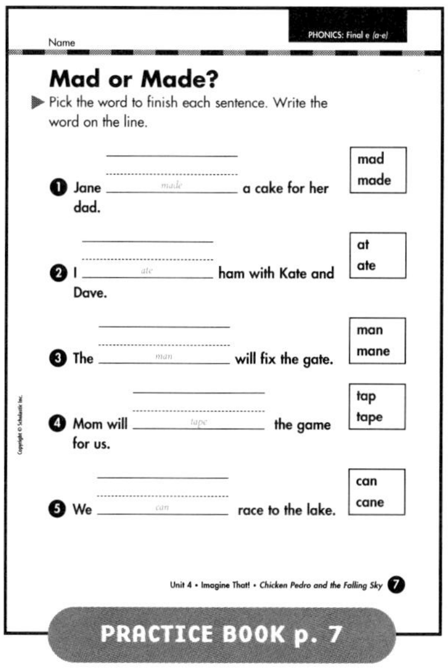

Name PHONICS: Final e (a-e)

Mad or Made?

Pick the word to finish each sentence. Write the word on the line.

1. Jane *made* a cake for her dad. (mad / made)
2. I *ate* ham with Kate and Dave. (at / ate)
3. The *man* will fix the gate. (man / mane)
4. Mom will *tape* the game for us. (tap / tape)
5. We *can* race to the lake. (can / cane)

Copyright © Scholastic Inc.

Unit 4 • Imagine That! • *Chicken Pedro and the Falling Sky* 7

PRACTICE BOOK p. 7

DECODABLE TEXT

For practice reading decodable text, see ***Scholastic Decodable Reader #44.***

For additional phonics instruction and review, see ***Scholastic Phonics A, pp. 167–168.***

COMPREHENSION

Preview and Predict

Tell children that *Chicken Pedro and the Falling Sky* is a version of the classic folk tale, *Chicken Licken,* which is also known as *Henny Penny* or *Chicken Little, the Sky Is Falling.* Ask children to look at the title page and preview the pictures in *Chicken Pedro and the Falling Sky.*

- **Who is this story about? How do you know?**
- **Do you think this is a story that is fact or make-believe? Why do you think so?**

Help children make predictions before they read by asking:

- **What do you think will happen to Chicken Pedro and his friends?**

JOURNAL

Make Predictions

Ask children to write their predictions in their Journals. As they discover what happens, have them record ideas about the story.

Set a Purpose

Help children set their own purposes for reading the story. For example, they might want to know how this story is different from folk tales they already know. Then have them read page 9.

8

FOLK TALE

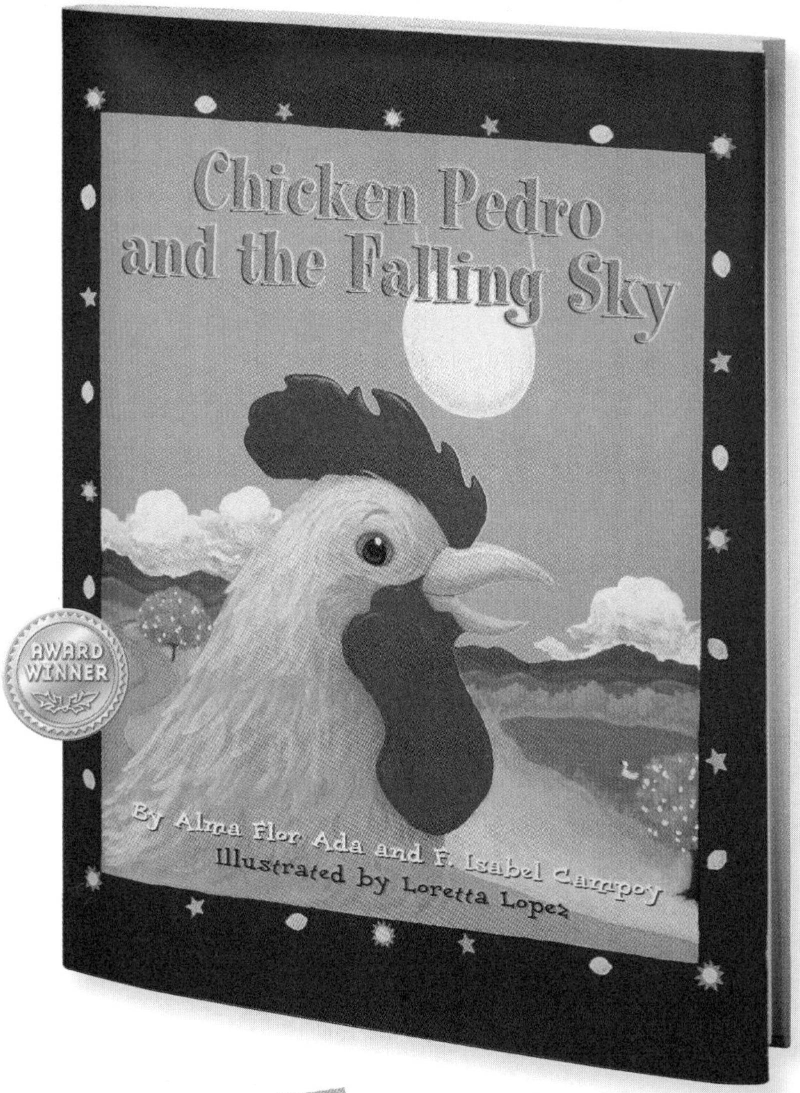
Chicken Pedro and the Falling Sky
AWARD WINNER
By Alma Flor Ada and F. Isabel Campoy
Illustrated by Loretta Lopez

8

CLASSROOM Management

WHOLE CLASS

On-Level Use the questions, Think Alouds, and Skills and Strategies lessons to guide children through a reading of the story.

Below-Level Have children listen to the story on audiocassette prior to the class reading to familiarize themselves with the story sequence and vocabulary.

INDEPENDENT

Above-Level You might choose to have above-level children read the story independently or with a partner while you do a guided reading of the story with the rest of the class. When completed, have the above-level children rejoin the group to participate in the story discussion.

9

Chicken Pedro opened the garden gate.
"What a nice morning!" he said.
"I am going for a walk."
And hip hop, hip hop, off he went.
Hip hop, hip hop down the lane.

9

SKILLS AND STRATEGIES

Revisit the selection for skills instruction.

✓ = Tested Skill

COMPREHENSION

✓ **Make Inferences** T27

DAILY PHONICS

✓ **Final *e* (*a-e*)** T29

Words With *-ing* T33

GENRE

Folk Tale T37

Recipe T41

SMALL GROUP TO WHOLE CLASS

ESL/ELD Have children listen to the story on the audiocassette prior to the whole class reading. This will help them to become familiar with the story sequence and vocabulary. Have children do the pre- and post-listening activities. **(USE AUDIO)**

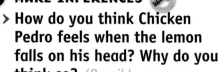

COMPREHENSION

1 MAKE INFERENCES

> **How do you think Chicken Pedro feels when the lemon falls on his head? Why do you think so?** *(Possible answer: Chicken Pedro probably feels surprised and frightened. He sounds very upset and scared when he says "Oh my! Oh my!")*

2 DRAW CONCLUSIONS

> **Why does Chicken Pedro think the sky is falling? Why does he think the sun hit him?** *(Possible answer: Chicken Pedro knows that something fell from above; he knows the sky is above. He sees that the lemon is yellow, like the sun, so he thinks the lemon is the sun.)*

INTERVENTION TIP

Onomatopoeia

Some children may have trouble understanding what the author means by ***Zum.*** Help children realize that ***Zum*** is the word the author made up to describe the sound of the lemon hitting Chicken Pedro. Drop a book or a ball on the floor and ask children to listen to the sound. Challenge children to invent a word that makes that sound.

10

Chicken Pedro went down the lane
all the way to the big blue lake.
He stopped under the shade
of the lemon tree.
Zum! A large lemon hit him on the face.

10

MODIFY Instruction

ESL/ELD

▲ Write the phrases *big blue lake* and *large lemon* on the chalkboard. Point to the lake and the lemon in the picture. Ask: *What is this? What color is it? What size is it?* Guide children to draw the conclusion that Chicken Pedro thinks the sun is a large lemon. **(GUIDED READING)**

GIFTED & TALENTED

✳ Have children work in pairs to make up other things that Chicken Pedro could tell the King about the lemon that hit him. For example, he could tell him that it was raining lemons. Have children role-play the new scene and share it with the class. **(ROLE-PLAY)**

11

1 Chicken Pedro picked up the lemon.
"Oh my! Oh my!" he cried.
"The sky is falling. **2**
The sun hit me on the face.
I must tell the King!"

11

CONNECTING TO FOLK TALES

Children may have enjoyed listening to *Chicken Little, the Sky Is Falling* and other folk tales. Ask children to bring in some of these stories to share with their classmates. Help them compare the stories and the illustrations in the various books. How are they similar and how are they different?

SCIENCE

Ask children to complete the **Find Out About the Sun** activity on **page R8.** Share with children that they will learn what the sun is and how big it really is.

SKILLS AND STRATEGIES

COMPREHENSION

Make Inferences

TEACH/MODEL

Explain to children that making inferences is making good guesses about things that an author does not say in a story.

> **Use story and picture clues along with what you already know to make guesses about things the author does not say.**

THINK ALOUD *When I read this part of the story, I know that Chicken Pedro thinks the sky is falling because he looks scared.*

PRACTICE/APPLY

Ask children to use the graphic organizer below to make inferences about why Chicken Pedro believes the sky is falling.

Clues from the story	+	What I already know	=	Inference

> **How might Chicken Pedro feel when he is hit on the face with a lemon?**

> **Why do you think Chicken Pedro wants to tell the King about the falling sky?**

INFORMAL ASSESSMENT
OBSERVATION

As children read, can they:

✔ use story and picture clues to make inferences?

✔ apply what they know about the story of *Chicken Licken* to make inferences about *Chicken Pedro*?

See pages T44–T45 for a full skills lesson on Make Inferences.

COMPREHENSION

3 FANTASY/REALITY

> **How do you know the characters in this story are make-believe?** *(Animals can't talk.)*

4 MAKE INFERENCES

> **Why do you think Daniel Duck wants to join Chicken Pedro on his trip to see the King?** *(Possible answers: Daniel Duck believes Chicken Pedro's story about the sky falling; Daniel Duck wants to help Chicken Pedro get to the King.)*

SELF-MONITORING STRATEGY

Relate to Literary Experience

THINK ALOUD *As I read through* Chicken Pedro and the Falling Sky, *I stop to think about what happens in the story about* Chicken Licken. *I know that story. Remembering what happened to the animals in it helps me understand what is happening in this story.*

- How is Chicken Pedro like Chicken Licken?

12

And hip hop, hip hop, off he went.
Hip hop, hip hop down the lane.
He soon came across Daniel Duck.

12

MODIFY Instruction

ESL/ELD

▲ Help children make inferences by asking yes/no questions. For example: *Do you think Daniel Duck believes Chicken Pedro's story? Do you think Daniel Duck can help Chicken Pedro to see the king?* **(GUIDED READING)**

EXTRA HELP

■ To encourage children to elaborate on their predictions about what will happen next in the story, read aloud a version of *Chicken Licken.* Point out the things that are alike in both stories. Ask children to predict what might happen at the end of the story. **(MAKE CONNECTIONS)**

13

"Chicken Pedro, where are you going with such a sad face?" asked Daniel Duck.

"The sky is falling.
The sun hit me on the face.
I'm on my way to tell the King!"

❸ "I will go with you," said Daniel Duck. ❹

13

ORAL LANGUAGE

Read aloud the words on page 12 that describe Chicken Pedro going to see the King: *Hip hop, hip hop, off he went. Hip hop, hip hop down the lane.* Ask children to describe what they see when they hear these words. Now have children echo read **page 12** with you and follow your phrasing.

WORD STUDY

Ask children to find the **high-frequency words** *soon* and *went* on page 12. Have children read aloud and spell each word. Ask children to think of a word that means the opposite of *soon.* (*later*) Next, have them think of the opposite of *went.* (*came*) Help them make up sentences using *soon* and *went.*

DAILY PHONICS

Final *e (a-e)*

CONNECT SOUND-SPELLING

TEACH/MODEL Write the words ***bake*** and ***cake*** on the chalkboard.

- **The long *a* sound in these words is made by adding an *e* at the end.**
- **Find and circle the *a-e* spelling pattern in each word.**

Phonics Maintenance Review the following sound-spellings: /ā/*a-e*, /sh/*sh*, /kw/*qu*, /v/*v*, /z/*s*, /th/*th*.

PRACTICE/APPLY

BLEND WORDS To practice using the sound-spellings list the following words on the chalkboard. Have children read each chorally. Model blending as needed.

lake	face	shade
made	quake	game
quit	vet	thin

INFORMAL ASSESSMENT
OBSERVATION

As children read, can they:

✔ recognize words with /ā/ (*a-e*)?

✔ blend words with /ā/ (*a-e*)?

COMPREHENSION

5 SUMMARIZE

> **What has happened so far in the story? Use the story map to talk about this.**

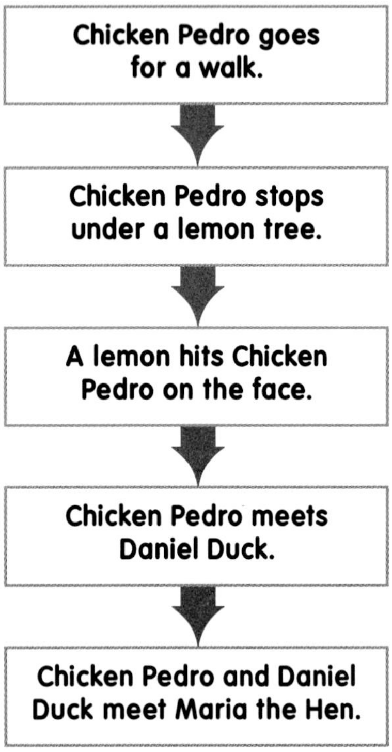
Chicken Pedro goes for a walk.
Chicken Pedro stops under a lemon tree.
A lemon hits Chicken Pedro on the face.
Chicken Pedro meets Daniel Duck.
Chicken Pedro and Daniel Duck meet Maria the Hen.

6 MAKE INFERENCES

> **Do you think Maria the Hen believes Chicken Pedro when he says the sky is falling? Why do you think so?**

(Possible answer: She must believe him because she looks worried and she agrees to go along with Daniel Duck and Chicken Pedro.)

OPTION You may end the first day's reading here or have children continue reading through the entire selection.

14

And hip hop, hip hop, off they went.
Hip hop, hip hop down the lane.
They soon came across Maria the Hen. 5

14

MODIFY Instruction

ESL/ELD

▲ Review story events with alternative questions such as: *Did Pedro meet a hen or a horse?* (a hen) *Was her name Maria or Sally?* (Maria) and so on. Have children point to art or words to verify their answers. Ask volunteers to describe the animals and the setting. **(GUIDED QUESTIONS)**

GIFTED & TALENTED

✷ Have children work in groups to develop dialogue and act out a new scene between Chicken Pedro and his friends. Tell children to imagine that the friends do not believe Chicken Pedro and try to convince him that the sky is not falling. **(ROLE-PLAY)**

15

"Chicken Pedro and Daniel Duck,
where are you going with such sad faces?"
asked Maria the Hen.

"The sky is falling.
The sun hit me on the face.
We're on our way to tell the King!"
said Chicken Pedro.

6 "I will go with you," said Maria the Hen.

15

Quickwrite

PREDICT

Ask children to describe anything they think is funny or surprising about the story. Children can also revise their predictions and predict what will happen next.

DAILY LANGUAGE PRACTICE

SPELLING

DAY 1:
Administer the Pretest for: Words With Final *e* (*a-e*). **See page R4.**

GRAMMAR, USAGE, MECHANICS

DAY 1:
Teach and Model Word Order in Complete Sentences. **See page R6.**

ORAL LANGUAGE

Write the following sentence on the chalkboard. Work with children to correct the errors.

The falling sky is.
(The sky is falling.)

DAY 1 WRAP-UP

READ ALOUD *To develop children's oral vocabularies, spend five to ten minutes reading from a selection of your choice.*

GUIDED READING *To extend reading, meet with the **red** and **blue** reading groups and assign Independent Center activities.* ***See pages R2–R3.***

TECHNOLOGY

Expanding Vocabulary Encourage children to learn the Spanish translations for the animals in the story. Use the **First Thousand Words** CD-ROM to hear pronunciations for the animal words.

CULTURAL CONNECTION

Pedro is the Spanish name for *Peter*. Many languages share similar names, adding their own spelling and pronunciation.

English	Spanish	French
Peter	Pedro	Pierre
George	Jorge	Georges
Helen	Elena	Hélène

Have children compare other names they might know.

COMPREHENSION

DAY 2 OBJECTIVES

CHILDREN WILL:

READ 35 MINUTES

- ***Chicken Pedro and the Falling Sky*, pp. 16–23**
- **Daily Phonics: Words With *-ing***

WRITE 25 MINUTES

- **Shared Writing: Prewrite Animal Characters**
- **Spelling: Words With *-ing*, Final *e* (*a-e*)**
- **Grammar, Usage, Mechanics: Word Order in Complete Sentences**
- **Oral Language**

EXTEND SKILLS 30 MINUTES

- **Integrated Curriculum**
- **Read Aloud**
- **Guided Reading**

RESOURCES

- **Spelling Resource Book, pp. 85–87**

Reread

You may wish to have children independently reread the first part of the story before beginning Day 2 reading.

7 SUMMARIZE

> **What has happened in the story so far?** *(When Chicken Pedro is hit on the face with a lemon, he decides to tell the King. On his way, he meets Daniel Duck and Maria the Hen, who agree to join Chicken Pedro.)*

8 PICTURE CLUES

> **Look at the picture of the characters on page 16. What is the same about Chicken Pedro and his friends?** *(Possible answer: They all have wings, beaks, and feathers.)*

16

7
And hip hop, hip hop, off they went.
Hip hop, hip hop down the lane.
They soon came across Raymond the Rooster.
8
16

MODIFY Instruction

ESL/ELD

▲ Review story sequence by asking questions such as: *What happened first? What happened next? Then what happened?* Invite children to take turns retelling the story. Whenever necessary, help children along by giving them single-word clues. For example: *What happened first with the lemon?* **(SEQUENCE)**

EXTRA HELP

■ Lead a discussion about birds. Draw a web such as the following. Ask them what birds look like and what they do. Write their responses in the web. **(USE VISUALS)**

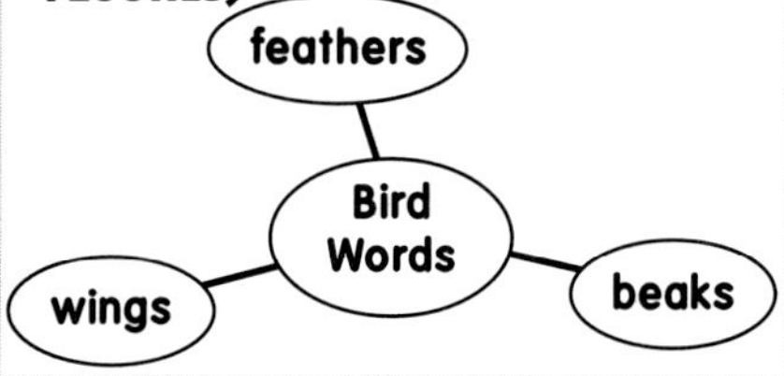
feathers
Bird Words
wings
beaks

17

"Chicken Pedro, Daniel Duck, and Maria the Hen, where are you going with such sad faces?" asked Raymond the Rooster.

"The sky is falling.
The sun hit me on the face.
We're on our way to tell the King!"
said Chicken Pedro.

"I will go with you," said Raymond the Rooster.

17

MATH

Ask children to complete the **Add It Up** activity on **page R8** where they will make up number stories based on *Chicken Pedro and the Falling Sky.*

THE ARTS

Ask children to complete the **Make Paintings of the Sky** activity on **page R9** where they will make drawings of the sky that show different times of day and night.

DAILY PHONICS

Words With *-ing*

TEACH/MODEL

Explain to children that often ***-ing*** is added to verbs, or action words. Have children find the word ***falling*** on page 17.

- Cover up the ***-ing*** ending and read the word. *(fall)*
- Uncover the ***-ing*** ending and blend the two word parts together. Use the word in a sentence.

THINK ALOUD When I cover the ***-ing*** in ***falling,*** I see a word I know—***fall.*** I can see that ***falling*** is made up of a word plus an ending, ***-ing.***

PRACTICE/APPLY

BLEND WORDS Write the words ***tell, pass, jump,*** and ***stand*** on the chalkboard.

- Ask a volunteer to select one of the words, add ***-ing*** to it, and use the new word formed in a sentence.
- Then give children word cards for ***help, play, miss,*** and ***look.*** Have children combine each word card with an ***-ing*** card, and read the new word formed. Model blending as necessary.

INFORMAL ASSESSMENT

OBSERVATION

As children read, can they:

✔ recognize words with ***-ing?***

✔ blend words with ***-ing?***

See pages T46–T47 for a full phonics lesson on Words With *-ing*.

COMPREHENSION

9 COMPARE/CONTRAST

> **How is the conversation between Rocky Fox and Chicken Pedro different from conversations between Chicken Pedro and the other animals?** *(Possible answer: Rocky Fox does not say "I'll go with you" to Chicken Pedro.)*

10 MAKE INFERENCES

> **Why do you think Rocky Fox says, "I know a shortcut. Come through my cave"? What do the story pictures tell you about what Rocky Fox is thinking?** *(Possible answer: Rocky Fox is trying to trick Chicken Pedro and his friends into the cave in order to eat them. The story picture shows Rocky Fox looking hungry.)*

18

And hip hop, hip hop, off they went.
Hip hop, hip hop down the lane.
They soon came across a cave.
And in front of the cave was Rocky Fox.

18

MODIFY Instruction

ESL/ELD

▲ Ask multi-level questions such as: *Show me the word* **Fox.** *Is Rocky Fox inside the cave or in front of the cave?* Point to the picture that shows where the fox lives. *How is Rocky Fox different from Chicken Pedro and his friends? (He has sharp teeth and a bushy tail.)* **(MULTI-LEVEL QUESTIONS)**

EXTRA HELP

■ Remind children that they can tell Rocky Fox is a tricky character by looking at the illustrations and using story clues. Have children act out the conversation between Chicken Pedro and Rocky Fox. Have them use facial expressions and special voices. **(ACT-IT-OUT)**

19

"Chicken Pedro, Daniel Duck, Maria the Hen, and Raymond the Rooster, where are you going with such sad faces?" asked Rocky Fox.

"The sky is falling.
The sun hit me on the face.
We're on our way to tell the King!"
said Chicken Pedro.

9 "I know a shortcut," said Rocky Fox.
He licked his lips.
"Come through my cave. I will take you to the palace." 10

19

SKILLS AND STRATEGIES

CONTEXT CLUES

Unfamiliar Words

TEACH/MODEL

Explain to children that when they come to a word they do not know, they can look at the words or pictures around the unknown word to help them figure out its meaning.

> **Look for clues in the sentences before and after the sentence with the unknown word.**

> **Use picture clues to confirm the meaning of the word.**

THINK ALOUD *If I didn't know the meaning of* **shortcut,** *I could look at the sentences and pictures around* **shortcut.** *I know that Chicken Pedro and his friends are trying to get to the King's palace. Rocky Fox says "I know a shortcut," and "Come through my cave. I will take you to the palace." From these sentences and the picture I can tell that Rocky Fox wants Chicken Pedro to think that he knows a faster way to the King's palace. From these clues I could figure out that a* **shortcut** *is a faster way to get somewhere.*

PRACTICE/APPLY

Ask children to work in small groups to figure out the meaning of an unfamiliar word such as ***shade*** on page 21 in the story. Have each group write or dictate story and picture clues they find.

FAMILY LITERACY RESOURCES

To find tips for choosing books and Web sites for children, families can use the Web site **www.Scholastic.com** on the Internet. Go to the "At Home" area.

VISUAL LITERACY

Ask children to look at the illustration on page 19. Discuss how the picture helps readers figure out what Rocky Fox is thinking. Ask children to make a list of words that describe Rocky Fox.

COMPREHENSION

11 MAKE INFERENCES

> **What do you think Chicken Pedro means when he says to Rocky Fox: "You are very clever, but we have wings."** *(Possible answer: Chicken Pedro knows that Rocky Fox wants to eat them. So, Chicken Pedro and his friends trick Rocky Fox by flying away from his cave.)*

12 VOCABULARY SUPPORT

> **Look at the illustrations. What is the King wearing? What is the scenery like? What is the palace garden like? What does this tell you about the King?** *(Possible answer: The King is wearing fancy clothes and the garden is beautiful. This tells me that the King must be an important man.)*

13 MAKE PREDICTIONS

> **Do you think the King and Queen will believe Chicken Pedro's story about the falling sky? Explain your answer.** *(Possible answer: I don't think they will believe Chicken Pedro. The King and Queen probably know that the lemon couldn't be the sun.)*

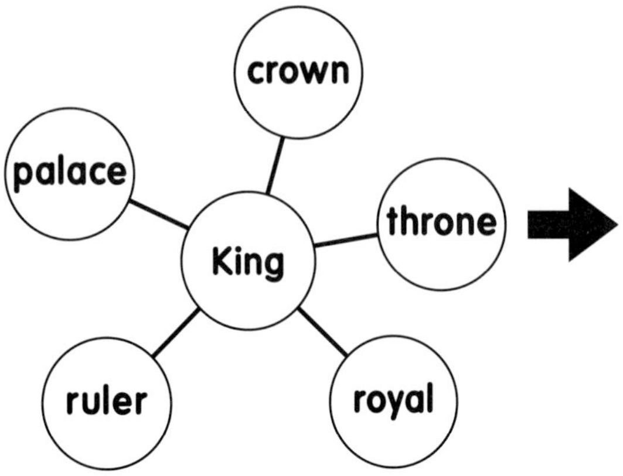
crown
palace
throne
King
ruler
royal

20

"Thank you, Rocky Fox," said Chicken Pedro. "You are very clever, but we have wings."
11 And flapping their wings, off they went. Flying, flying above the cave.

20

MODIFY Instruction

GIFTED & TALENTED

✷ Have children make a web for the word ***king.*** Have them name words that describe ***king.*** Write these words on the web. Then encourage children to list stories that have kings or queens in them. **(GRAPHIC DEVICE)**

ESL/ELD

▲ Invite children to do a mini role-play of the encounter with Rocky Fox. Give stage directions: *Fox, lick your lips. Chicken Pedro, flap your wings.* Ask children why the animals did **not** go hip hop. *(They were scared.)* Identify the words that tell how they went. *(flying, flying)* **(ACT IT OUT)**

21

They flew above the palace gates. They found the King and Queen in the garden, sitting under the shade of a green umbrella.

"Why do you all have such sad faces?" asked the King.

"The sky is falling.
The sun hit me on the face.
We came to tell you!" said Chicken Pedro.
And he handed the large yellow lemon to the King. 13

21

SOCIAL STUDIES

Ask children to do the **Spreading the News** activity on **page R9** where they discuss and illustrate different forms of modern communication.

TECHNOLOGY

Listening Skills Have children listen to the story on the audiocassette. Discuss what part of the story is predictable. How does the narrator change his or her voice to say the repetitive parts?

SKILLS AND STRATEGIES

GENRE

Folk Tale

TEACH/MODEL
Discuss folk tales with children. Point out the following:

- **Folk tales are stories that have been handed down from generation to generation by word of mouth.**
- **Folk tales often contain unusual characters, such as animals that speak.**
- **Many folk tales teach a lesson.**

THINK ALOUD *When I read this story I notice that the characters are animals. I also notice that this story is like* Chicken Licken, *which is a folk tale. Therefore, I think* Chicken Pedro and the Falling Sky *is a folk tale.*

PRACTICE/APPLY
Encourage children to talk about what makes *Chicken Pedro* a folk tale.

- **What clues about the characters tell you that this story is a folk tale?**
- **What has Chicken Pedro learned in this story?**

COMPREHENSION

14 COMPARE/CONTRAST

> **How do the King and Queen react to the news about the falling sky? How are their reactions different from the reactions of Chicken Pedro and his friends?** *(Possible answer: The King and Queen think it is funny that Chicken Pedro has everything so confused. They want to make lemonade because they don't believe the sky is falling.)*

15 MAKE INFERENCES

> **How do you think Chicken Pedro feels when he finds out the lemon is not the sun and that the sky is not falling? Why do you think so?** *(Possible answer: I think Chicken Pedro feels happy because he is smiling and enjoying the cake and lemonade party.)*

JOURNAL

Revisit Predictions

Ask children to look back at their predictions and record how they were or were not confirmed by the end of the story.

22

14
The Queen laughed: "This sun is a lemon!
Let's make lemonade."
The King said: "If we have lemonade
we will also have cake!
Let's bake a cake!"
22

MODIFY Instruction

ESL/ELD

▲ Have children work with English-speaking peers to compare how the characters looked and acted at the beginning and the end of the story. Encourage the mentor children to model language. For example: *At first, Chicken Pedro felt ______. At the end of the story, he felt ______.* **(MODEL)**

GIFTED & TALENTED

✳ Have pairs of children use school resources to find out about things that really do fall from the sky, such as meteors. Have children share their information with the rest of the class. **(WORK IN PAIRS)**

23

The King brought the cake on a large plate.
The Queen served the lemonade.
Chicken Pedro, Daniel Duck, Maria the Hen,
and Raymond the Rooster ate cake
and drank lemonade.
15 And they all had wonderful smiles
on their faces.

23

DECODING STRATEGIES

Write the word *lemonade* on the chalkboard. Say the word aloud. Cover *-ade* and help children pronounce the first part of the word. Point out that the second part of the word has the same final *e (a-e)* pattern as *made.* Uncover *-ade* and have children say the complete word: ***lemonade.***

WORKSHOP

You may wish to introduce the Workshop on this day. Set aside specific times over the next two weeks for children to work on this ongoing activity.

Stories With Animal Characters

SHARED WRITING

PREWRITE Using *Chicken Pedro and the Falling Sky* as a model, talk about using animals as characters in a story. Tell children that later they will be writing a story that uses animals as characters. Have children think about the animals they would like to have in their story and begin to complete the prewriting organizer on **Practice Book, page 13.**

DAILY LANGUAGE PRACTICE

SPELLING

DAY 2:
Practice Words With Final *e (a–e). **See page R4**.*

GRAMMAR, USAGE, MECHANICS

DAY 2:
Practice Word Order in Complete Sentences. ***See page R6.***

ORAL LANGUAGE

Queen will bake a cak the.
(The Queen will bake a cake.)

DAY 2 WRAP-UP

READ ALOUD *Spend five to ten minutes reading from a selection of your choice.*

GUIDED READING *Meet with the **green** and **yellow** reading groups and assign Independent Center activities. **See pages R2–R3.***

COMPREHENSION

DAY 3 OBJECTIVES

CHILDREN WILL:

READ 30 MINUTES

- **Lemonade Recipe, pp. 24–25**
- **Assess Comprehension**
- **Key Comprehension Skill: Make Inferences**
- **Daily Phonics: Words With *-ing***

WRITE 30 MINUTES

- **Respond: Recipe**
- **Spelling: Words With Final *e* (*a-e*)**
- **Grammar, Usage, Mechanics: Word Order in Complete Sentences**
- **Oral Language**

EXTEND SKILLS 30 MINUTES

- **Integrated Curriculum**
- **Read Aloud**
- **Guided Reading**

RESOURCES

- **Practice Book, pp. 8–12**
- **Spelling Resource Book, p. 88**

▶ Preview

Invite children to preview the recipe by reading the title and studying the illustration that goes with it.

1 STEPS IN A PROCESS

› **What is the first step in making lemonade?** *(Measure four cups of water and put it in a container.)*

2 MAKE INFERENCES

› **The recipe calls for lemon juice. Use the illustration to find out where the lemon juice comes from.** *(from squeezing the lemons)*

24

RECIPE

Lemonade Recipe

4 cups water
12 tablespoons lemon juice
12 tablespoons sugar
1/4 teaspoon salt

Add twelve tablespoons of lemon juice to four cups of water. Add twelve tablespoons of sugar and a quarter teaspoon of salt to the lemon juice and water. Stir well. 1

24

MODIFY Instruction

ESL/ELD

▲ Create a simple recipe for juice with children. Let each child choose a fruit, such as oranges, grapes, or grapefruit. Have them draw the fruit and list several numbered steps for making juice with it. Ask volunteers to read their recipes aloud, using the sequence words *first, next,* and *last.* **(STEP-BY-STEP)**

EXTRA HELP

■ Distribute measuring spoons and cups and let children examine them. Write the following measurements on the chalkboard: ***1 cup, 1 tablespoon, 1 teaspoon.*** Point to a measurement and help children find the correct cup or spoon. Repeat the procedure with the fractional measures. **(HANDS-ON LEARNING)**

25

SUGAR
2
SALT
25

TEACHER TIP

"Cooking in the classroom gives children an exciting way to apply what they are learning in both math and reading. When I cook with children, I work with small groups, so that everyone can get into the action. I assign everyone a job like reading the recipe aloud, measuring, preparing, or mixing the ingredients."

SKILLS AND STRATEGIES

GENRE
Recipe

TEACH/MODEL

Ask children if they have ever helped with cooking. Ask if they have ever seen or followed a recipe. Point out that a recipe is a list of ingredients and step-by-step directions on how to make something to eat or drink.

> **Before you use a recipe, read it all the way through, including the ingredients and the directions.**

> **Measure the ingredients carefully and follow the directions step-by-step.**

THINK ALOUD *When I read this recipe, I should read it from beginning to end. I have to know what ingredients to use, and what cooking tools I will need.*

PRACTICE/APPLY

If possible, help children follow the recipe as you make lemonade together.

> **What ingredients do we need?** *(lemons, water, sugar, salt)*

> **What is the first step in making lemonade?** *(The first step is to measure four cups of water.)*

> **How do you think the lemonade would taste if someone didn't read the ingredients carefully and put 12 tablespoons of salt and a quarter teaspoon of sugar instead of the correct amounts?** *(Possible answer: The lemonade would be salty and sour.)*

COMPREHENSION

Think About Reading

Below are the **answers** to the story map questions in *Think About Reading.*

First Chicken Pedro met Daniel Duck.

Next Chicken Pedro met Maria the Hen.

Then Chicken Pedro met Raymond the Rooster.

Then Chicken Pedro met Rocky Fox.

Last Chicken Pedro met the King and the Queen.

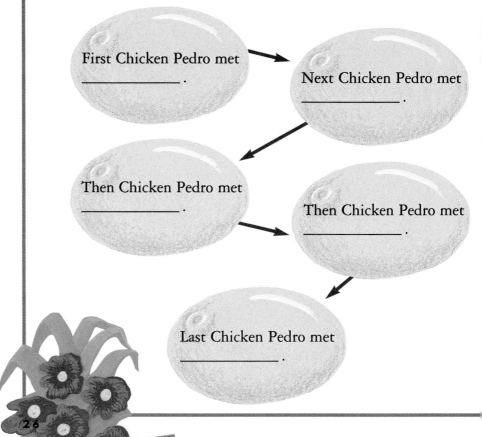

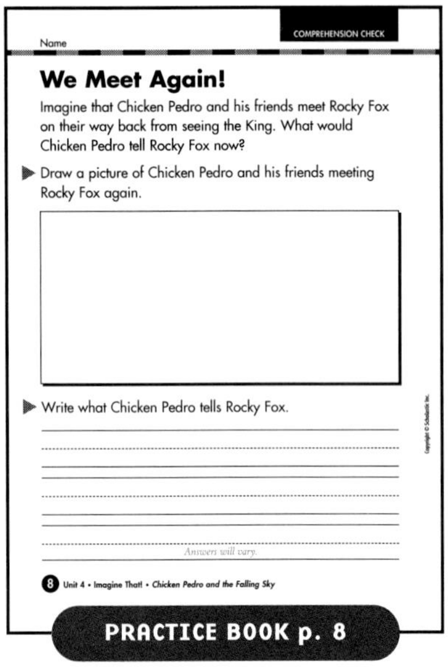
Name
COMPREHENSION CHECK

We Meet Again!

Imagine that Chicken Pedro and his friends meet Rocky Fox on their way back from seeing the King. What would Chicken Pedro tell Rocky Fox now?

▶ Draw a picture of Chicken Pedro and his friends meeting Rocky Fox again.

▶ Write what Chicken Pedro tells Rocky Fox.

Answers will vary.

8 Unit 4 • Imagine That! • Chicken Pedro and the Falling Sky

PRACTICE BOOK p. 8

26

RESPOND

Think About Reading

Think about Chicken Pedro and the Falling Sky. Finish each sentence on another piece of paper. Draw a picture to go with each sentence.

First Chicken Pedro met ______.

Next Chicken Pedro met ______.

Then Chicken Pedro met ______.

Then Chicken Pedro met ______.

Last Chicken Pedro met ______.

26

MODIFY Instruction

ESL/ELD

▲ Work with small groups, helping children create their own story map so they can retell the key events of the story. Ask children to answer these questions: *Who was scary in the story? Who was funny? Was this story real or make-believe?* **(RETELL)**

EXTRA HELP

■ Children can work in pairs to think of things that could drop from trees and could be made into something to eat. They can use a graphic organizer to chart their ideas. **(USE VISUALS)**

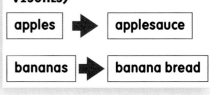

apples → applesauce

bananas → banana bread

27

Write a Recipe

What do you like to eat? Write a recipe for your favorite food. Write a list of all the things you need to make the food. Then write how to make it.

Peanut Butter and Jelly Sandwich
• peanut butter
• grape jelly
• 2 pieces of bread
Put peanut butter on one side of one piece of bread. Put jelly on one side of the other piece of bread. Put peanut butter side of bread against the jelly side of the other piece of bread. Now you have a sandwich!

Literature Circle

Why do Chicken Pedro, Daniel Duck, Maria the Hen, Raymond the Rooster, and the King and Queen make lemonade? What else could have fallen from a tree and hit Chicken Pedro on the head? What could he and his friends have made to eat from it? Talk about your ideas.

Author
Alma Flor Ada

Alma Flor Ada has been writing books for children for a long time. She writes poetry and stories for children. Some of her stories are written in English and in Spanish. You can learn another language when you read them!

More Books by Alma Flor Ada

- My Name is María Isabel
- Dear Peter Rabbit
- The Great-great-granddaughter of La Cucarachita Martina

27

TECHNOLOGY

Finding the Facts Food plays a part in many folk tales. Take the Internet Field Trip called Folk Tales on the Web at **www.scholasticnetwork.com**. Ask children to look for food in these stories, and think about recipes for these foods.

AUTHOR STUDY

Alma Flor Ada has been delighting young readers in both Spanish and English for years. Children can learn more about her by visiting **www.penguinputnam.com** and looking at the author biographies in the young readers section.

RESPOND

Write a Recipe

Before children start to write, have them think about these questions:

> **What are the things you need to make your favorite food?**
> **What cooking tools do you need?**
> **What are the steps in making the recipe?**

Children may want to demonstrate how to make a favorite recipe and share the finished product with the class.

Literature Circle

Encourage children to compare their ideas about what else could fall from a tree and what could be made to eat from it.

DAILY LANGUAGE PRACTICE

SPELLING
DAY 3:
Write Words with Final *e* (*a-e*). **See page R5.**

GRAMMAR, USAGE, MECHANICS
DAY 3:
Practice Writing Words in Correct Order and in Complete Sentences. **See page R7.**

ORAL LANGUAGE
cak Daniel Duck the ate.
(Daniel Duck ate the cake.)

SKILLS TRACE

MAKE INFERENCES TESTED

Introduce . . . . pp. T44–45
Practice . . . . pp. T27, T129
Review . . . . p. R43
Reteach . . . . p. R56

GOING HOME
by Margaret Wild
PIERRE
A cautionary tale
IN FIVE CHAPTERS
AND A PROLOGUE
MAURICE SENDAK

CONNECT TO THE TRADE BOOKS

Select one of the unit trade books. Read aloud the title, and discuss the cover illustration.

- Have children make predictions about what might happen in the story. Record their predictions on chart paper or the chalkboard.
- Then, read a few pages at a time, and stop to make inferences.
- Record children's inferences. Continue until the book is completed.

COMPREHENSION

Make Inferences

QUICKCHECK

Can children:

✔ use picture and word clues to make inferences?

✔ use personal experience and prior knowledge to make inferences?

If YES, go on to Practice/Apply.

If NO, start at Teach/Model.

A TEACH/MODEL

USE ORAL LANGUAGE

Hold up a picture of a specific scene, such as a long line of people near a movie theater. Ask children to tell you what is going on in the picture. Have them give reasons for their answers.

Making inferences is **using clues from the pictures and the story to understand information that is not given in the story.** What you already know also helps you to make inferences. To make inferences:

1. Read the story and look for important picture and word clues for information that is not given.
2. Use your own experiences and what you already know to make guesses about information that is not given.
3. Make an inference based on steps 1 and 2. Then ask yourself if your inference makes sense. Read on to check your inference, and change it if necessary.

MODIFY Instruction

ESL/ELD

▲ Have children use picture clues to make inferences. Pages 10–11: How do you know *Chicken Pedro is scared?* Page 11: *How do you know Rocky Fox is hungry?* Page 19: *How do you know the animals don't go "hip hop?"* **(CONTEXT CLUES)**

EXTRA HELP

■ Before children begin pages 9 and 10 in the Practice Book, have them make a list of the key points in both *Chicken Pedro and the Falling Sky* and *Chicken Licken.* **(MAKE CONNECTIONS)**

LITERATURE CONNECTION

Display page 11 of the Anthology and help children make inferences about what Chicken Pedro will do in the story.

THINK ALOUD *I can see from the picture of Chicken Pedro that he is upset by the lemon that hit him. The words* "Oh my! Oh my!" he cried *also tell me he is upset. I also know from reading* Chicken Licken *that when she was hit by an acorn, she wanted to tell the king the sky was falling. I can make the guess that Chicken Pedro is as scared as Chicken Licken.*

B PRACTICE/APPLY

USE PRACTICE BOOK

Looking at page 11 with children helped them to find the story and picture clues they needed to make inferences. Now have pairs of children practice the skill by completing **Practice Book page 9.**

C ASSESS

APPLY INSTRUCTIONAL ALTERNATIVES

Based on children's completion of **Practice Book** page 9, determine if they were able to make inferences in *Chicken Pedro and the Falling Sky*. The Instructional Alternatives below will aid you in pinpointing children's level of proficiency. Consider the appropriate instructional alternative to promote further skill development.

To reinforce the skill, distribute **page 10** of the **Practice Book.**

INSTRUCTIONAL ALTERNATIVES

	If the child . . .	Then
Proficient	Makes a valid inference.	• Have the child apply this skill independently to a more challenging story. • Present a new scenario. Have the child brainstorm possible inferences and provide a rationale for these inferences.
Apprentice	Makes an inference but cannot determine if it is valid or invalid based on text and picture information.	• Have the child work with other children to brainstorm inferences and then identify clues in the text and pictures that support or negate the inferences.
Novice	Makes an inference that does not fit the situation in either a real-world or text-based context.	• Provide the child with details of a scenario and work with the child to make possible inferences. • Complete the Reteach Lesson on R56.

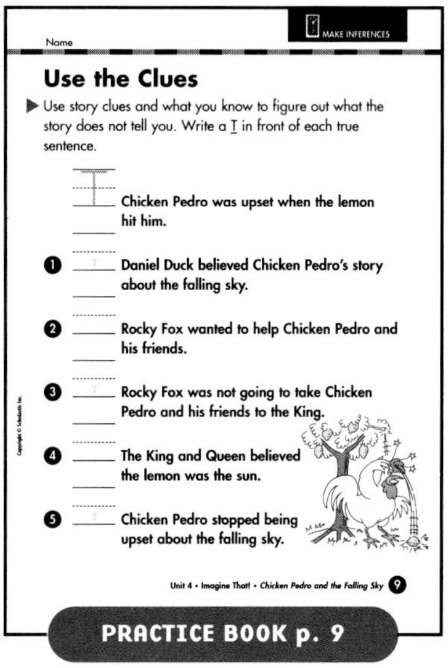
Name MAKE INFERENCES

Use the Clues

▶ Use story clues and what you know to figure out what the story does not tell you. Write a T in front of each true sentence.

T Chicken Pedro was upset when the lemon hit him.

1 ____ Daniel Duck believed Chicken Pedro's story about the falling sky.

2 ____ Rocky Fox wanted to help Chicken Pedro and his friends.

3 ____ Rocky Fox was not going to take Chicken Pedro and his friends to the King.

4 ____ The King and Queen believed the lemon was the sun.

5 ____ Chicken Pedro stopped being upset about the falling sky.

Unit 4 • Imagine That! • Chicken Pedro and the Falling Sky 9

PRACTICE BOOK p. 9

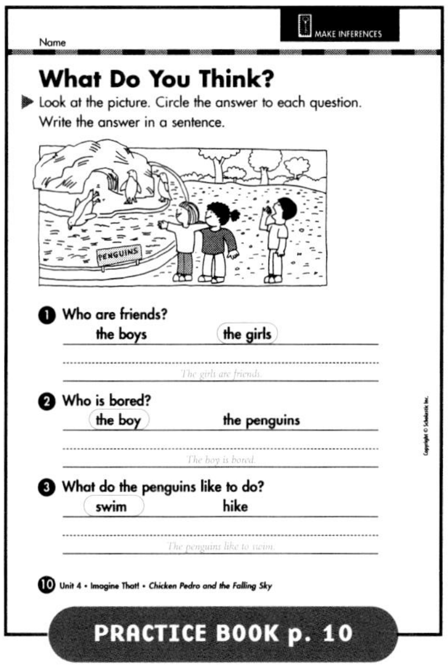
Name MAKE INFERENCES

What Do You Think?

▶ Look at the picture. Circle the answer to each question. Write the answer in a sentence.

PENGUINS

1 Who are friends? the boys / the girls

The girls are friends.

2 Who is bored? the boy / the penguins

The boy is bored.

3 What do the penguins like to do? swim / hike

The penguins like to swim.

10 Unit 4 • Imagine That! • Chicken Pedro and the Falling Sky

PRACTICE BOOK p. 10

Chicken Pedro and the Falling Sky

SELECTION WORDS With *-ing*

falling	flying
flapping	going

SKILLS TRACE

Words With *-ing* TESTED

Introduce . . . . p. T46–T47
Practice . . . . pp. T33, T137
Review . . . . p. R48
Reteach . . . . p. R58

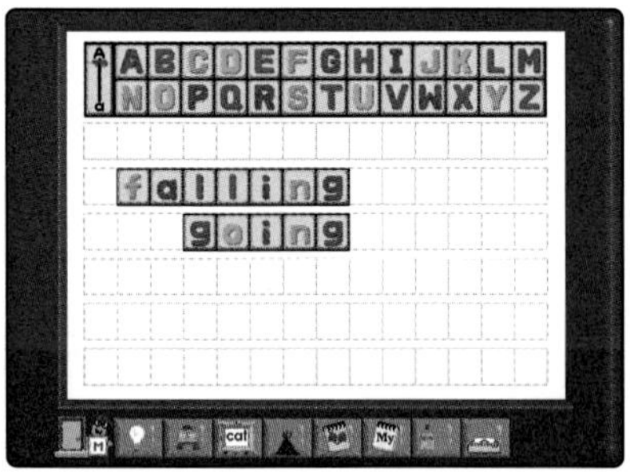
falling
going

TECHNOLOGY

Have children build words with *-ing* on the Magnet Board.

- Begin with the words *fall* and *go* to which children will add *-ing*.
- Have children search for words that end with *-ing* in classroom books and add the words to the list.

DAILY PHONICS

Words With -ing

A PHONOLOGICAL AWARENESS

SONG Write the song on the chalkboard and read it aloud. Then sing it to the tune of "Are You Sleeping?"

Mister Cat

Are you sleeping, are you sleeping,
Mister cat, mister cat?
All the mice are playing,
All the mice are playing,
Just like that, just like that.

Stress the words that contain *-ing,* such as ***sleeping.***

- As soon as children are familiar with the song, have them sing it along with you.
- Say the words ***sleeping*** and ***playing*** and have children repeat them. Point out the ***-ing*** ending in each word.

ORAL BLENDING Say the following word parts and ask children to blend them. Provide corrective feedback and modeling as needed.

- **fall . . . ing**
- **turn . . . ing**
- **plant . . . ing**
- **go . . . ing**
- **cook . . . ing**
- **tell . . . ing**

B CONNECT SOUND-SPELLING

INTRODUCE *-ing* Explain to children that words that describe actions sometimes end with ***-ing,*** such as ***falling*** and ***cooking.*** Write the word ***falling*** on the chalkboard and have a volunteer circle ***-ing.*** Then model how to blend the word.

THINK ALOUD *In this word, I see two parts. I see the smaller word* **fall** *and the ending* **-ing.** *I can put together the two parts to read the word.*

MODIFY Instruction

ESL/ELD

▲ Tell children that the ***-ing*** ending is a clue that means the word tells about something that is happening now. Before the song activity, play a question/answer game to prepare children. Ask questions like: *Are you sleeping?* Children reply: *No I'm (reading).* **(LINGUISTIC CLUES)**

EXTRA HELP

■ Write the words ***go, play, fall, tell, look,*** and the ending ***-ing*** on index cards, one word or ending per card. Ask children to place the word cards face down on a table. Have one child in the pair pick a word card and read it aloud. Have the second child add the ***-ing*** card and pronounce the new word. **(SMALL GROUPS)**

- Suggest other words that end with ***-ing.***
- List these words on a chart. Have volunteers circle the ***-ing*** ending.

Words With -ing

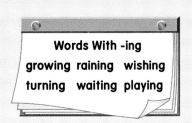

growing raining wishing
turning waiting playing

PHONICS MAINTENANCE Review the following sound-spellings: ***/sh/sh, /kw/qu, /v/v.*** Say one of these sounds. Have a volunteer write on the chalkboard the spelling that stands for the sound. Continue with all the sounds.

C PRACTICE/APPLY

BLEND WORDS To practice using the sound-spelling and review previous sound-spellings, list the following words and sentences on the chalkboard. Have children read each chorally. Model blending as needed.

go going fall falling
fly flying play playing

The sky is falling.
We are playing with a ball.

DICTATION Dictate the following words for children to spell: ***doing, ship, quick.***

BUILD WORDS Distribute the following word cards, and ***-ing*** card or have children use their own sets: ***-ing, fall, go, fly, play.*** Allow children time to build as many ***-ing*** words as possible using the cards. Children can write their words on a separate sheet of paper.

fall go -ing

Name
STRUCTURAL ANALYSIS: -ing

Make New Words

▶ Add **-ing** to make new words.

call + ing = calling jump + ing = jumping

pull + ing = pulling walk + ing = walking

▶ Use the best new word to complete each sentence.

1. Dan is pulling the wagon.
2. Ken and Maria are walking.
3. Lee is calling his sister.
4. She is jumping on the bed.

Copyright © Scholastic Inc.

Unit 4 • Imagine That! • *Chicken Pedro and the Falling Sky* 11

PRACTICE BOOK p. 11

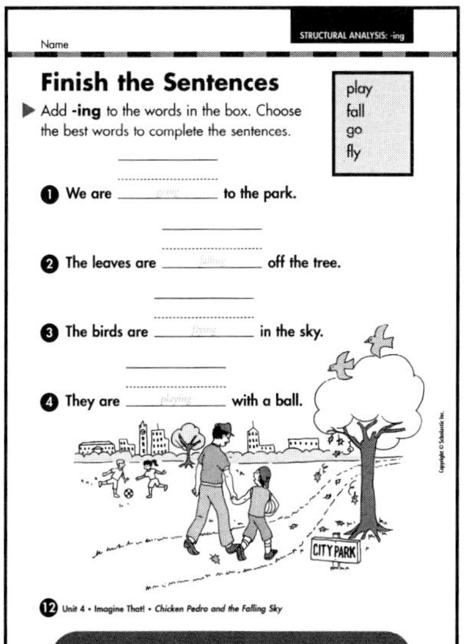
Name
STRUCTURAL ANALYSIS: -ing

Finish the Sentences

▶ Add **-ing** to the words in the box. Choose the best words to complete the sentences.

play
fall
go
fly

1. We are going to the park.
2. The leaves are falling off the tree.
3. The birds are flying in the sky.
4. They are playing with a ball.

CITY PARK

Copyright © Scholastic Inc.

12 Unit 4 • Imagine That! • *Chicken Pedro and the Falling Sky*

PRACTICE BOOK p. 12

DECODABLE TEXT

For practice reading decodable text, see ***Scholastic Decodable Reader #45.***

For additional phonics instruction and review, see ***Scholastic Phonics A, pp. 156–160.***

MAKE A WORD WHEEL

- Cut two wheels from paper, one smaller than the other. Help children make a word wheel for ***-ing*** by writing ***ing*** on the small "wheel" and ***go, sleep, play, yell, help, fall, call,*** and ***jump*** along the edge of the large "wheel."
- Place the small "wheel" on top of the large "wheel" so that partners or individual children can make new action words with ***-ing*** by turning the wheels.
- Suggest that children make a list of the words they make. Children can use the new words to make up a short story or write sentences.

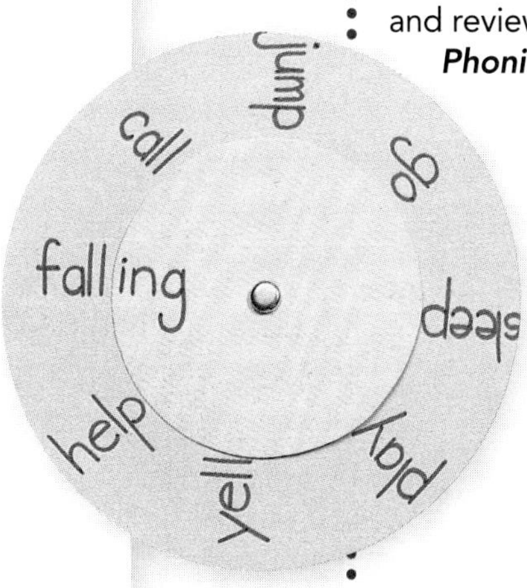
jump
go
sleep
play
yell
help
fall ing
call

Building Fluency

PHONICS READER

Guide children through a reading of **Phonics Reader #37,** *The Big Race.* For a detailed lesson plan, see **Phonics Reader Teacher's Guide Part B, pages 16–17.** While children read, note how well they:

- **blend words,**
- **recognize high-frequency words,**
- **read with speed, accuracy, and expression.**

You may wish to have children reread the story with a partner.

* See Phonics Readers Take-Home Books 37–72 for reproducible format.

The
BIG RACE
Book 37
START
a retelling by Nancy Hechinger
Illustrated by Renée Andriani
SCHOLASTIC

More Support Materials . . .

GOING HOME
PIERRE
A cautionary tale
IN FIVE CHAPTERS
AND A PROLOGUE
MAURICE SENDAK
JENNY'S JOURNEY
SCHOLASTIC

TRADE BOOK LIBRARY

For additional leveled reading practice, have children read one of the following:

Going Home
CHALLENGE

Pierre
AVERAGE

Jenny's Journey
EASY

PHONICS AND WORD BUILDING KIT

Have children build words with final ***e (a-e)*** using the letter and phonogram cards.

MAKE A FACE
by Cass Hollander
Illustrated by Ellen Joy Sasaki
SCHOLASTIC

MY BOOK

For additional practice with final *e (a-e)* have children read *Make a Face.* My Book is also available on the **WiggleWorks Plus** CD-ROM.

The
BIG RACE
MAKE A FACE

HOME-SCHOOL CONNECTION

Send home *The Big Race* and *Make a Face.* Have children read the books to a family member.

Intervention

For children who need extra help . . .

FOCUS ON HIGH-FREQUENCY WORDS

Write the words ***soon*** and ***went*** on note cards. Then follow this procedure:

- State each word aloud as children repeat it.
- Have children spell the word aloud as you point to each letter.
- Have children write each word in their Journals.
- Provide children with simple sentences containing each word. Help them to read the sentences. Then write the sentences on sentence strips for children to practice reading during center time.

Some children may need a large number of repetitions before these words become sight words. Brief, daily reviews and frequent rereadings of previous stories containing these words will be helpful.

FOCUS ON PHONICS

Provide time for children to play with the decodable words they encountered in the story such as ***cave*** and ***bake.*** To emphasize the importance of the silent *e,* also include minimal contrast pairs such as *mad/made* and *hat/hate.*

- Make each word using magnetic letters or letter cards as children observe.
- Remind children that the ***e*** is silent in ***cave*** and ***bake*** and other long ***a*** words spelled ***a-e.***
- Mix the letters and have children reform the words.
- Model blending as needed.

c
a
v
e
b
a
k
e

PROFESSIONAL DEVELOPMENT

GAY SU PINNELL

Using Minimal Contrasts

Minimal contrasts are word pairs that vary by only one letter, such as mad/made, run/sun, can/cat, *and* sat/sit. *Using minimal contrasts in instruction through word lists and sentence completion activities helps children see how one letter in a word can make all the difference. This technique is especially important for children who have difficulty fully analyzing words because it forces them to focus on and use every letter in a word.*

DAY 3 WRAP-UP

READ ALOUD *To conclude each reading session and develop children's oral vocabularies, read aloud a book of your choice. If the book contains chapters, you might choose to read only one chapter a day.*

GUIDED READING *Meet with the* ***red*** *and* ***blue*** *reading groups and assign Independent Center activities.* ***See pages R2–R3.***

DAY 4 OBJECTIVES

CHILDREN WILL:

READ 25 MINUTES

- **Reread *Chicken Pedro and the Falling Sky***

WRITE 35 MINUTES

- **Shared Writing: Animal Characters**
- **Spelling: Words With Final *e* (*a-e*)**
- **Grammar, Usage, Mechanics: Word Order in Complete Sentences**
- **Oral Language**

EXTEND SKILLS 30 MINUTES

- **Vocabulary**
- **Daily Phonics: Final *e* (*a-e*)**
- **Oral Language**
- **Read Aloud**
- **Guided Reading**

RESOURCES

- **Practice Book, p. 13**
- **Spelling Resource Book, p. 161**

Name

WRITING

Get Ready to Write

▶ Draw animals you like. Then write things the animals might do if they could act like people.

Things they might to do:

Copyright © Scholastic Inc.

To the Teacher: This is the prewriting organizer referenced in the lesson on using animal characters.

Unit 4 • Imagine That! • *Chicken Pedro and the Falling Sky* 13

PRACTICE BOOK p. 13

SHARED WRITING *Expressive Writing*

Stories With Animal Characters

Chicken Pedro and the Falling Sky

SELECTION CONNECTION Using *Chicken Pedro* as a model, children will write a class story with animal characters.

THINK ABOUT WRITING Ask children to describe animal characters in stories. Then ask children how the characters are like real animals. Help children discover that:

- in some stories, animals act like people and do things that people do.
- most of the characters in *Chicken Pedro and the Falling Sky* are animals that act like people.

INTRODUCE THE WRITING EVENT Let children know that they will work together to write a class story using animals as characters.

TEACH/MODEL

PUT IT IN CONTEXT Talk about the story *Chicken Pedro and the Falling Sky* and the characters in it.

> **How are Chicken Pedro and his friends like people?**

> **Find pages that show the animals acting like people.**

Have children think of animals to include in their story. Write their ideas on the chalkboard. Help children decide what the animals will do.

MODIFY Instruction

ESL/ELD

▲ Encourage children to act out their own version of the story. Use the visuals collected for the **Build Background** activity, or have children draw a few new simple characters. Children will color and act out the characters, and hold them up as props as they act out their own stories. **(ROLE-PLAY)**

EXTRA HELP

■ Have children tape-record *Chicken Pedro and the Falling Sky.* Then they can read along with the story as they play back the recording. Next, pairs of children can read the story together. **(RECORD)**

GRAMMAR CONNECTION Remind children to use complete sentences with words in the correct order as they write.

WRITE

WRITE A CLASS STORY

- Have children write or dictate on chart paper some sentences about their animal characters and what they do. Point out how more than one sentence makes up a paragraph.
- Then invite children to work in cooperative groups to draw pictures to go with the sentences. Each group can illustrate one sentence.
- Read the story aloud with children. Then ask them how their animal characters speak and act like people. Invite children to talk about how their animal characters make the class story interesting.

ASSESS

PERFORMANCE-BASED ASSESSMENT The following questions will help children assess their work.

✔ **Did we use animal characters in our story?**

✔ **Did our characters say and do things that people do?**

Children may wish to carry this piece through the writing process described on pages T278–T281.

DAILY LANGUAGE PRACTICE

SPELLING

DAY 4:
Review words with final *e* (*a*-*e*). Have children proofread sentences. **See page R5.**

GRAMMAR, USAGE, MECHANICS

DAY 4:
Apply writing words in correct order and in complete sentences. **See page R7.**

ORAL LANGUAGE

we cme to you tell. *(We came to tell you.)*

TECHNOLOGY

Writing Skills Encourage children to use the Unit Writer to create their story. Suggest that they use the Record Tool, the Paint Tools, and stamp art.

Extend Vocabulary

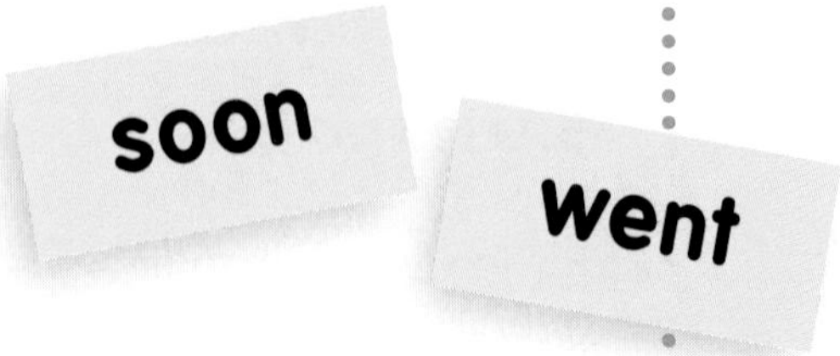
soon
went

TEACHER TIP

Make and distribute copies of the vocabulary cards on pages R66–R67. Children can use these cards for additional practice.

Review High-Frequency Words

Write the high-frequency words ***soon*** and ***went*** on note cards. For each word write a lowercase and uppercase version. **(*soon/Soon*)** Then write the following incomplete sentences on the chalkboard:

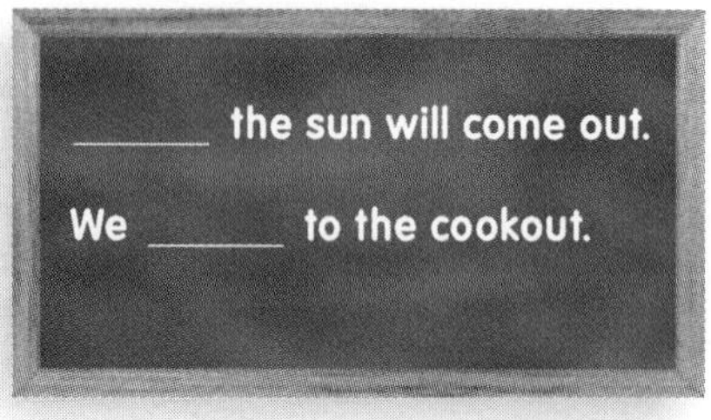
_____ the sun will come out.
We _____ to the cookout.

Read aloud the incomplete sentences and place the appropriate high-frequency word note card in the blank space. Then help children do a choral reading of the sentences.

Review Story Words

Write the story words ***lemon, sky, sun, king, cave,*** and ***cake*** on note cards. Then write the following incomplete sentences on sentence strips:

The _____ hit him on the face.

The fox will go in the _____ .

The sun is in the _____ .

Mom made a _____ for me.

The _____ is a big man.

Read aloud the incomplete sentences and place the appropriate story word note card in the blank space. Then help children to chorally read the sentences.

TELL IT AND SPELL IT

Put the word cards in a bucket. The first player picks a card out of the bucket, looks at it, and then conceals it from the rest of the class. Then the player gives clues about the word such as: *This word has three letters. It makes you hot.*

A child in the group tries to figure out what the word is and spells the word. If successful, he or she gets to choose the next word from the bucket.

king
cake
sun

Building Fluency

Phonics Reader

The
Pancake Man
Book 38
a retelling by Francie Alexander
Illustrated by Horacio Elena
SCHOLASTIC

Guide children through a reading of **Phonics Reader #38,** *The Pancake Man.* For a detailed lesson plan, **see Phonics Reader Teacher's Guide Part B, pages 18–19.** While children read, note how well they:

- **blend words,**
- **recognize high-frequency words,**
- **read with speed, accuracy, and expression.**

You may wish to have children reread the story with a partner.

★ See Phonics Readers Take-Home Books 37–72 for reproducible format.

More Support Materials . . .

GOING HOME
by Margaret Wild
PIERRE
A cautionary tale
IN FIVE CHAPTERS
AND A PROLOGUE
MAURICE SENDAK
JENNY'S JOURNEY
SCHOLASTIC

Trade Book Library

For additional leveled reading practice, have children read one of the following:

Going Home
Challenge

Pierre
Average

Jenny's Journey
Easy

Phonics Chapter Book

PHONICS
The
Puppet Club
SCHOLASTIC

For additional practice with final ***e*** **(*a-e*),** children read Chapter 1, "Jane and Jake" in **Phonics Chapter Book 4,** *The Puppet Club.*

Scholastic Phonics A

Scholastic
PHONICS
A
fish
pig
bus
globe
SCHOLASTIC

For additional practice with **final *e* (a-e)** and high-frequency words, have children read *At Home,* pages 175–176.

Home-School Connection

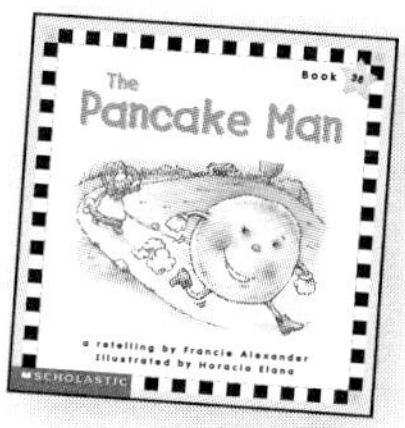
The
Pancake Man
SCHOLASTIC

Send home *The Pancake Man.* Have children read the book to a family member.

Listen to the Read Aloud

Curious George
Rides a Bike
by
H. A. REY

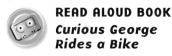

READ ALOUD BOOK
Curious George Rides a Bike

Introduce the Read Aloud

CREATE INTEREST

Spark children's interest in the Read Aloud by asking: *Is it possible to be too curious? What might happen to someone who is too curious?* Play the song "Pop! Goes the Weasel" and talk about the adventuresome monkey.

Write the questions on chart paper. Record children's responses below. Then explain that in the story they are about to listen to, they will meet a character who may be too curious.

Share the Read Aloud

MAKE PREDICTIONS

As you show children the cover of the book, read the title and the name of the author/illustrator. Talk about the cover picture and ask children to point out Curious George. Read aloud to the point where the man with the yellow hat leaves George alone with his new bike. Ask children to predict whether George will stay near the house. Continue reading, pausing occasionally so children can predict what George will do next.

Think About the Read Aloud

DISCUSSION

Give children a moment to share their thoughts about the story. You may want to prompt a conversation by asking questions such as:

> **What do you think of this story?**

> **Which parts did you think were funny? Which parts surprised you?**

> **Which word besides *curious* would you use to describe George?**

Return to the chart you made before reading the story. Encourage children to compare their responses and discuss whether someone can be too curious.

Handle with Care!

Focus on Language

SPECIAL WORDS

Reread pages 36–38 to children. Point out that the author uses special words, such as ***emergency*** and ***alarm*** to make this part of the story exciting. Ask children what other words the author uses to keep the story exciting. Record children's responses. The word list could include: ***rushed, grabbed, loud, dangerous, raced, naughty***.

ACTIVITY: WHAT'S GEORGE THINKING?

Ask a volunteer to pantomime George as you read one of the scenes aloud. Then ask children what George might be thinking and feeling. Invite children to ask "George" questions about himself. Repeat the activity with another volunteer and another scene.

Make Connections

ORAL LANGUAGE

To *Chicken Pedro and the Falling Sky*

DISCUSSION Chicken Pedro was not very curious when the lemon hit him on the face. Talk about how the story might be different if Chicken Pedro had asked some questions about the lemon. What could Chicken Pedro have asked about the lemon? How would the story have changed if he had asked questions about it?

To Children's Lives

DISCUSSION Ask children if they have ever been curious about something. Ask volunteers to tell about a time when they were curious.

DESCRIPTIVE WORDS

TEACH/MODEL Discuss the idea that children can learn more about George's character by paying attention to the words the author uses to describe him.

THINK ALOUD *I know about George because of the way the author describes him and what he does. The author uses words such as* curious *to describe George. The author also describes how George helps the newsboy and tries to save baby bear.*

PRACTICE/APPLY Ask children what other words they can think of to describe George. Brainstorm a list of words that describe George in this story. Have children draw a picture of George in a favorite scene from the story and write a sentence about it.

TECHNOLOGY

Speaking Skills Have children perform a choral reading of the predictable, repetitive parts of the story. Guide them to read aloud with style and drama choosing certain words and phrases to emphasize. Discuss what oral techniques make the story fun to hear. Record the choral presentation on an audiocassette and place it in the class or school library.

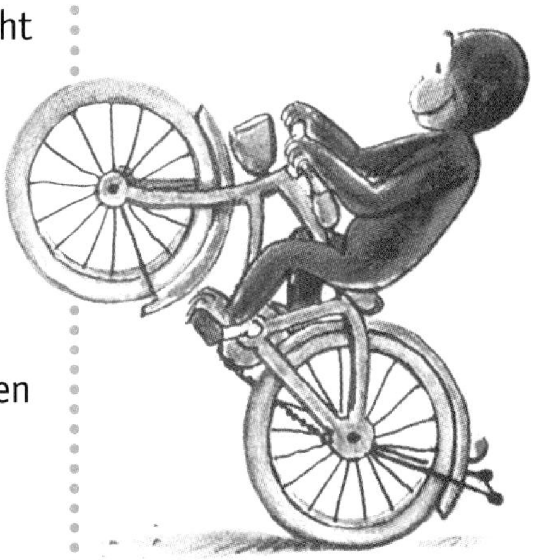

DAY 4 WRAP-UP

READ ALOUD *Spend five to ten minutes reading from a selection of your choice. Select nonfiction books at least twice a week.*

GUIDED READING *To extend reading, meet with the* ***green*** *and* ***yellow*** *reading groups and assign Independent Center activities.* ***See pages R2–R3.***

DAY 5 OBJECTIVES

CHILDREN WILL:

READ 30 MINUTES

- **Reading Assessment**
- **Daily Phonics: Final *e* (*a–e*), Words With *-ing***

WRITE 30 MINUTES

- **Writing Assessment**
- **Spelling: Words With Final *e* (*a–e*)**
- **Grammar, Usage, Mechanics: Word Order in Complete Sentences**
- **Oral Language**

EXTEND SKILLS 30 MINUTES

- **Integrated Language Arts**
- **Read Aloud**
- **Guided Reading**

RESOURCES

- **Selection Test**
- **Spelling Resource Book, p. 163**

REGROUPING TIP

- Assess and regroup children for leveled reading every six weeks.
- Use the results of your informal and formal assessments to regroup children as necessary.
- Be sure all children are involved in whole class and small group instruction throughout each day.

Reading Assessment

INFORMAL ASSESSMENT: OBSERVATION

PHONICS

Write the following spellings on note cards: ***-ate, -ade, -ame, -ing.*** Display one card at a time and have the class state aloud the sounds the spelling stands for. Continue with all the spellings. Note children who respond incorrectly or wait for classmates to respond before providing an answer.

HIGH-FREQUENCY WORDS

Write the following words on note cards: ***soon*, *went*.** Display one card at a time and have the class read the word. Note children who have difficulty recognizing either word.

soon
went

KEY STRATEGY: MAKE INFERENCES

Display a book children haven't read yet. Have them browse through the first part of the book. Then ask children to write a sentence or two that tells what the characters are doing or thinking, or what is going on, based on inferences they make.

CONFERENCE

Have children reread *Chicken Pedro and the Falling Sky*. As they reread, select several children to conference with. Ask them to do the following:

- read aloud a few pages of the story.
- retell the story in their own words.
- explain what they did to figure out an unfamiliar word.

Keep anecdotal records of the conferences. Be sure to monitor and record children's reading rate. Place your findings in each child's assessment folder. Use the information to determine which children need additional support.

Chicken Pedro and the Falling Sky

Chicken Pedro and the Falling Sky

FORMAL ASSESSMENT

DECODING TEST

Make two copies of the assessment below. The assessment piece is designed to be used individually.

- Give one to the child and keep the other to record each child's errors.
- As the child reads aloud the words and sentences in the assessment boxes, record his or her attempts, corrections, errors, and passes.
- Once completed, keep each assessment piece in the child's portfolio as a running record of his or her emerging reading skills.

NAME: ______________________ **DATE:** __________

A Have children read the following word list:

came	**shop**	**kick**	**went**	**over**
get	**thick**	**cake**	**soon**	**are**
fish	**sun**	**going**	**little**	**now**
bake	**falling**	**box**	**into**	**put**
van	**quit**	**telling**	**from**	**first**

B Have children read the following sentences.

- **Will the sun come out soon?**
- **The King went to get the cake.**

C On a separate sheet of paper, have children write the following words and sentences.

- **take made wish duck**
- **He likes to bake cakes.**
- **She will take a bag on the plane.**

SELECTION TEST

Use the selection test to obtain a formal measure of children's mastery of the week's reading objectives.

TIME MANAGEMENT

Part C of the assessment can be administered to the whole class. Assess children throughout the entire day on Parts A and B. Each assessment should take no more than 2–3 minutes.

You may choose to assess children during independent reading time or Independent Center time. If you have a teacher's aide, allow him or her to give the assessment.

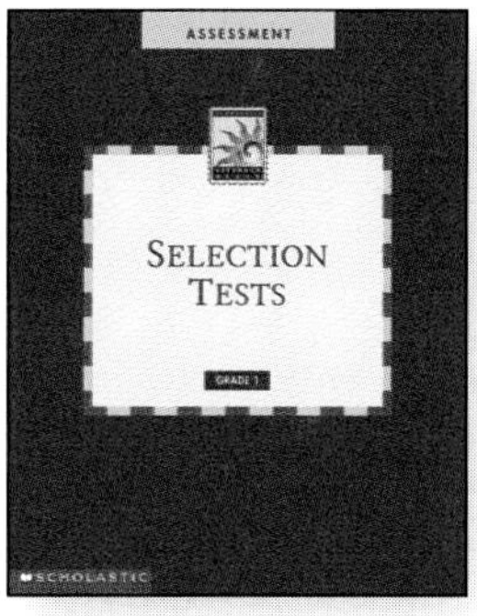
ASSESSMENT
SELECTION TESTS

SELECTION TEST

DAILY LANGUAGE PRACTICE

SPELLING

DAY 5:
Administer Posttest for Words With Final *e (a–e)*.
See page R5.

GRAMMAR, USAGE, MECHANICS

DAY 5:
Assess Word Order in Complete Sentences.
See page R7.

ORAL LANGUAGE

I'm on my way to the King tell.
(I'm on my way to tell the King.)

PORTFOLIO

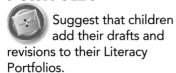

Suggest that children add their drafts and revisions to their Literacy Portfolios.

Writing Assessment

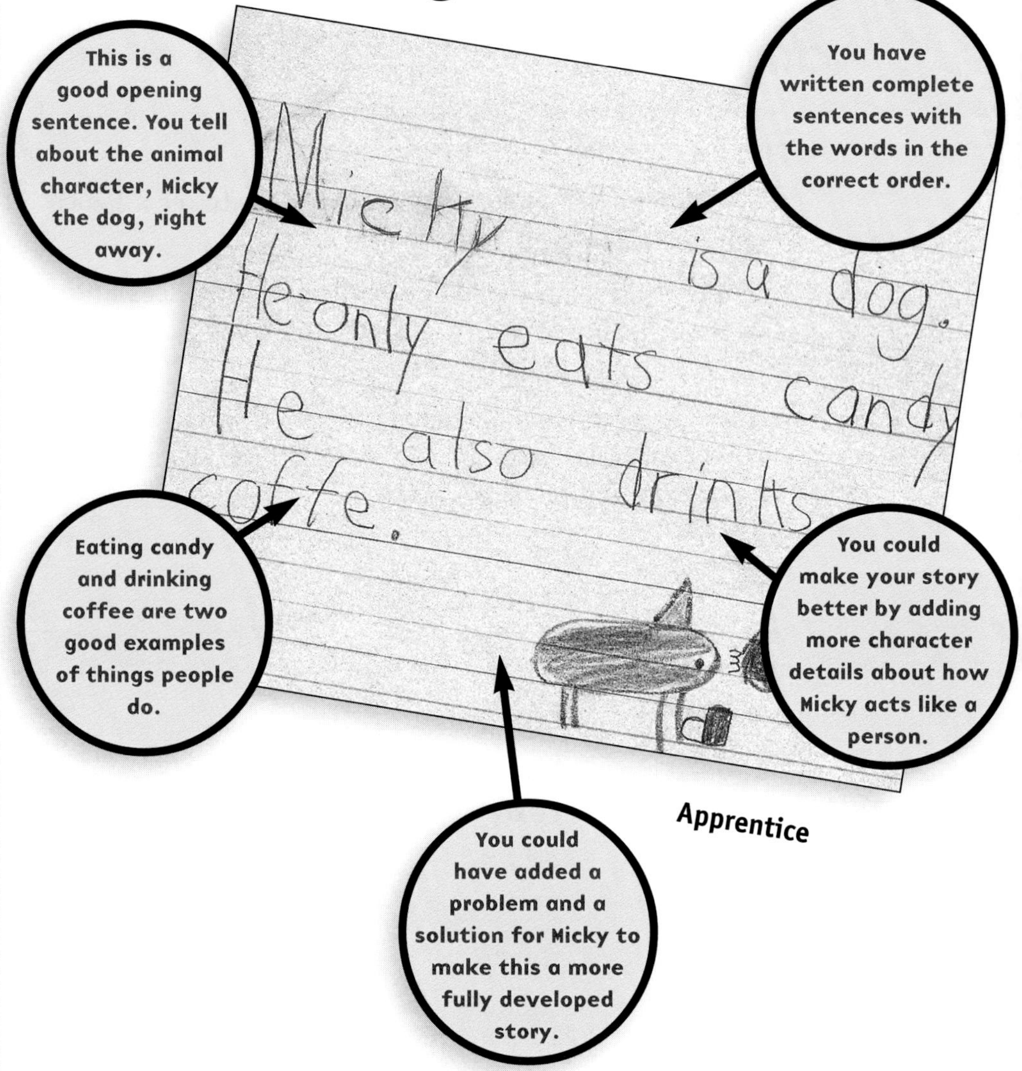
This is a good opening sentence. You tell about the animal character, Micky the dog, right away.
You have written complete sentences with the words in the correct order.
Micky is a dog.
He only eats candy
He also drints coffe.
Eating candy and drinking coffee are two good examples of things people do.
You could make your story better by adding more character details about how Micky acts like a person.
You could have added a problem and a solution for Micky to make this a more fully developed story.

Apprentice

Use the rubric below to assess children's writing.

CHILDREN'S WRITING RUBRIC

Proficient	• The story is developed with an animal character or characters. • The story includes animals doing what people do.	• All sentences are complete and the word order is correct. • The story is proofread and corrected for grammar, usage, and mechanics.
Apprentice	• The story may or may not be fully developed. • The story includes at least one animal character, but it may or may not act like a person.	• The story may be proofread but not completely corrected for errors.
Novice	• There is no developed story or animal characters. • The sentences are not complete and the word order is not correct.	• The story has not been corrected.

Integrated Language Arts

ORAL LANGUAGE

Make Up a Conversation

SUGGESTED GROUPING:
Partners

INTRODUCE the activity by asking children to think about the stories they have been told that they like to hear again and again. Are these stories always told in just the same way? Discuss how some of the small details in stories are likely to change when they are retold.

ASK children to think about which small details from *Chicken Pedro and the Falling Sky* might change if the story were retold. For example, Chicken Pedro could have been hit by a banana instead of a lemon. He might have thought he was hit by a crescent moon, instead of the sun.

INVITE children to work with a partner to change some small detail in *Chicken Pedro and the Falling Sky* and to retell the story to the class. Challenge children to listen carefully to identify the detail that was changed.

ORAL LANGUAGE

Radio News Broadcast

MATERIALS:
Paper, pencils

SUGGESTED GROUPING:
Small groups

INTRODUCE the activity by asking children to imagine that Chicken Pedro is a radio news reporter.

GET STARTED by having children work in small groups to brainstorm a list of key words Chicken Pedro would use to give a radio news report about the falling sky.

BROADCAST THE NEWS by having children act out a radio news report about the falling sky. Encourage them to use the words they listed and to add information such as where people should go for shelter from the falling sky.

banana
apple
Star
moon
flower

Integrated Language Arts

WRITING

Make a Class Book

MATERIALS: Paper, pencils, markers

SUGGESTED GROUPING: Individuals

BRAINSTORM with children a list of favorite folk tales or fairy tales.

INVITE children to make a class book of their favorite folk tales and fairy tales. Have each child draw a picture of a scene from his or her favorite story and write or dictate a sentence or two telling about the picture. Gather the papers into a class book.

PLACE the class book in the classroom library. Invite children to take turns looking at it and reading the captions to a partner.

Our Fairy Tales

WRITING/VIEWING

Make Up a Scene

SUGGESTED GROUPING: Small groups

INTRODUCE the activity by asking children to think about how Rocky Fox tried to trick Chicken Pedro and his friends.

ASK children to think of other ways he could have convinced them to go through the cave. For example, Rocky Fox could have told them that the King was in his cave, or that he had a cart and he would drive them to the King.

ACT OUT the scene. Have children choose a character and act out the scene with Rocky Fox, Chicken Pedro, and his friends.

TECHNOLOGY

Language Development Help children use **WiggleWorks Plus** Unit Writer to write a script for their scene. Show children how to set up the narrators' names on the left and the words each says to the right. Have them print out the scripts and use them to practice their scenes.

DAY 5 WRAP-UP

READ ALOUD *Spend five to ten minutes reading from a selection of your choice.*

GUIDED READING *Meet with the **red** and **blue** reading groups and assign Independent Center activities.* ***See pages R2–R3.***

The Night Sky

The Night Sky
Written by Alice Pernick
Illustrated by Lisa Desimini
AWARD WINNER
SCHOLASTIC

Main Selection
Genre: Nonfiction
Award-winning illustrator

Twinkle, Twinkle Little Star

Paired Selection
Genre: Song

WEEK 2 TESTED SKILLS

- **Key Comprehension Skill: Categorize Information**
- **Vocabulary**
- **Daily Phonics: Final *e*, Vowel /ē/ *(ea, ee)***
- **Spelling: Words With Final *e***
- **Grammar, Usage, Mechanics: Capitalizing Titles**

Technology Connection

BUILD BACKGROUND Visit **www.knowble.com** to find space-related games and activities. Guide children on a tour of the solar system through the spaceport and observatory areas.

Selection Summary

The wonders of the night sky are no longer mysterious, thanks to this nonfiction account. Here children learn all about the moon, stars, constellations, planets, and comets. The selection also provides tips for watching the night sky, including optimum conditions and locations to view.

PAIRED SELECTION The famous song "Twinkle, Twinkle Little Star" makes a great complement to nightwatching.

Illustrator

LISA DESIMINI'S artistic talent first surfaced when she was a young child. Her teachers, friends, and parents encouraged her to become an artist. Ms. Desimini is author and illustrator of *My House*.

Weekly Organizer

Visit Our Web Site
www.scholastic.com

The Night Sky

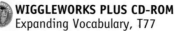

	DAY 1	DAY 2
READ and Introduce Skills • VOCABULARY • PHONICS • COMPREHENSION • LISTENING • SPEAKING • VIEWING The Night Sky Twinkle, Twinkle Little Star	**BUILD BACKGROUND,** p. T67 ▲ **VOCABULARY,** p. T68 ▲ ■ Practice Book, p. 15 **DAILY PHONICS:** ▲ ✷ Final *e*, pp. T70–T71 Practice Book, pp. 16, 17 **PREVIEW AND PREDICT,** p. T72 **READ:** ▲ ✷ ■ *The Night Sky*, pp. T72–T79 **COMPREHENSION:** Categorize Information, p. T75	**READ:** ▲ ■ ✷ *The Night Sky*, pp. T80–T85 **DAILY PHONICS:** Vowel /ē/ *ea, ee*, p. T81 Practice Book, p. 21 **GENRE:** Nonfiction, p. T83
WRITE and Respond • GRAMMAR • USAGE • MECHANICS • SPELLING • WRITING	**SHARED WRITING,** p. T67 **JOURNAL: High-Frequency Words,** p. T69 **QUICKWRITE: Predict,** p. T79 **SPELLING:** Pretest: Words With Final *e*, p. R12 Spelling Resource Book, p. 89 **GRAMMAR, USAGE, MECHANICS:** Teach/Model: Capitalizing Titles, p. R14 **ORAL LANGUAGE,** p. T79	**SHARED WRITING:** Prewrite, p. T85 **SPELLING:** Vocabulary Practice, p. R12 Spelling Resource Book, pp. 90–92 **GRAMMAR, USAGE, MECHANICS:** Practice, p. R14 **ORAL LANGUAGE,** p. T85
EXTEND SKILLS and Apply to Literature • SKILLS • INTEGRATED LANGUAGE ARTS • INTEGRATED CURRICULUM • GUIDED READING • INDEPENDENT READING	**READ ALOUD,** p. T79 **GUIDED READING,** pp. R10–R11 **INTEGRATED CURRICULUM:** Math, p. R16 The Arts, p. R17 **TRADE BOOKS** • *Pierre* • *Jenny's Journey* • *Going Home* PIERRE MAURICE SENDAK JENNY'S JOURNEY GOING HOME	**READ ALOUD,** p. T85 **GUIDED READING,** pp. R10–R11 **INTEGRATED CURRICULUM:** Science, p. R16 Social Studies, p. R17
TECHNOLOGY and **REAL-WORLD SKILLS**	**WIGGLEWORKS PLUS CD-ROM** Magnet Board, T68, T70 **WIGGLEWORKS PLUS CD-ROM** Expanding Vocabulary, T77 **WORKSHOP 1,** pp. T107–T110	**WIGGLEWORKS PLUS CD-ROM** Phonics, T85 **WORKSHOP 1,** pp. T107–T110

MODIFY INSTRUCTION

● INTERVENTION ▲ ESL/ELD ■ EXTRA HELP
✳ GIFTED & TALENTED ✓ = TESTED SKILL

DAY 3	DAY 4	DAY 5
READ: ▲ ■ "Twinkle, Twinkle Little Star," pp. T86–T87 ✓ **COMPREHENSION:** ▲ ■ Categorize Information, pp. T90–T91 Practice Book, pp. 19–20 ✓ **DAILY PHONICS:** ▲ ✳ Vowel /ē/ *ea, ee,* pp. T92–93 Practice Book, pp. 21–22 **BUILDING FLUENCY,** p. T94 **FOCUS ON HIGH-FREQUENCY WORDS,** p. T95 **FOCUS ON PHONICS,** p. T95	**VOCABULARY REVIEW,** p. T98 ✓ **DAILY PHONICS:** Vowel /ē/ *ea, ee,* p. T99	**READING ASSESSMENT,** p. T102 Selection Test Conference Decoding Test
RESPOND: ▲ ■ Think About Reading, p. T88 Practice Book, p. 18 **WRITE A CAPTION,** p. T89 ✓ **SPELLING:** Write/Proofread, p. R13 Spelling Resource Book, p. 93 ✓ **GRAMMAR, USAGE, MECHANICS:** Practice, p. R15 **ORAL LANGUAGE,** p. T89	**SHARED WRITING:** ▲ ■ List of Tips, p. T96 Practice Book, p. 23 ✓ **SPELLING:** Study/Review, p. R13 Spelling Practice Book, p. 161 ✓ **GRAMMAR, USAGE, MECHANICS:** Apply, p. R15 **ORAL LANGUAGE,** p. T97	**WRITING ASSESSMENT,** p. T104 Child Model Children's Writing Rubric ✓ **SPELLING:** Posttest, p. R13 Spelling Resource Book, p. 163 ✓ **GRAMMAR, USAGE, MECHANICS:** Assess, p. R15 **ORAL LANGUAGE,** p. T104
READ ALOUD, p. T95 **GUIDED READING,** pp. R10–R11 **OPTIONAL MATERIALS,** p. T94 Phonics Reader #39: *Lime Ice Is Nice* Phonics Reader #40: *Hen Pen's Joke*	**READ ALOUD,** p. T101 **GUIDED READING,** pp. R10–R11 **EXTEND VOCABULARY,** p. T98 **OPTIONAL MATERIALS,** p. T99 Phonics Reader #41: *The Three Little Pigs* Phonics Reader #42: *The Street Band* ✓ **STUDY SKILLS:** Sort/Organize Information, pp. T100–T101 Practice Book, p. 25	**READ ALOUD,** p. T106 **GUIDED READING,** pp. R10–R11 **INTEGRATED LANGUAGE ARTS:** Write About the Day Sky, p. T105 Write a Postcard, p. T105 Make a Mobile, p. T106 Write Directions, p. T106

WIGGLEWORKS PLUS CD-ROM Presentation Tools, T89 **WIGGLEWORKS PLUS CD-ROM** Magnet Board, T92 **WORKSHOP 1,** pp. T107–T110	**I SPY CD-ROM** Study Skills, T101 **WORKSHOP 1,** pp. T107–T110	**WIGGLEWORKS PLUS CD-ROM** Language Development, T106 **WORKSHOP 1,** pp. T107–T110

Weekly Assessment

ASSESSMENT PLANNING

USE THIS CHART TO PLAN YOUR ASSESSMENT OF THE WEEKLY READING OBJECTIVES.

- **Informal Assessment is ongoing and should be used before, during, and after reading.**
- **Formal assessment occurs at the end of the week on the selection test.**
- **Note that intervention activities occur throughout the lesson to support children who need extra help with skills.**

ASSESSMENT
ASSESSMENT HANDBOOK
SCHOLASTIC

YOU MAY CHOOSE AMONG THE FOLLOWING PAGES IN THE ASSESSMENT HANDBOOK.

- **Informal Assessment**
- **Anecdotal Record**
- **Portfolio Checklist and Evaluation Forms**
- **Self-Assessment**
- **Second -Language Learners**
- **Using Technology to Assess**
- **Test Preparation**

SKILLS AND STRATEGIES

Skills and Strategies	Informal Assessment
COMPREHENSION Categorize Information	OBSERVATION **p. T75** • Did children identify information? QUICKCHECK **p. T90** • Did children understand that the moon, stars, planets and comets can all be grouped as things seen in the night sky? CHECK PRACTICE BOOK **p. 19** CONFERENCE **p. 102**
PHONICS Final *e* Vowel /ē/ *ea, ee*	OBSERVATION **pp. T77, T81** • Did children recognize words with final *e*? • Did children recognize words with vowel /ē/ *ea, ee*? CHECK PRACTICE BOOK **pp. 16, 21** DICTATION **pp. T71, T93**
VOCABULARY Story Words **shine moon** **stars light** **planets night** High-Frequency **some many**	OBSERVATION **p. T102** • Did children identify story words? • Did children identify high-frequency words? CHECK PRACTICE BOOK **p. 15**

Formal Assessment	**INTERVENTION** and Instructional Alternatives	Planning Notes
SELECTION TEST • Questions 1–3 check children's mastery of the key strategy, categorize information. UNIT TEST	If children need help with categorize information, then go to: • **Instructional Alternatives, p. T91** • **Review, p. R44** • **Reteach, p. R62**	
DECODING TEST • See p. T103 SELECTION TEST • Questions 4–7 check children's ability to recognize words with final *e* and vowel /ē/ *ea, ee.* UNIT TEST	If children need help identifying words with final *e*, then go to: • **Intervention Activity, p. T95** • **Review, p. R49** • **Reteach, p. R58** If children need help identifying words with vowel /ē/ *ee, ea,* then go to: • **Review, p. R50** • **Reteach, p. R59**	
SELECTION TEST • Questions 8–10 check children's recall of high-frequency words and story words. UNIT TEST	If children need additional practice with the vocabulary words, then go to: • **Intervention Activity, p. T95** • **Extend Vocabulary, p. T98** • **Integrated Language Arts Activity, p. T105**	

Technology

Exploring the WiggleWorks Plus Selection

Children can interact with an electronic version of the literature selection in this lesson. Use this activity to direct children as they explore the WiggleWorks Plus CD-ROM.

Millions of stars twinkle in the night sky. Some look brighter than others. Some look blue and some look white.

WiggleWorks Plus CD-ROM

STEP 1
Listen

First, have the children listen to the story using the **WiggleWorks Plus** Source Book. Guide them to listen to the words, but to focus on the simplicity and beauty of the illustrations.

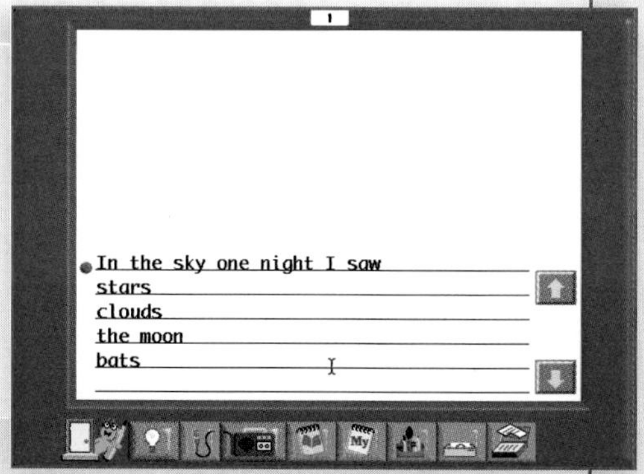
In the sky one night I saw
stars
clouds
the moon
bats

WiggleWorks Plus CD-ROM

STEP 2
Illustrate

When the reading is complete, inquire how they might have illustrated the story. Discuss types of media such as water colors, pen and ink, crayons, and computer art. Allow the children to use the art tools in the My Book version of the story to create and color their own version of the Source Book.

STEP 3
Write

Next, have the children open the Write area of *The Night Sky*. Find the Story Starter, "In the sky one night, I saw . . ." Have children make a list of what they saw under the story starter.

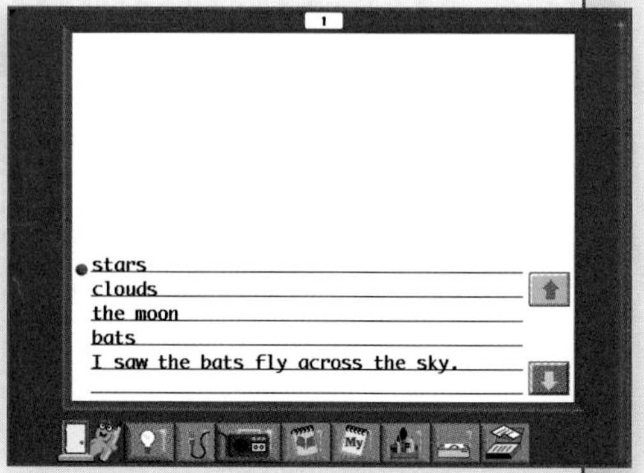
stars
clouds
the moon
bats
I saw the bats fly across the sky.

WiggleWorks Plus CD-ROM

STEP 4
Extend

Finally, ask children to write a sentence to describe each sky item on the list. Compare the original lists to the items found in the sky in the Source Book. You may wish to use an electronic encyclopedia to do some further research on new items not found in the story.

For more activity suggestions, see the **WiggleWorks Plus** Teaching Guide.

Build Background

There are many things that can be seen in the sky at night. This selection gives information about many of the real objects that can be observed.

The Night Sky

Activate Prior Knowledge

DISCUSS NONFICTION Share with children that a nonfiction selection gives facts and information about a subject.

ORAL LANGUAGE Talk about the night sky with children. Ask them if they have ever sat outdoors at night and looked at the sky. Invite them to tell about their experiences. You may want to prompt the discussion with the following questions:

> **What have you seen in the night sky?**

> **What is the most unusual or most interesting thing you have seen?**

> **What have you noticed about the moon's shape?**

SHARED WRITING *A List of Tips*

INTRODUCE Explain that a tip is written to help someone do or understand something. Invite children to write or dictate a note that will help someone to find things in the night sky.

DAY 1 OBJECTIVES

CHILDREN WILL:

READ 30 MINUTES

- **Build Background**
- **Vocabulary**
- **Daily Phonics: Words With Final *e***
- ***The Night Sky*, pp. 29–35**
- **Key Comprehension Skill: Categorize Information**

WRITE 30 MINUTES

- **Shared Writing: Introduce Writing a List of Tips**
- **Quickwrite: Set a Purpose**
- **Spelling: Words With Final *e***
- **Grammar, Usage, Mechanics: Capitalizing Titles**
- **Oral Language**

EXTEND SKILLS 30 MINUTES

- **Integrated Curriculum**
- **Read Aloud**
- **Guided Reading**

RESOURCES

- **Practice Book, pp. 15–17**
- **Spelling Resource Book, p. 89**

MODIFY Instruction

ESL/ELD

▲ To verify that children understand the concept, show pictures of the daytime and nighttime sky. Create a chart with two columns. Label one column *Day* and the other *Night*. Ask children what they see in the sky during the day and during the night. Have children draw pictures on the chart. **(GRAPHIC DEVICE)**

VOCABULARY

VOCABULARY

HIGH-FREQUENCY

some many

STORY WORDS

night shine
stars planets
moon light

VOCABULARY
High-Frequency Words

Ⓐ TEACH/MODEL

INTRODUCE HIGH-FREQUENCY WORDS Write the high-frequency words ***some*** and ***many*** in sentences on the chalkboard. Read the sentences aloud, underline the high-frequency words, and ask children if they recognize them. You may wish to use these sentences:

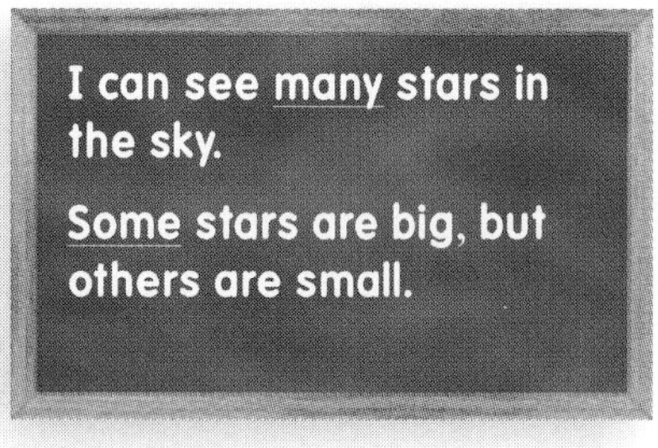
I can see many stars in the sky.
Some stars are big, but others are small.

Ask volunteers to dictate sentences using the high-frequency words. Add these to the chalkboard.

Ⓑ PRACTICE/APPLY

FOCUS ON SPELLING Write each high-frequency word on a note card. Read each aloud. Then do the following:

ROUTINE

1. **Display one card at a time, and ask children to state each word aloud.**
2. **Have children spell each word aloud.**
3. **Ask children to write each word in the air as they state aloud each letter. Then have them write each word on a sheet of paper or in their Journals.**

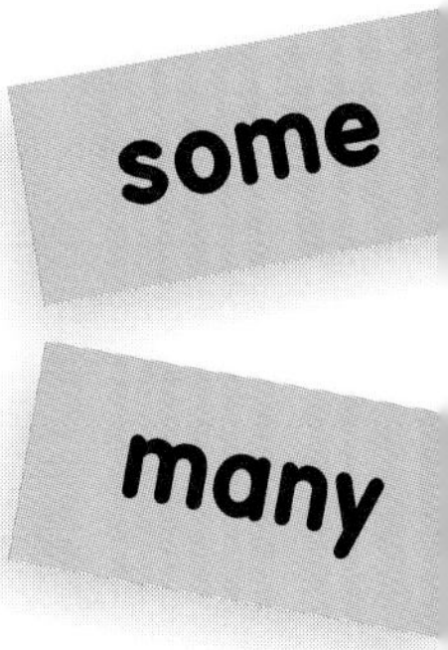
some
many

MAINTAIN VOCABULARY Add the note cards to the **Word Wall.** Then review the following high-frequency words on the Wall: ***went, soon, from,*** and ***over.***

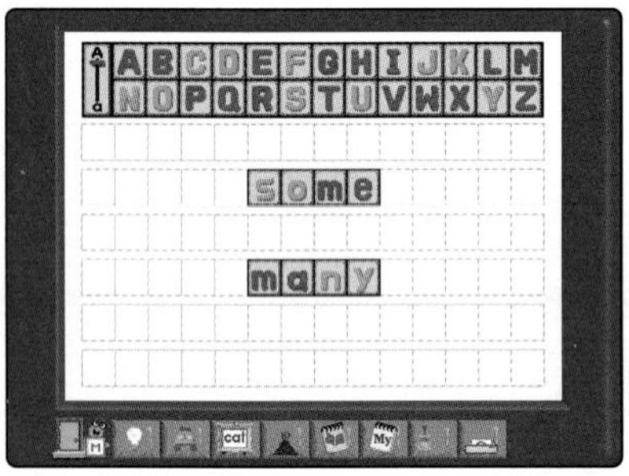
ABCDEFGHIJKLM
NOPQRSTUVWXYZ
some
many

TECHNOLOGY

For children needing additional practice with high-frequency words prior to reading the story, have them build, explode, and rebuild each high-frequency word on the **WiggleWorks Plus** Magnet Board.

MODIFY Instruction

ESL/ELD

▲ Preview the story and use the pictures to teach and practice key vocabulary: *night, sky, moon, stars, planets, light, constellations, Venus, comets.* Several of these words are very similar in Spanish: *constelación, planeta, cometa.* **(USE VISUALS)**

EXTRA HELP

■ Provide additional support during the discussion of the night sky by assembling and displaying a collection of books and posters that deal with stars. Seeing pictures of stars and star patterns may help children recall and talk about their own experiences. **(USE VISUALS)**

Story Words

Ⓐ TEACH/MODEL

INTRODUCE STORY WORDS

The story also contains the following story words—***stars, planets, night, shine, moon, light.***

- Write these words on the chalkboard, read them aloud, and discuss their meanings if necessary.
- Point out previously taught sound-spelling correspondences, such as ***/ē/e*** and ***/k/c,k.***
- If possible, provide a visual clue for each. For example, draw stars on the chalkboard or have children wiggle their fingers in a "twinkle" motion.

Ⓑ PRACTICE/APPLY

BUILD STORY BACKGROUND

Discuss objects in the night sky.

- Ask children to name what they might see in a night sky.
- Have them imagine what it would be like to see all these things at once.
- Have children draw a picture of the night sky with all the different objects they might see.

WRITE TO READ

- When the drawing is completed, have children write a sentence about their picture using one or more of the story words.

Name VOCABULARY

Up Above the World So High

▶ Write a word from the box to complete each sentence.

light	shine
moon	stars
night	many

1. In the daytime, the sun gives us light.
2. But at night I can see many things in the sky.
3. When the moon is full, it seems to have a face.
4. I like to see all the stars, too.
5. I don't know how many stars are in the sky.
6. I like to see them twinkle and shine.

Unit 4 • Imagine That! • The Night Sky 15

PRACTICE BOOK p. 15

SAturn

VENUS

I SEE STARS, PLANETS, AND THE MOON AT NIGHT.

SPILL IT/SPELL IT

Write the story words and high-frequency words on note cards and place them in a container.

- Pairs of children take turns shaking the container, spilling out the cards, and dictating the face-up words for their partners to spell.

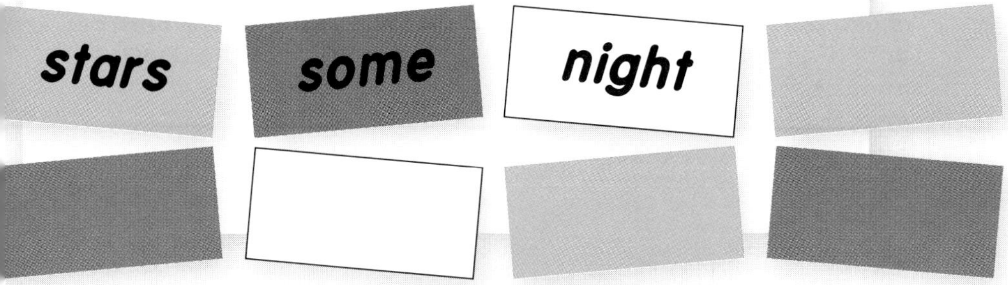
stars
some
night

JOURNAL

Ask children to write a sentence in their Journals using each **high-frequency word.** You might suggest the following sentence starters:

Do you have some _____ ?

I have many _____ .

The Night Sky

SELECTION WORDS With Final *e*

close	times
like	used
rises	white
shine	

SKILLS TRACE

FINAL *e* TESTED

Introduce	pp. T70–T71
Practice	pp. T77, T94, T95
Review	p. R49
Reteach	p. R58

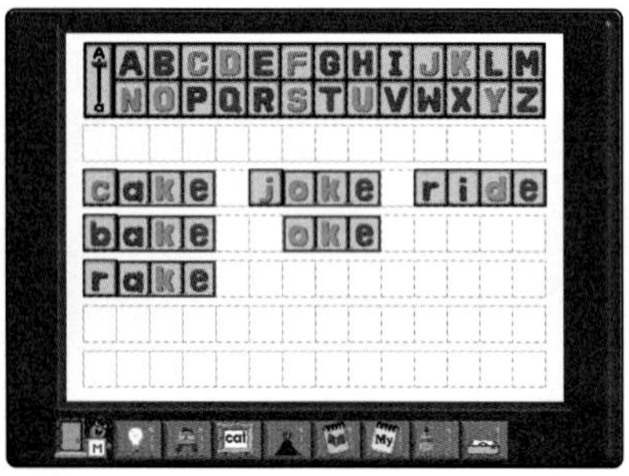
ABCDEFGHIJKLM
NOPQRSTUVWXYZ
cake
joke
ride
bake
oke
rake

TECHNOLOGY

Have children build words with final *e* on the **WiggleWorks Plus** Magnet Board.

- Begin with the words ***cake, joke,*** and ***ride*** or write rows of final ***e*** phonograms ***(-ake, -ate, -ide, -ime, -oke, -ope).***
- Have children add or change one letter to make new words.

DAILY PHONICS

Words With Final e

A PHONOLOGICAL AWARENESS

RHYME Read aloud the rhyme "I Eat My Peas With Honey" from the *Big Book of Rhymes and Rhythms 1B,* page 5. As you read, stress the words that contain final ***e: knife, life.***

- When children are familiar with the rhyme, ask them to read along with you.
- Frame the words ***knife*** and ***life*** and point out the long ***i*** sound in each word.

I Eat My Peas With Honey
I eat my peas with honey,
I've done it all my life.
It makes the peas taste funny,
But it keeps them on the knife.
life

***Big Book of Rhymes and Rhythms 1B,* p. 5**

ORAL BLENDING Say the following word parts and ask children to blend them. Provide modeling and corrective feedback when needed.

- /l/ . . . ike
- /g/ . . . ate
- /k/ . . . ite
- /h/ . . . ome
- /r/ . . . ide
- /r/ . . . ose

B CONNECT SOUND-SPELLING

INTRODUCE Final *e* Write the words ***tap, bit, rob,*** and ***us*** on the chalkboard. Have children read each word, add an ***e***, and read the new word formed. Note the importance of the ***e***-marker as you model how to blend each word.

THINK ALOUD *I can add the letter **e** to the word **tap** to make a new word **tape**. Let's say the sounds slowly as I move my finger under the letters. Note how the final **e** changes the vowel sound /a/ in **tap** to /ā/ in **tape**.*

MODIFY Instruction

ESL/ELD

▲ Gather picture cards for the words *cap, cape* and *pin, pine*. As you show each item, say the word, stressing the vowel sound. Then write each word on the chalkboard as you say it. Underline the vowel sounds and the final *e*, and encourage children to say each word aloud. **(PICTURE CARDS)**

EXTRA HELP

■ Encourage children to select two rhyming *i_e, o_e,* and *u_e* words and pantomime them for their classmates to guess. The first child to guess the rhyme can perform another rhyming pair. **(PANTOMIME)**

- Then write the following final ***e*** phonograms on the chalkboard: ***-ice, -ide, -ike, -ime, -ine, -ite, -oke, -ome, -one, -ope, -ose.***
- Have children add consonants to each phonogram to make words. List the words in separate columns.

PHONICS MAINTENANCE Review the following sound-spellings: ***/ā/a-e, /sh/sh, /u/u, /th/th, /e/e, /kw/qu*** and final ***e.*** Say one of the sounds and have a volunteer write on the board the spelling that stands for the sound. Continue with all the sounds.

C PRACTICE/APPLY

BLEND WORDS To practice using the sound-spelling and review previous sound-spellings, list the following words and sentence on the chalkboard. Have children read each chorally. Model blending as needed.

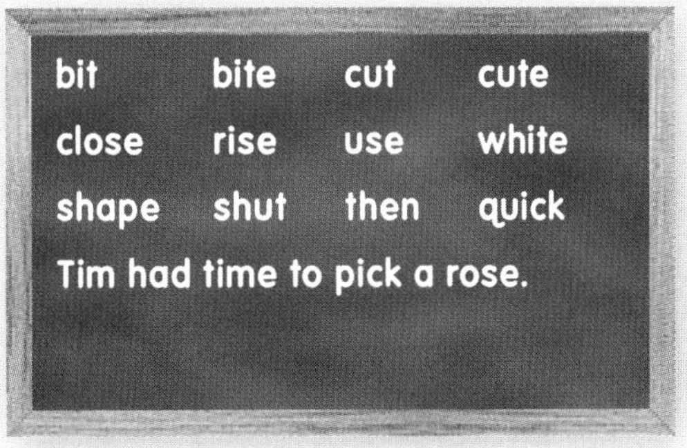
bit bite cut cute
close rise use white
shape shut then quick
Tim had time to pick a rose.

DICTATION Dictate the following words: ***tap, tape, cub, cube, this, shed, quack.***

BUILD WORDS Distribute the following letter and phonogram cards, or have children use their own sets: ***s, d, f, k, b, h, t, c, a, u, -ime, -ine, -ite, -one, -ome, -uge, -ute.*** Allow children time to build words using the letter cards. Children can write their words on a separate sheet of paper. **(INDEPENDENT WORK)**

c
ute

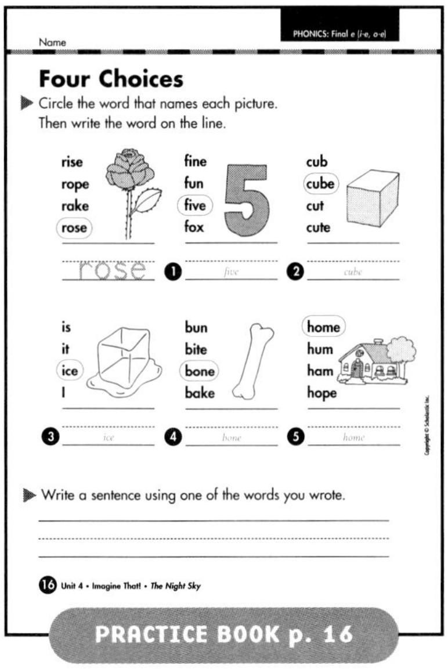

Name

PHONICS: Final e (i-e, o-e)

Four Choices

▶ Circle the word that names each picture. Then write the word on the line.

rise rope rake rose — rose

fine fun five fox — ❶ five

cub cube cut cute — ❷ cube

is it ice I — ❸ ice

bun bite bone bake — ❹ bone

home hum ham hope — ❺ home

▶ Write a sentence using one of the words you wrote.

16 Unit 4 • Imagine That! • The Night Sky

PRACTICE BOOK p. 16

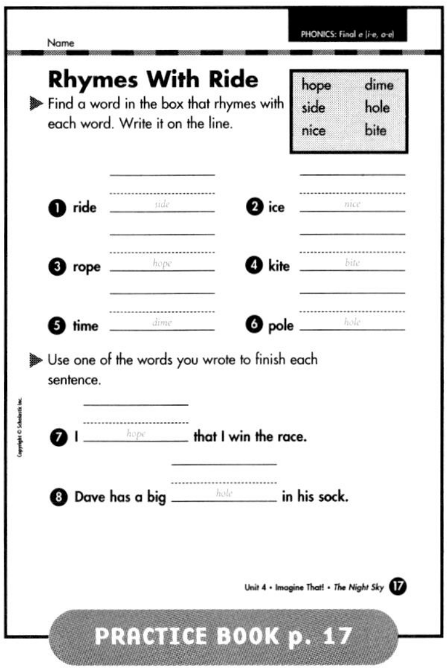

Name

PHONICS: Final e (i-e, o-e)

Rhymes With Ride

▶ Find a word in the box that rhymes with each word. Write it on the line.

hope	dime
side	hole
nice	bite

❶ ride side ❷ ice nice

❸ rope hope ❹ kite bite

❺ time dime ❻ pole hole

▶ Use one of the words you wrote to finish each sentence.

❼ I hope that I win the race.

❽ Dave has a big hole in his sock.

Unit 4 • Imagine That! • The Night Sky 17

PRACTICE BOOK p. 17

DECODABLE TEXT

For practice reading decodable text, see ***Scholastic Decodable Reader #46.***

For additional phonics instruction and review, see ***Scholastic Phonics A, pp. 169–174, 177–180.***

THE DIFFERENCE AN *e* MAKES

Have children form small groups to make a long/short-vowel poster.

- Provide each group with the following words: ***bit, can, cub, cut, fin, hat, hid, hop, kit, mad, not, pin, rid, rip, tap, us.***
- Have children add an ***e*** to each word. Ask them to write both the long and short vowel words on their posters.
- Suggest that they add illustrations where appropriate.

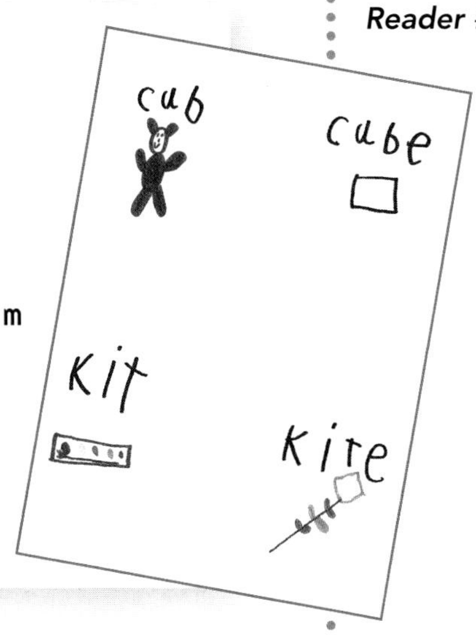
cub
cube
kit
kite

COMPREHENSION

Preview and Predict

Invite children to preview the selection by reading the title and looking at the pictures. Talk about what they see. Help children determine that this selection gives information about what is in a night sky.

> **What do the pictures in this selection show?**

> **What do you think this selection is about?**

JOURNAL

Make Predictions

Ask children to write about or draw pictures in their Journals of something they hope to discover when they read *The Night Sky*.

Set a Purpose

Help children contribute to a K-W-L chart to set a purpose for reading. Invite children to write or dictate what they know and what they want to find out about the night sky. Children can complete the chart as they read. Then have children read page 29.

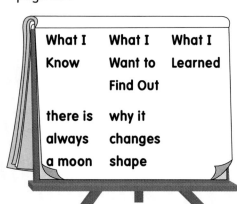

What I Know	What I Want to Find Out	What I Learned
there is always a moon	why it changes shape	

28

NONFICTION

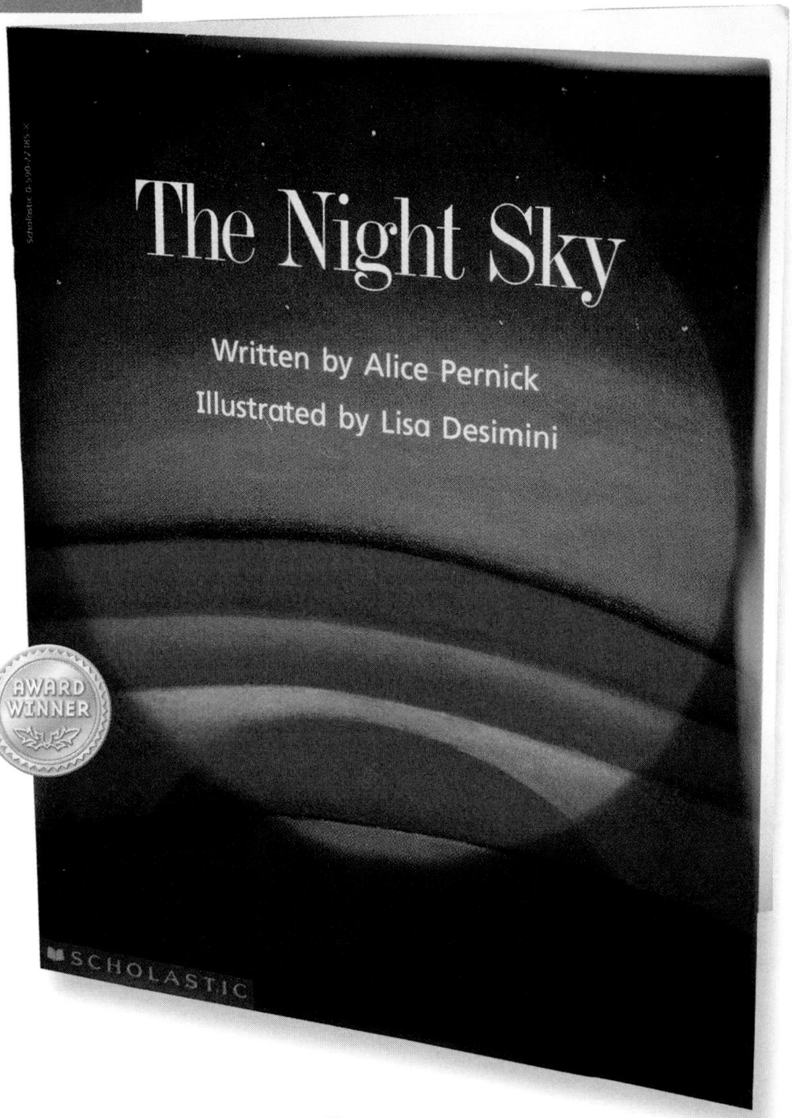
The Night Sky
Written by Alice Pernick
Illustrated by Lisa Desimini
AWARD WINNER
SCHOLASTIC

28

CLASSROOM Management

WHOLE CLASS

On-Level Use the questions, think alouds, and the Skills and Strategies lessons to guide children through a reading of the selection.

Below-Level Have children listen to the selection on audiocassette prior to the whole-class reading to familiarize themselves with the selection sequence and vocabulary.

COOPERATIVE

Above-Level You might choose to have above-level children read the story independently or with partners while you do a guided reading of the story with the rest of the class. When the above-level children finish, they can rejoin the group to participate in the selection discussion.

29

When the sun sets at the end of the day, the night sky begins to twinkle and shine.

There are many things to see in the night sky.

29

SKILLS AND STRATEGIES

Revisit the selection for skills instruction.

✓ = Tested Skill

COMPREHENSION
Categorize Information T75

DAILY PHONICS
✓ Final *e* T77
Vowel /ē/ *(ea, ee)* T81

GENRE
Nonfiction T83

GENRE
Song T87

SMALL GROUP TO WHOLE CLASS

ESL/ELD Have children who need extra help or who are acquiring English listen to the story on the audiocassette prior to the class reading. This will help them to become familiar with the story sequence and vocabulary. Have children do the pre- and post- listening activities. **(AUDIO CLUES)**

COMPREHENSION

1 CATEGORIZE INFORMATION

> **The title of this selection is *The Night Sky*. What have you already learned that should be included in the category of Things in the Night Sky?** *(The moon should be included in the category of* Things in the Night Sky.*)*

2 COMPARE/CONTRAST

> **Look at the pictures of the moon on these pages. How is the moon different in each picture? What does this tell you about the moon?** *(Possible answer: The picture of the full moon and the picture of the curved moon show how the shape of the moon changes.)*

INTERVENTION TIP

Picture Clues

Some children may think that the pages show two separate moons in the sky. To help them understand that the pictures show one moon at different times, point out the text and picture clues that refer to the moon sometimes being round while other times it looks curved. Reread the last sentence on page 31 with children.

30

(1) The moon is the brightest light in the night sky. Sometimes the moon looks full and round.
(2)
30

MODIFY Instruction

ESL/ELD

▲ Point out the two moons. Tell children that the full moon is *bigger*, *rounder*, and *brighter* than the other moon. Write each adjective and its comparative on the board, underlining in color the *-er* ending. **(LINGUISTIC CLUES)**

EXTRA HELP

■ Children may be interested in showing all the phases of the moon. Invite them to work with a partner to illustrate and tell the class about the way the moon changes over each month. **(ORAL LANGUAGE)**

31

Sometimes the moon looks thin and curved. It looks different at different times of the month.
31

MATH

Ask children to do the **Count the Days** activity on **page R16.** Have them use a calendar to count the days between phases of the moon.

THE ARTS

Ask children to do the **Make a Space Mobile** activity on **page R17** to build a mobile that shows the relative positions of the moon and the stars.

SKILLS AND STRATEGIES

Categorize Information

TEACH/MODEL

Explain to children that when they read a lot of information, they should put it into groups or categories. Doing this could make the information easier to remember.

> **Think about the information you are reading.**

> **Ask yourself what category each piece of information would fit into.**

THINK ALOUD *When I read about the moon and how it changes shape, I think about what category this information might fit into. I know that no matter what shape the moon is, it is always in the night sky. Remembering the larger category of* Things in the Night Sky *will help me remember what I learned.*

PRACTICE/APPLY

Explain that there are many things in the category of *Things in the Night Sky*. Ask children to suggest objects other than the moon that might fit into this category.

INFORMAL ASSESSMENT
OBSERVATION

Did children:

✔ identify information?

✔ select categories in which to place pieces of information?

See pages T90–T91 for a full skill lesson on Categorizing Information.

COMPREHENSION

3 CATEGORIZE INFORMATION

> **Think about the information on page 33. What category would you put this information in?** *(Possible answer: I would put this information in the category of stars.)*

4 COMPARE/CONTRAST

> **How are the stars alike? How are they different?** *(Possible answer: Stars are alike because they all twinkle; they are different because some are brighter than others and some look blue while others look white.)*

32

32

MODIFY Instruction

ESL/ELD

▲ Continue the lesson on comparative forms. Show children three similar classroom items that can be described by the words *big* or *round*. Write *big, bigger, biggest* on separate word cards. Have them use the cards to label the items. **(LINGUISTIC CLUES)**

EXTRA HELP

■ Write the sentence *Some stars look brighter than others* on the chalkboard or on chart paper. Read it aloud with children. Then erase the word *brighter*. Have children name other words that could complete this sentence. You may wish to have children illustrate their new sentences. **(INNOVATE)**

33

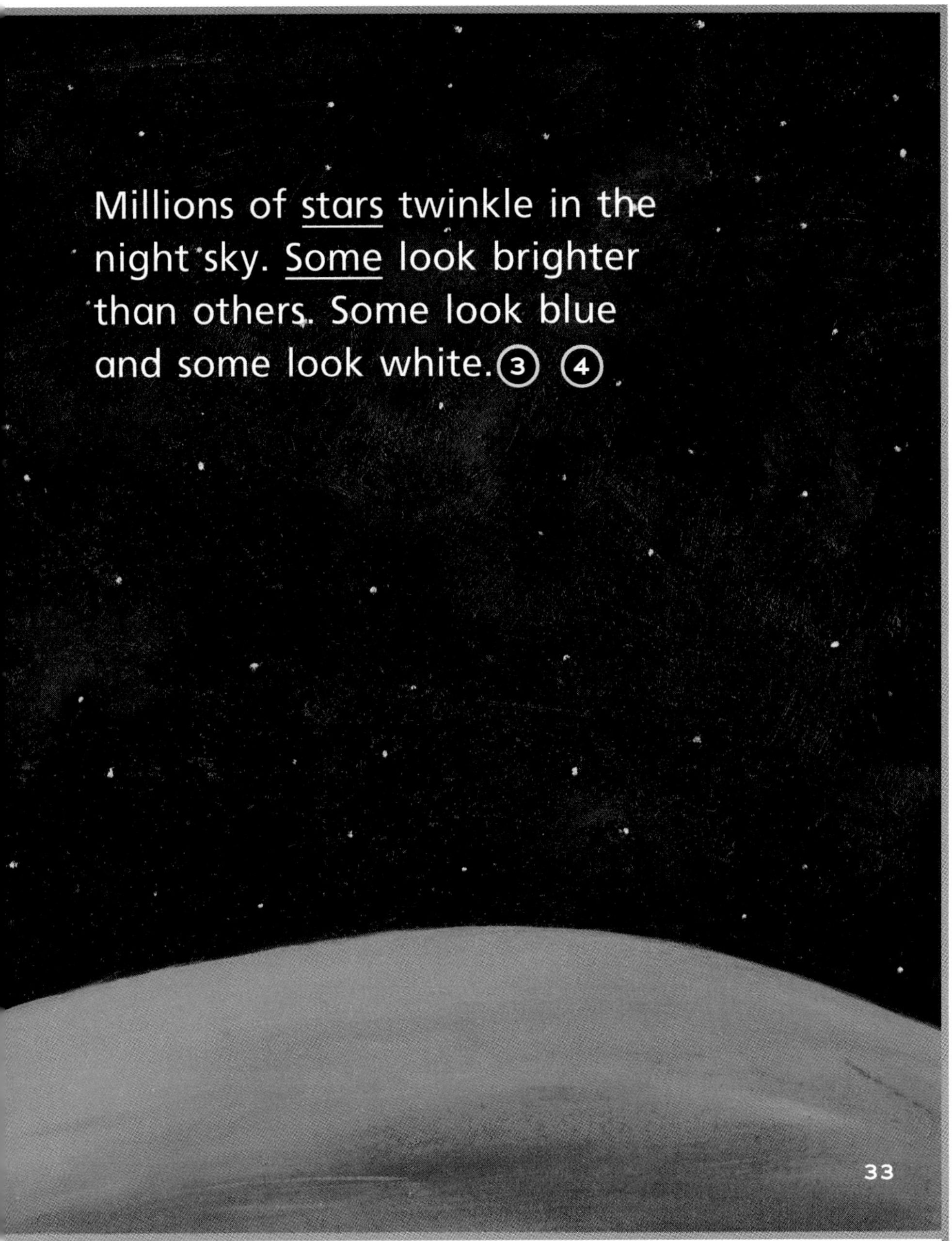
Millions of stars twinkle in the night sky. Some look brighter than others. Some look blue and some look white. ③ ④
33

DAILY PHONICS

Final *e*

CONNECT SOUND-SPELLING

Teach/Model Write the words ***bit*** and ***bite*** on the chalkboard. Remind children that the letter ***e*** at the end of a word can signal that the vowel has a long sound.

- Have children find the word ***white*** on page 33.
- Have them pronounce the word and identify the long vowel sound.
- Encourage them to search the story for other final ***e*** words.

Phonics Maintenance Review the following sound-spellings: ***/ā/a-e, /sh/sh, /th/th, /u/u, /e/e, /kw/qu,*** and final ***e.***

PRACTICE/APPLY

Blend Words To practice using the sound-spellings and review previous sound-spellings, list the following words and sentence on the chalkboard. Have children read each chorally. Model blending.

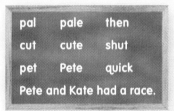

pal	pale	then
cut	cute	shut
pet	Pete	quick

Pete and Kate had a race.

INFORMAL ASSESSMENT
OBSERVATION

Did children:

✔recognize and blend words with final ***e?***

IF children need more support with final ***e,***
THEN see **page R58.**

TECHNOLOGY

Expanding Vocabulary Have children go to the My Book area of The Night Sky on the **WiggleWorks Plus** CD-ROM. Ask them to erase the story text and then rewrite it using words from the Story Words list.

CRITICAL THINKING

Ask children why some stars may appear brighter than others. Encourage them to give possible explanations. List their ideas on chart paper. Then read aloud star-related books during Read Aloud time. Encourage children to listen for the answer to this question as you read.

COMPREHENSION

5 CATEGORIZING INFORMATION

> **What have you learned about stars? What information would you put under the heading *Things I Know About Stars*?** *(Possible answer: Stars twinkle, can look blue or white, and can form patterns in the sky.)*

SELF-MONITORING STRATEGY

Use Illustrations to Understand Text

Point out the illustration of the stars forming the Big and Little Dippers. Discuss how the artist made it easier to see the patterns of stars that form the constellations.

OPTION You may end the first day's reading here or have children continue reading the entire selection.

34

Groups of stars that form patterns in the sky (5) are called constellations.

34

MODIFY Instruction

ESL/ELD

▲ Have children point to the constellation. Ask: *What is the name of this constellation?* Continue by asking: *What other star patterns do you know?* Ask volunteers to come to the chalkboard to draw and label the constellations they know. **(BUILD ON SUCCESS)**

GIFTED & TALENTED

✳ Tell children that long ago people gave names to the constellations and told stories about them. Suggest that children find other constellations and draw pictures of them. Then have children share their drawings with the class. **(RESEARCH)**

35

Little Dipper
Big Dipper
35

Quickwrite

PREDICT

Invite children to write something they found interesting in the selection so far. Have them revise the predictions they made about the selection and add any new ones. You may also wish to have children revisit the K-W-L chart to write what they have learned so far.

DAILY LANGUAGE PRACTICE

SPELLING

DAY 1:
Administer the Pretest for Words With Final *e*. **See page R12.**

GRAMMAR, USAGE, MECHANICS

DAY 1:
Teach and Model Capitalizing Titles. **See page R14.**

ORAL LANGUAGE

I lik to read the Night sky.
(I like to read The Night Sky.)

MENTOR CONNECTION

Show the mentor video of muralist William Walsh. Ask children to think about his work. Discuss how William Walsh might paint the night sky.

ORAL LANGUAGE

Ask children to use black paper and white or yellow chalk to draw their own constellations. Have them give their constellations names. Then invite children to show their drawings and tell the class about them.

DAY 1 WRAP-UP

READ ALOUD *To develop children's oral vocabularies, spend five to ten minutes reading from a selection of your choice.*

GUIDED READING *To extend reading, meet with the **green** and **yellow** reading groups and assign Independent Center activities.* ***See pages R10–R11.***

DAY 2

COMPREHENSION

DAY 2 OBJECTIVES

CHILDREN WILL:

READ 30 MINUTES

- ***The Night Sky*, pp. 36–41**
- **"Twinkle, Twinkle Little Star," pp. 42–43**
- **Daily Phonics: Vowel /ē/ *(ea, ee)***

WRITE 30 MINUTES

- **Shared Writing: Prewrite**
- **Spelling: Words With Final *e***
- **Grammar, Usage, Mechanics: Capitalizing Titles**
- **Oral Language**

EXTEND SKILLS 30 MINUTES

- **Integrated Curriculum**
- **Read Aloud**
- **Guided Reading**

RESOURCES

- **Spelling Resource Book, pp. 90–92**

Reread

You may wish to have children independently reread the first part of the selection before beginning Day 2 reading.

6 SUMMARIZE

> **What have we learned so far?**
(The moon is the brightest object; its shape is different at different times. The stars twinkle; patterns of stars are called constellations.)

7 CATEGORIZING INFORMATION

> **What information might you list under the category *Things I Know About Planets?***
(Planets do not twinkle; some of the brightest points of light are planets.)

36

⑥ Some of the brightest points of light in the night sky are planets. They look like stars, but they do not twinkle.

Look at the sky just before the sun rises. You might see Venus shining brightly in the east. ⑦

36

MODIFY Instruction

ESL/ELD

▲ Help children process the new information by creating a chart with two lists, one headed *Stars* and one headed *Planets.* Have children work with a peer partner to look back through the story and choose words or phrases to add to each list. **(PEER PARTNERS)**

GIFTED & TALENTED

✷ Ask children to find and list the names of other planets. Children may wish to draw pictures of these planets. Give children an opportunity to share what they learned with the rest of the class. **(RESEARCH)**

37

Venus
37

SCIENCE

Ask children to do the **Model Sun, Earth, and Moon** activity on **page R16**. Children will role-play the relative positions of the sun, moon, and earth to understand how the planets orbit around the sun.

WORD STUDY

Point out the high-frequency word *some* and write it on the chalkboard. Ask children to raise their hands if they would like some ice cream, some asparagus, some friends to play with. Call on volunteers to make up sentences using *some*. Then have children spell the word aloud with you as you touch each letter.

DAILY PHONICS

Vowel /ē/*ea, ee*

CONNECT SOUND-SPELLING

Teach/Model Explain to children that the letters ***ea*** and ***ee*** often stand for /ē/, as in the words ***feet*** and ***eat.***

- Write the words ***feet, eat, bean, need, keep,*** and ***team*** on the chalkboard, and read them aloud.
- Ask a volunteer to circle the letters in each word that stand for the long ***e*** sound.

Phonics Maintenance Review the following sound-spellings: /ā/*a-e,* /sh/*sh,* /kw/*qu,* /v/*v,* /th/*th,* and final ***e.***

PRACTICE/APPLY

Blend Words List the following words and sentences on the chalkboard. Have children read chorally. Model blending as needed.

seat	sheet	teeth
quack	vase	cave

We keep the room neat.

INFORMAL ASSESSMENT
OBSERVATION

Did children:

✔ recognize words with vowel /ē/ *ea, ee?*

✔ blend words with vowel /ē/ *ea, ee?*

IF children need more support with vowel /ē/ *ea, ee,*

THEN see **pages T92–T93** for a full skills lesson on vowel /ē/ *ea, ee.*

COMPREHENSION

8 CATEGORIZE INFORMATION

> **This page gives information about comets. What facts would you put under a heading *What I Know About Comets*?** *(Possible answers: Comets look like they have long tails; comets don't pass by often.)*

9 COMPARE/CONTRAST

> **How are comets like stars? How are comets different from stars?** *(Comets look like stars but comets have long tails. Comets blaze across the sky, but stars do not.)*

38

38

MODIFY Instruction

ESL/ELD

▲ Help each child draw and label pictures of a *comet*, the *moon*, *planets*, and *stars*. Show the art on each spread of the story, asking, *What did we learn first (next, then, last)?* Encourage children to answer by holding up the appropriate picture. **(CATEGORIZE)**

EXTRA HELP

■ Some children may have difficulty understanding the meaning of *it's your lucky night*. Discuss why it would be lucky to see something that is very rare, like a comet. Help children rephrase the sentence to mean *someone would be lucky to see a comet.* **(PARAPHRASE)**

39

Comets blaze across the sky. They look like stars with long tails. Comets don't pass by often. If you see a comet, it's your lucky night! ⑧ ⑨
39

WORD STUDY

Discuss the meanings of the word *blaze,* pointing out that it can mean both "to burn brightly," and "to mark a trail." Have children look at the picture on page 38 and discuss how this picture illustrates both meanings of the word *blaze.*

CULTURAL CONNECTIONS

The Night Sky gives facts about the moon, stars, and planets. But people have also created legends or stories about the moon, the stars, and planets. For example, the Inca peoples of South America told that the moon was a queen, living close to her handmaidens, the stars.

SKILLS AND STRATEGIES

GENRE
Nonfiction

TEACH/MODEL
Explain to children that a nonfiction selection gives facts and information about a subject.

THINK ALOUD *I read nonfiction selections because I enjoy learning new information. The text and pictures give me facts and details about things I've always wanted to know about. I often learn things that I can use every day.*

PRACTICE/APPLY
Invite children to look back through the selection and mention any facts they learned from it. Display the K-W-L chart again. Point out information children already know, want to know, and have learned. Ask children to write or dictate any new information they have learned.

COMPREHENSION

10 CATEGORIZE INFORMATION

> **We have talked about the different kinds of information we have learned in the selection. What kind of information is given here?**
(Possible answer: Tips for watching the night sky.)

40

Tips for Watching
40

MODIFY Instruction

ESL/ELD

▲ Offer English-language learners the opportunity to contribute to the Cultural Connection. Encourage children to draw or tell a "sky story" they know. You might ask family members who are interested to make a presentation to the class. **(COMMUNITY INVOLVEMENT)**

EXTRA HELP

■ Pair children who are having difficulty with an above-level reading partner to read page 41. Have the partner read each tip while the other child pantomimes it to show its meaning. **(WORK IN PAIRS)**

41

he Night Sky ⑩

Go out on a night when the moon is not bright.

Pick a spot where buildings and trees won't get in the way.

Close your eyes and get used to the dark.

Open your eyes and look up. What do you see?

41

TECHNOLOGY

Phonics Have children use the **WiggleWorks Plus** Magnet Board to expand on the story word *bright*. Copy the pattern *ight* and create rhyming words. Ask children which of the new words *(light, sight, night)* could be used in a story about the sky.

SOCIAL STUDIES

Invite children to do the **Retell Moon Tales** activity on **page R17**. Help them to find a moon tale to tell and have them discuss what is real and what is fantasy in the tale.

A List of Tips

SHARED WRITING

PREWRITE Using the information on page 41 as a guide, tell children that they will be writing a list of tips for doing something. Have them think about something they might give tips for. Encourage children to begin listing some of the tips they might give.

DAILY LANGUAGE PRACTICE

SPELLING

DAY 2:
Practice Words With Final e. **See page R12.**

GRAMMAR, USAGE, MECHANICS

DAY 2:
Practice Capitalize Titles. **See page R14.**

ORAL LANGUAGE

Can we take goodnight moon hom?
(Can we take Goodnight Moon home?)

DAY 2 WRAP-UP

READ ALOUD *Spend five to ten minutes reading from a selection of your choice.*

GUIDED READING *Meet with the **red** and **blue** reading groups and assign Independent Center activities. **See pages R10–R11.***

COMPREHENSION

DAY 3 OBJECTIVES

CHILDREN WILL:

READ 30 MINUTES

- **"Twinkle, Twinkle Little Star," on pp. 42–43**
- **Assess Comprehension**
- **Key Comprehension Skill: Categorize Information**
- **Daily Phonics: Final *e***

WRITE 20 MINUTES

- **Respond: Caption**
- **Spelling: Words With Final *e***
- **Grammar, Usage, Mechanics: Capitalizing Titles**
- **Oral Language**

EXTEND SKILLS 30 MINUTES

- **Integrated Curriculum**
- **Read Aloud**
- **Guided Reading**

RESOURCES

- **Practice Book, pp. 18–22**
- **Spelling Resource Book, p. 93**

▶ Preview

Invite children to preview the song by reading the title and studying the pictures that go with it.

❶ **COMPARE/CONTRAST**

> **How is what the song says about stars the same or different from what you learned about stars in *The Night Sky*?** *(Possible answer: Both say that the stars twinkle. The song says stars are like diamonds; the selection tells about the colors of stars and the way they form patterns.)*

42

TRADITIONAL SONG

Twinkle, Twinkle Little Star

Twinkle, twinkle, little star,
how I wonder what you are.
Up above the world so high,
like a diamond in the sky.
Twinkle, twinkle, little star,
how I wonder what you are. ❶

42

MODIFY Instruction

ESL/ELD

▲ Work with children in a small group to teach them the song. Clarify the meaning of key words and model hand motions. Some children may know this song in their first language. Encourage them to teach their song to the class. **(RHYTHM)**

EXTRA HELP

■ Ask children if they have sung the song before. Help them suggest hand motions to go with the words. **(MULTISENSORY TECHNIQUES)**

43

EFG
43

TEACHER TIP

"I use simple songs to get children's attention and to help them remember simple routines. For example, I sing 'Time to stop and put away all the things we used today,' to the tune of 'Twinkle, Twinkle Little Star,' at the end of our center time, or whenever I need to have children return to their seats."

SKILLS AND STRATEGIES

GENRE
Song

TEACH/MODEL
Explain that songs are poetry set to music.

- Explain that the music for "Twinkle, Twinkle Little Star" was written many years ago by a famous composer named Wolfgang Mozart.
- Point out that songs often have one or more lines that repeat.

PRACTICE/APPLY
Sing the song with the class. Have children echo each line after you, following your phrasing and expression.

> **Which line of the song repeats?** *(Twinkle, twinkle little star, how I wonder what you are.)*

> **What are the rhyming words?** *(star, far; high, sky)*

> **What other songs are sung to the music of "Twinkle, Twinkle Little Star?"** *(Possible answer: the "Alphabet Song.")*

COMPREHENSION

Think About Reading

Below are the **answers** to the questions in *Think About Reading.*

1. *The moon is the brightest light in the night sky.*
2. *The stars and the moon make the night sky twinkle and shine.*
3. *One constellation is called the Big Dipper. Another is called the Little Dipper.*
4. *Comets don't pass by often.*
5. *Possible response: Yes, because it twinkles and shines. [Paired Selection]*

44

RESPOND

Think About Reading

1. What is the brightest light in the night sky?
2. What makes the night sky twinkle and shine?
3. What is the name of one constellation in the night sky?
4. Why would you be lucky to see a comet in the night sky?
5. Do you think that a star looks like a diamond in the night sky? Why or why not?

44

Name COMPREHENSION CHECK

High in the Sky

▶ Draw things in the night sky. Then write two things you learned about the night sky.

❶

❷

18 Unit 4 • Imagine That! • *The Night Sky*

PRACTICE BOOK p. 18

MODIFY Instruction

ESL/ELD

▲ Simplify the questions by rephrasing them as yes/no or either-or questions. For example: *Do stars twinkle in the night sky? Is the moon the brightest light in the night sky?* Have children reread the story as they listen to the recording of it. Children can also record themselves reading a favorite page. **(USE AUDIO)**

EXTRA HELP

■ Have children work in pairs to brainstorm objects in a night sky and the words that describe them. Help children use simple graphic organizers to record their ideas. **(BRAINSTORM)**

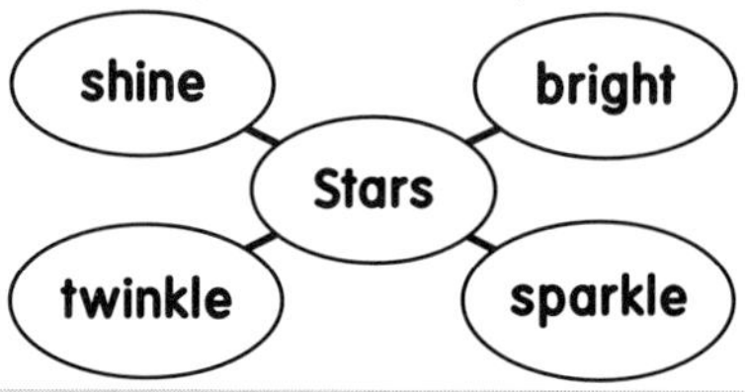
shine
bright
Stars
twinkle
sparkle

45

Write a Caption

The Night Sky tells facts about things in the sky. Draw your own picture of the night sky. Write a sentence to go with your picture. Include facts that will help people understand your picture.

Literature Circle

Think about what is in a night sky. What do you most like to see there? Why? Share your ideas.

Illustrator
Lisa Desimini

When Lisa Desimini was a child, she liked to look at the moon and the stars. She still likes looking at the night sky. That's why she was so happy to draw the pictures for The Night Sky.

More Books Illustrated by Lisa Desimini

- How the Stars Fell Into the Sky
- In a Circle Long Ago: A Treasury of Native Lore From North America

45

TECHNOLOGY

Presentation Tools Guide children as they use **WiggleWorks Plus PlaceMaker** to create pictures of a night sky. Use the text tool to label the sky objects in the illustrations. Print and share the drawings. Ask children whether the sky might look different at a different time of year.

CULTURAL CONNECTION

In July, the Japanese have a Star Festival, called *Tanabata*. The festival commemorates a legend about the meeting of two stars on either side of the Milky Way. Poems on colored paper are used to decorate bamboo branches which children then take to a stream to be carried away.

RESPOND

Write a Caption

Before children begin writing, have them think about these questions:

- **What do you want to include in your picture?**
- **What information do you want to give about your picture?**

Children may wish to display their illustrations and captions on a bulletin board.

Literature Circle

Encourage small groups of children to discuss what they most like to see in the night sky.

DAILY LANGUAGE PRACTICE

SPELLING

DAY 3: Write the Words With Final *e*. **See page R13.**

GRAMMAR, USAGE, MECHANICS

DAY 3: Practice Capitalizing Titles. **See page R15.**

ORAL LANGUAGE

We sang "twinkle, twinkle little star."

(We sang "Twinkle, Twinkle Little Star.")

PIERRE
MAURICE SENDAK
GOING HOME
JENNY'S JOURNEY

CONNECT TO THE TRADE BOOKS

Select one of the unit trade books. Read aloud the title and discuss the cover illustration.

- Have children make predictions about what might happen in the story. Record their predictions on chart paper or on the chalkboard.
- Then, read a few pages at a time, and stop to categorize information.
- Record children's categories and information. Continue until the book is completed.

COMPREHENSION
Categorize Information

QUICKCHECK

Can children:

✔ understand that the moon, stars, planets, and comets can all be grouped as things seen in the night sky?

✔ recall specific facts about each topic or category?

If YES, go on to Practice/Apply.

If NO, start at Teach/Model.

A TEACH/MODEL

USE ORAL LANGUAGE

Ask children how they would sort a banana, a sandwich, a shirt, and gloves. What two groups would these things fit into? Point out that the banana and sandwich might be in a category such as *Things to Eat,* while the shirt and gloves might be in a category such as *Things to Wear.*

Explain that to categorize is to sort things or information into groups. Tell children that when they categorize, they should:

1. think about the objects or information to be categorized.
2. decide what is the same about the objects or information.
3. decide what category or categories the objects or information best fits into.

MODIFY Instruction

ESL/ELD

▲ Have children categorize information under a board list with the headings "Things to Do During the Day" and "Things to Do at Night." Volunteers will act out or pantomime actions (*eat breakfast, look at stars*). Children figure out what the action is, and tell you under which list to write it. **(ACT IT OUT)**

EXTRA HELP

■ Use classroom objects for additional practice categorizing information. Encourage children to organize objects into categories, such as *Things We Write On*, and *Things We Read From.* Then have children discuss the similarities and differences in each list. **(USE REALIA)**

LITERATURE CONNECTION

THINK ALOUD *As I read* The Night Sky, *I categorized, or sorted, what I learned. I put facts about the moon under the category of* The Moon. *I categorized the Big Dipper and constellations under* Stars. *And now I know that the whole selection fits into the category of* Things in the Night Sky.

B PRACTICE/APPLY

USE PRACTICE BOOK

Look at page 29 of *The Night Sky* with children. Read aloud the sentence *There are many things to see in the night sky.* Point out how putting these things into categories made the selection easier to understand. Now have pairs of children practice categorizing information by completing Practice Book page 19.

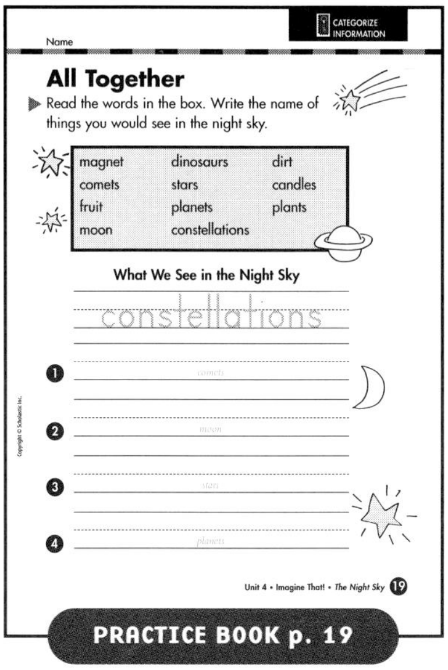

Name

CATEGORIZE INFORMATION

All Together

Read the words in the box. Write the name of things you would see in the night sky.

magnet	dinosaurs	dirt
comets	stars	candles
fruit	planets	plants
moon	constellations	

What We See in the Night Sky

constellations

1

2

3

4

Unit 4 • Imagine That! • The Night Sky 19

PRACTICE BOOK p. 19

C ASSESS

APPLY INSTRUCTIONAL ALTERNATIVES

Based on children's completion of **Practice Book page 19,** determine if children were able to categorize information in *The Night Sky*. The Instructional Alternatives below will aid you in pinpointing children's levels of proficiency. Consider the appropriate instructional alternative to promote further skill development.

To reinforce the skills, distribute **page 20** of the **Practice Book.**

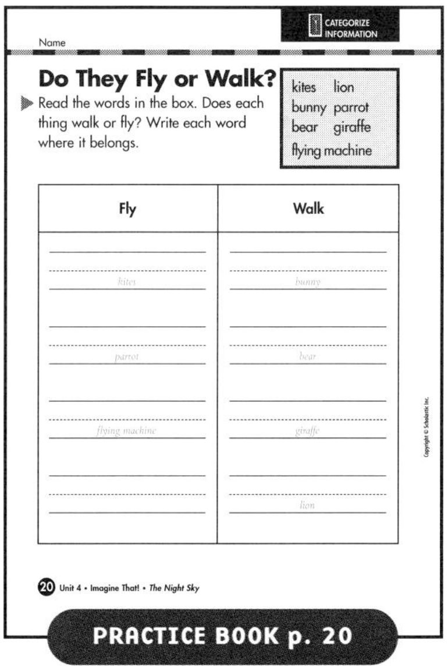

Name

CATEGORIZE INFORMATION

Do They Fly or Walk?

Read the words in the box. Does each thing walk or fly? Write each word where it belongs.

kites	lion
bunny	parrot
bear	giraffe
flying machine	

Fly	Walk

20 Unit 4 • Imagine That! • The Night Sky

PRACTICE BOOK p. 20

INSTRUCTIONAL ALTERNATIVES

	If the child . . .	Then
Proficient	Places objects or ideas in valid categories	• Have the child apply this skill independently to a more challenging story. • Present a new scenario and have the child brainstorm possible categories and present a rationale for the categories.
Apprentice	Has difficulty sorting information into valid categories	• Have the child work with others to sort objects or ideas and to explain why they belong together.
Novice	Cannot sort objects or information into categories	• Work with the child to see similarities and differences among objects or ideas. • Complete the Reteach lesson on R62.

Foods to Eat
Things to Wear
bananas
apples
Sandwich
hats
mittens
Shoes

The Night Sky

SELECTION WORDS With /ē/ *ea, ee*

see

east

trees

SKILLS TRACE

VOWEL /ē/
ea, ee TESTED

Introduce . . . . pp. T92–T93
Practice . . . . pp. T81, T99
Review . . . . p. R50
Reteach . . . . .p. R59

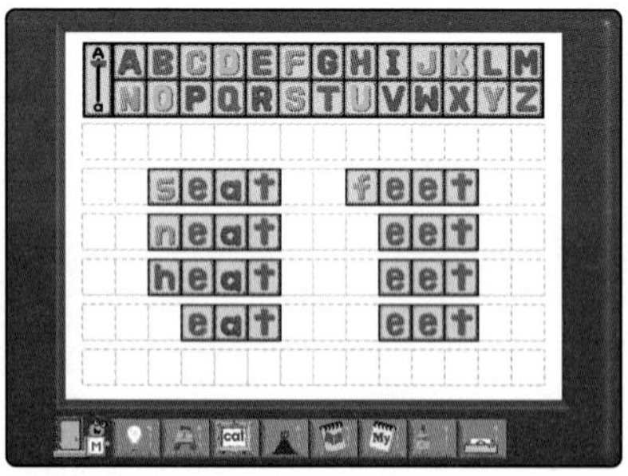

TECHNOLOGY

Have children build words with vowel /ē/ *ea, ee* on the **WiggleWorks Plus** Magnet Board.

- Begin with the words **seat** and **feet**.
- Have children change one letter to make new words.

DAILY PHONICS

Vowel /ē/ ea, ee

A PHONOLOGICAL AWARENESS

RHYME Read aloud the rhyme "Stop! Look! Listen!" from *The Big Book of Rhymes and Rhythms 1B*, page 8. As you read, stress the words with the long *e* sound: ***each, street, feet***.

- On a second reading, ask children to read along with you.
- Frame the words ***each*** and ***feet*** and point out the long *e* sound in each word.

Stop! Look! Listen!
Stop!
Look!
Listen!
Each time you cross the street,
Use your eyes,
Use your ears,
Before you use your feet.
each street

Big Book of Rhymes and Rhythms, 1B, p. 8

ORAL BLENDING Say the following word parts and ask children to blend them. Provide modeling and corrective feedback as needed.

- /s/ /ē/ /d/
- /f/ /ē/ /t/
- /m/ /ē/ /t/
- /l/ /ē/ /f/
- /k/ /ē/ /p/
- /b/ /ē/ /n/

B CONNECT SOUND-SPELLING

INTRODUCE Vowel /ē/ *ea, ee* Explain to children that the letters ***ea*** and ***ee*** often stand for **/ē/**, as in the words ***leaf*** and ***wheel***. Write the words on the chalkboard and underline ***ea*** and ***ee***.

THINK ALOUD *I can put the letters **l**, **ea**, and **f** together to make the word **leaf**. Listen to the sound that **ea** stands for in the word **leaf**. Now let's listen for the sound **ee** stands for in **wheel**.*

MODIFY Instruction

ESL/ELD

▲ Write *beat*, *feet*, and *seat* on the chalkboard, underlining *ea* or *ee*. Have children read the words aloud. Then teach them the following Total Physical Response chant: *Listen to the beat* (cup your ear); *Stamp your feet* (stand up and stamp feet); *Now take your seat!* (sit down). **(USE RHYME)**

GIFTED & TALENTED

✷ Ask children to find long *e* homophones, such as *meet* and *meat*, and to compile a list of the words. Suggest that they choose two homophone words and illustrate each one. **(PEER PARTNERS)**

PHONICS MAINTENANCE Review the following sound-spellings: ***/a/a-e, /sh/sh, /kw/qu, /v/v, /th/th.*** Say one of the sounds and have a volunteer write on the board the spelling that stands for the sound. Continue with all the sounds.

C PRACTICE/APPLY

BLEND WORDS To practice using the sound-spelling and review previous sound-spellings, list the following words and sentence on the chalkboard. Have volunteers read each aloud. Model blending as needed.

meat	east	seed
sheet	teeth	bean
queen	leaves	save

I need to eat my lunch.

DICTATION Dictate the following words: ***eat, see, leaf, shut, then, queen, cave.***

BUILD WORDS Distribute the following letter cards, or have children use their own sets: ***ee, ea, b, n, m, t, f, l, q, u, a, i, e.*** Allow children time to build words using the letter cards. Children can write their words on a separate sheet of paper. **(INDEPENDENT WORK)**

l
ea
f

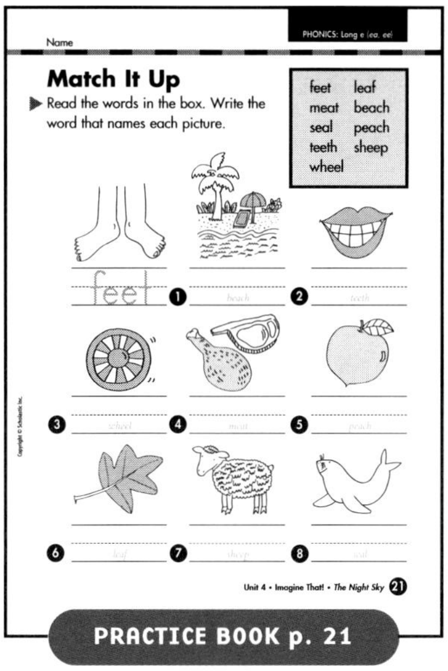
Name

PHONICS: Long e (ea, ee)

Match It Up

▶ Read the words in the box. Write the word that names each picture.

feet leaf meat beach seal peach teeth sheep wheel

feet

Unit 4 • Imagine That! • The Night Sky 21

PRACTICE BOOK p. 21

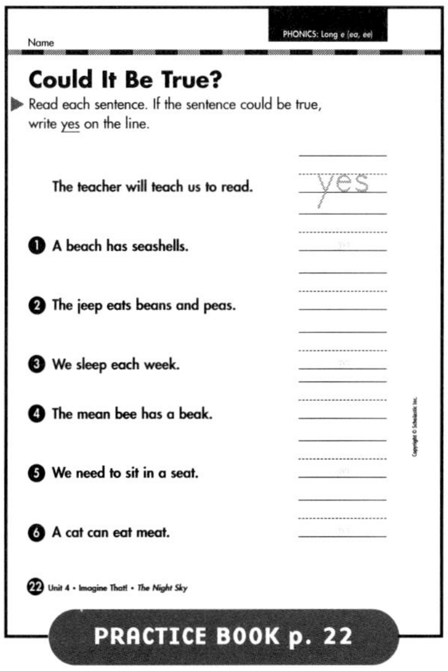
Name

PHONICS: Long e (ea, ee)

Could It Be True?

▶ Read each sentence. If the sentence could be true, write yes on the line.

The teacher will teach us to read. yes

1. A beach has seashells.
2. The jeep eats beans and peas.
3. We sleep each week.
4. The mean bee has a beak.
5. We need to sit in a seat.
6. A cat can eat meat.

22 Unit 4 • Imagine That! • The Night Sky

PRACTICE BOOK p. 22

DECODABLE TEXT

For practice reading decodable text, see ***Scholastic Decodable Reader #47.***

For additional phonics instruction and review, see ***Scholastic Phonics A, pp. 181–186.***

TWO PEAS IN A POD

Have children cut out large pea pods from green construction paper. Ask children for words that rhyme with *pea* (or other long *e* words) and write them on the chalkboard. Then have children write two of these words on their pea pods.

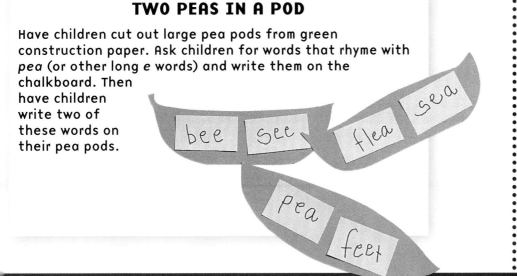

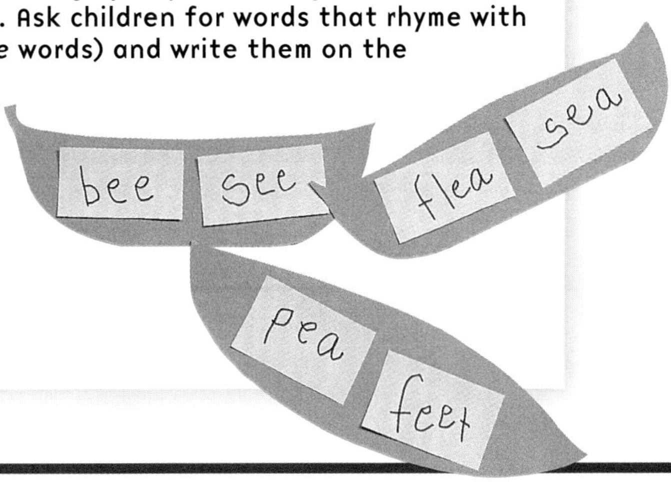
bee
see
flea
sea
pea
feet

Building Fluency

Phonics Reader

Book 39
Lime Ice Is Nice
a retelling by Francie Alexander and Nancy Hechinger
Illustrated by Jackie Snider
SCHOLASTIC

Guide children through a reading of **Phonics Reader #39** *Lime Ice Is Nice* or **#40** *Hen Pen's Joke.* For a detailed lesson plan, see **Phonics Reader Teacher's Guide Part B, pages 20–23.** While children read, note how well they:

- **blend words,**
- **recognize high-frequency words,**
- **read with speed, accuracy, and expression.**

You may wish to have children reread the story with a partner.

* See Phonics Readers Take-Home Books 37–72 for reproducible format.

More Support Materials . . .

GOING HOME
PIERRE
A cautionary tale
IN FIVE CHAPTERS
AND A PROLOGUE
MAURICE SENDAK
JENNY'S JOURNEY
SCHOLASTIC

Trade Book Library

For additional leveled reading practice, have children read one of the following:

Going Home
Challenge

Pierre
Average

Jenny's Journey
Easy

Phonics Chapter Book

PHONICS
The
Puppet Club

For additional practice with final *e*, have children read Chapter 1, "Jane and Jake" in ***Phonics Chapter Book 4,*** *The Puppet Club.*

Home-School Connection

Hen Pen's Joke
Lime Ice Is Nice
ALONE

Send home *Lime Ice Is Nice, Hen Pen's Joke,* and *Alone.* Have children read the books to a family member.

My Book

ALONE

For additional practice with high-frequency words and words with final *e*, have children read *Alone.* This book is also available on **WiggleWorks Plus.**

Intervention

For children who need extra help . . .

FOCUS ON HIGH-FREQUENCY WORDS

Write the words ***many*** and ***some*** on note cards. Then follow this procedure:

- Read each word and have children repeat it.
- Have children write each word in their Journals.
- Provide children with simple sentences containing each word. Help them read the sentences. Allow time for them to practice reading the words and sentences before rereading *The Night Sky*.

Some children may need a large number of repetitions before these words become sight words. Brief daily reviews and frequent rereadings of previous stories containing these words will be helpful.

FOCUS ON PHONICS

Provide time for children to play with the decodable words they encountered in the story, such as ***shine*** and ***white***.

- Make each word using magnetic letters or letter cards as children observe.
- Have children trace the letters in each word with their fingers, as you say the sounds with them.
- Mix the letters and have children respell the words.
- Model blending as needed.

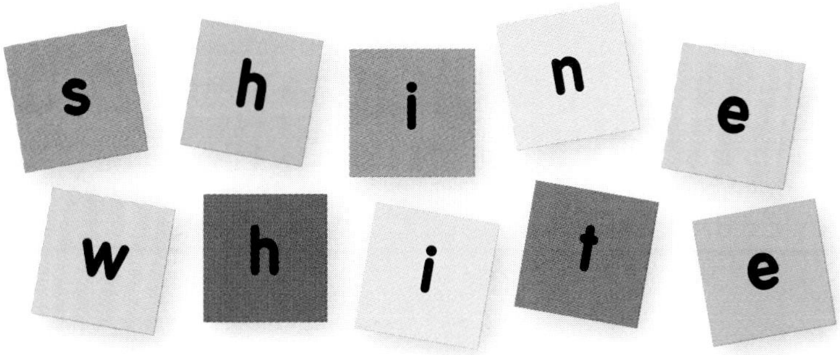
s h i n e
w h i t e

PROFESSIONAL DEVELOPMENT

JOHN SHEFELBINE

When to Adjust the Instructional Pace

When children are far behind in their knowledge of sound-spelling relationships or high-frequency (sight) words, it is best to go back to where the new information was first presented and then proceed at an appropriate pace. For blending problems, going back is not as useful as providing extra practice in blending. Remember, blending is easier when there are no stop sounds at the beginning or in the middle of the word.

DAY 3 WRAP-UP

READ ALOUD *To conclude each reading session and to develop children's vocabularies, read aloud from a book or a chapter of a book of your choice.*

GUIDED READING *Meet with the **green** and **yellow** reading groups and assign Independent Center activities.* ***See pages R10–R11.***

DAY 4 OBJECTIVES

CHILDREN WILL:

READ 15 MINUTES

- **Reread *The Night Sky***

WRITE 30 MINUTES

- **Shared Writing: List of Tips**
- **Spelling: Words With Final *e***
- **Grammar, Usage, Mechanics: Capitalize Titles**

EXTEND SKILLS 45 MINUTES

- **Vocabulary**
- **Daily Phonics: Vowel /ē/ *ea, ee***
- **Study Skills: Sort/Organize Information**
- **Read Aloud**
- **Guided Reading**

RESOURCES

- **Practice Book, pp. 23, 25**

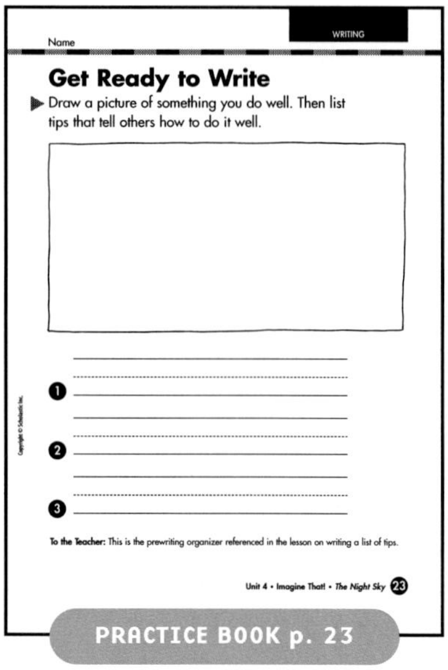
Name

WRITING

Get Ready to Write

▶ Draw a picture of something you do well. Then list tips that tell others how to do it well.

1

2

3

To the Teacher: This is the prewriting organizer referenced in the lesson on writing a list of tips.

Unit 4 • Imagine That! • The Night Sky 23

PRACTICE BOOK p. 23

SHARED WRITING

List of Tips

The Night Sky

SELECTION CONNECTION *The Night Sky* ends with a list of tips. Children will write their own list of tips for doing something they know how to do.

THINK ABOUT WRITING Help children see that the tips in *The Night Sky* are written:

- to help someone do something.
- to explain something new.

INTRODUCE THE WRITING EVENT Tell children they will write a list of tips for something they know how to do. They will be writing the list for someone who has never done the activity.

TEACH/MODEL

PUT IT IN CONTEXT Have children turn to pages 40-41 to review "Tips for Watching the Night Sky." Ask:

> **Who do you think wrote these tips? Why do you think the person wrote them?**

Ask children to think about something they know how to do and can write a list of tips for.

- Ask children to think about what tips they would suggest to someone to help that person do the activity.
- Write these suggestions on the chalkboard.
- Ask children to suggest the order these tips should be in.

MODIFY Instruction

ESL/ELD

▲ Help children think about the order of their tips by asking, *What step comes first? What happens next? What is the last step?* Have them repeat the tips aloud in order before writing them in a list. Accept short-phrase answers as long as children demonstrate understanding. **(SEQUENCE)**

EXTRA HELP

■ Support children who need extra help deciding what to write about by encouraging them to brainstorm a list of things they especially enjoy. Help them realize that the things they enjoy doing are usually the things they do well. **(BRAINSTORM)**

GRAMMAR CONNECTION

- Have children suggest a title for their list of tips. Encourage them to point out which letters in the title should be capitalized.

WRITE

CREATE A CLASS LIST OF TIPS

- Model how to write a tip. Have small groups of children write or dictate tips onto strips of paper, one tip per strip.
- Have children draw pictures to illustrate their tips.
- Create a class list of tips. Compile the tips into a single list by pasting the strips onto a large sheet of paper. Help children number the tips.

ASSESS

PERFORMANCE-BASED ASSESSMENT

The following questions will help children assess their work:

✔ Will the tips help someone do the thing well?

✔ Are the tips written in a list?

Children may wish to carry this piece through the writing process described on pages T278–T281.

DAILY LANGUAGE PRACTICE

SPELLING

DAY 4:

Review Words With Final *e*.

Have children proofread the tips. **See page R13.**

GRAMMAR, USAGE, MECHANICS

DAY 4:

Apply Capitalizing Titles.

See page R15.

ORAL LANGUAGE

I want to read a book called *moon soup.*

(I want to read a book called Moon Soup.)

TECHNOLOGY

Writing Skills

Encourage children to use the cut and paste options in a familiar word processing program to help them revise their writing.

Extend Vocabulary

TEACHER TIP

Make and distribute copies of the vocabulary Cards on pages R68–R69. Have children use these cards for additional practice.

Review High-Frequency Words

Write the high-frequency words ***some*** and ***many*** on note cards. For each word write a lowercase and uppercase version **(some/Some).** Then write the following incomplete sentences on the chalkboard:

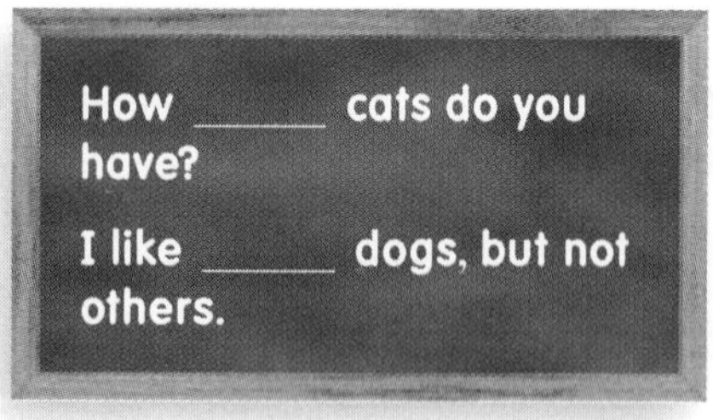
How _____ cats do you have?
I like _____ dogs, but not others.

some
Some
many
Many

Read aloud each incomplete sentence, and have children tape the appropriate high-frequency word card in the blank space. Then help children to choral read the sentences.

Review Story Words

Write the story words ***stars, planets, night, shine, moon,*** and ***light*** on note cards. Then write the following incomplete sentences on sentence strips.

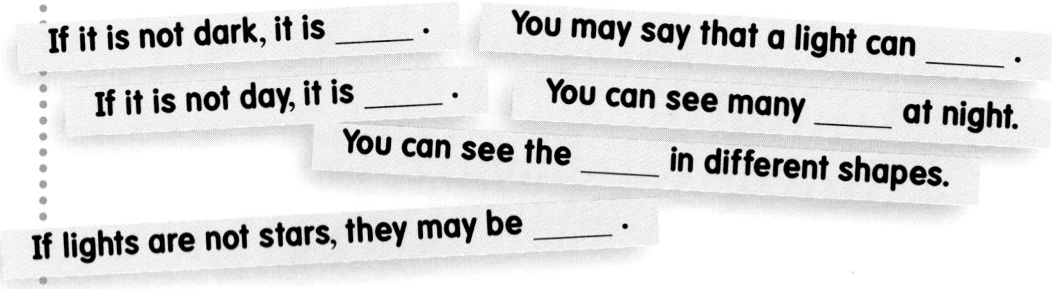
If it is not dark, it is _____ .
You may say that a light can _____ .
If it is not day, it is _____ .
You can see many _____ at night.
You can see the _____ in different shapes.
If lights are not stars, they may be _____ .

Read aloud the incomplete sentences and place the appropriate story word note card in the blank space. Then help children to chorally read the sentences.

SKY FACTS

Have children select as a topic one of the vocabulary words that names something they learned about in the selection. Ask children to make little books by drawing and writing about their topic. Encourage children to include facts and other vocabulary words in their writing.

Building Fluency

Phonics Reader

The Street Band
Book 42
The Three Little Pigs
Book 41
a retelling by Gail Tuchman
Illustrated by Tony Griego
SCHOLASTIC

Guide children through a reading of **Phonics Reader #41** *The Three Little Pigs* or **#42** *The Street Band.* For a detailed lesson plan, see **Phonics Reader Teacher's Guide Part B, pages 24–27.** While children read, note how well they:

- **blend words,**
- **recognize high-frequency words,**
- **read with speed, accuracy, and expression.**

You may wish to have children reread the story with a partner.

★ See Phonics Reader Take-Home Book 37–72 for reproducible format.

More Support Materials . . .

GOING HOME
PIERRE
A cautionary tale
IN FIVE CHAPTERS
AND A PROLOGUE
JENNY'S JOURNEY
SCHOLASTIC

Trade Book Library

For additional leveled reading practice, have children read one of the following:

Going Home
Challenge

Pierre
Average

Jenny's Journey
Easy

PHONICS
CHAPTER BOOK 4
The Puppet Club
SCHOLASTIC

Phonics Chapter Book

For additional practice with vowel ***/ē/ ea, ee,*** have children read Chapter 2, "A Good Team" in ***Phonics Chapter Book 4,*** *The Puppet Club.*

The Three Little Pigs
The Street Band
WHAT DO YOU SEE?

Home-School Connection

Send home *The Three Little Pigs, The Street Band,* and *What Do You See?* Have children read the books to a family member.

WHAT DO YOU SEE?
by Cass Hollander
Illustrated by Mavis Smith
SCHOLASTIC

My Book

For additional practice with high-frequency words and words with vowel ***/ē/ ea, ee,*** have children read *What Do You See?* This book is also available on **WiggleWorks Plus.**

STUDY SKILLS

Sort/Organize Information

Ⓐ TEACH/MODEL

DEFINE SORT/ ORGANIZING INFORMATION Explain that it is usually easier to remember information if it is sorted and put together in such a way that all the facts about one topic are together.

PRESENT HOW TO SORT AND ORGANIZE INFORMATION Remind children that the author of *The Night Sky* gave information about many things that can be seen in the sky at night. Ask children:

> **What things did you learn about from reading the selection?**

As children suggest things in the night sky that they learned about, make them headings on the chalkboard or on chart paper. Then point to and read each heading, one at a time. Encourage children to share one fact from *The Night Sky* about each heading as you point to it. Write that fact under the heading.

Moon
The moon is bright tonight
Stars
Stars seem to twinkle

B PRACTICE/APPLY

Ask children to work in small groups to select a topic from *The Night Sky*. Then have each group write a list of facts about their topic.

When the groups have written their lists, help them add the information to the appropriate columns on the chart. When the chart is completed ask:

> **How have you sorted and organized the information from *The Night Sky?***

> **Where is it easier to find information, in the selection *The Night Sky* or on the chart? Why do you think so?**

INFORMAL ASSESSMENT: PERFORMANCE-BASED

✔ Did children correctly identify the main topics in *The Night Sky*?

✔ Did children correctly identify the facts about a single topic?

✔ Did children correctly sort and organize the topics and facts?

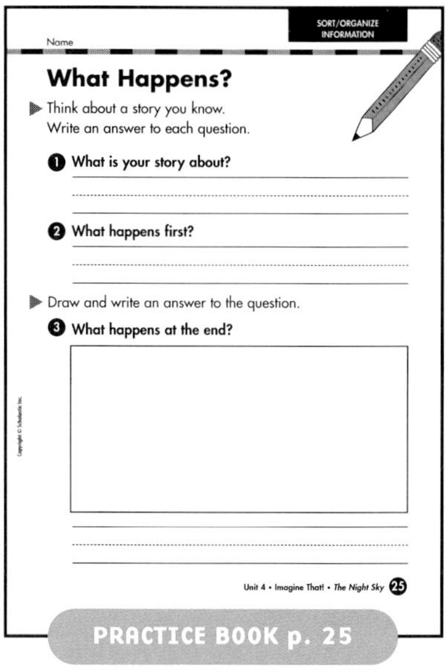
SORT/ORGANIZE INFORMATION

Name

What Happens?

▶ Think about a story you know. Write an answer to each question.

1 What is your story about?

2 What happens first?

▶ Draw and write an answer to the question.

3 What happens at the end?

Unit 4 • Imagine That! • The Night Sky 25

PRACTICE BOOK p. 25

TECHNOLOGY

Study Skills Before children begin classifying sky objects, they might practice sorting and classifying more common items. Use the **I Spy** CD-ROM and choose *Oops Hoops!* In these activities children practice sorting using a Venn diagram.

DAY 4 WRAP-UP

READ ALOUD *Spend five to ten minutes reading from a selection of your choice. Try to read nonfiction selections each week.*

GUIDED READING *Meet with the **red** and **blue** reading groups and assign Independent Center activities.* ***See pages R10–R11.***

DAY 5 OBJECTIVES

CHILDREN WILL:

READ 20 MINUTES

- **Reading Assessment**
- **Daily Phonics: Final *e*, Vowel /ē/ *ea*, *ee***

WRITE 30 MINUTES

- **Writing Assessment**
- **Spelling: Words With Final *e***
- **Grammar, Usage, Mechanics: Capitalize Titles**
- **Oral Language**

EXTEND SKILLS 40 MINUTES

- **Integrated Language Arts**
- **Read Aloud**
- **Guided Reading**

RESOURCES

- **Selection Test**
- **Spelling Resource Book, p. 163**

TEACHER SELF-ASSESSMENT

✓Did I frequently model how to blend words with long vowels?

✓Did I regroup children according to skill needs and reading level?

✓Did I provide children with successful daily reading and writing opportunities?

Reading Assessment

INFORMAL ASSESSMENT: OBSERVATION

PHONICS

Write the following spellings on note cards: ***i_e, a_e, o_e, u_e, ea, ee.*** Display one card at a time and have the class state the sound the spelling stands for. Note children who respond incorrectly or wait for classmates to respond before providing an answer.

HIGH-FREQUENCY WORDS

Write the following words on note cards: ***many, some.*** Display one card at a time and have the class read the word. Note children who have difficulty recognizing either word.

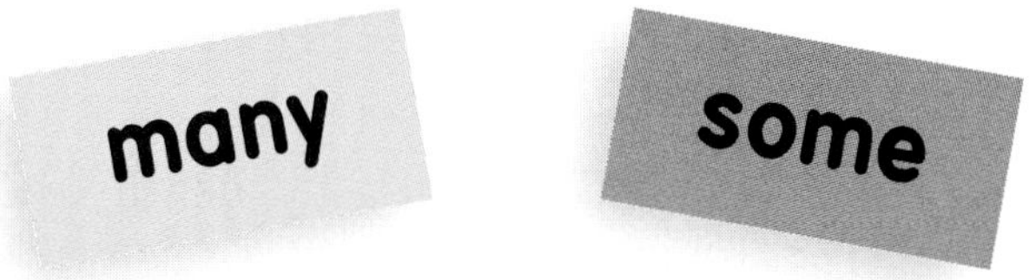
many
some

KEY STRATEGY: CATEGORIZE INFORMATION

Read a few pages of a nonfiction book. You may wish to choose one about stars. Have children decide on categories they might use to list the information provided in the book.

CONFERENCE

Have children reread *The Night Sky*. As they reread, select several children to conference with. Ask them to do the following:

- read aloud a few pages of the story.
- tell facts about the night sky they learned from the story.
- explain what they do to figure out an unfamiliar word.

Keep anecdotal records of the conferences. Place your findings in each child's assessment folder. Use the information to determine which children need additional support.

The Night Sky
Written by Alice Pernick
Illustrated by Lisa Desimini

The Night Sky

FORMAL ASSESSMENT

DECODING TEST

Make two copies of the assessment below. The assessment piece is designed to be used with one child at a time.

- Give one to the child and keep the other to record each child's errors.
- As the child reads aloud the words and sentences in the assessment boxes, record his or her attempts, corrections, errors, and passes.
- Once completed, keep each assessment piece in the child's portfolio as a running record of his or her emerging reading skills.

NAME: ______________________ **DATE:** ____________

A Have children read the following word list:

luck	**feet**	**cake**	**me**	**some**
fine	**use**	**time**	**went**	**from**
rope	**seat**	**note**	**through**	**over**
leaf	**shut**	**quick**	**soon**	**put**
made	**see**	**safe**	**little**	**many**

B Have children read the following word sentences:

- **Many pigs sleep in the mud.**
- **I need some green pens.**

C On a separate sheet of paper, have children write the following words and sentences:

- **hide take read see**
- **We had a fine bus ride.**
- **I did not keep the note.**

SELECTION TEST

Use the selection test to obtain a formal measure of children's mastery of the week's reading objectives.

SELF-SELECTION

Have children select one or two pieces of work from the week that they would like to place in their portfolios.

Suggest that children write sentences telling why they chose each piece. You may also wish to select a piece that best illustrates the child's work.

Periodically review the pieces in the portfolio and remove any that no longer seem appropriate.

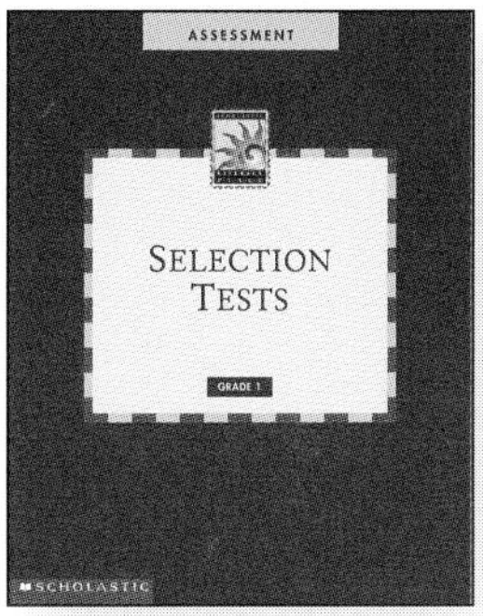
ASSESSMENT
SELECTION TESTS
SCHOLASTIC

SELECTION TEST

DAILY LANGUAGE PRACTICE

Spelling

DAY 5:

Administer the Posttest for Words With Final e. **See page R13.**

Grammar, Usage, Mechanics

DAY 5:

Assess Capitalizing Titles. **See page R15.**

Oral Language

Sue read Lime Ice is nice to me.

(Sue read Lime Ice Is Nice to me.)

PORTFOLIO

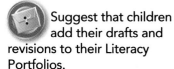

Suggest that children add their drafts and revisions to their Literacy Portfolios.

Writing Assessment

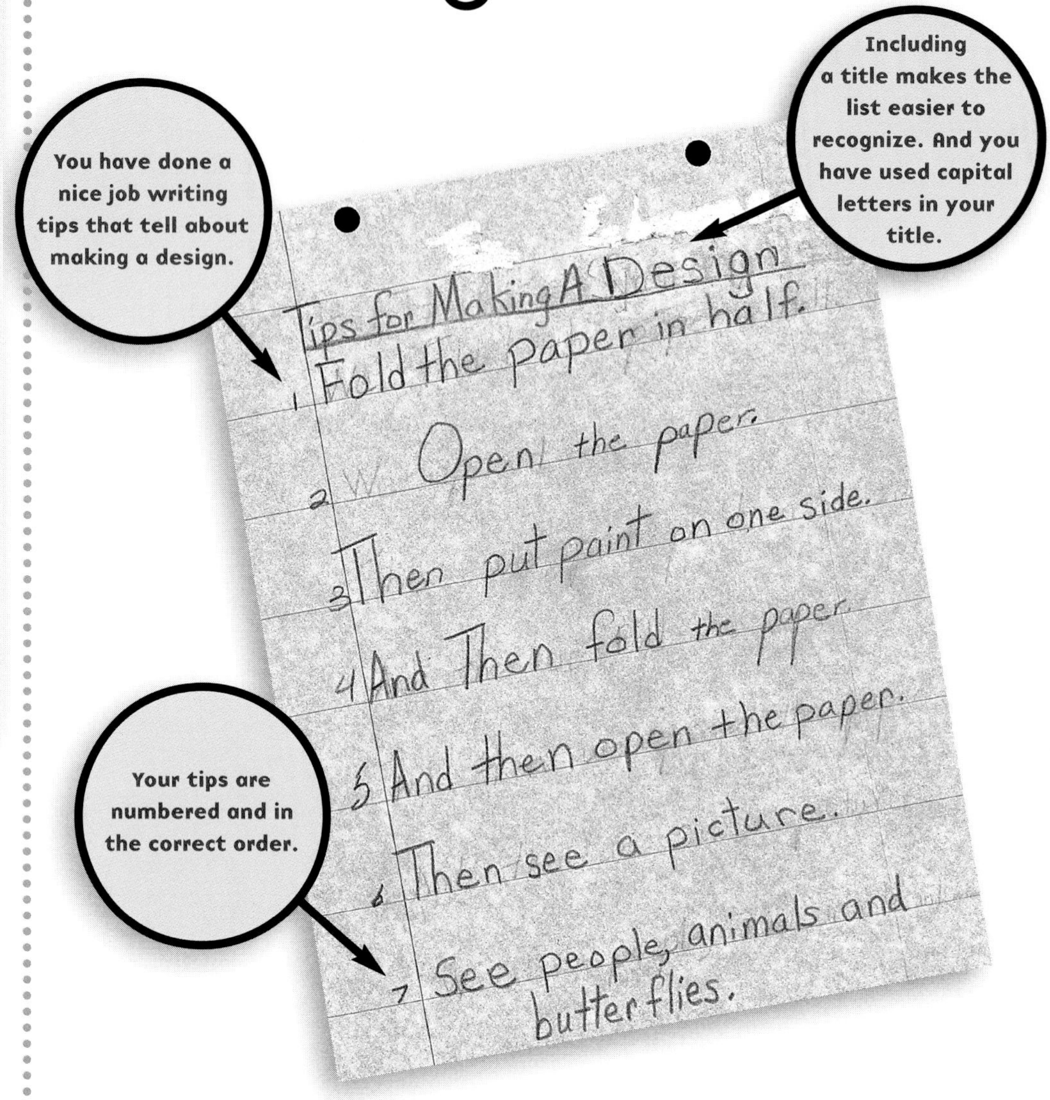
Including a title makes the list easier to recognize. And you have used capital letters in your title.
You have done a nice job writing tips that tell about making a design.
Your tips are numbered and in the correct order.
Tips for Making A Design
1 Fold the paper in half.
2 Open the paper.
3 Then put paint on one side.
4 And Then fold the paper
5 And then open the paper.
6 Then see a picture.
7 See people, animals and butterflies.

Proficient

Use the rubric below to assess children's writing.

CHILDREN'S WRITING RUBRIC

Proficient	• The tips explain how to do something. • The tips are in a numbered list that clearly shows a sequence of activities.	• The tips include a title. • The list has been proofread and corrected for grammar, usage, and mechanics.
Apprentice	• The tips may not show how to do something. • The list may not be numbered or show a sequence of activities.	• The tips may not include a title. • The list may have been proofread but not completely corrected.
Novice	• The tips do not show how to do something. • The tips are not written in a numbered list.	• The tips do not include a title. • The tips have not been corrected for errors.

Integrated Language Arts

WRITING/VIEWING

Write About the Day Sky

Good For Grading

MATERIALS:
Drawing paper
Crayons or markers

SUGGESTED GROUPING:
Individuals or cooperative groups

SUGGEST that children contribute to a class book about what they see in the daytime sky.

HAVE children look out the window and note what they see in the sky. Then ask them to write or dictate a sentence about what they see. Help children focus by giving an example such as: *I see two gray clouds that look like a baby elephant chasing a mouse.*

ASK children to illustrate their sentences. Then gather their pages into a big book.

HOW TO GRADE When grading these sentences, look for sentences that show a complete thought.

my Kite and
the bird are in
the Sky

Dear Mom,
Mars is rocky
and red. Love
AMY

WRITING/VIEWING/VOCABULARY

Write a Postcard

MATERIALS:
Large index cards
Crayons or markers
Books or other resources with pictures of planets

SUGGESTED GROUPING:
Independent

SUGGEST that children use their imaginations to picture themselves on another planet. Their job is to send a postcard home.

ASK children to share what they know about postcards. Talk about their form and how they are written.

CHILDREN can draw a picture of the planet on one side of a large index card. On the other side, they can name the planet, tell about it, or tell about their trip getting there. Encourage children to use the story words whenever possible.

Children might want to include their postcards in their Literacy Portfolios.

Address Envelopes

TEACH/MODEL Write an address such as the following on the chalkboard: ***123 Schoolroom Lane, West End, Texas, 10001.*** Read aloud the address. Explain that when they send a letter or postcard to someone, they must write the person's address and where the person lives on the envelope or postcard.

PRACTICE/APPLY Encourage children to write or dictate each other's addresses or made-up addresses for their postcards or envelopes.

Integrated Language Arts

WRITING/VIEWING

Make a Mobile

MATERIALS: Collage materials such as aluminum foil, glitter, cardboard, colored tissue, paper, markers, scissors, tape, string

SUGGESTED GROUPING: Cooperative groups

HAVE cooperative groups of children work together to make night-sky objects for mobiles.

ENCOURAGE the groups to first list different objects that can be found in the night sky. Then groups can work together to plan and create the objects, using various collage materials.

ASK groups to write the name of the night-sky object on the back of their collages.

GROUPS can tape string to their objects and have an adult hang them from the ceiling of the classroom.

DAY 5 WRAP-UP

READ ALOUD *Spend five to ten minutes reading aloud from a selection of your choice.*

GUIDED READING *Meet with the **green** and **yellow** groups and assign Independent Center activities.* ***See pp. R10–R11.***

WRITING/VIEWING/READING

Write Directions

MATERIALS: Drawing paper, Crayons or markers, Stapler or tape

SUGGESTED GROUPING: Partners

ASK children to look at the tips listed on the last page of *The Night Sky*. Using them as a model, ask partners to think of an activity they like to do. Then have children list tips and directions for doing the activity.

CHILDREN can make minibooks for their tips by folding a piece of paper in half, then in half again. Each tip can be written or dictated on a separate page of the mini-book. The children can illustrate each tip.

CREATE a "How-To" corner to display and share the books.

TECHNOLOGY

Language Development Have children create direction booklets using **WiggleWorks Plus** PlaceMaker. Use the card format to create a booklet with an illustrated cover. The inside should be text in a list format—children note the steps needed to accomplish a simple task.

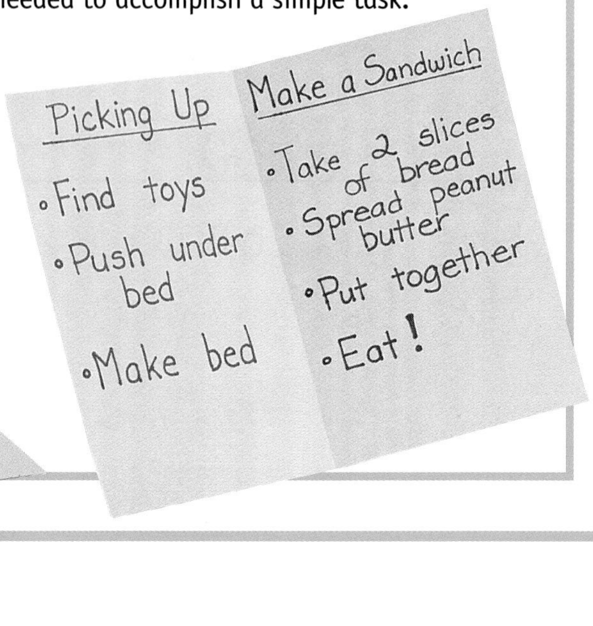
Picking Up
• Find toys
• Push under bed
• Make bed
Make a Sandwich
• Take 2 slices of bread
• Spread peanut butter
• Put together
• Eat!

How to Make a Story Plan

WHY DO THIS WORKSHOP?

When children read a story, they may not be aware of the many elements—such as characters, setting, and plot—that make it up. One good tool for helping children identify what the elements are and be able to discuss a piece of writing is the story plan. When children make a story plan after they've read a selection, they're engaged in the process of comprehending someone else's ideas. When they make a story plan before they start writing, they begin the process of making their own ideas concrete.

This Workshop gives children a chance to be creative and develop a plan for a story. They will make decisions about the characters, setting, and plot for their stories and talk over their ideas with each other to clarify and refine them. They'll use their artistic skills to sketch their ideas and use these ideas to write their stories.

WORKSHOP OBJECTIVES

CHILDREN WILL:

- **Recognize that a story is made up of characters, setting, and plot**
- **Create a story plan and use it to write a story**

MATERIALS

- **Paper and pencil**

TECHNOLOGY

Organizing Information Have children use a tape recorder to record their thoughts about their story plans. Encourage them to rewind and rerecord as their plans change.

GETTING STARTED

Make Your Own Story Plan

To focus your children on the task, read through side 1 of the Workshop Card with the class. You could also ask any of the following questions:

> **What do the author's notes tell you about the characters?**

> **Where does the story take place? What do you think the children do there?**

> **What are the children doing in the story?**

> **Why do you think authors make notes before writing a story?**

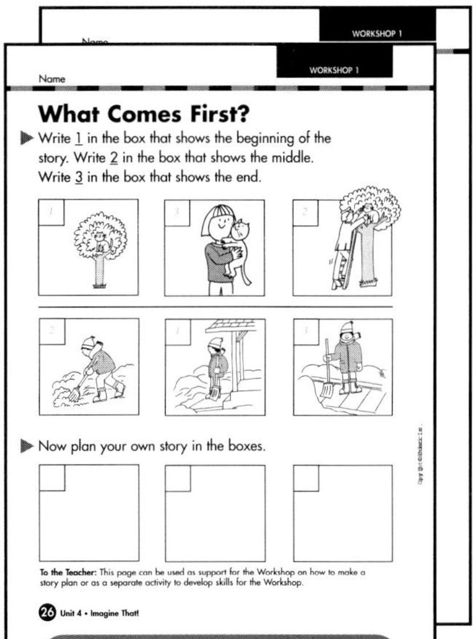
WORKSHOP 1

Name

What Comes First?

▶ Write 1 in the box that shows the beginning of the story. Write 2 in the box that shows the middle. Write 3 in the box that shows the end.

▶ Now plan your own story in the boxes.

To the Teacher: This page can be used as support for the Workshop on how to make a story plan or as a separate activity to develop skills for the Workshop.

26 Unit 4 • Imagine That!

PRACTICE BOOK pp. 26, 27

Use **Practice Book pages 26 and 27** as practice for the Workshop or as a separate activity.

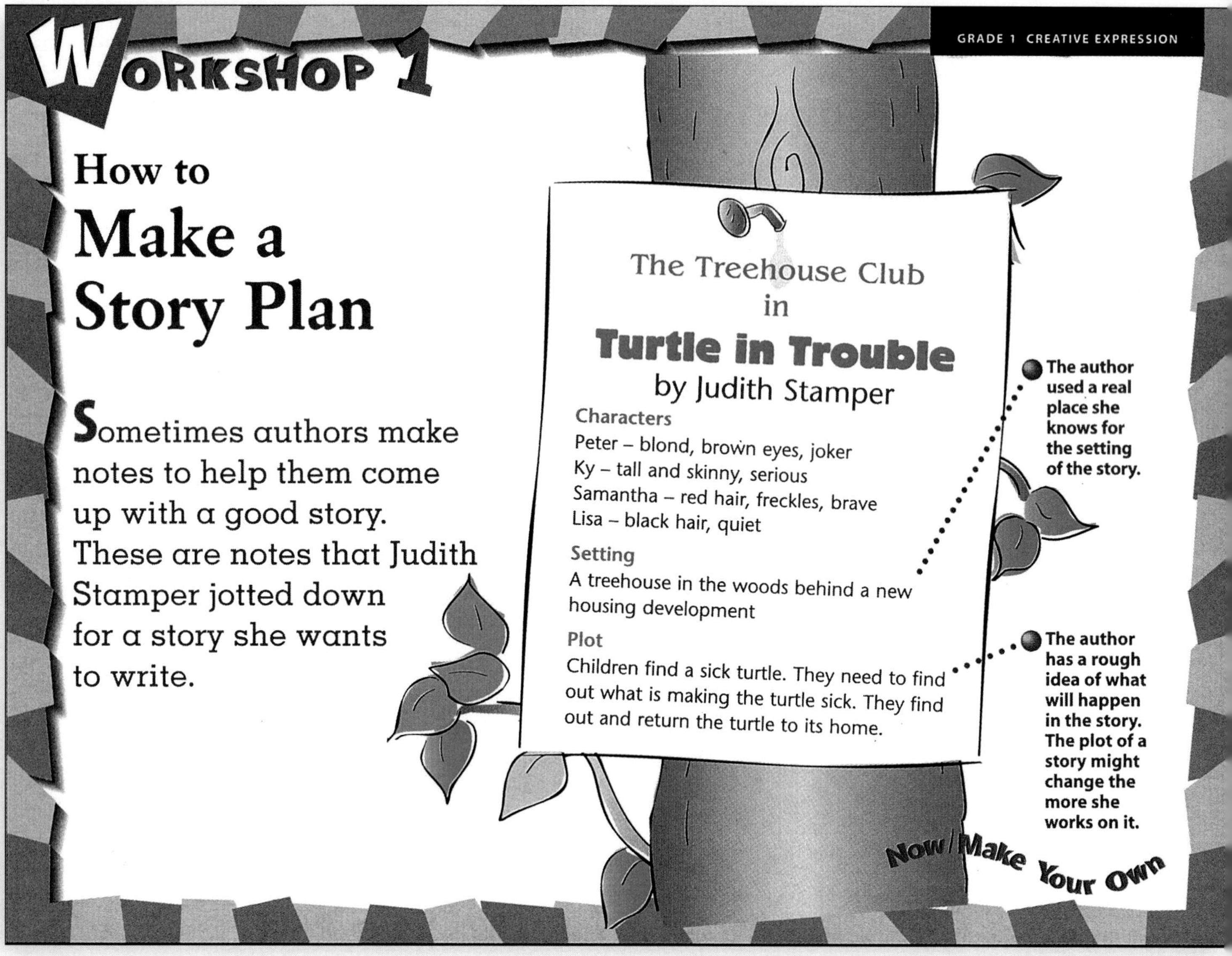

GRADE 1 CREATIVE EXPRESSION

WORKSHOP 1

How to Make a Story Plan

Sometimes authors make notes to help them come up with a good story. These are notes that Judith Stamper jotted down for a story she wants to write.

The Treehouse Club in

Turtle in Trouble

by Judith Stamper

Characters

Peter – blond, brown eyes, joker
Ky – tall and skinny, serious
Samantha – red hair, freckles, brave
Lisa – black hair, quiet

Setting

A treehouse in the woods behind a new housing development

Plot

Children find a sick turtle. They need to find out what is making the turtle sick. They find out and return the turtle to its home.

The author used a real place she knows for the setting of the story.

The author has a rough idea of what will happen in the story. The plot of a story might change the more she works on it.

Now Make Your Own

1 Write a Story Plan

To get children started, begin a list of story ideas. You might have a group storytelling session in which one child comes up with the first event or problem and a second child picks up from there. Write a story plan for the class's story on the chalkboard. Then have children write, draw, or dictate some ideas for their own story plans. Have them use the questions on their Workshop cards to get ideas.

WORI

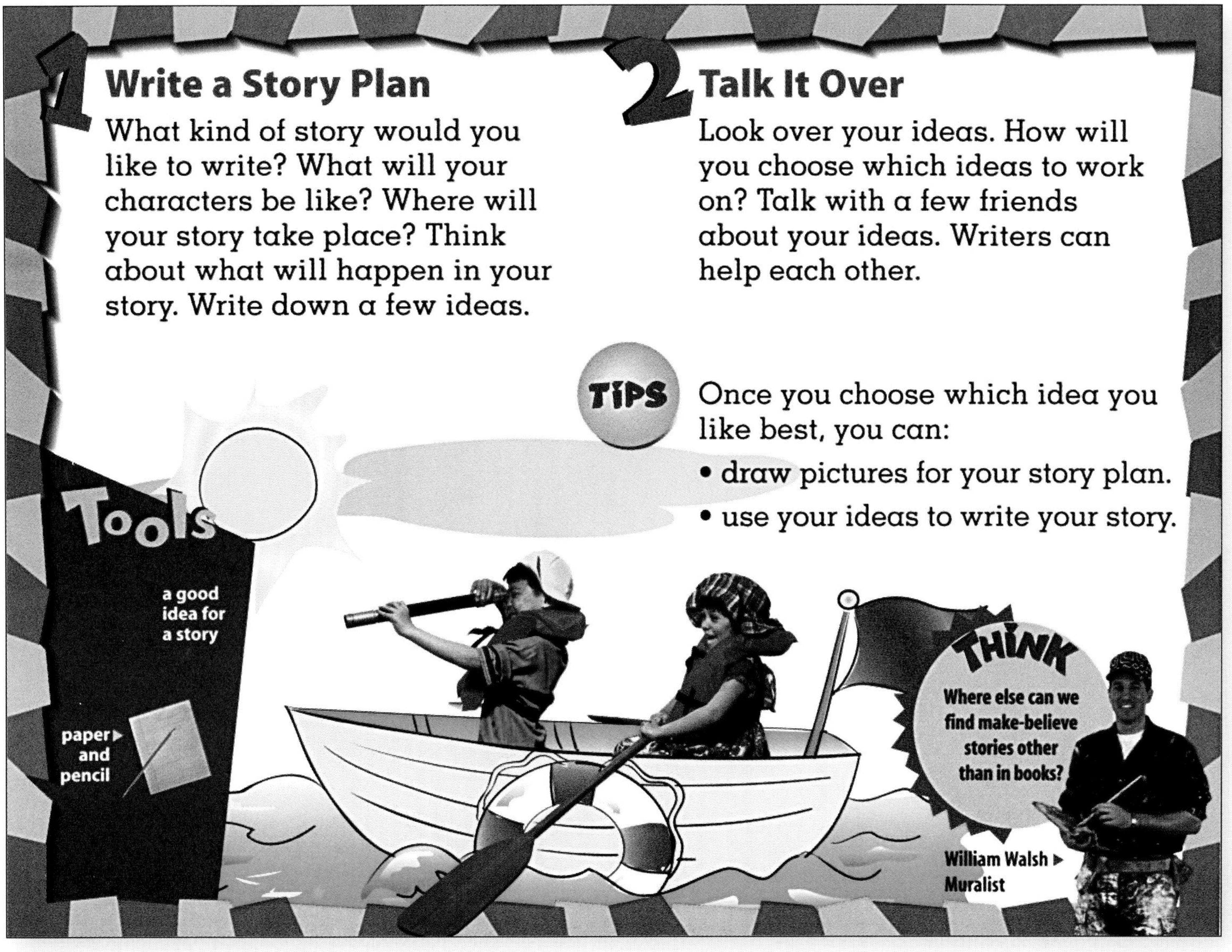

1 Write a Story Plan

What kind of story would you like to write? What will your characters be like? Where will your story take place? Think about what will happen in your story. Write down a few ideas.

2 Talk It Over

Look over your ideas. How will you choose which ideas to work on? Talk with a few friends about your ideas. Writers can help each other.

TIPS Once you choose which idea you like best, you can:

- draw pictures for your story plan.
- use your ideas to write your story.

Tools
a good idea for a story
paper and pencil
THINK
Where else can we find make-believe stories other than in books?
William Walsh
Muralist

2 Talk It Over

Children can work in cooperative groups to talk about the parts they want to use in their story plans. When children are ready, have them work independently to write, draw, or dictate their stories.

SELF-SELECTION

When the children have completed this Workshop, they may want to keep a copy of their story plans in their Portfolios. In addition, reviewing the story plan will help them do the Project, in which they'll produce a story mural.

Connect to Home and Community

Instead of imagining new characters, settings, and plots, children may find it helpful to use real people they know—such as friends, neighbors, and family members—as models for story characters. They may also refer to places they know, such as a park or playground, and tell about something that really happened.

ASSESSMENT

INFORMAL ASSESSMENT

OBSERVATION

Review children's work. Ask yourself:

✔ Did children's plans include characters, setting, and plot?

✔ Did children use their plans to write their stories?

✔ How did children present their stories? Did they draw, write, or dictate them?

IF NOT, TRY THIS:

Have children look at a favorite story in the Anthology and make a story plan for that selection.

CHILDREN'S SELF-ASSESSMENT

> **Does my story plan have characters, setting, and plot?**

CHILDREN'S WORKSHOP RUBRIC

Proficient	**Children's story plans include characters, setting, and events; children write a story or draw pictures based on their story plans.**
Apprentice	**Children's story plans include characters and some details of setting and plot. Their stories or drawings may not follow their story plans exactly.**
Novice	**Children's story plans may include characters but details of setting and plot may be unclear; their stories or drawings may have little to do with their story plans.**

In the Attic

IN THE ATTIC
HIAWYN ORAM
SATOSHI KITAMURA
AWARD WINNER
BY MYSELF

Main Selection
Genre: Fantasy
New York Times Notable Book Award

Paired Selection
Genre: Poem

WEEK 3 TESTED SKILLS

- **Vocabulary**
- **Daily Phonics:** ***l*-Blends** ***r*-Blends**
- **Key Comprehension Skill: Plot**
- **Study Skills: Graphic Aids: Pictures**
- **Spelling: Words With *l*-Blends**
- **Grammar, Usage, Mechanics: Irregular Verbs**

Technology Connection

Build Background Have children use **WiggleWorks Plus** Place-Maker to create a four-sided card. Children can draw an object or choose a piece of clip art for each side of the card. Challenge children to use the text tool and describe functions each object might have other than its original use.

Selection Summary

A young boy, bored with his toys, searches for something else to do. He uses the ladder from his toy fire engine truck to go up into the attic. There he discovers—with help from his imagination—many exciting things to do and see. When he returns from the attic, he tells his mother where he's been playing. That's when she reminds him that they don't have an attic.

PAIRED SELECTION In this poem, the narrator talks about the power of imagination and the importance of being yourself.

Illustrator

Illustrator **SATOSHI KITAMURA** is interested in the different angles of looking at things. He finds that picture books have great potential because visual and verbal elements come together. Mr. Kitamura has also collaborated with author Hiawyn Oram on the book *Ned and the Joybaloo.*

Weekly Organizer

Visit Our Web Site
www.scholastic.com

In the Attic

	DAY 1	**DAY 2**
READ and Introduce Skills • VOCABULARY • PHONICS • COMPREHENSION • LISTENING • SPEAKING • VIEWING 	**BUILD BACKGROUND,** p. T117 ▲ **VOCABULARY,** p. T118 ▲ ■ Practice Book, p. 28 **DAILY PHONICS:** ▲ ✱ Words With *l*-Blends, pp. T120–T121 Practice Book, pp. 29, 30 **PREVIEW AND PREDICT,** p. T122 **READ:** ▲ ✱ ■ *In the Attic*, pp. T122–T133 **COMPREHENSION:** Plot, p. T125	**READ:** ▲ ■ ✱ *In the Attic*, pp. T134–T146 "By Myself," p. T147 **DAILY PHONICS:** Inflectional Ending *-ing*, p. T137 Practice Book, p. 11 *r*-Blends, p. T141 **COMPREHENSION:** Categorize Information, p. T135 **GENRE:** Fantasy, p. T145
WRITE and Respond • GRAMMAR • USAGE • MECHANICS • SPELLING • WRITING	**SHARED WRITING,** p. T117 **JOURNAL: High-Frequency Words, p. T119** **QUICKWRITE: Predict, p. T133** **SPELLING:** Pretest: Words With *l*-Blends, p. R20 Spelling Resource Book, p. 94 **GRAMMAR, USAGE, MECHANICS:** Teach/Model: Irregular Verbs, p. R22 **ORAL LANGUAGE,** p. T133	**SHARED WRITING:** Prewrite, p. T147 **SPELLING:** Vocabulary Practice, p. R20 Spelling Resource Book, pp. 95–97 **GRAMMAR, USAGE, MECHANICS:** Practice, p. R22 **ORAL LANGUAGE,** p. T147
EXTEND SKILLS and Apply to Literature • SKILLS • INTEGRATED LANGUAGE ARTS • INTEGRATED CURRICULUM • GUIDED READING • INDEPENDENT READING	**READ ALOUD,** p. T133 **GUIDED READING,** pp. R18–R19 **INTEGRATED CURRICULUM:** Math, p. R24 **TRADE BOOKS** • *Pierre* • *Jenny's Journey* • *Going Home* 	**READ ALOUD,** p. T147 **GUIDED READING,** pp. R18–R19 **INTEGRATED CURRICULUM:** Social Studies, p. R25 Science, p. R24 The Arts, p. R25
TECHNOLOGY and **REAL-WORLD SKILLS**	**VIDEO** Viewing Skills, p. T127 **WIGGLEWORKS PLUS CD-ROM** Magnet Board, pp. T118, T120	**WIGGLEWORKS PLUS CD-ROM** Speaking Skills, p. T143 **WORKSHOP 2,** pp. T227–T230

MODIFY INSTRUCTION

● INTERVENTION ▲ ESL/ELD ■ EXTRA HELP
✳ GIFTED & TALENTED ✓ = TESTED SKILL

<table>
<tr><th>DAY 3</th><th>DAY 4</th><th>DAY 5</th></tr>
<tr>
<td>**COMPREHENSION:** ▲ ■
Plot, pp. T150–T151
Practice Book, pp. 32–33
✓ **DAILY PHONICS:** ▲ ■
Words With *r*-Blends, pp. T152–T153
Practice Book, pp. 34–35
BUILDING FLUENCY, p. T154
FOCUS ON HIGH-FREQUENCY WORDS, p. T155
FOCUS ON PHONICS, p. T155</td>
<td>**VOCABULARY REVIEW,** p. T158
✓ **DAILY PHONICS:**
Words With *r*-Blends, p. T152</td>
<td>**READING ASSESSMENT,** p. T162
Selection Test
Conference
Decoding Test</td>
</tr>
<tr>
<td>**RESPOND:** ▲
Think About Reading, p. T148
Practice Book, p. 31
WRITE A POSTCARD, p. T149
✓ **SPELLING:**
Write/Proofread, p. R21
Spelling Resource Book, p. 98
✓ **GRAMMAR, USAGE, MECHANICS:**
Practice, p. R23
ORAL LANGUAGE, p. T149</td>
<td>**SHARED WRITING:** ▲ ■
Fantasy Story, p. T156
Practice Book, p. 36
✓ **SPELLING:**
Study/Review, p. R21
Spelling Resource Book, p. 161
✓ **GRAMMAR, USAGE, MECHANICS:**
Apply, p. R23
ORAL LANGUAGE, p. T157</td>
<td>**WRITING ASSESSMENT,** p. T164
Child Model
Children's Writing Rubric
✓ **SPELLING:**
Posttest, p. R21
Spelling Resource Book, p. 163
✓ **GRAMMAR, USAGE, MECHANICS:**
Assess, p. R23
ORAL LANGUAGE, p. T164</td>
</tr>
<tr>
<td>**READ ALOUD,** p. T161
GUIDED READING, pp. R18–R19
OPTIONAL MATERIALS, p. T154
Phonics Reader #44:
Play the Animal Game</td>
<td>**READ ALOUD,** p. T161
GUIDED READING, pp. R18–R19
EXTEND VOCABULARY:
Review High-Frequency Words, p. T158
Review Story Words, p. T158
✓ **STUDY SKILLS:**
Use Pictures to Acquire Information, p. T160
Practice Book, p. 38</td>
<td>**READ ALOUD,** p. T166
GUIDED READING, pp. R18–R19
INTEGRATED LANGUAGE ARTS:
Imagine Your Own Story, p. T165
Make a Rhyming Chain, p. T165
Retell the Story, p. T166
Write Dialogue, p. T166</td>
</tr>
<tr><td></td><td></td><td></td></tr>
<tr>
<td>**WIGGLEWORKS PLUS CD-ROM**
Presentation Skills, p. T149
WIGGLEWORKS PLUS CD-ROM
Magnet Board, p. T152
WORKSHOP 2, pp. T227–T230</td>
<td>**WIGGLEWORKS PLUS CD-ROM**
Matching Technology to Task, p. T157
I SPY CD-ROM
Comprehension Skills, p. T161
WORKSHOP 2, pp. T227–T230</td>
<td>**WORD PROCESSING**
Language Development, p. T166
WORKSHOP 2, pp. T227–T230</td>
</tr>
</table>

Weekly Assessment

ASSESSMENT PLANNING

USE THIS CHART TO PLAN YOUR ASSESSMENT OF THE WEEKLY READING OBJECTIVES.

- **Informal Assessment is ongoing and should be used before, during, and after reading.**
- **Formal assessment occurs at the end of the week on the selection test.**
- **Note that intervention activies occur throughout the lesson to support students who need extra help with skills.**

ASSESSMENT
Assessment Handbook

YOU MAY CHOOSE AMONG THE FOLLOWING PAGES IN THE ASSESSMENT HANDBOOK.

- **Informal Assessment**
- **Anecdotal Record**
- **Portfolio Checklist and Evaluation Forms**
- **Self-Assessment**
- **Second-Language Learners**
- **Using Technology to Assess**
- **Test Preparations**

SKILLS AND STRATEGIES	Informal Assessment
COMPREHENSION Plot	OBSERVATION p. T125 • Did children identify the main character and his problem? QUICKCHECK p. T150 • Did children understand that important events, problems, and solutions provide the pattern for the plot? CHECK PRACTICE BOOK p. 32 CONFERENCE p. T162
PHONICS *l*-Blends *r*-Blends	OBSERVATION pp. T131, T141 • Did children recognize and blend words with *l*-blends? • Did children recognize and blend words with *r*-blends? CHECK PRACTICE BOOK pp. 29, 34
VOCABULARY Story Words **bored** **attic** **toys** **talk** **ladder** **game** High-Frequency **look** **about**	OBSERVATION p. T162 • Did children identify story words? • Did children indentify high–frequency words? CHECK PRACTICE BOOK p. 28

Formal Assessment	INTERVENTION and Instructional Alternatives	Planning Notes
SELECTION TEST • Questions 1–3 check children's mastery of the key strategy, plot. **UNIT TEST**	**If children need help with plot, then go to:** • **Instructional Alternatives, p. T151** • **Review, p. R45** • **Reteach, p. R56**	
DECODING TEST • See p. T163 **SELECTION TEST** • Questions 4–7 check children's ability to recognize words with *l*-blends and *r*-blends. **UNIT TEST**	**If children need help identifying words with *l*-blends, then go to:** • **Intervention, p. T155** • **Review, p. R51** • **Reteach, p. R59** **If children need help identifying words with *r*-blends, then go to:** • **Intervention, p. T155** • **Review, p. R52** • **Reteach, p. R60**	
SELECTION TEST • Questions 8–10 check children's recall of high-frequency and story words. **UNIT TEST**	**If children need additional practice with the vocabulary words, then go to:** • **Intervention Activity, p. T155** • **Extend Vocabulary, p. T158** • **Integrated Language Arts Activity, p. T166**	

Technology

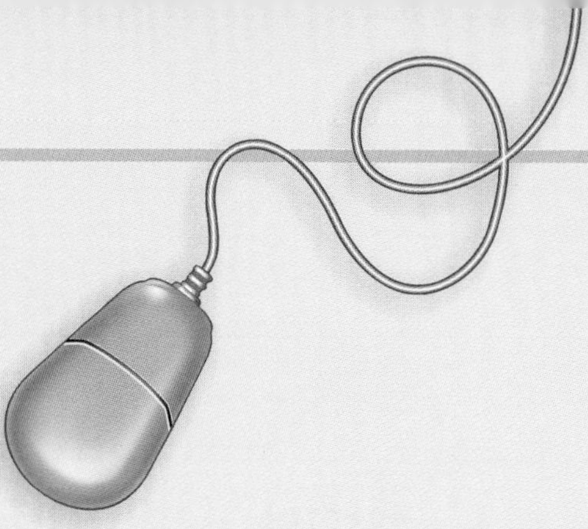

The technology in this lesson helps teachers and children develop the skills they need for the 21st Century. Look for integrated technology activities on every day of instruction.

DAY 1 Viewing Skills	• Children enjoy the Weston Woods video *Harold and the Purple Crayon,* and discuss how Harold used his vivid imagination.
DAY 2 Speaking Skills	• Children use the **WiggleWorks Plus** Unit Writer to record interviews in which they discover the answer to the question, "What do **you** do when you're bored?"
DAY 3 Presentation Skills	• Children use **WiggleWorks Plus** PlaceMaker to create a postcard from Harold describing the attic's contents.
DAY 4 Comprehension Skills	• Children use the Chalkboard activity on the **I Spy** CD-ROM to locate things that could be found in an attic.
DAY 5 Language Development	• Children use a table to create a rhyming word game.

When I'm bored I ...
...I read books about
spaceships. Then I pretend my
room is a spaceship. I make a
Record
Stop
Cancel
OK

WiggleWorks Plus CD-ROM

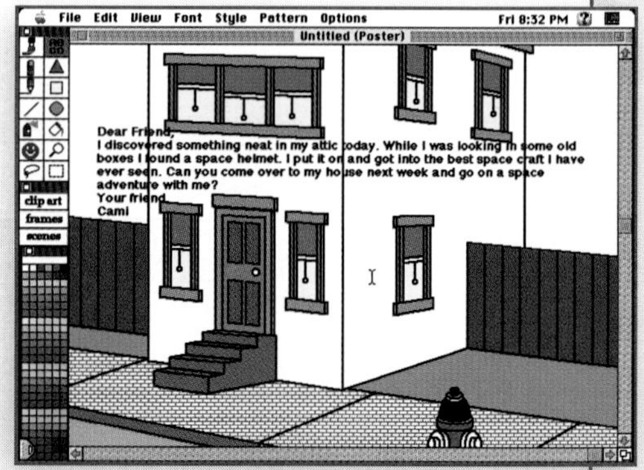
File Edit View Font Style Pattern Options
Fri 8:32 PM
Untitled (Poster)

WiggleWorks Plus CD-ROM

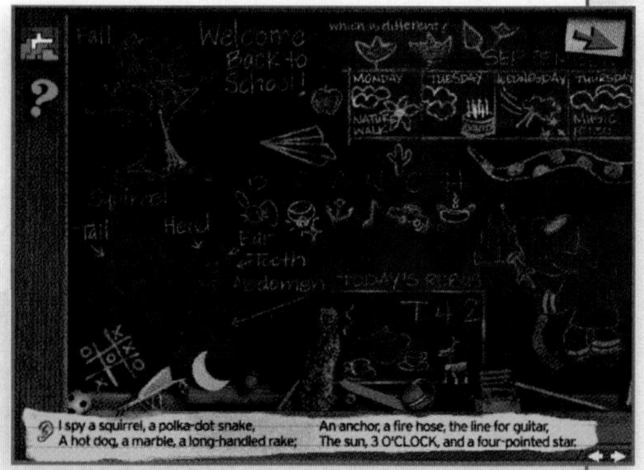
I spy a squirrel, a polka-dot snake,
A hot dog, a marble, a long-handled rake;
An anchor, a fire hose, the line for guitar,
The sun, 3 O'CLOCK, and a four-pointed star.

I Spy CD-ROM

Build Background

Artists and authors aren't the only people who use their imaginations. The story In the Attic *shows how one child uses his imagination to have fun while playing alone.*

IN THE ATTIC

Activate Prior Knowledge

DISCUSS FANTASY

Explain that fantasy stories deal with events that could not happen in real life. They can take place in make-believe places or in real places in which people or objects do make-believe things.

BRAINSTORM IMAGINARY PLAY

Have children brainstorm ways in which they use imagination for enjoyment. Ask them to tell what they imagine when they play alone.

> **How do you use your imagination to make being by yourself more fun?**

SHARED WRITING *Fantasy Story*

INTRODUCE Build background for writing a fantasy story by asking children to think about a real place that could be the setting for a fantasy story. Have them write a note to a classmate about what they imagine.

DAY 1 OBJECTIVES

CHILDREN WILL:

READ 35 MINUTES

- **Build Background**
- **Vocabulary**
- **Daily Phonics: Words With *l*-Blends**
- ***In the Attic*, pp. 46–57**
- **Key Comprehension Skill: Plot**

WRITE 25 MINUTES

- **Shared Writing: Introduce Writing a Fantasy Story**
- **Quickwrite: Predict**
- **Spelling: Words With *l*-Blends**
- **Grammar, Usage, Mechanics: Irregular Verbs**
- **Oral Language**

EXTEND SKILLS 30 MINUTES

- **Integrated Curriculum**
- **Read Aloud**
- **Guided Reading**

RESOURCES

- **Practice Book, pp. 28–30**
- **Spelling Resource Book, p. 94**

MODIFY Instruction

ESL/ELD

▲ Discuss the difference between *real* and *make-believe.* List some real events on the chalkboard, asking children to give you more examples. Have children draw or tell about a make-believe place they would like to visit. Ask: *Who will you take with you when you go there? What will you do there?* **(MAKE CONNECTIONS)**

VOCABULARY

High-Frequency Words

A TEACH/MODEL

INTRODUCE HIGH-FREQUENCY WORDS

Write the high-frequency words ***look*** and ***about*** in sentences on the chalkboard. Read the sentences aloud, underline the high-frequency words, and ask children if they recognize them. You may wish to use these sentences:

I went to look for Mom.
I want to tell her about my game.

Ask volunteers to dictate sentences using the high-frequency words. Add these to the chalkboard.

B PRACTICE/APPLY

FOCUS ON SPELLING

Write each high-frequency word on a note card. Read each word aloud. Then do the following:

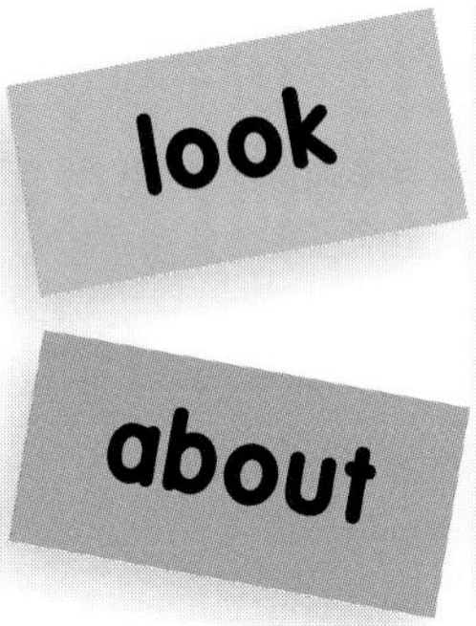
look
about

ROUTINE

1. **Display one card at a time, and ask children to state each word aloud.**
2. **Have children spell each word aloud.**
3. **Ask children to write each word in the air as they state aloud each letter. Then have them write each word on a sheet of paper or in their Journals.**

MAINTAIN VOCABULARY

Add the note cards to the **Word Wall.** Then review the following high-frequency words on the wall: ***soon, went, some, many.***

MODIFY Instruction

ESL/ELD

▲ Review with children the vocabulary of the parts of a *real* house. Review vocabulary words and include prepositions such as *up/down, top/bottom.* Draw and label the rooms of a house on the chalkboard, including *basement* and *attic.* Help children list activities that might take place in each room. **(BRAINSTORM)**

EXTRA HELP

■ Give children word cards on which you have written the words *look* and *about,* as well as the words you reviewed on the **Word Wall.** Mix up the cards and have partners use them as flash cards. Children can take turns showing the words as their partners read them aloud. **(USE VISUALS)**

VOCABULARY

HIGH-FREQUENCY

look about

STORY WORDS

bored attic
toys talk
ladder game

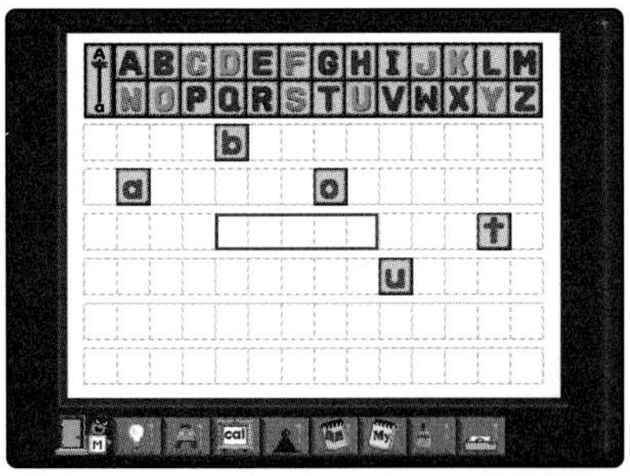

TECHNOLOGY

For children needing additional practice with high-frequency words prior to reading the story, have them build, explode, and rebuild each high-frequency word on the **WiggleWorks Plus** Magnet Board.

Story Words

Ⓐ TEACH/MODEL

INTRODUCE STORY WORDS

The story also contains the following story words—***bored, attic, toys, game, talk, ladder.***

- Write these words on the chalkboard, read them aloud, and discuss their meanings if necessary.
- Point out previously taught sound-spelling correspondences such as final ***e (a-e).***
- Have children join you in acting out the words. For example, yawn for ***bored,*** point to the ceiling for ***attic,*** pretend to climb a ***ladder,*** then play with a ***toy*** and a board ***game.***

Ⓑ PRACTICE/APPLY

BUILD STORY BACKGROUND

Discuss with children the concept of being bored.

- Have children tell how they would use their imagination if they were bored.
- Ask them to close their eyes and imagine being bored and climbing a ladder to an empty attic.
- Have children draw a picture of what they would imagine in the attic. Point out that children would probably imagine things that would keep them from being bored.

WRITE TO READ

- When completed, have children write a sentence about their picture using one or more of the story words.

Name

VOCABULARY

What's in the Attic?

▶ Use the words from the box to fill in the blanks.

look	bored
about	attic
toys	ladder
talk	game

1. I was ___bored___ with my toys.
2. I went to the attic to ___look___ for more.
3. The ___attic___ is at the top of the house.
4. I went up a ___ladder___ to get to the attic.
5. I saw new ___toys___!
6. I saw a ___game___ for Mom and me to play.
7. I will ___talk___ to her about it.

28 Unit 4 • Imagine That! • In the Attic

PRACTICE BOOK p. 28

I am not bored in this attic.

ATTIC PICTURES

Have children write ***attic*** vertically on a large sheet of paper. Invite them to draw a picture beside each letter in the word. Each picture name should begin with the letter it is beside. The pictures should also show things that might be in an attic, such as art, toy, tent, insect, and cage. If time permits, have children repeat the activity with ***ladder.***

a
t
t
i
c

JOURNAL

Ask children to write a sentence using each **high-frequency word** in their Journals. You might suggest the following sentence starters:

We can _____ .

The book is _____ .

IN THE ATTIC

SELECTION WORDS With *l*-Blends

climbed

flying

place

SKILLS TRACE

Words With *l*-Blends TESTED

Introduce . . . . . . pp. T120–121
Practice . . . . . . pp. T131, T154
Review . . . . p. R51
Reteach. . . . . p. R60

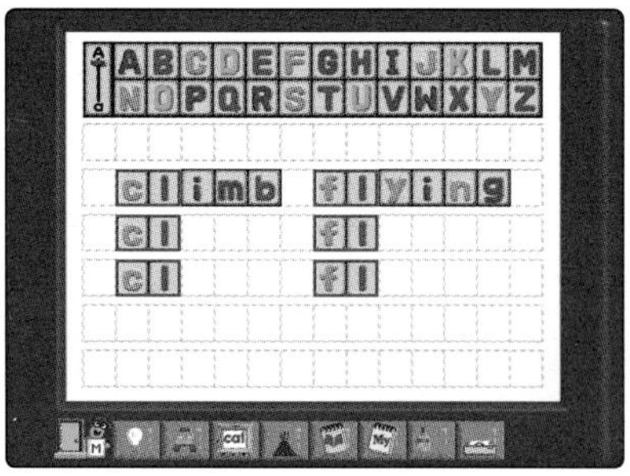
climb
flying
cl
fl
cl
fl

TECHNOLOGY

- Have children build words with *l*-blends on the **WiggleWorks Plus** Magnet Board.
- Begin with the words *climb, flying,* and *place* or write rows of *l*-blends (*cl, fl, pl*).
- Have children add letters to the *l*-blends to make new words.

DAILY PHONICS

Words With *l*-Blends

A PHONOLOGICAL AWARENESS

SONG Sing "If You're Happy and You Know It" from the *Big Book of Rhymes and Rhythms 1B*, pages 10–11. Stress the word ***clap.***

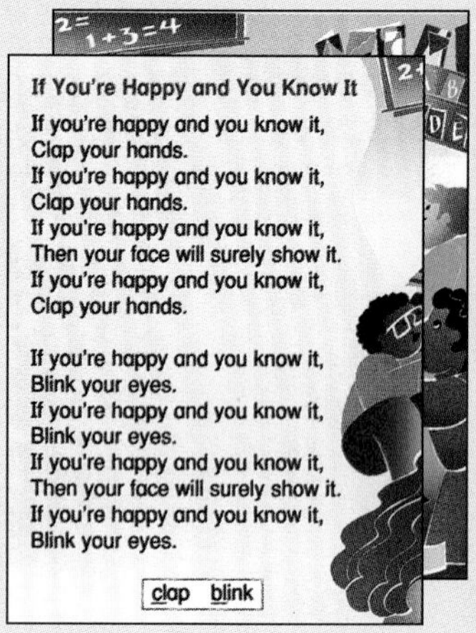
If You're Happy and You Know It
If you're happy and you know it,
Clap your hands.
If you're happy and you know it,
Clap your hands.
If you're happy and you know it,
Then your face will surely show it.
If you're happy and you know it,
Clap your hands.
If you're happy and you know it,
Blink your eyes.
If you're happy and you know it,
Blink your eyes.
If you're happy and you know it,
Then your face will surely show it.
If you're happy and you know it,
Blink your eyes.
clap blink

***Big Book of Rhymes and Rhythms 1B*, pp. 10–11**

- When children are familiar with the song, ask them to sing along with you.
- They may want to clap when they hear "clap your hands."
- Then say the following words and have children clap when they hear **/kl/** as in ***clap: clown, car, clock, cat, clever, clue, climb.***

ORAL BLENDING Say the following word parts, and have children blend them. Model as needed.

• **cl . . .ap**	• **fl . . .at**	• **pl . . .op**
• **cl . . .ock**	• **fl . . .ag**	• **pl . . .ant**

B CONNECT SOUND-SPELLING

INTRODUCE *l*-blends Write the words ***clap, flag,*** and ***plop*** on the chalkboard. Underline the *l*-blend in each word and model how to blend the sounds. Then model how to blend the word ***clap.***

THINK ALOUD *I can put the letters* ***cl, a,*** *and* ***p*** *together to make the word* ***clap.*** *Let's say the sounds slowly as I move my finger under the letters:* ***clap.*** *Listen to the sounds that* ***cl*** *stand for in the word* ***clap.*** *The sound of* ***cl*** *is* **/kl/.**

MODIFY Instruction

ESL/ELD

▲ Consonant *l*-blends may be difficult to pronounce. Model the different tongue/teeth positions. Have children chant each word you say in chorus. As the story unfolds, ask them to be the first to raise their hands and volunteer to say *l*-blend words. **(MODEL)**

EXTRA HELP

■ Challenge children to invent two-word combinations in which both words use the *cl, fl,* or *pl* blend, such as *clapping clown,* or *flapping flag.* Then have children pantomime their word combinations for their classmates. **(PANTOMIME)**

- Ask children to suggest other words that begin with ***cl, fl,*** and ***pl.*** List them on a chart.
- Have volunteers circle the ***l***-blend in each word.

clap	**flag**	**play**
clown	**flap**	**place**
cloud	**floor**	**plant**

PHONICS MAINTENANCE Review the following sound-spellings: ***l***-blends; ***/ē/ ea, ee;*** final ***e (a-e, i-e, o-e).*** Say one of these sounds. Have a volunteer write on the chalkboard the spelling or spellings that stand for the sound. Continue with all the sounds.

C PRACTICE/APPLY

BLEND WORDS To practice using the sound-spellings and review previous sound-spellings, list the following words and sentences on the chalkboard. Have children read each chorally. Model blending.

clap	flame	place
close	flea	heat
fine	feet	tree

I like to climb.

A flying game is fun, too!

DICTATION Dictate the following words: ***clap, place, flame, pine, cone, team, tree.***

BUILD WORDS Distribute the following letter cards, or have children use their own sets: ***p, c, f, l, a, o, i, e, s, t, b, n, m, y.*** Allow children time to build ***l***-blend words using the letter cards. Children can write their words on a separate sheet of paper. **(INDEPENDENT WORK)**

c
l
a
p

TONGUE TWISTERS

Direct groups to make up tongue twisters with *cl, fl,* or *pl.* Share the following example: *Clever clowns climb and clap.* Have children dictate their tongue twisters and challenge each other to say them as quickly as possible.

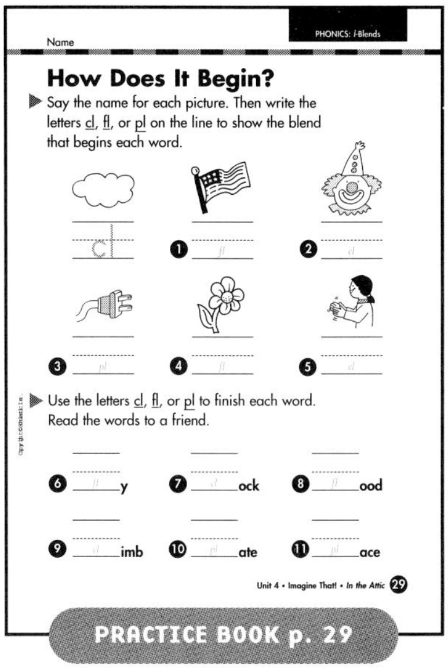

Name PHONICS: l-Blends

How Does It Begin?

▶ Say the name for each picture. Then write the letters cl, fl, or pl on the line to show the blend that begins each word.

▶ Use the letters cl, fl, or pl to finish each word. Read the words to a friend.

6 ___y 7 ___ock 8 ___ood

9 ___imb 10 ___ate 11 ___ace

Unit 4 • Imagine That! • In the Attic 29

PRACTICE BOOK p. 29

Name PHONICS: l-Blends

Make a Rhyme!

▶ Read each word. Find a word in the box that rhymes with each word. Write the rhyming word on the line.

clean flat plate cloud flag

wag flag

1 bean

2 date

3 loud

4 hat

▶ Write a sentence using rhyming words you wrote.

5

30 Unit 4 • Imagine That! • In the Attic

PRACTICE BOOK p. 30

DECODABLE TEXT

For practice reading decodable text, see ***Scholastic Decodable Reader #48.***

For additional phonics instruction and review, see ***Scholastic Phonics A, pp. 191–192.***

COMPREHENSION

Preview and Predict

Tell children that *In the Attic* is a fantasy story about a boy who has a very good imagination. Encourage them to look through the selection to preview it.

> **Where does the story take place? How do you know?**

> **Do you think the boy has a million toys? Why or why not?**

Help children make predictions before they read by asking questions:

> **What do you think the boy is going to do in the attic?**

> **What do you think he will find there?**

JOURNAL

Make Predictions

Before reading, ask children to write their predictions in their Journals. Encourage them to record what the boy does in the attic and what he finds there.

Set a Purpose

Help children set their own purposes for reading the story. They might want to find out how the boy uses his imagination in the story. Then have them read the first page of the story.

1 POINT OF VIEW

> **Who is telling the story? How do you know?** *(The boy is telling the story. He uses the word I.)*

46

FANTASY

IN THE ATTIC
HIAWYN ORAM
SATOSHI KITAMURA
AWARD WINNER

46

CLASSROOM Management

WHOLE CLASS

On-Level Use the questions, think alouds, and the skills and strategies lessons to guide children through a reading of the story.

Below-Level Have children look at the pictures prior to the whole class reading to familiarize themselves with the story sequence.

PARTNERS

Above-Level You might have children read the story independently or with a partner while you read the story with the rest of the class. When completed, have these children rejoin the group to participate in the story discussion.

47

1 I had a million toys, but I was bored.

47

SKILLS AND STRATEGIES

Revisit the selection for skills instruction.

✓ = Tested Skill

✓ COMPREHENSION

Plot T125

✓ DAILY PHONICS

***l*-Blends** T131

***r*-Blends** T141

GENRE

Fantasy T145

SMALL GROUP TO WHOLE CLASS

ESL/ELD Have children who need extra help or who are acquiring English listen to the story on the audiocassette prior to the whole class reading. This will help them to become familiar with the story sequence and vocabulary. Make sure that the children pay attention to the pre- and post-learning activities. **(AUDIO CLUES)**

COMPREHENSION

❷ PLOT

> **What's the problem in this story? What does the boy do to begin to solve the problem?** *(The boy is bored. He climbs into the attic.)*

❸ MAKE INFERENCES

> **Look at how the boy is getting into the attic. He's using the ladder on his fire truck! Could he really do that? What do you think this means?** *(Possible answer: He could not really use the tiny fire truck ladder. He is imagining that he is climbing up into the attic.)*

INTERVENTION TIP

Understand an Exaggeration

On page 47, the boy says he has a million toys. Write the numeral 1,000,000 on the board and explain that it is a million. Point out that a million is a very large number, and that a thousand groups of one thousand things make a million. Ask children if they think the boy really has a million toys.

48

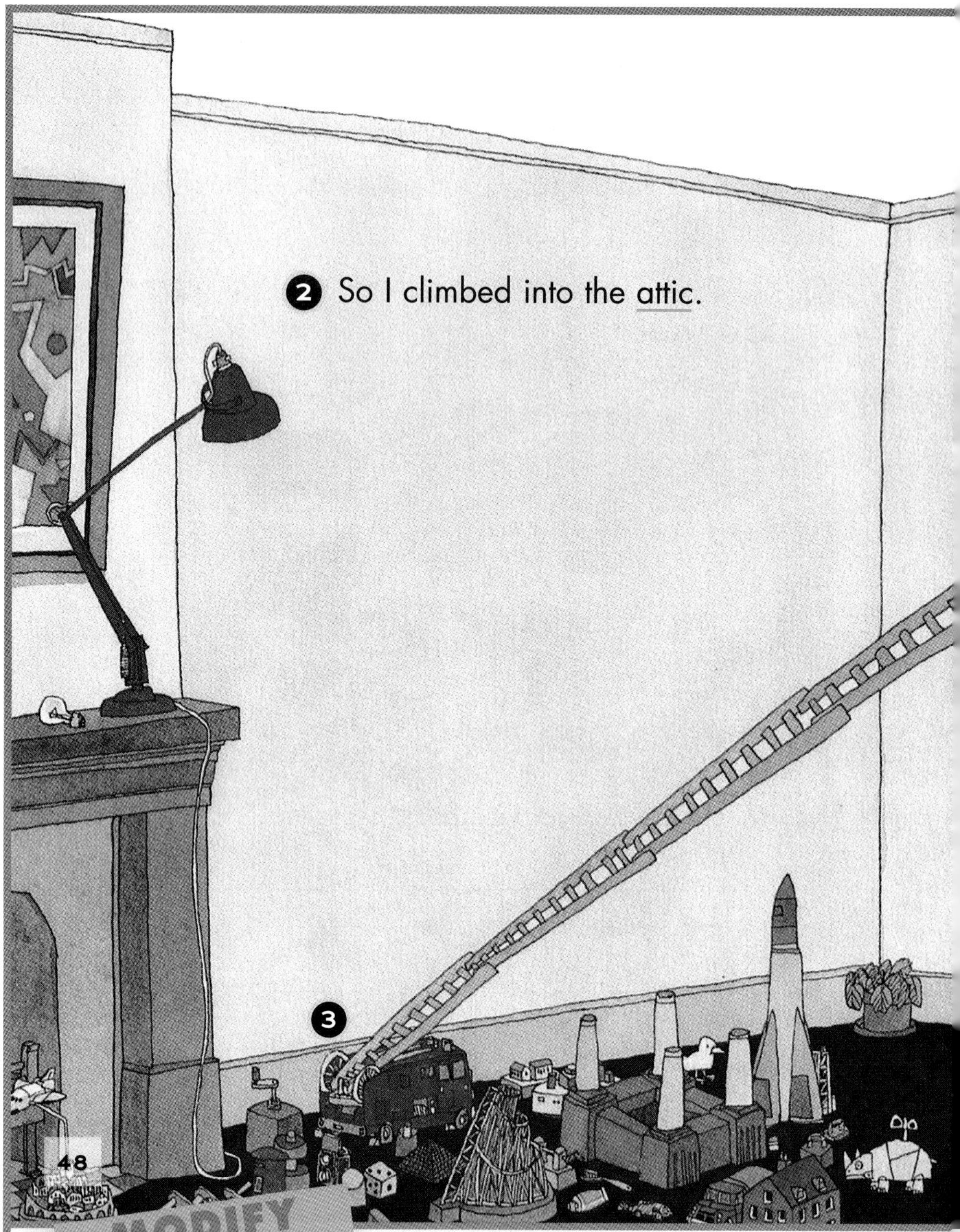
❷ So I climbed into the attic.
❸
48

MODIFY Instruction

ESL/ELD

▲ Explain that the pronoun *I* is always capitalized. Follow by pointing out that in this case, the *I* refers to the boy telling the story. Ask questions that require *I* answers: *What do you like to do on weekends? I like to play soccer.* **(ASSIST IN PROCESS)**

EXTRA HELP

■ Have children act out the beginning of the story to help them understand what the little boy is doing. Encourage children to pretend to pull out a ladder on a fire truck, climb up the ladder into an attic, and peek in. Then ask children to describe what they might see. **(ACT-IT-OUT)**

49

3
49

FAMILY TALK

Have children discuss attics with their family. Encourage them to talk about where attics are found in homes.

If the family has an attic in their home, ask family members to talk about how they get into their attic and what is in the attic. **(15-MINUTE LITERACY BYTE)**

SKILLS AND STRATEGIES

COMPREHENSION
Plot

TEACH/MODEL
Explain that all stories have a plot. Important events, problems, and solutions provide the pattern for the plot.

> **Think about the boy in the story. He has a problem.**
> **Ask yourself how the boy tries to solve his problem.**
> **Use story clues and picture clues to help you list what the boy goes through.**

THINK ALOUD *When I read this story, I learn that the boy is bored. The plot is the plan or the series of events the boy goes through to solve this problem.*

PRACTICE/APPLY
Have children use the graphic organizer below to determine elements of plot in *In the Attic.*

Character Problem	+	Solution	=	Plot

> **Who is the main character?**
> **What is his problem?**
> **How does the boy solve his problem?**

INFORMAL ASSESSMENT
OBSERVATION

Did children:

✔ identify the main character and his problem?

✔ use story clues and their imagination to suggest how the boy began to solve his problem?

See pages T150–T151 for a full skills lesson on Plot.

COMPREHENSION

4 MAKE INFERENCES

> **Look at this picture of the attic. What makes it unusual? Why doesn't it look like a real attic?** *(Possible answer: The floor is floating. The walls and ceiling are stone. Real attics don't have floating floors and usually don't have stone walls and ceilings.)*

5 USE PICTURE CLUES

> **Let's look closely at the picture again. Is the attic really empty? Point to anything that you see in the attic.** *(The attic isn't empty. There is a group of mice near the ladder.)*

6 MAKE PREDICTIONS

> **What do you think the boy will find in the attic?** *(Answers should reflect the understanding that the attic is imaginary.)*

50

The attic was empty.

50

MODIFY Instruction

ESL/ELD

▲ Help children relate the question "Or was it?" to "The attic was empty." Supply the meaning that is "understood." For example, *Or was the attic empty?* Help children to understand the relation by using picture clues. Point to the mice and say: *The attic was empty. Or was it?* Repeat using other examples. **(FOLLOW PATTERNS)**

GIFTED & TALENTED

✳ Challenge partners to work together to write several sentences to describe the pictures on these pages. **(WORK IN PAIRS)**

51

Or was it? 6

51

SKILLS AND STRATEGIES

COMPREHENSION
Picture Clues

TEACH/MODEL
Explain to children that pictures can give important information that's not in the story.

> **Look carefully at the pictures.**

> **Think about what the pictures tell you that the words in the story do not.**

THINK ALOUD *The boy is unhappy because he thinks the attic is empty. When I look at the picture on this page, I see that the attic is not empty; there are little mice near the ladder.*

PRACTICE/APPLY
Ask children to use the graphic organizer below to draw conclusions about the story.

Pictures	+	Words	=	My Conclusion

> **What do the pictures show?**

> **What does the story say?**

> **What story clues did you learn?**

TECHNOLOGY

Viewing Skills Have children view the *Weston Woods* video *Harold and the Purple Crayon,* the story of an imaginative boy who, with his magic crayon, draws himself in and out of adventures. Brainstorm a list of qualities shown by creative, imaginative children like Harold.

CONNECTING TO TELEVISION

Ask children to connect the imaginary events of the boy in this story to a favorite television character who uses his or her imagination. If children like pets, they may want to connect the boy's imagination to the imagination of the precocious terrier in the series "Wishbone."

COMPREHENSION

7 MAKE INFERENCES

> **There are lots of things going on in this picture! What do you think is really happening?** *(Possible answer: The boy is looking at the mice and imagining all the things that they might do.)*

8 PLOT

> **Do you remember the problem the boy had at the beginning of the story? How is he solving it now? How do you think the way he feels has changed?** *(The boy is now adding imaginary things to the attic to make it more fun. He does not feel bored anymore.)*

INTERVENTION TIP

Recognize a Change in Setting

Some children may have trouble following the abrupt changes of setting that occur in this story. Help them use picture and text clues to understand that when the boy imagines things in the attic, the setting changes.

52

ABC
DEFGH
7
8

52

MODIFY Instruction

ESL/ELD

▲ Assess children's understanding of what the boy is imagining by using Total Physical Response commands, such as: *Point to a real mouse. Show me an imaginary mouse. Show me what this mouse is doing. Show me what these mice are doing.* **(TOTAL PHYSICAL RESPONSE)**

EXTRA HELP

■ Point out the ellipses at the end of the sentence on page 53. Ask children if they know why the sentence ends with these three dots. Help them understand that the dots tell the reader that the sentence is not yet finished and will continue on the next page. **(USE TEXT FEATURES)**

53

I found a family of mice . . .

53

VISUAL LITERACY

Discuss with children how the artist shows what the mice really do and what the boy imagines they do. Discuss what the mice are doing in the boy's imagination and have children point to the mice that could be real.

MATH

Have children use this and other illustrations in the story to complete the **Solve Picture Problems** activity on **page R24.** Children will learn to use mathematical reasoning as they use the pictures to solve simple math problems.

SKILLS AND STRATEGIES

COMPREHENSION

Make Inferences

TEACH/MODEL

Explain to children that they can use pictures and words to help them understand what they read in a story.

> **Combine what you know with clues from the pictures and clues from the story to help you make inferences about the story.**

THINK ALOUD *When I read this story, I know that the boy uses a tiny ladder to climb to the attic. I know he can't really climb to the attic on this tiny ladder, so I can guess that the boy is imagining this. Maybe he's bored.*

PRACTICE/APPLY

Have children use the following graphic organizer to make inferences about the story.

Story & Picture Clues	+	What You Know	=	Inference

> **How many mice did the boy find in the attic?**

> **How many mice do you see in the picture?**

> **Based on what you know, what can you infer about the boy in the story?**

Assign **Practice Book page 39** for skill maintenance.

IF children need more support with Make Inferences,

THEN see page R43.

COMPREHENSION

9 PLOT

> **How has the attic changed? How is it different from the last place? How does the new setting help the boy solve his problem?** *(Now the attic looks like a garden. It was filled with mice, now it is a big garden. The boy is using his imagination to create a new place.)*

SELF-MONITORING STRATEGY

Recalling Plot

THINK ALOUD *I know that the plot is made up of the events in a story. Things are beginning to change quickly. One way I can remember what has happened in the story is to write a sentence or draw a picture of the events in the story.*

- **Why do you think things are changing so quickly in this story?**

54

54

MODIFY Instruction

ESL/ELD

▲ Help children identify elements of fantasy in the story. You may ask, *Is the boy still in the attic? How do you know? Can you find the attic floor? What plants and bugs do you see? Are they real or imaginary?* Help children with key vocabulary as you ask each question. **(GUIDED QUESTIONS)**

EXTRA HELP

■ Reinforce story plot by helping children review what has happened so far. Look at the first five spreads and have volunteers take turns retelling in their own words what happens on each. **(RETELL)**

55

. . . and a cool, quiet place to rest and think.

55

MENTOR CONNECTION

Tell children that the muralist William Walsh says imagination is the most important tool we have. Ask children if they think the boy in the story would agree with William Walsh. Why or why not?

DECODING STRATEGIES

Write the word *place* on the chalkboard. Ask a volunteer to circle the vowels. Remind children that in words with final *e* (*a-e*), the vowel *a* is a long vowel sound. Have them say the word *place* and tell what the vowel sound is. Then have them find examples of final *e* (*a-e*) words in the story.

DAILY PHONICS

l-Blends

CONNECT SOUND-SPELLING

TEACH/MODEL Review that some words begin with a consonant plus *l*. Write ***clap, flake,*** and ***plate*** on the chalkboard and underline the *l*-blends.

> **What two letters are at the beginning of each word?**

> **What sound does each letter stand for?**

THINK ALOUD *I know that when I see* ***pl*** *at the beginning of a word, I have to say the sounds of both letters. For example, when I see the word* ***plate,*** *I blend the sounds of* ***p*** *and* ***l*** *with the sounds for* ***-ate.*** *The word is* ***plate.***

PHONICS MAINTENANCE Review the following sound-spellings: final ***e;*** /ē/ ***ea, ee;*** *l*-blends.

PRACTICE/APPLY

BLEND WORDS Ask children to find the word ***place*** on page 55.

- Write ***place*** on the chalkboard. Have a volunteer underline the *l*-blend at the beginning of the word.
- Encourage children to look for other words in the story with *l*-blends. (*climbed,* p. 48; *flying,* p. 60)

INFORMAL ASSESSMENT
OBSERVATION

As children read, can they:

✔ recognize words with *l*-blends?

✔ blend words with *l*-blends?

COMPREHENSION

10 Make Inferences

> **Remember the mice? The mice were something that you might really find in an attic, but what the boy imagined about them was quite fantastic. How do you think this spider is like the mice?** *(Answers should reflect an understanding of the elements of fantasy in this story.)*

INTERVENTION TIP

Imaginary Events

Some children might need help understanding what's happening in this picture. It would appear that the boy has left the attic and is floating in the sky. Help children understand that we see just what the boy is imagining–that he is helping a spider make a web.

OPTION You may end the first day's reading here or have children continue reading the selection.

56

56

MODIFY Instruction

ESL/ELD

▲ Help children understand that the boy has begun to imagine things outside of the attic. Define the word *pyramids*. Then ask children where there are some real pyramids. Are there pyramids in the attic? Is there a spider in the attic? Do you think the boy saw a spider? Make a list of things that can be found in an attic. **(GUIDED READING)**

EXTRA HELP

■ Help children understand what is real and what is imaginary in the scene. Ask: *Is he inside or outside? Do you see a spider? Is it really making a web? What else do you see?* **(GUIDED QUESTIONS)**

57

10

I met a spider and we made a web.

57

CULTURAL CONNECTION

Share information about the pyramids on these pages. Explain that pyramids are structures with four sloping sides. The sides either meet at the top or are cut off to make a platform. People built pyramids as monuments in many places around the world, including Egypt, Greece, India, Thailand, and Mexico.

You may wish to have children make their own pyramids. Provide them with a triangular template and heavy paper or cardboard. Tell them to trace four triangles, cut them out and then tape the sides of the triangles together.

Quickwrite

PREDICT

Ask children to write how the boy has used his imagination so far in the story. Encourage them to refine the predictions they made before reading.

DAILY LANGUAGE PRACTICE

SPELLING

DAY 1:

Administer the Pretest for Words With *l*-Blends. **See page R20.**

GRAMMAR, USAGE, MECHANICS

DAY 1:

Teach and Model Irregular Verbs. **See page R22.**

ORAL LANGUAGE

When I cimbed into the attic, I find some mice.

(When I climbed into the attic, I found some mice.)

DAY 1 WRAP-UP

READ ALOUD *To develop children's oral vocabularies, spend five to ten minutes reading from a selection of your choice.*

GUIDED READING *To extend reading, meet with the **blue** and **green** reading groups and assign Independent Center activities. **See pages R18–R19.***

COMPREHENSION

DAY 2 OBJECTIVES

CHILDREN WILL:

READ 40 MINUTES

- ***In the Attic*, pp. 58–70**
- **"By Myself," p. 71**
- **Daily Phonics: Words With *r*-Blends, *-ing***

WRITE 30 MINUTES

- **Shared Writing: Prewrite a Fantasy Story**
- **Spelling: Words With *l*-Blends**
- **Grammar, Usage, Mechanics: Irregular Verbs**
- **Oral Language**

EXTEND SKILLS 20 MINUTES

- **Integrated Curriculum**
- **Read Aloud**
- **Guided Reading**

RESOURCES

- **Practice Book, p. 36**
- **Spelling Resource Book, pp. 95–97**

Reread

You may wish to have children independently reread the first part of the story before beginning Day 2 reading.

11 **SUMMARIZE**

> **How has the boy used his imagination so far in the story?** *(He climbed into the attic using the ladder on his fire truck. In his imagination he saw mice, a garden, a spider, pyramids, and windows to other worlds.)*

58

58

MODIFY Instruction

ESL/ELD

▲ Have children work in pairs and use the chart from the "Categorize Information" activity to summarize the story so far. Ask them to take an item from each category, and make up the scenes in the story. Have them repeat the activity until they have summarized what they've read. **(CATEGORIZE)**

EXTRA HELP

■ Help children interpret the pictures. Focus their attention by using pieces of paper to mask everything but one window. Encourage them to look through that window and describe what they see. Relate this experience to the idea of "windows to other worlds." **(STEP BY STEP)**

59

11 I opened windows to other worlds.

59

VISUAL LITERACY

Help children identify the picture of Earth. If possible, show them pictures of Earth in the encyclopedia. Then discuss where they think the boy imagines himself to be now. Help children to understand that the boy is imagining himself in space somewhere looking down at Earth.

ORAL LANGUAGE

Have children close their eyes and imagine that they are the boy in the story looking out the windows. Ask them what the boy might be thinking. Have them share their ideas with the class.

SKILLS AND STRATEGIES

COMPREHENSION

Categorize Information

TEACH/MODEL

Share with children that when they categorize, they sort things or information into groups that have something in common.

THINK ALOUD *As I read* In the Attic, *I categorized, or sorted, what I saw in the pictures. I put the real-life things that can be found in the attic under the category* real. *I categorized the garden, pyramids, and windows to other worlds under* imaginary. *Everything I read about in the story falls into the category of* "Things in the Attic."

PRACTICE/APPLY

Have children make a chart of the real and imaginary things in the attic. Ask children to draw and cut out things that the boy saw in the attic.

Assign **Practice Book page 69** for skill maintenance.

COMPREHENSION

12 CONTEXT CLUES

> **There are all different kinds of machines. What do you think a flying machine is? What is another name for a flying machine?** *(Possible answer: A flying machine could be called an airplane.)*

13 PICTURE DETAILS

> **This flying machine is made of something we've seen before. Do you know what it is?** *(The flying machine is the attic floor.)*

SELF-MONITORING STRATEGY

Relate to Literary Experiences

THINK ALOUD *As I read this story, I stop to think about how I use my own imagination when I play. I also make-believe. If I use my imagination, I can understand how the boy might have built the flying machine.*

- How is your own imagination like the boy's?
- How would you have built the flying machine?

60

12
13

I found an old flying machine

60

MODIFY Instruction

ESL/ELD

▲ Point out the word *flying* in front of the word *machine*. Ask: *Do you know the name of any other flying machines?* Play a game and provide context clues to help them decide what kind of machine you are thinking of. For example, you may ask: *I am a driving machine. What am I?* (a car) **(MAKE CONNECTIONS)**

GIFTED & TALENTED

Invite children to spend a few minutes studying the picture on pages 60–61. Then have them write about what they see. Challenge them to use words that end in ***-ing*** as in ***flying***. Have them underline each word with ***-ing***. Ask them to share their work with the class. **(DESCRIBE VISUALS)**

61

and I made it work.

61

WORD STUDY

Ask children to look at the last word on page 61. The boy made the flying machine fly. But the word begins with a *w*, not an *f*. Ask children what means the same thing as *fix*, but begins with a *w*.

SOCIAL STUDIES

Have children complete the **What's Real and What's Not?** activity on **page R25** by drawing an imaginary scene and identifying what is real and what is not. Children will develop an awareness of the real world as they note relevant details in their drawings.

DAILY PHONICS

Inflectional Ending -ing

TEACH/MODEL

Review with children that action words sometimes end with ***-ing.*** Write the words ***fixing, resting, thinking,*** and ***working*** on the chalkboard.

> **Find and circle the ending *-ing* in the words.**

> **List other words that end in *-ing.***

THINK ALOUD *If I cover the* ***-ing*** *in* resting, *I see a small word that I know—****rest.*** *When I add* ***-ing*** *to* ***rest,*** *I get a new word,* ***resting.***

PRACTICE/APPLY

Ask children to point to the word ***flying*** on page 60.

- Write ***flying*** on the chalkboard. Ask a volunteer to say the word and draw a line under the ending ***-ing.***
- Write the sentences *I* ***fly*** and *I am* ***flying*** on the chalkboard. Discuss what is the same and what is different about the underlined words.
- Encourage children to continue to look for words with ***-ing*** as they read other stories in this book.

Assign **Practice Book page 11** for skill maintenance.

IF children need more support with Inflectional Ending ***-ing,***

THEN use the review lesson on page R48.

COMPREHENSION

14 PLOT

> **Where was the boy when we last saw him? Where is the boy now? How do you think he got here?** *(The boy was flying over a city. Now he is in a field. He got here using his imagination.)*

15 CRITICAL THINKING: APPLY

> **Why do you think the ladder is in the picture? Why do you think the boy is carrying a window?** *(The boy flew his machine here and used the ladder to climb down. The window is one of the windows from the attic. It shows the world the boy is visiting now.)*

16 MAKE PREDICTIONS

> **The boy is looking for someone so he can share what he has found. Who do you predict he will find?** *(Answers should reflect an understanding of the elements of fantasy in this story.)*

62

14
15

I went out to look for someone

62

MODIFY Instruction

ESL/ELD

▲ Help children make predictions by posing alternative questions: *Will the boy find a person or an animal? Will it be a pet? Will the person be a boy or girl? Will the animal be wild? Do you hope he will find an elephant or a kitten? A tiger or a dog?* **(GUIDED QUESTIONS)**

EXTRA HELP

■ Encourage children to elaborate on what will happen next. Have them recall previous imaginary events in the story to help them predict what the boy will find next. **(MAKE CONNECTIONS)**

63

to share what I had found . . .

63

SCIENCE

Ask children to complete the **Explore Structures** activity on **page R24** in which partners will build models of ladders.

WORD STUDY

Ask children to find the word ***look*** on page 62. Have them think about what the word means in the sentence. Then ask children what word could take the place of ***look for*** in the sentence: ***I went out to _____ someone. . . .***

COMPREHENSION

17 MAKE PREDICTIONS

> **Look what the boy found! Did you predict he would find a tiger?** *(Answers should reflect the predictions made on the previous pages.)*

18 MAKE INFERENCES

> **Look at the speech balloons. The tiger's speech balloon is filled with stripes that match his skin. The boy's speech balloon is filled with stripes that match his shirt. What do you think they are saying to each other?** *(Possible answer: "We both have stripes!" "We can be friends!")*

64

17
18

64

MODIFY Instruction

ESL/ELD

▲ Create mixed-up dialogue for the speech balloons. For example, the tiger might say, "Hello, little girl." The boy might say, "Come and play, monkey." Ask children to correct the dialogue so it makes sense. Then invite them to pair up to make up dialogue of their own. **(PARAPHRASE)**

GIFTED & TALENTED

✷ Partners can pretend to be the boy and the tiger. Invite them to imagine the meeting that takes place in this picture. Challenge children to create a dialogue between these new friends. **(CREATE DIALOGUE)**

65

. . . and I found a friend I could talk to.

65

CULTURAL CONNECTION

Share information with children about the tiger. Explain to children that in China, tiger symbols were often carved into stone or wood to protect homes and farms. In China, people born in the Year of the Tiger (every 12 years: 1984, 1996, 2008) are said to be intelligent and brave.

Have children create a Year of the Tiger corner where they can display pictures and information about tigers. Children can cut out large letters to spell "Year of the Tiger" and decorate them with tiger colors and tiger markings.

DAILY PHONICS

r-Blends

CONNECT SOUND-SPELLING

TEACH/MODEL Write ***crib, frame,*** and ***prize*** on chart paper. Read the words with children, stressing the *r*-blend at the beginning of each word. Ask volunteers to underline the *r*-blend in each word.

THINK ALOUD *When I see a word like **crib,** I notice the **cr** at the beginning of the word. I know that I have to blend the sounds of **c** and **r** together to pronounce the word.*

PHONICS MAINTENANCE Review the following Sound-Spellings: *r*-blends; final ***e***; **/ē/ *ea, ee***.

PRACTICE/APPLY

BLEND WORDS Ask children to find the word ***friend*** on page 65.

- On the chalkboard, write ***friend.*** Have a volunteer say the word and underline the *r*-blend.
- Display the blends ***cr, fr,*** and ***pr*** in a pocket chart, or write them on the chalkboard. Have children take turns adding letters to each blend to make *r*-blend words.

INFORMAL ASSESSMENT
OBSERVATION

As children read, can they:

✔ recognize words with *r*-blends?

✔ blend words with *r*-blends?

See pages T152–T153 for a full skills lesson on *r*-blends.

COMPREHENSION

19 CRITICAL THINKING: EVALUATE

> **Look at all the interesting shapes and lines in this picture! What do you think these shapes are?** *(Answers should reflect children's own imaginations.)*

20 USE PICTURE CLUES

> **Let's see what we can recognize in this picture—what we know and what we've seen before. Then let's use our imagination and see if we can figure out what kind of game the boy and his friend found.** *(Possible answer: A board game in which they use a die to move along the squares on the floor.)*

21 COMPARE/CONTRAST

> **How is this attic like other attics you have seen? How is it different?** *(Possible answer: Like other attics, it has a window and it is up high. It is different because there is a ladder to the sky, a large die, a tiger, and many imaginary shapes.)*

INTERVENTION TIP

Understanding Picture Details

Some children might find this picture confusing. Help them locate familiar details, such as the boy, the tiger, and the ladder. Next, point out things that might be part of a game, such as the checkered floor and die. Then invite them to use their imagination and describe the "squiggles" and shapes.

66

21
19

My friend and I found a game that could

66

MODIFY Instruction

ESL/ELD

▲ Continue the discussion about the attic and what it looks like. Ask: *Is there an attic in your house? Does it have old toys in it? What does your family keep in the attic?* **(RELATE TO REAL LIFE)**

GIFTED & TALENTED

✳ Challenge partners to write or dictate directions for a game that the boy and the tiger might play while in this setting. Encourage them to include as many details from the picture as possible when creating the game. **(INNOVATE)**

67

go on forever, but it was time for dinner.

67

THE ARTS

Have partners complete the **What Do You Get When . . .** activity on **page R25.** Children will create an imaginary creature by combining two animals. As partners work together they will learn how to combine relevant details.

TECHNOLOGY

Speaking Skills Use the teacher options to edit the Story Starter in the **WiggleWorks Plus** Unit Writer to help children begin an interview. Have the interviewer use the Record Tool to record the interviewee's response.

COMPREHENSION

22 MAKE INFERENCES

> **The boy's mother says they don't have an attic. If there isn't an attic, where has the boy been all day? What is the attic?** *(He has been in an imaginary attic that he made up in his mind.)*

23 PICTURE CLUES

> **What toy does the boy have with him? Where have we seen the fire engine before?** *(The boy has a toy fire engine. We saw it at the very beginning of the story.)*

24 GENRE: FANTASY

> **There is often some kind of magical thing that helps a character get from the real world to the world of fantasy. What magical thing helped the boy get from the real world to the world of fantasy or imagination?** *(The magical thing was the ladder on the fire truck.)*

68

So I climbed out of the attic, and told my mother where I'd been all day.
"But we don't have an attic," she said. 22

68

MODIFY Instruction

ESL/ELD

▲ Help children distinguish between what is real and what is imaginary. Ask: *Is the kitchen real or imaginary?* Then, ask children to find a sentence on these pages that lets them know the attic is imaginary. **(COMPARE/CONTRAST)**

EXTRA HELP

■ Prepare a two-column chart to help children distinguish fact from fantasy. Ask children to look through the story and identify what is real and what is imaginary in each picture. For example, the fire truck is real but the big ladder that the boy uses to get into the attic is imaginary. **(GRAPHIC DEVICE)**

69

23
24
69

CONNECTING TO FILMS

Show the video or film version of *James and the Giant Peach.* As children watch, have them compare the elements of fantasy in *James and the Giant Peach* to fantasy elements in *In the Attic.*

TEACHER TIP

"Children love fantasy stories! I use them often in my classroom to stimulate young imaginations. With fantasy stories, children open up to the reading experience and look upon reading as adventuresome fun!"

SKILLS AND STRATEGIES

GENRE

Fantasy

TEACH/MODEL

Discuss key elements of fantasy with children.

- **A fantasy can happen in a real or make-believe place.**
- **In a fantasy, objects often come to life.**
- **The characters in a fantasy can often do things they can't do in real life.**

THINK ALOUD *I know this story is a fantasy because at the beginning, the boy climbs up a toy fire truck ladder. The boy also imagines things that could never be found in a real attic. Some look like places I've seen, but others are unreal!*

PRACTICE/APPLY

Help children make a Venn diagram to illustrate what is real and what is fantasy in *In the Attic.*

Real Life | **Imaginary but seem real** | **Fantasy**

- **Which things in the story could happen in real life?**
- **Which things could only happen in a fantasy?**
- **Which things are imaginary, but seem real?**

COMPREHENSION

25 MAKE INFERENCES

> **What do you think the boy means when he says that his mother "hasn't found the ladder"?** *(She hasn't imagined a ladder and an attic.)*

26 PLOT

> **What is the plot of *In the Attic?*** *(The boy is bored so he takes an imaginary trip to the attic.)*

JOURNAL

Revisit Predictions

Ask children to look back at their predictions and record how they were or were not confirmed.

Preview

Invite children to preview the poem by reading the title and discussing the photograph.

1 MAKE INFERENCES

> **What makes it possible for the speaker to be "whatever I want to be"?** *(Her imagination makes this possible.)*

2 ANALYZE

> **Have you ever imagined being any of the things mentioned in the poem? Which ones would you like to try?** *(Answers should reflect an understanding of the poem.)*

70

I guess she doesn't know
about the attic.
She hasn't found the ladder. 25

70

MODIFY Instruction

ESL/ELD

▲ Bring the poem closer to children by pantomiming the words, and changing the point of view to third person. Replace *I'm* with children's names. Encourage children to repeat the poem and movements together with you. **(PANTOMIME; PERSONALIZING)**

EXTRA HELP

■ Help children understand the poem. Invite them to act out some of the things that the poet imagines herself to be. **(PANTOMIME)**

71

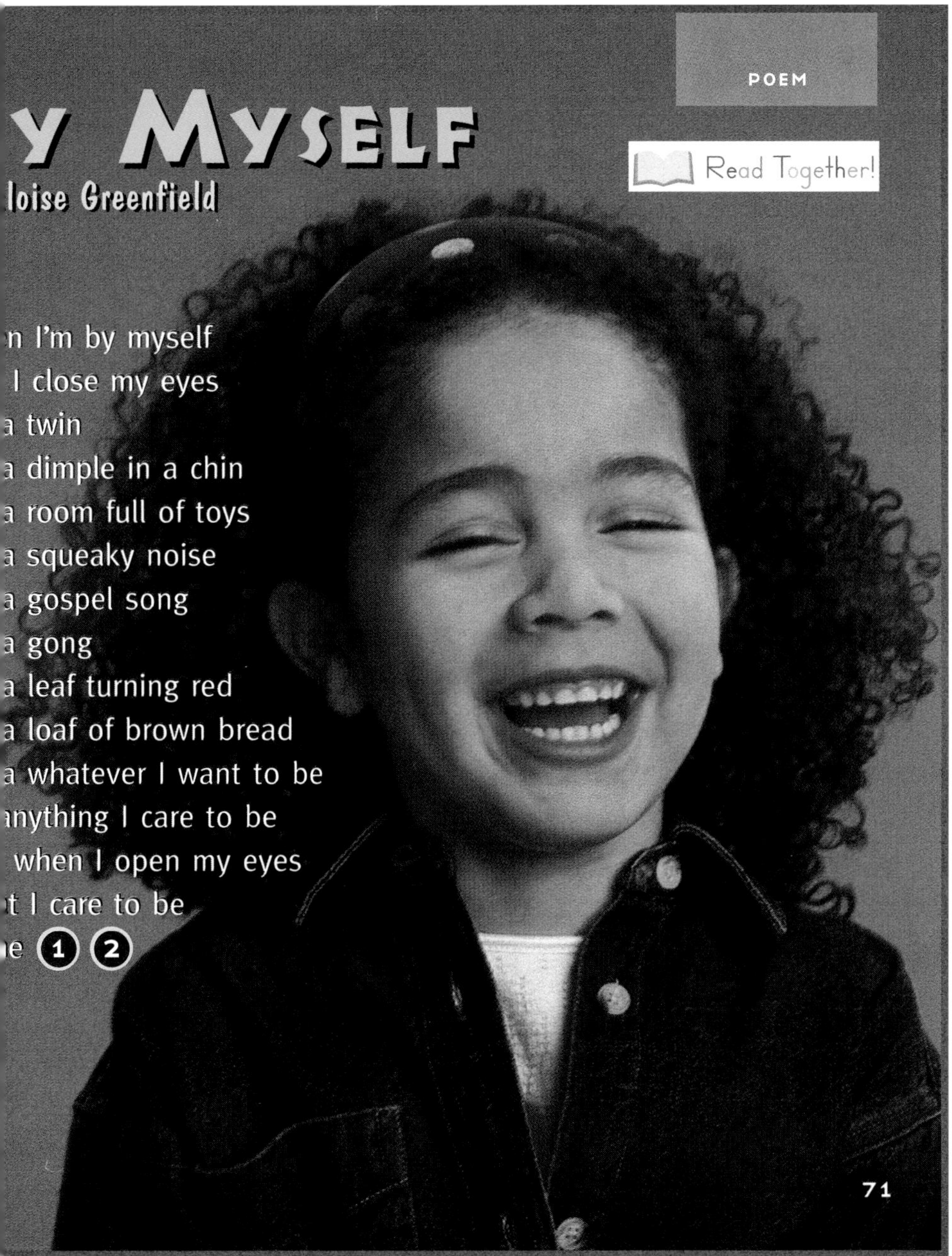

POEM

y Myself

loise Greenfield

Read Together!

n I'm by myself
I close my eyes
a twin
a dimple in a chin
a room full of toys
a squeaky noise
a gospel song
a gong
a leaf turning red
a loaf of brown bread
a whatever I want to be
anything I care to be
when I open my eyes
t I care to be
ne ① ②

71

ORAL LANGUAGE

Explain to children that lines in poems sometimes end with rhyming words. Have them find pairs of rhyming words in the poem, such as *twin/chin*. Suggest that they use some of the rhyming word pairs to write a short poem of their own.

Rhyming Words	
twin	chin
song	gong
red	bread

Fantasy

SHARED WRITING

PREWRITE Using *In the Attic* as a model, discuss the elements of plot in a fantasy story, such as setting, problem/solution, and events. Tell children that later they will be writing a fantasy story. Ask them to imagine that their own classroom is the setting for a fantasy story. Have them begin to complete the prewriting organizer.

Use Practice Book page 36.

DAILY LANGUAGE PRACTICE

SPELLING PRACTICE

DAY 2:

Practice Words With *l*-Blends. **See page R20.**

GRAMMAR, USAGE, MECHANICS

DAY 2:

Practice Irregular Verbs. **See page R22.**

ORAL LANGUAGE

I will kry when I saw the movie.

(I will cry when I see the movie.)

DAY 2 WRAP-UP

READ ALOUD *Spend five to ten minutes reading from a selection of your choice.*

GUIDED READING *Meet with the **green** and **red** reading groups and assign Independent Center activities. **See pages R18–R19.***

COMPREHENSION

DAY 3 OBJECTIVES

CHILDREN WILL:

READ 40 MINUTES

- **Assess Comprehension**
- **Key Comprehension Skill: Plot**
- **Daily Phonics: *l*-Blends**

WRITE 20 MINUTES

- **Respond: Postcard**
- **Spelling: Words With *l*-Blends**
- **Grammar, Usage, Mechanics: Irregular Verbs**
- **Oral Language**

EXTEND SKILLS 30 MINUTES

- **Integrated Curriculum**
- **Read Aloud**
- **Guided Reading**

RESOURCES

- **Practice Book, pp. 31–35**
- **Spelling Resource Book, p. 98**

Think About Reading

Below are the **answers** to the **Think About Reading** questions.

1. *The boy is bored.*
2. *He opens make-believe windows to other worlds. The pictures help me to know that the windows are not real.*
3. *Possible response: I would like to play with a friend my age.*
4. *Possible response: He can help her imagine where the ladder might be.*
5. *They both play by themselves and use their imagination.*

72

RESPOND

Think About Reading

1. Why does the boy climb into the attic?
2. Does the boy open real windows or make-believe windows in the attic? How do you know?
3. What kind of friend would you want to find in the attic?
4. How can the boy help his mother find the ladder to the attic?
5. How do you think the boy in In the Attic and the girl in "By Myself" are the same?

72

Name COMPREHENSION CHECK

Imagine It!

▶ The girl in the poem "By Myself" is alone. Draw a picture of one thing she thinks about when she closes her eyes.

▶ The boy in the story In the Attic is also alone. Draw a picture of one make-believe thing he does.

Copyright © Scholastic Inc.

Unit 4 • Imagine That! • In the Attic 31

PRACTICE BOOK p. 31

MODIFY Instruction

ESL/ELD

▲ Have children work in pairs to brainstorm pictures and messages that could be on postcards. You may wish to have them write or dictate their ideas on the chalkboard or on chart paper. **(WORK IN PAIRS)**

73

/rite A Postcard

lp the boy in the story make a stcard to tell a friend about the ic. Draw a picture of something ꞉ boy saw or did in the attic. en write about the picture and at the boy saw or did.

iterature Circle

th In the Attic and "By Myself" (about kids playing alone. ıat do you like about playing ɒne? What do you like about ɪying with friends?

Author
Satoshi Kitamura

Satoshi Kitamura grew up in Japan where he learned to speak, read, and write Japanese. Now he lives in England, where he speaks, reads, and writes in English. In any language, pictures help make a story such as In the Attic come to life.

More Books Illustrated by
Satoshi Kitamura

- Angry Arthur
- A Boy Wants a Dinosaur
- Sheep in Wolves' Clothing (He's the author, too.)

73

RESPOND

Write a Postcard

Before children begin to write, encourage children to participate in a conversation about these questions:

- **What was the most unusual thing the boy saw in the attic?**
- **What friends did the boy meet in the attic?**

Literature Circle

Encourage children to help you fill in the chart that follows. Children can use the chart to have a conversation with a classmate about the differences between playing alone and playing with a friend.

What I Like	
About Playing Alone	About Playing With Others

DAILY LANGUAGE PRACTICE

SPELLING

DAY 3:
Write sentences for Words With *l*-Blends. **See page R21.**

GRAMMAR, USAGE, MECHANICS

DAY 3:
Practice Irregular Verbs.
See page R23.

ORAL LANGUAGE

The boy see a tiger behind the tee.
(The boy saw a tiger behind the tree.)

FAMILY LITERACY

Suggest that families do echo reading using the whole story or a part of the story that their child enjoyed. Each older family member should read one page aloud and have the child read back the same page. Encourage families to give guidance and support while their children read. **(10-Minute Literacy Byte)**

TECHNOLOGY

Presentation Skills
Have children use **WiggleWorks Plus** PlaceMaker to create their postcard. Use either the poster or card format and include at least one illustration complete with text description. Encourage proper sentence format and look for capitals and ending punctuation.

COMPREHENSION
Plot

SKILLS TRACE

PLOT TESTED

Introduce. . . . . . . pp. T150–T151
Practice. . . . . p. T125
Review. . . . . p. R45
Reteach. . . . . p. R56

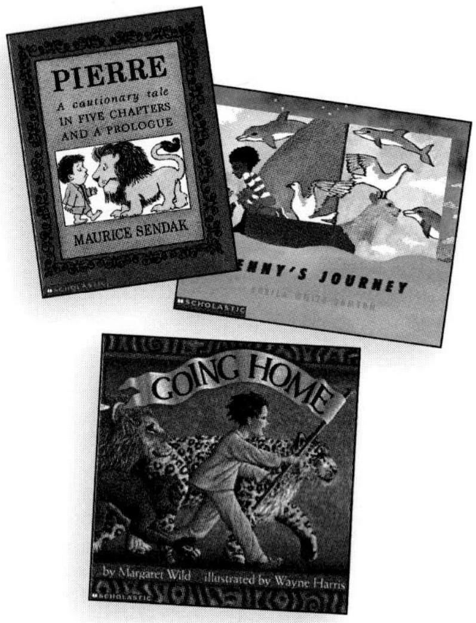
PIERRE
A cautionary tale IN FIVE CHAPTERS AND A PROLOGUE
MAURICE SENDAK
JENNY'S JOURNEY
GOING HOME
by Margaret Wild illustrated by Wayne Harris

CONNECT TO TRADE BOOKS

Select one of the unit trade books. Read aloud the title, and discuss the cover illustration.

- Have children make predictions about what might happen in the story. Record their predictions on chart paper or on the chalkboard.
- Then, read a few pages at a time, and stop to discuss plot.
- Record children's ideas about the problem, any solution, and events in the story. Continue this procedure until the book is completed.

QUICKCHECK

Can children:

✔ understand that important events, problems, and solutions provide the pattern for the plot?

✔ understand that plot is the plan or series of events that the character or characters go through?

If YES, go on to Practice/Apply.

If NO, start at Teach/Model.

A TEACH/MODEL

USE ORAL LANGUAGE

Talk about a familiar story or fairy tale with children. Encourage them to discuss the series of events, the problems and solutions, and the characters in the story.

The plot of a story is made up of **the main events and usually involves a problem and solution.** The plot is the plan or the series of events that the character or characters go through to solve the problem. To determine the plot, tell children to:

1. Read the story and think about the series of events.
2. Ask what problem the character or characters have.
3. Read to find out how the character or characters solve the problem.

MODIFY Instruction

ESL/ELD

▲ Pose true/false statements to make sure children understand the plot. Can children correct false statements? For example: *The boy was bored. He had a thousand toys. The boy climbed a mountain to get to the attic. He found mice in the attic.* **(TASK LISTENING)**

EXTRA HELP

■ Before children begin **pages 32 and 33** in the **Practice Book**, help them recall another favorite story or fairy tale. Have them use the steps described above to determine the plot. **(RECALL)**

LITERATURE CONNECTION

THINK ALOUD *When I think about plot, I think about the problems, solutions, and events in a story. At the beginning of* In the Attic, *the boy is bored. That is his problem. In order to solve that problem, the boy climbs up an imaginary ladder into an imaginary attic. Everything he does in that attic helps him solve the problem of being bored!*

B PRACTICE/APPLY

USE PRACTICE BOOK Have children practice what they learned about plot by completing **Practice Book page 32. (INDIVIDUALS)**

C ASSESS

APPLY INSTRUCTIONAL ALTERNATIVES Based on children's completion of **Practice Book page 32**, determine if they were able to identify elements of plot in *In the Attic*. The Instructional Alternatives below will aid you in pinpointing children's level of proficiency. Consider the appropriate instructional alternatives to promote further skill development.

To reinforce the skill, distribute **page 33** of the **Practice Book**.

INSTRUCTIONAL ALTERNATIVES

	If the child . . .	Then
Proficient	Recognizes all elements of plot	• Have the child summarize the plot of the story. • Have the child apply this skill independently to a more challenging story.
Apprentice	Recognizes characters, events, problems, and solution, but may not identify how they come together to form the plot pattern	• Have the child work with others to identify the series of events that the character goes through in the story.
Novice	Does not identify any of the elements of plot	• Review with the child the plot of a simple, familiar story. • Complete the Reteach lesson on R56.

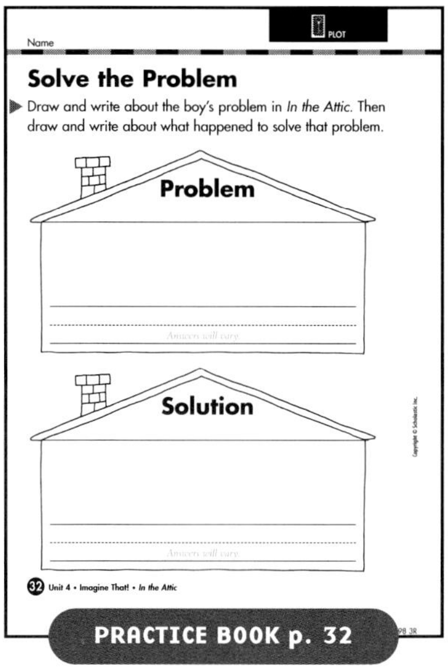

Name PLOT

Solve the Problem

▶ Draw and write about the boy's problem in *In the Attic*. Then draw and write about what happened to solve that problem.

Problem

Solution

32 Unit 4 • Imagine That! • In the Attic

PRACTICE BOOK p. 32

Name PLOT

What Happened?

▶ Look at the pictures. Draw a line under the answer to each question.

1 What is this about?
Friends that fly a kite.
Friends that play soccer.

2 What is their problem?
A hole is in the kite.
They want a basketball.

3 What do the friends do to fix this?
They sew the kite.
They fly a kite.

4 What do the friends do after that?
Buy a kite.
Fly the kite.

Unit 4 • Imagine That! • In the Attic 33

PRACTICE BOOK p. 33

IN THE ATTIC
HIAWYN ORAM
SATOSHI KITAMURA

SELECTION WORDS With *r*-Blends

friend

SKILLS TRACE

***r*-Blends** TESTED

Introduce . . . . . . pp. T152–153
Practice . . . pp. T141, T159, T195
Review . . . . p. R52
Reteach. . . . . p. R60

DAILY PHONICS

Words With *r*-Blends

A PHONOLOGICAL AWARENESS

Rhyme Read aloud "Five Little Peas" from the *Big Book of Rhymes and Rhythms* 1A, page 9. As you read, stress the ***r***-blend in ***grew.***

- On a second reading, ask children to read along with you.
- Frame the words ***pressed*** and ***grew*** and point out the ***r***-blend in each word.

Five Little Peas
Five little peas
In a pea pod pressed.
One grew, two grew,
And so did all the rest.
They grew and they grew,
And they did not stop.
Then all of a sudden,
The pod went POP.
pressed grew

Big Book of Rhymes, 1A, p. 9

ORAL BLENDING Say the following word parts and have children blend them. Provide corrective feedback and modeling as needed.

- **br. . .ake**
- **br. . .own**
- **gr. . . een**
- **gr. . . ape**
- **fr . . .ee**
- **fr . . .esh**

B CONNECT SOUND-SPELLING

INTRODUCE *r*-blends Write the words ***grab, brick,*** and ***fresh*** on the chalkboard. Underline the ***r***-blend in each word and model how to blend the sounds formed by the consonant blend.

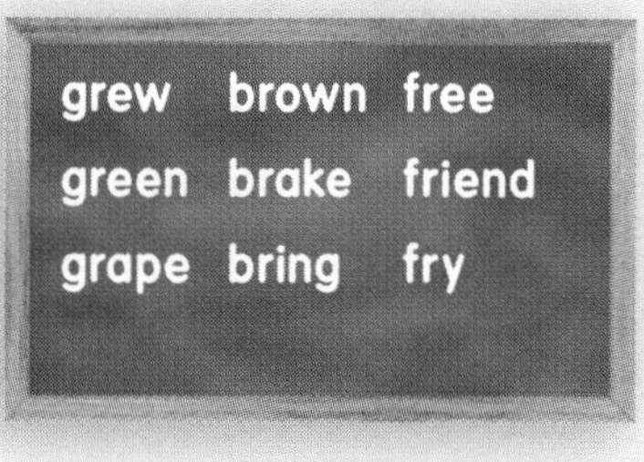
grew brown free
green brake friend
grape bring fry

THINK ALOUD *I can put the letter **g, r, a,** and **b** together to make the word **grab.** Let's say the sounds slowly, as I move my finger under the letters: **grab.** Listen to the sounds that **gr** stand for in **grab.** The sound of **gr** is **/gr/.***

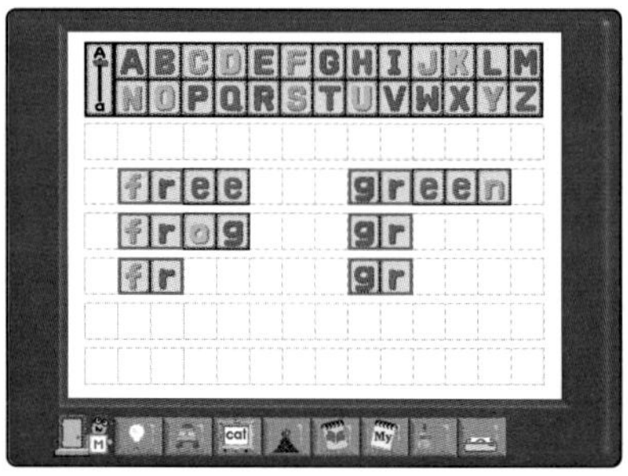
ABCDEFGHIJKLM
NOPQRSTUVWXYZ
free green
frog gr
fr gr

TECHNOLOGY

Have children build words with *r*-blends on the **WiggleWorks Plus** Magnet Board.

- Begin with the words *free* and *green.*
- Children can also begin with *fr, gr,* and *br* and add letters to make new words.

MODIFY Instruction

ESL/ELD

▲ Words with *r*-blends may be difficult for children to pronounce. Teach children some simple rhymes, which they may then practice for fun, perhaps as jump rope rhymes on the playground. For example, "Fred, Fred, here's some bread!" **(RHYTHM)**

EXTRA HELP

■ Have children work in groups to answer these color riddles with words that begin with *r*-blends. *This is the color of the grass.* (green) *The sky is this color just before it rains.* (gray) *Peanut butter is this color.* (brown) **(SMALL GROUPS)**

- Ask children to suggest other words that begin with ***gr, br,*** and ***fr.*** List the words in separate columns on the chalkboard.
- Have volunteers circle the ***r***-blend in each word.

PHONICS MAINTENANCE Review the following sound-spellings: ***r***-blends; ***l***-blends; final ***e; /ē/ ea, ee.***

C PRACTICE/APPLY

BLEND WORDS To practice using the sound-spellings and review previous sound-spellings, list the following words and sentences on the chalkboard. Have children read each chorally. Model blending.

brake	free	grape
team	bike	froze

Look at all the green grass.
I need a friend to play with.

DICTATION Dictate the following words: ***frame, green, eat, broke.***

BUILD WORDS Distribute the following letter cards, or have children use their own sets: ***a, y, ee, f, g, r, n.*** Allow children time to build ***r***-blend words using the letter cards. Children can write their words on paper. **(INDEPENDENT WORK)**

f
r
y

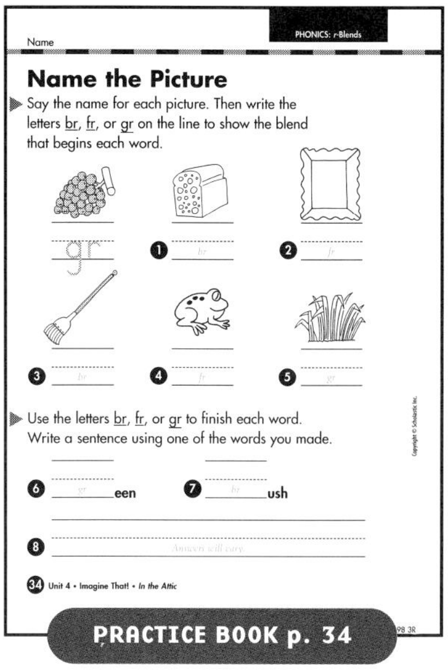
Name
PHONICS: r-Blends
Name the Picture
Say the name for each picture. Then write the letters br, fr, or gr on the line to show the blend that begins each word.
Use the letters br, fr, or gr to finish each word. Write a sentence using one of the words you made.
6 ___een 7 ___ush
8
34 Unit 4 • Imagine That! • In the Attic

PRACTICE BOOK p. 34

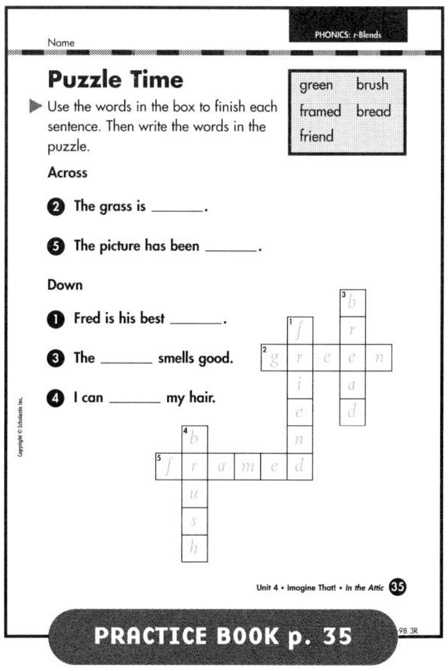
Name
PHONICS: r-Blends
Puzzle Time
Use the words in the box to finish each sentence. Then write the words in the puzzle.
green brush framed bread friend
Across
2 The grass is ___.
5 The picture has been ___.
Down
1 Fred is his best ___.
3 The ___ smells good.
4 I can ___ my hair.
Unit 4 • Imagine That! • In the Attic 35

PRACTICE BOOK p. 35

DECODABLE TEXT

For practice reading decodable text, see ***Scholastic Decodable Reader #49.***

For additional phonics instruction and review, see ***Scholastic Phonics A, pp. 189–190.***

THE *R* TRAIN

Cut out construction paper train boxcars. Have small groups write or dictate words with ***r***-blends in these boxcars. Then have children read the words aloud. Join the boxcars together on a bulletin board to make a train.

brown
bread
crown
free
tray
tree

Building Fluency

PHONICS READER

Play the Animal Game!
Book 44
by Anne Schreiber and Gail Tuchman
Illustrated by Tim Haggerty
SCHOLASTIC

Guide children through a reading of **Phonics Reader #44** *Play the Animal Game!* For a detailed lesson plan, see **Phonics Reader Teacher's Guide Part B, pages 30–31.** While children read, note how well they:

- **blend words,**
- **recognize high-frequency words,**
- **read with speed, accuracy, and expression.**

You may wish to have children reread the story with a partner.

* See Phonics Readers Take-Home Books 37–72 for reproducible format.

More Support Materials . . .

GOING HOME
PIERRE
A cautionary tale IN FIVE CHAPTERS AND A PROLOGUE
JENNY'S JOURNEY
SCHOLASTIC

TRADE BOOK LIBRARY

For additional leveled reading practice, have children read one of the following:

Going Home
CHALLENGE

Pierre
AVERAGE

Jenny's Journey
EASY

PHONICS
CHAPTER BOOK 4
The Puppet Club
SCHOLASTIC

PHONICS CHAPTER BOOK

For additional practice with *l*-blends, have children read Chapter #4, "Things Click," in Phonics Chapter Book #4, ***The Puppet Club.***

HOME-SCHOOL CONNECTION

Play the Animal Game!
MAGGIE BLOOM'S MESSY ROOM

Send home ***Play the Animal Game!*** and ***Maggie Bloom's Messy Room***. Have children read the books to a family member.

MAGGIE BLOOM'S MESSY ROOM
by Cass Hollander
Illustrated by Deborah Sims

MY BOOK

For additional practice with *l*-blends have children read ***Maggie Bloom's Messy Room.*** The *My Book* is also available on **WiggleWorks Plus.**

Intervention

or children who need extra help . . .

FOCUS ON HIGH-FREQUENCY WORDS

Write the following sentences on sentence strips. Each sentence focuses on one of the high-frequency words.

Look at the plane.

We are about to play a game.

I am about five feet tall.

Did you look at the new book?

- Read aloud each sentence. Help children find or draw a picture to match each sentence. Attach the pictures to index cards.
- Then have children chorally read each sentence and match the sentence to the picture card.
- Continue by mixing the cards and strips for children to practice reading and matching.

FOCUS ON PHONICS

Write the words ***fly, friend, place, flag, cry, clap, free, blade, grape,*** and ***brick*** on index cards.

- Help children read the word on each card.
- Then mix the cards. Have children sort the cards into two piles: one with *r*-blends and one with *l*-blends.
- Ask children to read the words in each group. Challenge them to add words to each pile.

f
l
y
c
l
a
p

PROFESSIONAL DEVELOPMENT

DELORES STUBBLEFIELD SEAMSTER

What About Reading Rate?

The speed with which children read is an important indicator of a child's reading fluency and a great predictor of reading success. Periodically monitor a child's reading rate. To do so, you might provide children with a 100 word portion of a story they have not read. Ask children to read aloud the text for one minute. Count and record the number of words read. The goal by the end of first grade is a reading rate of @ 60 words per minute.

DAY 3 WRAP-UP

READ ALOUD *To conclude each reading session and develop children's oral vocabularies, read aloud a book of your choice. If the book contains chapters, you might choose to read only one chapter a day.*

GUIDED READING *Meet with the* ***red*** *and* ***blue*** *reading groups and assign Independent Center activities.* ***See pages R18–R19.***

DAY 4 OBJECTIVES

CHILDREN WILL:

READ 20 MINUTES

- **Reread *In the Attic***

WRITE 40 MINUTES

- **Shared Writing: Fantasy Story**
- **Spelling: Words With *l*-Blends**
- **Grammar, Usage, Mechanics: Irregular Verbs**
- **Oral Language**

EXTEND SKILLS 30 MINUTES

- **Vocabulary**
- **Daily Phonics: *r*-Blends**
- **Study Skills: Graphic Aids: Pictures**

RESOURCES

- **Practice Book pp. 36, 38**
- **Spelling Resource Book, p. 161**

Name

WRITING: Fantasy Story

Get Ready to Write

▶ Draw a picture of something in your classroom that might come to life. Then write about what it might do.

Answers will vary.

To the Teacher: This is the prewriting organizer referenced in the lesson on writing a fantasy story.

36 Unit 4 • Imagine That! • *In the Attic*

PRACTICE BOOK p. 36

SHARED WRITING

Fantasy Story

IN THE ATTIC
HIAWYN ORAM
SATOSHI KITAMURA

SELECTION CONNECTION Using *In the Attic* as a model, children will write a fantasy story.

THINK ABOUT WRITING Ask children to describe the imaginative adventures of *In the Attic*. Help children discover that in fantasy stories objects can change in size and shape and make-believe things happen.

INTRODUCE THE WRITING EVENT Explain to children that they will work together to write a class fantasy story.

TEACH/MODEL

PUT IT IN CONTEXT Look back at *In the Attic* with children. Talk about how real objects helped create the fantasy. Ask the following:

> **Which real toy changes and helps the boy create his fantasy?**

> **How do other real objects change in the boy's imagination? How do they remain the same?**

GRAMMAR CONNECTION Have children list action words that describe how imaginary objects move. Help children to identify the irregular verbs in the list.

MODIFY Instruction

ESL/ELD

▲ Help children make sentence innovations on the story. Write key sentence starters on the chalkboard: *I climbed into a . . ., I saw a . . ., I jumped up to . . . .* Brainstorm and complete several innovations orally. Then ask pairs of children to complete others on their own. **(GUIDED WRITING)**

EXTRA HELP

■ Allowing visual learners to move around the room and examine objects may help them more readily think of ideas during the writing event. **(MULTISENSORY TECHNIQUES)**

WRITE

CREATE A FANTASY STORY

- Have children list classroom objects that could come to life in a fantasy. Have them write on sticky notes, for example, "The plant could come to life." and post them on the appropriate objects.
- Ask children to choose the fantasy object or objects they will write about in their class fantasy story.
- Have a volunteer begin the story by writing a sentence about the story problem. Encourage children to add sentences to the story. As children continue, remind them to add details that make the object seem lifelike.
- Encourage children to add other make-believe elements to the story.
- Have children write the story on chart paper or dictate it to you. Remind them to include make-believe elements. When finished, have children point to an indent that shows a paragraph.
- Encourage children to illustrate the story. Gather the pages into a class book to keep in the classroom library.

ASSESS

PERFORMANCE-BASED ASSESSMENT

The following questions will help children assess their work.

✔ **How is our story like *In the Attic*? How is it different?**

✔ **How did we make our object come to life?**

✔ **Does our story have a plot?**

Children may wish to carry this piece through the writing process described on pages T278–T281.

DAILY LANGUAGE PRACTICE

SPELLING

DAY 4:
Review Words With *l*-Blends. **See page R21.**

GRAMMAR, USAGE, MECHANICS

DAY 4:
Apply writing Irregular Verbs. **See page R23.**

ORAL LANGUAGE

He go to the attic yesterday and see a cat with the back fur.
(He went to the attic yesterday and saw a cat with black fur.)

TECHNOLOGY

Matching Technology to Task Encourage children to use the **WiggleWorks Plus** Unit Writer to create their story. Suggest that they use the Record Tool, the Paint Tools, and stamp art.

Tiger

Extend Vocabulary

look

about

Review High-Frequency Words

Write the high-frequency words ***look*** and ***about*** on note cards. Then write the following incomplete sentences on sentence strips:

I _____ for my toy truck.

I see a book _____ mice.

Read aloud the incomplete sentences, and have children place the appropriate card in each blank space. Then help children to chorally read the sentences.

TEACHER TIP

Make and distribute copies of the vocabulary cards on **pages R70–R71.** Have children use these cards for additional practice.

Review Story Words

Write the story words ***bored, attic, toys, game, talk,*** and ***ladder*** on note cards. Then write the following incomplete sentences on the chalkboard:

I am _____ with no toys.
I want _____ to play with.
I want to play a _____
I will look in the _____
I can get there with a _____
I will _____ to Mom about this.

Read aloud the incomplete sentences and have children place the appropriate story word note card in the blank space. Then help children chorally read the sentences.

SORT IT

Use the note cards on which you wrote the story words and the high-frequency words in lowercase letters. Mix them up and distribute them to groups of children. Have each group sort the words into words that begin with vowels and words that begin with consonants. Then mix up the words again and have each child choose one. Ask children to use that word in an oral sentence.

about

attic

bored

look

Building Fluency

PHONICS READER

Book 43
Troll Tricks
by Gail Tuchman and Anne Schreiber
Illustrated by Vincent Andriani
SCHOLASTIC

Guide children through a reading of **Phonics Reader #43,** *Troll Tricks.* For a detailed lesson plan, see **Phonics Reader Teacher's Guide Part B, pages 28–29.** While children read, note how well they:

- **blend words,**
- **recognize high-frequency words,**
- **read with speed, accuracy, and expression.**

You may wish to have children reread the story with a partner.

★ See Phonics Readers Take-Home Books 37–72 for reproducible format.

More Support Materials . . .

GOING HOME
PIERRE
A cautionary tale
IN FIVE CHAPTERS
AND A PROLOGUE
JENNY'S JOURNEY
SCHOLASTIC

Trade Book Library

For additional leveled reading practice, have children read one of the following:

Going Home
Challenge

Pierre
Average

Jenny's Journey
Easy

PHONICS
CHAPTER BOOK 4
The Puppet Club
by Mike Thaler and Janelle Cherrington
Illustrated by Ana López Escrivá
SCHOLASTIC

Phonics Chapter Book

For additional practice with ***r***-blends, have children read Chapter 3, "A Breeze," in **Phonics Chapter Book 4, *The Puppet Club.***

Home-School Connection

Troll Tricks
GRANDPA GRAY

Send home ***Troll Tricks*** and ***Grandpa Gray.*** Have children read the books to a family member.

GRANDPA GRAY
by Cass Hollander
Illustrated by Elliot Kreloff
SCHOLASTIC

My Book

For additional practice with ***r***-blends, have children read ***Grandpa Gray.*** The *My Book* is also available on **WiggleWorks Plus.**

STUDY SKILLS

Graphic Aids: Pictures

SKILLS TRACE

PICTURES TESTED

RESEARCH IDEA

Provide children with wordless picture books. Have them use the pictures to tell the story shown in each book.

A TEACH/MODEL

EXPLAIN THE IMPORTANCE OF PICTURES Explain to children that pictures can give a lot of information. In a story, pictures can give information about plot, setting, characters, and even the type of story being read.

PRESENT PICTURES Review the pictures in *In the Attic* with children. Discuss one or two of the pictures. Encourage children to suggest the kinds of information that each picture conveys. Ask children:

- > **What does the picture tell about the boy?**
- > **What does it tell about the setting?**
- > **How does the picture show that the story is a fantasy?**
- > **What else does the picture tell you about the story?**

DRAW A PICTURE Ask each of the children to draw a picture showing his or her favorite part of *In the Attic*. Remind children to show the boy in the picture. You may wish to suggest that children draw the boy in one of the fantasy settings.

B PRACTICE/APPLY

DISCUSS DRAWINGS Have partners review each other's drawings and have a conversation about the information in each picture.

> **What information does this picture give you about the boy?**

> **Does this picture show that the story is a fantasy? Why or why not?**

> **What information does this picture give about the plot of the story?**

INFORMAL ASSESSMENT: PERFORMANCE-BASED

✔ **Did children identify what is happening in each picture?**

✔ **Did children acquire story information from each picture?**

✔ **Can children explain which elements in the pictures helped them understand what is happening in the story?**

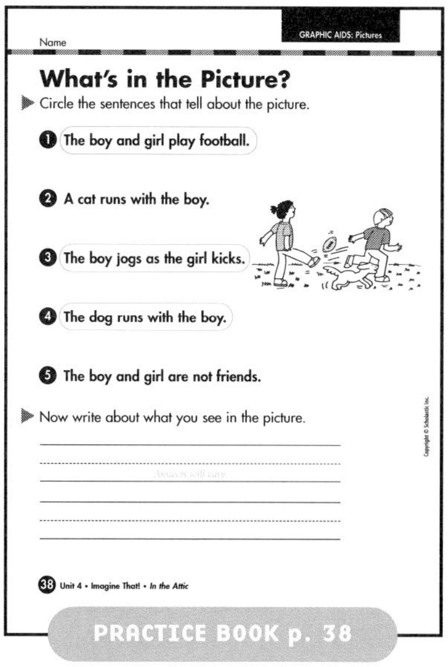
Name

GRAPHIC AIDS: Pictures

What's in the Picture?

▶ Circle the sentences that tell about the picture.

1. The boy and girl play football.
2. A cat runs with the boy.
3. The boy jogs as the girl kicks.
4. The dog runs with the boy.
5. The boy and girl are not friends.

▶ Now write about what you see in the picture.

Answers will vary.

Copyright © Scholastic Inc.

38 Unit 4 • Imagine That! • *In the Attic*

PRACTICE BOOK p. 38

TECHNOLOGY

Comprehension Skills Use the **I Spy** CD-ROM and have the children explore Chalkboard to search and sort through items that might be found in an attic. Children might want to create their own virtual attic treasure hunt in the Find Me section of the program.

DAY 4 WRAP-UP

READ ALOUD *Spend five to ten minutes reading from a selection of your choice.*

GUIDED READING *To extend reading, meet with the* ***blue*** *and* ***green*** *reading groups and assign Independent Center activities.* ***See pages R18–R19.***

DAY 5 OBJECTIVES

CHILDREN WILL:

READ 40 MINUTES

- **Reading Assessment**
- **Daily Phonics: Words With *l*- and *r*-Blends**

WRITE 30 MINUTES

- **Writing Assessment**
- **Spelling: Words With *l*-Blends**
- **Grammar, Usage, Mechanics: Irregular Verbs**
- **Oral Language**

EXTEND SKILLS 20 MINUTES

- **Integrated Language Arts**
- **Read Aloud**
- **Guided Reading**

RESOURCES

- **Selection Test**
- **Spelling Resource Book, p. 163**

TEACHER SELF-ASSESSMENT

- Did I frequently model how to blend words?
- Did I regroup children according to skill needs and reading level?
- Did I provide children with successful, daily reading and writing opportunities?

Reading Assessment

INFORMAL ASSESSMENT: OBSERVATION

PHONICS

Write the following spellings on note cards: ***cl, fl, pl, gr, fr, br***. Display one card at a time and have the class state aloud the sound the spelling stands for. Note children who respond incorrectly or wait for classmates to respond before providing an answer.

HIGH-FREQUENCY WORDS

Write the following words on note cards: ***look, about***. Display one card at a time and have the class read the word. Note children who have difficulty recognizing either word.

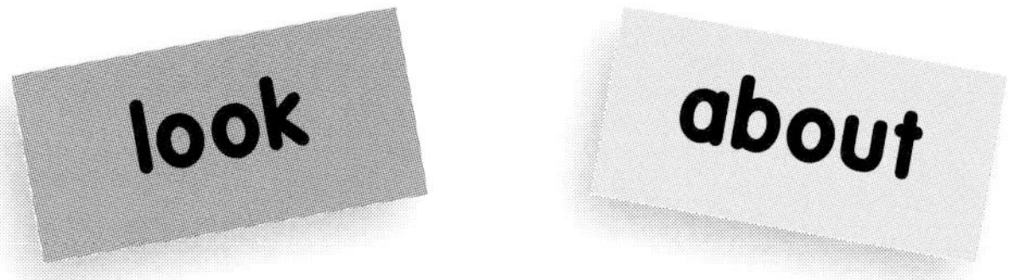
look
about

KEY STRATEGY: PLOT

Ask children to choose a book that is appropriate to their reading level. Have them read the book individually or in a small group. Then ask each child to write or dictate sentences that tell who the main character was, what kind of problem he or she faced, and how the problem was solved.

CONFERENCE

Have children reread *In the Attic*. As they reread, select several children to conference with. Ask them to do the following:

- read aloud a few pages of the story.
- retell the story in their own words.
- explain what they did to figure out an unfamiliar word.

IN THE ATTIC
HIAWYN ORAM
SATOSHI KITAMURA

In the Attic

Keep anecdotal records of the conferences. Place your findings in each child's assessment folder. Use the information to determine which children need additional support.

FORMAL ASSESSMENT

DECODING TEST

Make two copies of the assessment below. The assessment piece is designed to be used individually.

- Give one to the child and keep the other to record each child's errors.
- As the child reads aloud the words and sentences in the assessment boxes, record his or her attempts, corrections, errors, and passes.
- Once completed, keep each assessment piece in the child's portfolio as a running record of his or her emerging reading skills.

NAME: ______________________________ **DATE:** ______________

A Have children read the following word list:

mat	**teeth**	**duck**	**frog**	**brake**
sun	**thin**	**click**	**clock**	**mixing**
wide	**quick**	**flying**	**price**	**plane**
many	**look**	**soon**	**has**	**from**
about	**when**	**went**	**little**	**how**

B Have children read the following sentences.

- **I know all about planes.**
- **I look at them flying in the sky.**

C On a separate sheet of paper, have children write the following words and sentences.

- **flying climb lane playing**
- **Please look at the pretty flowers.**
- **They came from a friend.**

SELECTION TEST

Use the selection test to obtain a formal measure of children's mastery of the week's reading objectives.

SELF-SELECTION

Have children select one or two pieces of work from the week that they would like to place in their Portfolios.

Suggest that children write a sentence telling why they chose each piece. You may also wish to select a piece that best illustrates the child's work.

Periodically review the pieces in the Portfolio and remove any that no longer seem appropriate.

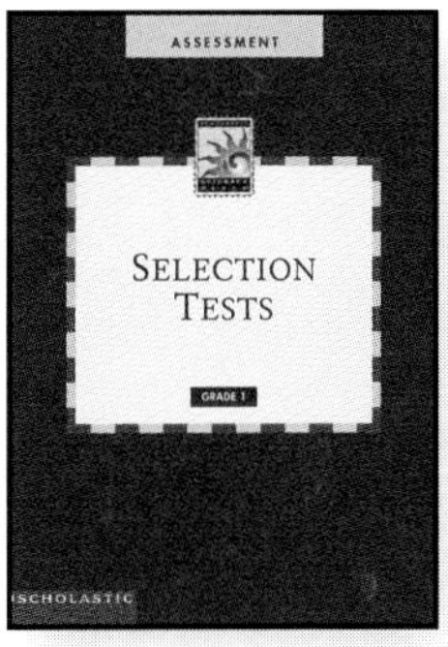
ASSESSMENT
SELECTION TESTS
SCHOLASTIC

SELECTION TEST

DAILY LANGUAGE PRACTICE

SPELLING

DAY 5:

Administer the Posttest for Words With *l*-Blends.

See page R21.

GRAMMAR, USAGE, MECHANICS

DAY 5:

Assess Irregular Verbs.

See page R23.

ORAL LANGUAGE

What was you doing with that pant?

(What were you doing with that plant?)

PORTFOLIO

Suggest that children add their drafts and revisions to their Literacy Portfolios.

Writing Assessment

This is a good opening sentence. You really made the stuffed animal come to life.
This is a good make-believe event for the story.
You used the correct form of irregular verbs.
You did a good job of proofreading your sentences.
You might make your story better by describing a problem more clearly.
It was a cold, dark,
rainy day when our
stuffed animal came to
He danced around A-3
acted like a real
ey. The teacher left the
ssroom and didn't come
back. The monkey became
our teacher. He did a pupp
show and made us all laugh
Our classroom turned into a

Apprentice

Use the rubric below to assess children's writing.

CHILDREN'S WRITING RUBRIC

Proficient	• The fantasy story shows an object coming to life.	• Many fantasy or make-believe things happen in the story. • The story is proofread and corrected for errors.
Apprentice	• The fantasy story may or may not show an object coming to life.	• There are few if any make-believe things in the story. • The story is proofread, but may not be corrected for errors.
Novice	• The story does not show an object coming to life.	• The story is not corrected for errors.

Integrated Language Arts

ORAL LANGUAGE

Imagine Your Own Story

MATERIALS:
Construction paper
Crayons

SUGGESTED GROUPING:
Whole class and individuals

INTRODUCE the activity by asking children to imagine their own story about visiting the boy's attic.

PROMPT children to close their eyes and imagine that they are climbing the ladder on the fire truck and entering the attic. Children can think about what they see and do in the attic. Ask what they could do in there that they would not be able to do in their own rooms. You may wish to have children write, dictate, and draw story maps to outline the story events.

ENCOURAGE children to use the story words. Children may elaborate on their adventures by answering classmates' questions.

READING/WRITING

Make a Rhyming Chain

MATERIALS:
Poem "By Myself"
Strips of colored paper 1" x 6"
Glue or a stapler
Marking pens
Chart paper

SUGGESTED GROUPING:
Small groups or partners

INTRODUCE the activity by having children return to the poem "By Myself." Ask children to identify the rhyming words in the poem.

GET STARTED by having small groups or partners copy pairs of their own rhyming words onto paper strips. Ask children to add their rhyming words to their My Words lists. Have children loop and fasten the strips into a chain so the words show. Display the chain in the writing area.

SUGGEST that small groups or partners use the rhyming words in the chain to write their own two or four line poems.

PUBLISH by displaying children's poems and the rhyming chain in the writing area.

TECHNOLOGY

Language Development Use a familiar word processor to create a rhyming word table. Have one child fill in words in the first column while a second matches rhyming words in the second column. Print the table and share the rhyming pairs.

toys
noise
be
me

Integrated Language Arts

VIEWING/SPEAKING

Retell the Story

MATERIALS:
Anthology pp. 46–70

SUGGESTED GROUPING:
Partners or small groups

ENCOURAGE children to talk about *In the Attic* after reading it. Have them use the illustrations to ask each other questions about the story. Children should also use the text and illustrations to answer each other's questions.

PROMPT children to take turns looking at the illustrations. Then have them use the illustrations to retell the story to each other. Encourage children to point to the illustrations as they retell the story. Point out that the child who is listening may ask questions as the story is being retold.

SUGGEST children elaborate on:

- what it's like to climb a ladder.
- the animals the boy sees.
- how the boy feels as he travels.

WRITING/SPEAKING/LISTENING

Write Dialogue

Good For Grading

MATERIALS:
Anthology pp. 46–70
Beanbag chairs, carpet squares, or big pillows (optional)

SUGGESTED GROUPING:
Partners or Cooperative groups

INTRODUCE the activity by reminding children that the boy in the story found a friendly tiger in his make-believe attic. Ask children to think of what the boy and the tiger might say to each other.

SUGGEST that in one conversation, the boy might tell the tiger that he will bring him back home to meet his mother. Children can take turns thinking of questions that the boy and the tiger might ask each other.

DRAMATIZE/PUBLISH Have partners act out their short scenes between the characters. Children can then draw pictures of the characters and write words in speech balloons.

HOW TO GRADE When grading, make sure children are able to create a related exchange of thoughts in the dialogue.

DAY 5 WRAP-UP

READ ALOUD *To develop students' oral vocabularies, spend five to ten minutes reading from a selection of your choice.*

GUIDED READING *To extend reading, meet with the **green** and **red** reading groups and assign Independent Center activities.* ***See pages R18–R19.***

Starring First Grade

A DELL YOUNG YEARLING
Starring First Grade
AWARD WINNER
Miriam Cohen
Pictures by Lillian Hoban

Main Selection
Genre: Realistic Fiction
Parents Choice Award

MENTOR
William Walsh
Muralist

Paired Selection

WEEK 4
TESTED SKILLS

- **Vocabulary**
- **Daily Phonics: *s*-Blends, Digraphs *ch, wh***
- **Key Comprehension Skill: Sequence**
- **Spelling: Words With *s*-Blends**
- **Grammar, Usage, Mechanics: Describing Words**

Technology Connection

Build Background
Go to the Read Aloud area of **WiggleWorks Plus** to share *The Three Billy Goats Gruff* with children. After listening to the story, turn to a page that shows the play format. Discuss with the children how plays are formatted, noting the character introductions and stage directions called out from the dialogue. You might brainstorm a few stage directions for the play.

Selection Summary

The First Grade decides to perform the folk tale *The Three Billy Goats Gruff*. When Jim isn't cast as Troll, he makes trouble at rehearsal and angers his friend Paul. But in the end, Jim is recast as water under Troll's bridge and helps Paul with his stage fright on opening night.

PAIRED SELECTION Everyone has different ways to tell stories. The First Grade chose to tell a folk tale in the form of a play. Mentor William Walsh uses murals to tell his stories.

Author

MIRIAM COHEN has written more than one book about Jim and his friends. Her first book, *Will I Have a Friend?*, is about Jim and his friends going to school for the first time. Another book in her *First Grade* series is *First Grade Takes a Test.*

Weekly Organizer

Visit Our Web Site www.scholastic.com

Starring First Grade

	DAY 1	DAY 2
READ and Introduce Skills • VOCABULARY • PHONICS • COMPREHENSION • LISTENING • SPEAKING • VIEWING STARRING FIRST GRADE Story by Miriam Cohen Pictures by Lillian HobanWilliam Walsh Muralist	**BUILD BACKGROUND, p. T173** ▲ **VOCABULARY, p. T174** ▲ ✱ Practice Book, p. 44 **DAILY PHONICS:** ▲ ■ *s*-Blends, pp. T176–T177 Practice Book, pp. 45, 46 Long *e: ee, ea,* p. T185 **PREVIEW AND PREDICT, p. T178** **READ:** ▲ ✱ ■ *Starring First Grade*, pp. T178–T187 **COMPREHENSION:** Sequence, p. T181	**READ:** ▲ ■ ✱ *Starring First Grade*, pp. T188–T205 **DAILY PHONICS:** *r*-Blends and *l*-Blends, p. T189 Practice Book, pp. 58, 59 Final *e*, p. T191 Digraphs *ch* and *wh*, p. T197 Practice Book, pp. 51, 52 **COMPREHENSION:** Plot, p. T201 **GENRE:** Realistic Fiction, p. T203
WRITE and Respond • GRAMMAR • USAGE • MECHANICS • SPELLING • WRITING	**SHARED WRITING,** p. T173 **JOURNAL:** High-Frequency Words, p. T175 **SPELLING:** Pretest: Words With *s*-Blends, p. R28 Spelling Resource Book, p. 99 **GRAMMAR, USAGE, MECHANICS:** Teach/Model: Describing Words, p. R30 **ORAL LANGUAGE,** p. T187	**SHARED WRITING:** Prewrite, p. T205 Practice Book, p. 53 **SPELLING:** Vocabulary Practice, p. R28 Spelling Resource Book, pp. 100–102 **GRAMMAR, USAGE, MECHANICS:** Practice, p. R30 **ORAL LANGUAGE,** p. T205
EXTEND SKILLS and Apply to Literature • SKILLS • INTEGRATED LANGUAGE ARTS • INTEGRATED CURRICULUM • GUIDED READING • INDEPENDENT READING	**READ ALOUD,** p. T187 **GUIDED READING,** pp. R26–R27 **INTEGRATED CURRICULUM:** Math, p. R32 Social Studies, p. R33 **TRADE BOOKS** • *Pierre* • *Jenny's Journey* • *Going Home* PIERRE MAURICE SENDAK JENNY'S JOURNEY	**READ ALOUD,** p. T205 **GUIDED READING,** pp. R26–R27 **INTEGRATED CURRICULUM:** The Arts, p. R33 Science, p. R32
TECHNOLOGY and **REAL-WORLD SKILLS**	**WIGGLEWORKS PLUS CD-ROM** Magnet Board, pp. T174, T176 **ART PROGRAM** Comprehension Skills, p. T187 **WORKSHOP 2,** pp. T227–T230	**WIGGLEWORKS PLUS CD-ROM** Language Development, p. T193 **WORKSHOP 2,** pp. T227–T230

MODIFY INSTRUCTION

● INTERVENTION ▲ ESL/ELD ■ EXTRA HELP
✷ GIFTED & TALENTED ✓ = TESTED SKILL

DAY 3	DAY 4	DAY 5
READ: ▲ ■ "Mentor William Walsh," pp. T206–T207 ✓ **COMPREHENSION:** ▲ ■ Captions, p. T207 Sequence, pp. T210–T211 Practice Book, pp. 48, 49 ✓ **DAILY PHONICS,** Digraphs /hw/*wh*, /ch/*ch*, p. T212 **FLUENCY,** p. T214 **FOCUS ON HIGH-FREQUENCY WORDS,** p. T215 **FOCUS ON PHONICS,** p. T215	**VOCABULARY REVIEW,** p. T218 ✓ **DAILY PHONICS:** Digraphs /hw/*wh*, /ch/*ch*, p. T219	**READING ASSESSMENT,** p. T222 Selection Test Conference Decoding Test
RESPOND: ▲ ■ Think About Reading, p. T208 Practice Book, p. 47 **WRITE A POSTER,** p. T209 ✓ **SPELLING:** Write/Proofread, p. R29 Spelling Resource Book, p. 103 ✓ **GRAMMAR, USAGE, MECHANICS:** Practice, p. R31 **ORAL LANGUAGE,** p. T209	**SHARED WRITING** ▲ ■ Description, p. T216 Practice Book, p. 53 ✓ **SPELLING:** Study/Review, p. R29 Spelling Resource Book, p. 161 ✓ **GRAMMAR, USAGE, MECHANICS:** Apply, p. R31 **ORAL LANGUAGE,** p. T217	**WRITING ASSESSMENT,** p. T224 Child Model Children's Writing Rubric ✓ **SPELLING:** Posttest, p. R29 Spelling Resource Book, p. 163 ✓ **GRAMMAR, USAGE, MECHANICS:** Assess, p. R31 **ORAL LANGUAGE,** p. T224
READ ALOUD, p. T215 **GUIDED READING,** pp. R26–R27 **OPTIONAL MATERIALS,** p. T214 Phonics Reader #45: *Slip Slide Baseball Jokes* Phonics Reader #46: *Say It and Smile!*	**READ ALOUD,** p. T221 **GUIDED READING,** pp. R26–R27 **EXTEND VOCABULARY:** Review High-Frequency Words, p. T218 Review Story Words, p. T218 ✓ **STUDY SKILLS:** Test-Taking Strategies, pp. T220–T221	**READ ALOUD,** p. T226 **GUIDED READING,** pp. R26–R27 **INTEGRATED LANGUAGE ARTS:** Add to the Story, p. T225 Act Out a Play, p. T225 Be a Reporter, p. T226 Interview a Character, p. T226
WIGGLEWORKS PLUS CD-ROM Presentation Skills, p. T209 **WIGGLEWORKS PLUS CD-ROM** Magnet Board, p. T212 **WORKSHOP 2,** pp. T227–T230	**WORD PROCESSING** Test-Taking Skills, p. T221 **WORKSHOP 2,** pp. T227–T230	**WIGGLEWORKS PLUS CD-ROM** Speaking Skills, p. T226 **ASSESS WORKSHOP 2**

Weekly Assessment

ASSESSMENT PLANNING

USE THIS CHART TO PLAN YOUR ASSESSMENT OF THE WEEKLY READING OBJECTIVES.

- **Informal Assessment is ongoing and should be used before, during and after reading.**
- **Formal assessment occurs at the end of the week on the selection test.**
- **Note that intervention activities occur throughout the lesson to support children who need extra help with skills.**

ASSESSMENT
Assessment Handbook
SCHOLASTIC

YOU MAY CHOOSE AMONG THE FOLLOWING PAGES IN THE ASSESSMENT HANDBOOK.

- **Informal Assessment**
- **Anecdotal Record**
- **Portfolio Checklist and Evaluation Forms**
- **Self-Assessment**
- **Second-Language Learners**
- **Using Technology to Assess**
- **Test Preparations**

SKILLS AND STRATEGIES

SKILLS AND STRATEGIES	Informal Assessment
COMPREHENSION Sequence	**OBSERVATION p. T181** • Did children identify the first important story events? **QUICKCHECK p. T210** • Can children follow the sequence of events? **CHECK PRACTICE BOOK p. 48** **CONFERENCE p. T222**
DAILY PHONICS *s*-Blends Digraphs *ch, wh*	**OBSERVATION pp. T183, T197** • Did children recognize words with /sn/? • Did children recognize words with digraphs *wh* and *ch?* **CHECK PRACTICE BOOK pp. 45, 51** **DICTATION pp. T177, T213**
VOCABULARY Story Words **actors play story** **troll first goat** High-Frequency **which make**	**OBSERVATION p. T222** • Did children identify Story words? • Did children identify high-frequency words? **CHECK PRACTICE BOOK p. 44**

Formal Assessment	INTERVENTION and Instructional Alternatives	Planning Notes
SELECTION TEST • Questions 1–3 check children's mastery of the key strategy, sequence. UNIT TEST	**If children need help with sequence, then go to:** • **Instructional Alternatives, p. T211** • **Review, p. R46** • **Reteach, p. R57**	
DECODING TEST • See p. T223 SELECTION TEST • Questions 4–7 check children's ability to read words with *s*-blends and digraphs *ch, wh*. UNIT TEST	**If children need help identifying words with *s*-blends, then go to:** • **Reteach, p. R60** **If children need help identifying words with digraphs *ch,wh,* then go to:** • **Intervention, p. T215** • **Review, p. R53** • **Reteach, p. R61**	
SELECTION TEST • Questions 8–10 check children's recall of high-frequency and story words. UNIT TEST	**If children need additional practice with the vocabulary words, then go to:** • **Intervention, p. T215** • **Extend Vocabulary, p. T218** • **Integrated Language Arts, p. T226**	

Technology

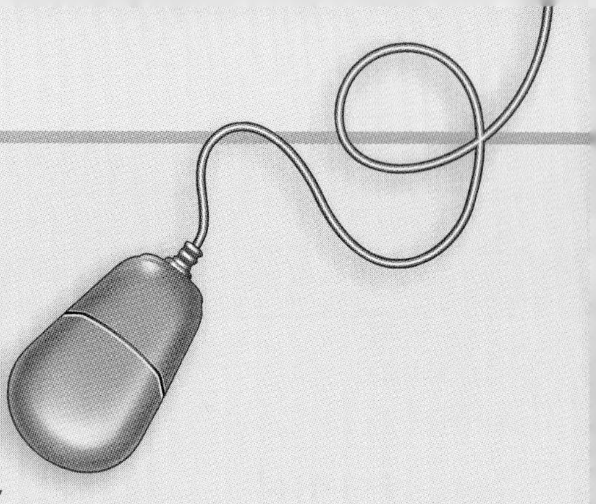

The technology in this lesson helps teachers and students develop the skills they need for the 21st Century. Look for integrated technology activities on every day of instruction.

DAY 1 Comprehension Skills	• Children create a Venn diagram to organize and compare the characteristics of story characters.
DAY 2 Language Development	• Children revise *The Three Billy Goats Gruff* by using the **WiggleWorks Plus** My Book area to add story characters' dialogue.
DAY 3 Presentation Skills	• Children use **WiggleWorks Plus** Placemaker to make a poster advertising the class play.
DAY 4 Test-Taking Skills	• Children use a word processor to create and format answers to a multiple-choice test question.
DAY 5 Speaking Skills	• Children create, record, and illustrate interview questions using the **WiggleWorks Plus** Unit Writer.

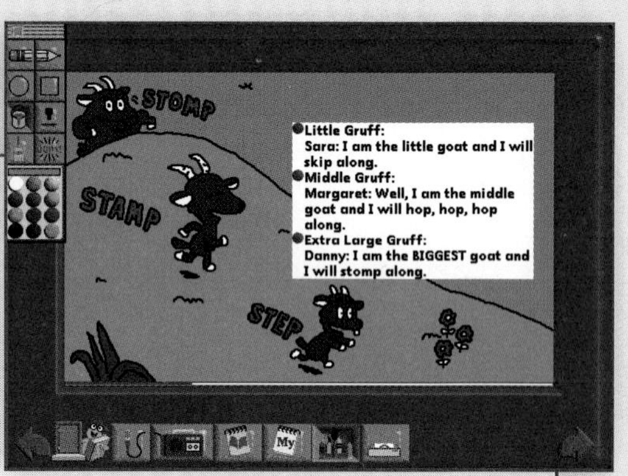
STOMP
STAMP
STEP
Little Gruff:
Sara: I am the little goat and I will skip along.
Middle Gruff:
Margaret: Well, I am the middle goat and I will hop, hop, hop along.
Extra Large Gruff:
Danny: I am the BIGGEST goat and I will stomp along.

WiggleWorks Plus CD-ROM

Untitled (Poster)
clip art
frames
scenes
COME ONE!!
COME ALL!!
WE ARE HAVING A PLAY

WiggleWorks Plus CD-ROM

What was the best part of being in a play?
Was it fun acting like a Gruff?
Record
Stop
Cancel
OK

WiggleWorks Plus CD-ROM

Build Background

The First Grade decides to perform a play of the folk tale The Three Billy Goats Gruff. *Imagine what happens when hurt feelings and stage fright get in the way, all on opening night!*

A DELL YOUNG YEARLING
Starring First Grade
Miriam Cohen
Pictures by Lillian Hoban

Activate Prior Knowledge

DISCUSS IMAGINATION Suggest some ways people use their imaginations. Include solving problems, making up stories, and playing pretend games. Encourage children to tell how they use their imaginations.

RETELL THE STORY Ask children if they know *The Three Billy Goats Gruff.* Have volunteers help you retell the story.

> **Where did the Billy Goats Gruff want to go?**

> **What was keeping them from getting there?**

> **How did they use their imaginations to solve their problem?**

SHARED WRITING *Description*

INTRODUCE Have children imagine the troll in the folk tale *The Three Billy Goats Gruff.* Ask children to describe what the troll looks like and what the troll does. Have children write a sentence or two describing the troll.

DAY 1 OBJECTIVES

CHILDREN WILL:

READ 30 MINUTES

- **Build Background**
- **Vocabulary**
- **Daily Phonics: *s*-Blends**
- ***Starring First Grade*, pp. 74–83**
- **Key Comprehension Skill: Sequence**

WRITE 30 MINUTES

- **Shared Writing: Introduce Writing a Description**
- **Quickwrite: Predict**
- **Spelling: Words With *s*-Blends**
- **Grammar, Usage, Mechanics: Describing Words**
- **Oral Language**

EXTEND SKILLS 30 MINUTES

- **Integrated Curriculum**
- **Read Aloud**
- **Guided Reading**

RESOURCES

- **Practice Book, pp. 44–46**
- **Spelling Resource Book, p. 99**

MODIFY Instruction

ESL/ELD

▲ Choose a classic version of *The Three Billy Goats Gruff* to read aloud to children so they will be familiar with the "story within the story" in this selection. Use the illustrations to introduce key vocabulary, such as *goat, troll, bridge,* and *river,* as well as lesson vocabulary. **(READ ALOUD)**

VOCABULARY
High-Frequency Words

VOCABULARY

HIGH-FREQUENCY

which make

STORY WORDS

actors play
first troll
story goat

Ⓐ TEACH/MODEL

INTRODUCE HIGH-FREQUENCY WORDS Write ***which*** and ***make*** in sentences on the chalkboard. Read the sentences aloud, underline the high-frequency words, and ask children if they recognize them. You may wish to use these sentences:

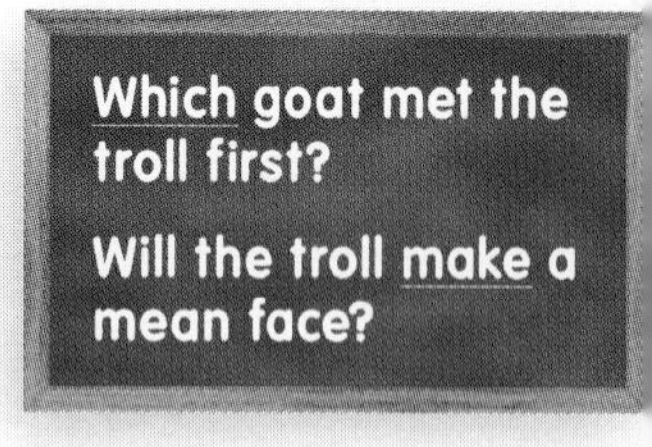
Which goat met the troll first?
Will the troll make a mean face?

Ask volunteers to dictate sentences using the high-frequency words. Add these to the chalkboard.

Ⓑ PRACTICE/APPLY

FOCUS ON SPELLING Write each high-frequency word on a note card. Read each aloud. Then do the following:

ROUTINE

1. Display one card at a time, and ask children to state each word aloud.
2. Have children spell each word aloud.
3. Ask children to write each word in the air as they state aloud each letter. Then have them write each word on a sheet of paper or in their Journals.

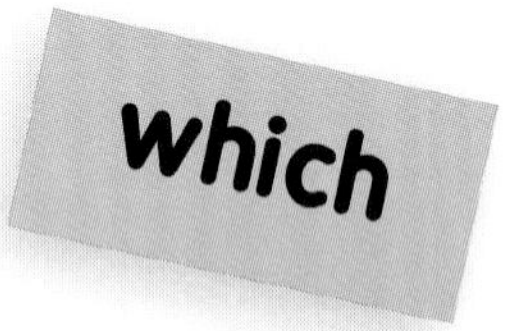
which

make

MAINTAIN VOCABULARY Add the note cards to the **Word Wall.** Then review the following high-frequency words on the wall: ***look, about, some, many, soon, went.***

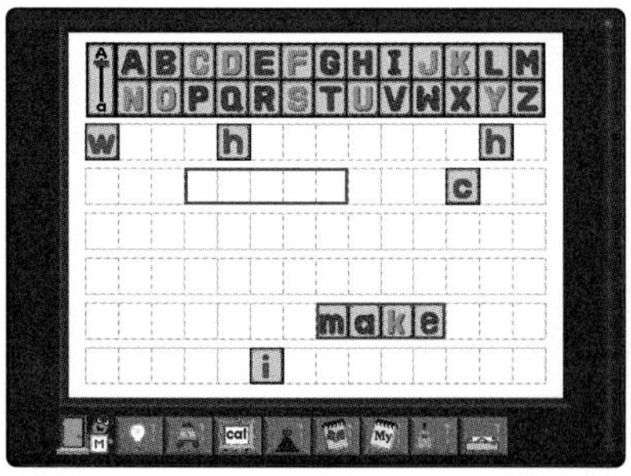

TECHNOLOGY

Have children use the **WiggleWorks Plus** Magnet Board to scramble and rebuild the high-frequency words *which* and *make*.

MODIFY Instruction

ESL/ELD

▲ Use photos or a video of a children's play that shows actors in performance on stage to help English language learners understand the basic story vocabulary. Point to the *stage*, the *curtain*, the *costumes*, and the *actors*. Say: *A play is a story. Actors act out the story on a stage.* **(KEY WORDS)**

GIFTED & TALENTED

✳ Have children write these high-frequency words on index cards, one word per card: ***which, make, look, about, some, many, soon,*** and ***went.*** Working with partners, children can take turns choosing a card, reading the word, and using it in a sentence. **(WORK IN PAIRS/USE VISUALS)**

Story Words

Ⓐ TEACH/MODEL

INTRODUCE STORY WORDS

The story also contains the following story words—***actors, first, story, play, troll, goat.***

- Write these words on the chalkboard, read them aloud, and discuss their meanings if necessary.
- Point out previously taught sound-spelling correspondences, such as ***l***-blends and ***r***-blends.
- If possible, provide a visual clue for each of the words. For example, show a first place ribbon for *first;* show a picture of a play being performed.

Ⓑ PRACTICE/APPLY

BUILD STORY BACKGROUND

Discuss the concept of a play with children.

- Ask children if they have ever seen a play. Talk about plays and compare them to movies or television shows.
- Encourage children to point out the important elements of a play, such as the actors, the props, the stage, and the audience.
- Discuss how actors in a play use their hands and other movements, as well as words, to tell a story.
- Discuss how a folk tale such as *The Three Billy Goats Gruff* could be performed as a play.

WRITE TO READ

- Have children draw pictures of plays being performed. When children have completed their pictures, have them write sentences, using one or more of the story words.

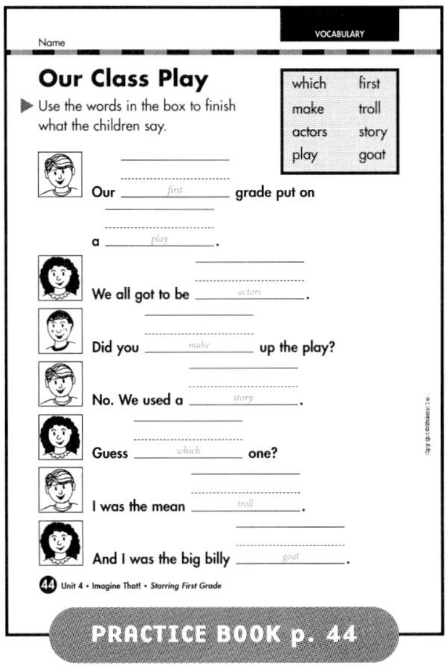

Name VOCABULARY

Our Class Play

▶ Use the words in the box to finish what the children say.

which	first
make	troll
actors	story
play	goat

Our first grade put on a play.

We all got to be actors.

Did you make up the play?

No. We used a story.

Guess which one?

I was the mean troll.

And I was the big billy goat.

44 Unit 4 • Imagine That! • Starring First Grade

PRACTICE BOOK p. 44

The goat is on the bridge.

TIC-TAC-TOE

Draw a tic-tac-toe grid. In each grid space, write a high-frequency or story word. Use all the words at least once.

- Partners can be either **X** or **O**. Have them take turns choosing words in the grid and reading them aloud.
- If children correctly read the words, they can replace them with **X** or **O**. Three **X**'s or **O**'s in a row wins.

troll
first
play
troll
first
first
troll
goat
goat

JOURNAL

Ask children to write a sentence using each **high-frequency word** in their Journals. You might suggest the following sentence starters:

Which ____ ?

We make ____ .

Starring First Grade

SELECTION WORDS With *s*-Blends

scare	stayed
snowflake	stopped
speech	story
stage	stupid
started	

SKILLS TRACE

***s*-Blends** TESTED

Introduce ....p. T182
Practice ....p. T189
Review ....p. R52
Reteach ....p. R60

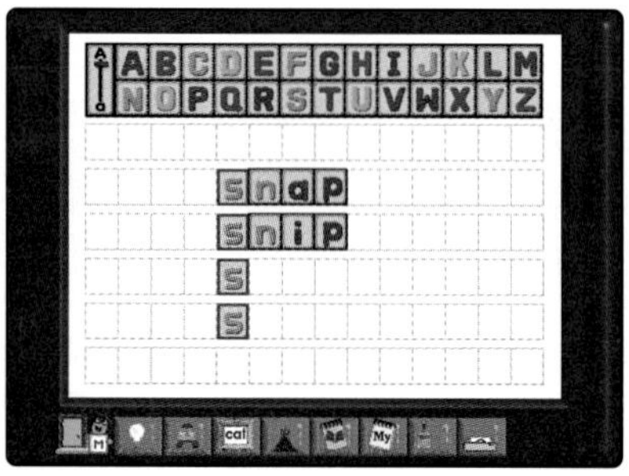
A B C D E F G H I J K L M
N O P Q R S T U V W X Y Z
snap
snip
s
s

TECHNOLOGY

Have children build words with *s*-blends on the Magnet Board.

• Begin with the word *snap*. Have children change one letter to form new words: for example, *slap, snip, snag*.

DAILY PHONICS

s-Blends

A PHONOLOGICAL AWARENESS

RHYME Read aloud "Hey, Diddle, Diddle" from the *Big Book of Rhymes and Rhythms 1B,* pages 12–13. As you read, stress the words with *s*-blends.

- As soon as children are familiar with the rhyme, have them read along with you.
- Isolate the words ***sport*** and ***spoon*** and have children repeat them. Point out the *s*-blend in each word.

The little dog laughed to see such sport,
Hey, Diddle, Diddle
Hey, diddle, diddle, the cat and the fiddle,
The cow jumped over the moon.

***Big Book of Rhymes and Rhythms 1B*, pp. 12–13**

ORAL BLENDING Say the following word parts, and ask children to blend them. Provide corrective feedback and modeling as needed.

/sn/...ap /st/...op /sn/...ail

/sp/...ill /sp/...ort /st/...amp

B CONNECT SOUND-SPELLING

INTRODUCE *s*-BLENDS Write ***snap, stand,*** and ***spill*** on the chalkboard. Underline the consonant blend at the beginning of each word as you say each aloud. Model how to blend the sounds formed by each consonant blend. Then model how to blend the word ***snap.***

THINK ALOUD *I can put the letters* ***s, n, a,*** *and* ***p*** *together to make the word* ***snap.*** *Let's say the sounds slowly as I move my finger under the letters. Listen to the sounds that* ***sn*** *stands for in the word* ***snap****. The sounds of* ***sn*** *are* **/sn/**.

MODIFY Instruction

ESL/ELD

▲ Write the words ***nap, pin, top, lip, pot***. Make sure children understand the meaning of all the words used. Tell them that when you point to a word, they will say it out loud. Then they will add the letter **s** and say the word again. Write each resulting **s**-blend word. **(STEP-BY-STEP)**

EXTRA HELP

■ Kinesthetic learners can build words by holding large index cards with **s** and these words: ***nap, nip, top, lap, pill.*** The child with **s** stands next to a child with a word and says **/s/**. The child with the word reads it aloud. Then they blend the two together to say the new word formed. **(HANDS-ON LEARNING)**

- Ask children to suggest other words that begin with ***sn, st,*** and ***sp.*** List these words on chart paper.

Words With *s*-Blends		
sniff	stop	spin
snake	stack	speed

PHONICS MAINTENANCE Review the following sound-spellings: ***s***-blends ***(sn, st, sp), l***-blends ***(cl, bl, pl), r***-blends ***(br, gr, pr), /ē/ea, ee.*** Say one of these sounds. Have a volunteer write on the chalkboard the spelling or spellings that stand for the sounds. Continue with all the sounds.

C PRACTICE/APPLY

BLEND WORDS To practice using the sound-spellings and to review previous sound-spellings, list the following words and sentences on the chalkboard. Have children read each chorally. Model blending.

nap snap sand stand
place snake friend see
Do not stop reading that book.
Put a stamp on the letter.

DICTATION Dictate the following words for children to spell: ***stop, seat, clap.***

BUILD WORDS Distribute the following letter cards, or have children use their own sets: ***st, sp, sn, a, i, o, t, n, p, ck.*** Allow children time to build words using the letter cards. Children can write their words on separate sheets of paper. **(INDEPENDENT WORK)**

sp i n

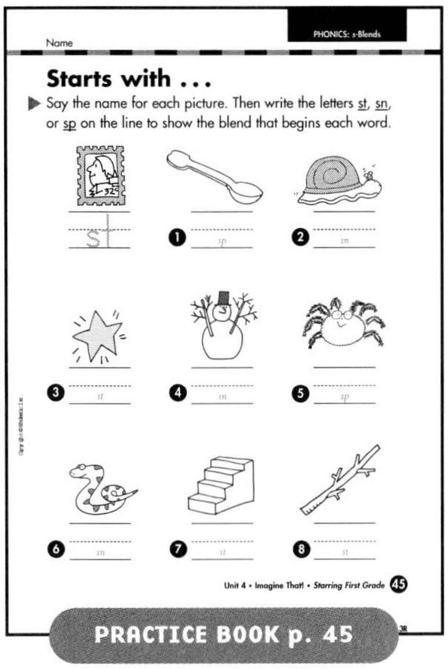
Name
PHONICS: s-Blends
Starts with . . .
Say the name for each picture. Then write the letters st, sn, or sp on the line to show the blend that begins each word.
Unit 4 • Imagine That! • Starring First Grade 45

PRACTICE BOOK p. 45

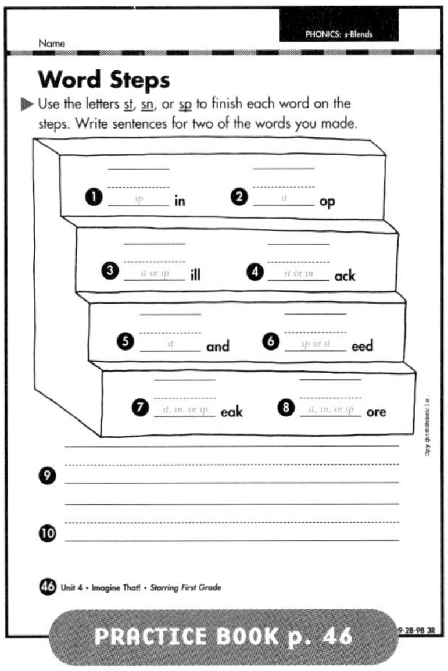
Name
PHONICS: s-Blends
Word Steps
Use the letters st, sn, or sp to finish each word on the steps. Write sentences for two of the words you made.
in
op
ill
ack
and
eed
eak
ore
46 Unit 4 • Imagine That! • Starring First Grade

PRACTICE BOOK p. 46

DECODABLE TEXT

For practice reading decodable text, see ***Scholastic Decodable Reader #50.***

For additional phonics instruction and review, see ***Scholastic Phonics A, pp. 195–196, 201–202.***

STEVE LIKES . . .

Have children sit in a circle for this activity. Each child in turn completes the sentence *Steve likes...* with a word that begins with an *s*-blend—for example, *Steve likes stamps; Steve likes snails; Steve likes spinach.* For a real memory challenge, make the game accumulative. Challenge children to repeat all the things that Steve likes before adding their own *s*-blend words.

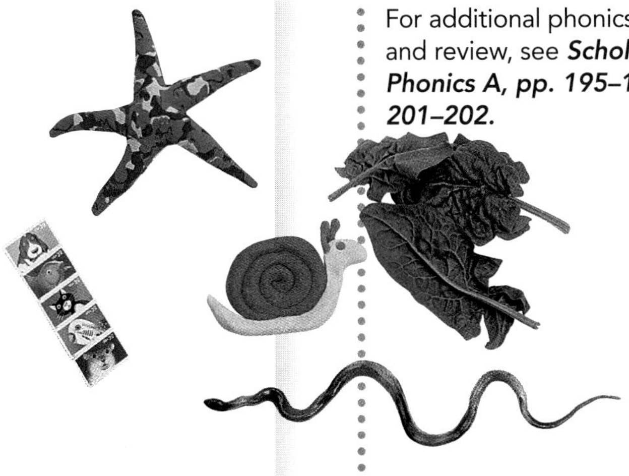

COMPREHENSION

Preview and Predict

Tell children that *Starring First Grade* is about a first-grade class that puts on a play. Encourage children to look at the illustrations on the first few pages.

> **Where does this story take place?**

> **Could this story really happen or is it make-believe?**

Help children make predictions before they read by asking a question:

> **How will the children in this story use their imaginations?**

JOURNAL

Make Predictions

Ask children to write their predictions in their Journals. They might also think of a play they would like to do and record that, too.

Set a Purpose

Discuss with children a purpose for reading. They may want to learn more about how to put on a play. Then have them read page 75 of the story.

74

POPULAR FICTION

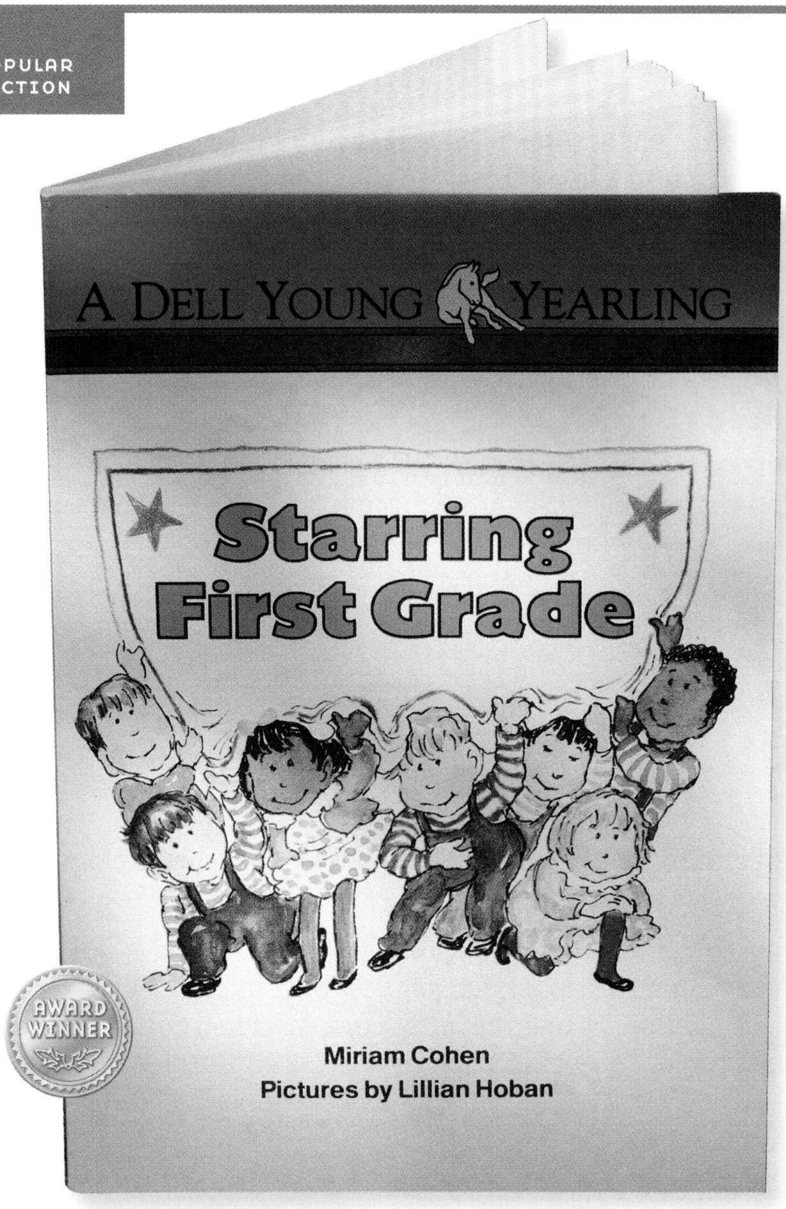
A DELL YOUNG YEARLING
Starring First Grade
AWARD WINNER
Miriam Cohen
Pictures by Lillian Hoban

74

CLASSROOM Management

WHOLE CLASS

On-Level Use the questions, think alouds, and the Skills and Strategies lessons to guide children through a reading of the story.

Below-Level Have children listen to the story on audiocassette before reading so they can familiarize themselves with story vocabulary, characters, and events.

PARTNERS

Above-Level You may wish to have some children read the story independently or with a partner while you read with the rest of the class. Encourage them to take roles and read aloud some of the dialogue in the story. Invite these children to rejoin the group to participate in the story discussion.

75

"First Grade has been asked to put on a play for the school," the teacher said. "Which story should we do?"

75

SKILLS AND STRATEGIES

Revisit the selection for skills instruction.

✓ = Tested Skill

COMPREHENSION

✓ **Sequence** T181

PHONICS

✓ ***s*-Blends** T183

Digraphs *ch, wh* T197

GENRE

Realistic Fiction T203

SMALL GROUP TO WHOLE CLASS

ESL/ELD Have children who need extra help or who are acquiring English listen to the story on the audiocassette prior to the class reading. This will help them to become familiar with the story sequence and vocabulary. Have children do the pre- and post-listening activities. **(AUDIO CLUES)**

COMPREHENSION

1 SEQUENCE

> **Let's keep track of what happens. What happened first in this story? Now what's happening?** *(The teacher said the first grade was going to put on a play and asked what story they wanted to do. The children want to do* The Three Billy Goats Gruff. *Now the teacher is assigning parts.)*

2 MAKE INFERENCES

> **Why do you think everybody wanted to do *The Three Billy Goats Gruff?*** *(Possible answer: Because the troll would be fun to act out.)*

SELF-MONITORING STRATEGY

THINK ALOUD

Sometimes when I see a play, it is the retelling of a story or folk tale I already know. When I watch the play, I try to remember what happens in that story. The first graders in this story are trying to remember the story of The Three Billy Goats Gruff *as they plan for their class play.*

- What story would you like to act out in a play? What character would you want to be in the play?

76

Everybody wanted "The Three Billy Goats Gruff," especially Danny. He said, "I want to be the biggest goat that knocks off the troll's ears!" 1 2

76

MODIFY Instruction

ESL/ELD

▲ Talk about the steps of planning a play. Start a list on the board with these words: *1. Choose play. 2. Assign actors.* Ask children to read or point to the words on pages 76 and 77 that show the class doing these steps. You may want to add to the list as the story goes on to help children follow sequence. **(GRAPHIC DEVICE)**

EXTRA HELP

■ Review the story of *The Three Billy Goats Gruff* with children. Help them identify and count the characters in the traditional story. **(MAKE CONNECTIONS)**

77

The teacher picked Paul to be the troll, and Danny to be the biggest billy goat. She picked Sara and Margaret to be the other two goats. "We will have to make up more parts so everyone can be in the play," she said.

77

MATH

Ask children to complete the **Count Characters** activity on **page R32** where they'll do computations using the characters in the first grade play. The activity will help children use mathematical reasoning.

PLAYS FROM STORIES

Ask children to discuss what story they would like to perform as a play. Have children suggest titles and talk about who in the class might play the parts in each story.

SKILLS AND STRATEGIES

COMPREHENSION

Sequence

TEACH/MODEL

Explain to children that story events happen in a certain order. This order is called sequence. The sequence tells what important things happen first, next, and last in a story.

> **Think about what's happened so far in the story.**

> **Ask yourself what happens next and then read to find out the answer.**

THINK ALOUD *When I read, I keep track of what happens. The first important thing that happens in this story is that the teacher tells the class they are going to put on a play. Then the class decides to do* The Three Billy Goats Gruff.

PRACTICE/APPLY

Work with children to begin recording the sequence of events on a chart like this one:

Events
First
Next
Then
Last

INFORMAL ASSESSMENT

OBSERVATION

Did children:

✔identify the first important story events?

✔identify the next important event in the story?

See pages T200–T201 for a full skills lesson on Sequence.

COMPREHENSION

3 MAKE INFERENCES

> **Why do you think Anna Maria wants a girl snowflake to be part of the play?** *(Anna Maria wants to be a girl snowflake.)*

4 CRITICAL THINKING: EVALUATE

> **What extra parts would you add to *The Three Billy Goats Gruff* so that everyone can be in it?** *(Answers will vary but should support the idea that everyone can be in the play.)*

78

Anna Maria said, "We could have a little girl snowflake that dances. I'm the only one that knows how to do it, because we have snowflakes at my dancing class." 3

78

MODIFY Instruction

ESL/ELD

▲ Say: *Anna Maria wants to be a snowflake in the play.* Some children may not know what a snowflake is. Show pictures of snow, and explain that a flake is one tiny piece of snow. Then ask: *Would you like to be a snowflake in a play? A goat? A troll? A tree? Why?* **(MAKE CONNECTIONS)**

GIFTED & TALENTED

✷ Have children write or record descriptions of the extra parts they create for the play in the computer writing area. **(NOTE TAKING)**

79

Danny said, "*No* snowflakes!"
But the teacher said Anna Maria could be one. 4

ORAL LANGUAGE

Have children do a dramatic reading of pages 75–80. Ask volunteers to take the roles of the teacher, Danny, Anna Maria, and Willy. Encourage children to say the lines with expression, the way they think that characters would say them. When they have practiced, they can tape-record their readings for the class.

MENTOR

Ask children to imagine how William Walsh might help the first-graders get ready for their play. Brainstorm the things he might do.

DAILY PHONICS

s-Blends

CONNECT SOUND-SPELLING

Teach/Model Remind children that some words begin with ***s*** and another consonant letter.

- Write the word ***snap*** on the chalkboard and read it aloud, emphasizing the beginning sounds **/sn/**. Have a volunteer underline the beginning consonant letters ***sn.***

Phonics Maintenance Review the following sound-spellings: ***s***-blends, ***l***-blends, ***r***-blends, **/ē/** ***ea, ee.***

PRACTICE/APPLY

Blend Words Write these words on the chalkboard: ***nap, nail, pin, pot, top, tone.***

- Have children read them aloud.
- Ask a volunteer to add ***s*** to the beginning of the word.
- Say **/s/** and the word. Have children blend them together to say the new word.

Ask children to find the word ***snowflake*** on pages 78 and 79.

- Write ***snowflake*** on the chalkboard. Ask a volunteer to read the word and underline the ***s***-blend ***sn.***
- Ask children to look for other words that begin with the ***s***-blend ***sn.***

INFORMAL ASSESSMENT
OBSERVATION

Did children:

✔ recognize words with **/sn/**?
✔ blend words with **/sn/**?

COMPREHENSION

5 MAKE INFERENCES

> **How do you think Willy feels about being a tree? Do you think Willy will make a good tree? Why or why not?** *(Possible answer: Willy is not happy about being a tree. He may not be a good tree since he is not happy about being a tree.)*

6 PROBLEM/SOLUTION

> **Things usually happen in a story because a character has a problem to solve. What is the problem in this story?** *(Jim doesn't want to be a tree. He wants to be the troll.)*

80

"We need some trees to stand by the bridge," said the teacher. "Jim, you'd make a good, strong tree. And George, and Louie, and Willy, and Sammy too."

"Well, somebody has got to be the trees," Willy said to Sammy. 5

80

MODIFY Instruction

ESL/ELD

▲ Make sure children understand that Jim has a problem. Ask: *Which children are going to be trees? Does Jim want to be a tree? Why not? Is Jim happy or unhappy? What would you do if you were Jim?* **(GUIDED QUESTIONS)**

EXTRA HELP

■ Use a character map to help children organize information about trolls. Write ***troll*** in a circle on the chalkboard. Using the information on page 81 and their prior knowledge, have children make suggestions about what a troll looks like and what a troll does. **(GRAPHIC DEVICE)**

81

But Jim didn't want to be a tree. He wanted to be the troll and make awful faces and scare everybody. He wanted to shout, "Who is going over *my* bridge?" 6

81

SOCIAL STUDIES

Ask children to do the **Cooperation!** activity on **page R33** where they'll work together to make a cooperative plan for choosing roles in a play. Children will work cooperatively to come up with a reasonable plan.

TEACHER TIP

"Acting out stories, the way Miriam Cohen's first-graders do, is a fantastic way to help children 'own' a story. Not only is it a great way for children to master story sequence, it helps them understand the structure of stories and how dialogue works."

DAILY PHONICS

Vowel /ē/ *ee, ea*

CONNECT SOUND-SPELLING

Teach/Model Remind children that the letters ***ee*** and ***ea*** stand for **/ē/** as in ***see*** and ***read.***

- Write the words ***see*** and ***read*** as column heads on chart paper. Have a volunteer circle ***ee*** and ***ea.***

PRACTICE/APPLY

Blend Words Write the following words on index cards: ***feed, feel, green, seem, teach, clean, team, mean.***

- Display the cards in random order.

feed	clean	feel
green	seem	teach
team	mean	

- Have a volunteer read the word, identify the letters that spell **/ē/**, then tape the word under the word with the same spelling for **/ē/**—***see*** or ***read***.
- Ask children to find more words with **/ē/** spelled ***ee*** or ***ea*** on pages 80 and 81 of the selection. ***(need, trees, teacher, tree)***

IF children need more support with vowel **/ē/ ee, ea,**

THEN see page **R50.**

COMPREHENSION

7 SEQUENCE

> **What does Jim do when they start to rehearse the play?** *(He starts singing when he's not supposed to.)*

8 DRAW CONCLUSIONS

> **Paul gets mad when Jim's singing interrupts him. Why did Jim start singing when Paul was saying his lines?** *(Jim starts to sing when Paul is saying his lines because he does not want to be a tree.)*

9 MAKE INFERENCES

> **What do you think the teacher means when she says to Jim, "It's not like you to act this way"?** *(She means that Jim is not usually uncooperative.)*

INTERVENTION TIP

Character

Some children may not understand why Jim starts singing. Help them recall that Jim doesn't want to be a tree; he wants to be the troll. Jim is angry and jealous of Paul's role and he makes noise when Paul is trying to rehearse his part. Ask children if the way they usually act has ever changed because of how they were feeling.

OPTION You may end the first day's reading here or have children continue reading the entire selection.

82

They began to rehearse. Suddenly, the tree that was Jim started singing, "This Land Is Your Land." 7
"A singing tree! That's stupid," Anna Maria said.

82

MODIFY Instruction

ESL/ELD

▲ Help children infer what the teacher means. Ask: *Why do you think Jim is singing? Does Jim usually act this way?* Use the intervention tip to help English language learners with this question. **(PARAPHRASE)**

EXTRA HELP

■ To help children understand how Jim is feeling, ask them if they have ever wanted to do something and couldn't. Ask:

- *How did that make you feel?*
- *What did you do to show your feelings?* **(GUIDED QUESTIONS)**

83

Paul was mad. "He's interrupting me!" he complained. **8**

"It's not like you to act this way, Jim," the teacher said. **9**

83

CONNECTING TO SONGS

Play a recording of the Woody Guthrie song "This Land Is Your Land" or sing it with children. Words and music are found in *The Reader's Digest Children's Songbook*.

TECHNOLOGY

Comprehension Skills Guide the class to use a familiar art program to create a Venn diagram. Have children label one circle *Jim* and the other *Paul*, and place words describing the boys in the proper areas of the circles. Discuss with children what is different about the boys and what is the same.

Quickwrite

PREDICT

Ask children to write about the children in the story. Do they remind them of children they know? They may also refine the predictions they made before reading and predict what will happen next.

DAILY LANGUAGE PRACTICE

SPELLING

DAY 1:

Administer the Pretest for Words With **s**-Blends. **See page R28.**

GRAMMAR, USAGE, MECHANICS

DAY 1:

Teach and Model Describing Words. **See page R30.**

ORAL LANGUAGE

We found a big sail in the garden

(We found a big snail in the garden.)

DAY 1 WRAP-UP

READ ALOUD *To develop children's oral vocabularies, spend five to ten minutes reading from a selection of your choice.*

GUIDED READING *Meet with the* ***green*** *and* ***yellow*** *reading groups and assign Independent Center activities.* ***See pages R26–R27.***

COMPREHENSION

DAY 2 OBJECTIVES

CHILDREN WILL:

READ 30 MINUTES

- ***Starring First Grade*, pp. 84–101**
- **Mentor Profile: William Walsh, Muralist, pp. 102–103**
- **Key Comprehension Skill: Sequence**
- **Daily Phonics: Digraphs *ch, wh***

WRITE 30 MINUTES

- **Shared Writing: Prewrite a Description**
- **Spelling: Words with *s*-Blends**
- **Grammar, Usage, Mechanics: Describing Words**
- **Oral Language**

EXTEND SKILLS 30 MINUTES

- **Integrated Curriculum**
- **Read Aloud**
- **Guided Reading**

RESOURCES

- **Practice Book, p. 53**
- **Spelling Resource Book, pp. 100–102**

Reread

You may wish to have children orally reread the first part of the story before beginning Day 2 reading. Make sure children read with appropriate phrasing and attention to punctuation.

10 SUMMARIZE

> **What has happened so far in the story?** *(The first grade is putting on a play of* The Three Billy Goats Gruff. *Jim wanted to be the troll, but the teacher gave that part to Paul. When they start rehearsing, Jim sings and interrupts Paul.)*

84

10 Jim didn't sing anymore, but he began telling the others what to do. And he kept telling Paul how to be the troll.

"Make him be quiet!" Paul shouted.

Finally, the teacher said, "Jim, go and sit down."

84

MODIFY Instruction

ESL/ELD

▲ Go back through the story to summarize what has happened so far. Be sure children understand that now the children are rehearsing, or practicing the play. Ask if any of the children practice anything at home, such as a musical instrument. **(MAKE CONNECTIONS)**

GIFTED & TALENTED

✷ The teacher tells Jim, "It's not like you to act this way." Challenge children to read Miriam Cohen's other stories about First Grade to find out what Jim is usually like. Then have them brainstorm words that describe how Jim usually is. **(MAKE CONNECTIONS)**

85

Jim began talking to himself. "I might not even be here for the play. I'll probably be going to Disney World."

Anna Maria heard him. She said, "You're just making that up."

"You don't know what my father said!" Jim shouted.

85

DAILY PHONICS

r-Blends and *l*-Blends

CONNECT SOUND-SPELLING

Teach/Model Write the words ***tree*** and ***class*** on the chalkboard and read them aloud. Have a volunteer underline the letters ***tr*** and ***cl*** and blend them.

PRACTICE/APPLY

Blend Words Ask children to find the word ***troll*** on page 84 and ***play*** on page 85.

- Write ***troll*** and ***play*** on the chalkboard. Underline the consonant blend in each word. Ask children to suggest other words that begin with ***tr*** and ***pl.*** List them on the chalkboard.
- Encourage children to look for other words in the story with *r*-blends and *l*-blends. Add these words to the list on the chalkboard. (***bridge, Friday, principal, grade, bright, trees, trip-trop, fright, troll, grinned, cloth, played, classes, play, places***)
- Using a pointer, have children take turns pointing to a word on the chalkboard, reading it aloud, and then calling on a classmate to use the word in a sentence.

VISUAL LITERACY

Ask children to look back at the illustrations in the story. Help children recognize that often the picture shows who is speaking. On page 85, you know that the little boy is talking because his mouth is open.

TEACHER TIP

"Composing stories in comic strip form and giving characters speech balloons can help children understand how the pictures, text, and dialogue are connected."

COMPREHENSION

11 PLOT

> **What would you tell someone about the plot or story events in *Starring First Grade?* How has the teacher used her imagination to solve the problem in the story?** *(The teacher uses her imagination to solve the problem when she asks Jim to be the river under the troll's bridge.)*

12 PLOT

> **There is still a problem. What is it?** *(Paul is still mad at Jim.)*

13 DRAW CONCLUSIONS

> **How do you think the teacher's idea changes the story?** *(Jim is happy to be the river, and he stops bothering the other children.)*

86

The teacher came over. "Jim, how would you like to be the river that goes under the troll's bridge? You could hide under this blue cloth and move around so it looks like water." 11

86

MODIFY Instruction

ESL/ELD

▲ Help children follow the plot. Say: *Look at the picture on page 87. Is Jim happy now? Does he like being the river? Are Paul and Jim friends again? Look for words or phrases that give you the answers to these questions. When you find them, read them to me.* **(PICTURE/CONTEXT CLUES)**

GIFTED & TALENTED

✷ Challenge children to use their imaginations to dramatically represent a river, a tree, or some other inanimate objects. Children may want to add words or sounds to make their representations more expressive. **(ACT IT OUT)**

87

Jim stayed under the cloth and stopped bothering the other actors. But Paul was still mad at him. 12 13

87

THE ARTS

Ask children to complete the **Design a Set** activity on **page R33.** Children will design and build a miniature stage set for *The Three Billy Goats Gruff* based on the selection's illustrations. Children will learn how to create a set for a play.

VISUAL LITERACY

To help children recall the sequence of story events, complete a story map as they reread *Starring First Grade. (See p. R87 for the Story Map form.)*

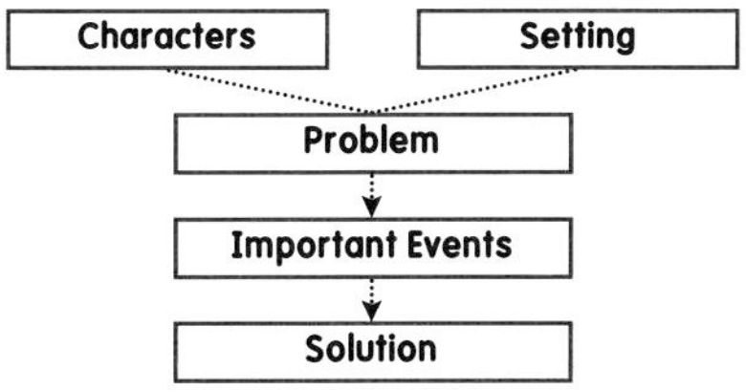
Characters
Setting
Problem
Important Events
Solution

DAILY PHONICS

Final *e*

CONNECT SOUND-SPELLING

Teach/Model Demonstrate how final ***e*** affects the vowel sound in a word.

- Write ***hid*** on the chalkboard and read it aloud. Add final ***e*** and read the new word ***hide.***

PRACTICE/APPLY

Blend Words Ask children to find the word ***hide*** on page 86.

- Have children suggest words that rhyme with ***hide.*** Write these words on the chalkboard, pointing out the final ***e*** in each one. ***(ride, side, tide, wide)***
- Have children locate two more final ***e*** words with long vowels on pages 86 and 87. ***(came, like)***

Write the following words on the chalkboard: ***fin, mad, not, cap, hat, rod.***

- Have children read each word aloud.
- Have a volunteer add final ***e*** and read the new word aloud.
- Help children compare the vowel sound in the original word and the new word.

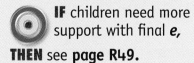

IF children need more support with final ***e,*** **THEN** see **page R49.**

COMPREHENSION

14 MAKE INFERENCES

> **Paul tells Jim that he's bossy. Paul doesn't talk to Jim for one whole week. Why do you think Paul is acting this way?** *(He's still mad at Jim for interrupting and trying to tell him how to be a troll.)*

88

After school, Paul said, "You think you're the boss of everybody!"

88

MODIFY Instruction

ESL/ELD

▲ Ask: *How does Jim look on pages 88 and 89?* (sad) Ask children why they think he looks sad. Direct them to think about Paul's feelings. Ask: *Why is Paul mad at Jim? Do you get mad when your friends act "bossy" with you?* **(VISUAL CLUES)**

EXTRA HELP

■ Have volunteers act out what Jim did to make Paul so mad at him. Children can perform the events for the class. **(ACT IT OUT)**

89

THE
3 BILLY GOATS
GRUFF
STARRING
FIRST GRADE

He didn't talk to Jim for a whole week,
not even on Friday, the day of the play. 14

89

WORD STUDY

Have children locate the contraction *didn't* on page 89. Write *didn't* on the chalkboard. Remind children that it is made up of two smaller words. Ask children what smaller words make up the word *didn't* (*did not*). Emphasize that the apostrophe replaces the letter *o* in *not* when the two words are combined.

TECHNOLOGY

Language Development Have children add trees and water as characters in *The Three Billy Goats Gruff.* Using the My Book area on **WiggleWorks Plus**, children can add pictures of trees and color the water, and then create dialogue for them.

COMPREHENSION

15 SETTING

> **The setting has changed. Where are the characters, and what day is it?** *(The characters are in the school auditorium because it is Friday, the day of the play.)*

16 PLOT

> **This is the big moment the whole story has been leading up to. What has happened with the events, characters, and problems so that they arrive at this point?** *(The first graders are about to perform their play.)*

90

On Friday the school band played as hard as it could. All the classes marched in. 15

90

MODIFY Instruction

ESL/ELD

▲ Help establish the new setting with multi-level questions: Show me the stage. Point to the school band. Do you see the first grade class? Are they on the stage or off the stage? What are they going to do today? **(MULTI-LEVEL QUESTIONS)**

EXTRA HELP

■ To reinforce children's understanding of the sequence of events, have children turn back to the beginning of the story. Guide them as they retell in their own words what happens on each page. **(RETELL)**

91

on the auditorium was full of people waiting
r the play to begin. The principal made a long
eech about the play. 16

91

VISUAL LITERACY

Read page 91 aloud. Ask children who is waiting for the play to begin. Ask them who they think would come to see them in a school play. Guide children to understand that the people in the auditorium are probably parents and grandparents of the children in the first grade.

ORAL LANGUAGE

According to the story, the principal made a long speech about the play. Have children share ideas about what she might have said in this speech. Encourage volunteers to pretend to be the principal and give the speech she might have given. Remind children to use their hands as they speak.

COMPREHENSION

17 Make Inferences

> **Where is the first grade now? Why is their teacher whispering?** *(The first grade is backstage. The teacher is whispering because she doesn't want the audience to hear her.)*

18 Draw Conclusions

> **The play is about to begin. How do you think the first-grade children feel right now?** *(They are probably excited and maybe a little nervous.)*

92

Backstage, the teacher whispered, 17

92

MODIFY Instruction

ESL/ELD

▲ Help children to draw conclusions about the first grade children's feelings. First remind them who is playing each part: *Find Jim. Which part is he playing? Does he think he will be a good river? Where is Paul? How does he feel?* **(GUIDED QUESTIONS)**

GIFTED & TALENTED

✷ The curtain is going up in one minute! Challenge children to work with a partner and make up their own ending to the story. Remind them that the ending must somehow solve the story's big problem: Paul is still mad at Jim. Something needs to happen that will make Paul and Jim friends again. **(INNOVATE)**

93

"Get ready, First Grade. The curtain is going up in one minute!" 18

93

VISUAL LITERACY

Have children look closely at the first graders in the picture. Everyone is smiling in the picture except for Sara and Paul. Ask children why they think Sara is peeking out at the audience and why Paul has a funny look on his face. Then ask children to predict what they think will happen when the curtain opens.

DAILY PHONICS

Digraphs *ch* and *wh*

CONNECT SOUND-SPELLING

Teach/Model Review that sometimes two consonants together stand for one sound.

- Write ***which*** on the chalkboard. Point out that ***which*** begins and ends with a consonant digraph.
- Read the word aloud, stressing the initial sound **/hw/** and the final sound **/ch/.** Have a volunteer circle the digraphs ***wh*** and ***ch.***

Phonics Maintenance Review the following sound-spellings: digraphs ***ch*** and ***wh***, ***s***-blends, ***l***-blends, and ***r***-blends.

PRACTICE/APPLY

Blend Words Write ***ch*** and ***wh*** on letter cards.

- Say these words aloud and hold up the digraph indicated: ***care (ch); hair (wh); win (ch); kite (wh); pick (ch); high (wh).***
- Have children substitute the digraph for the beginning sound and say the new word. ***(chair; where; chin; white; chick; why)***

INFORMAL ASSESSMENT
OBSERVATION

Did children:

✔ recognize words with ***wh*** and ***ch***?

✔ blend words with ***wh*** and ***ch***?

See pages T212–T213 for a full skills lesson on digraphs ***ch*** and ***wh***.

COMPREHENSION

19 SEQUENCE

> **It's time for the play to begin. What happens first? Then what happens?** *(The troll waited under the bridge. The trees were in their places. The snowflake twirled. Sara started across the bridge, but Paul the troll didn't say anything.)*

20 DRAW CONCLUSIONS

> **Isn't Paul supposed to say his lines now? Why is Paul quiet? How do you think he is feeling right now?** *(The troll is supposed to jump up and look scary and ask who is crossing his bridge. Paul is quiet because he is so nervous.)*

94

Then the curtain went up. On the bright stage, the troll waited under the bridge. The trees were in their places. The snowflake twirled about near the river.

94

MODIFY Instruction

ESL/ELD

▲ Have children imagine they are watching the play. Ask them to describe the sequence of events. Model if necessary: *The curtain is up. Paul is the troll. He is under the bridge. He looks nervous. Jim is the river. He is hiding under the blue cloth. Paul does not talk.* **(SUMMARIZE)**

EXTRA HELP

■ To help children understand the problem in the story, invite two volunteers to act out what was supposed to happen when the troll hears the first goat go over his bridge. Then have another volunteer read aloud page 95 and discuss what the problem is. **(ACT IT OUT)**

95

ara started across the bridge, Trip-trop, rip-trop. But Paul didn't say anything. He ust stared at the lights and people. 19 20

95

WORD STUDY

The story says that the snowflake *twirled*. What did the snowflake do? Some dictionaries say that *twirl* is a blend of two words: *twist* and *whirl*. When someone or something *twirls*, it spins around in a circle. Ask children if this is what the snowflake does. Have them demonstrate how to *twirl*.

SCIENCE

Have children complete the **Build Model Bridges** activity on **page R32** where they experiment with different materials to build model bridges that can support a small amount of weight. They will build bridges and test their ability to hold weight using balls of clay.

COMPREHENSION

21 MAKE INFERENCES

> **Why do you think the teacher whispers, "Who is going across my bridge?"** *(She is whispering Paul's line so he will hear her and say it aloud for the audience.)*

22 PLOT

> **This is an exciting part of the story. What is the problem?** *(Paul has stage fright and can't say his line.)*

23 SEQUENCE

> **I'm busy keeping track of what's happening. First Paul didn't talk when he was supposed to. What happened after that? Then what happened?** *(Jim pretends that the river can speak to the troll and makes up lines for the river to say.)*

24 MAKE PREDICTIONS

> **What do you think Paul will do next?** *(Possible answer: Paul will start to speak and act out his part.)*

96

The teacher whispered, "Who is going across my bridge?" But Paul just stared and stared. "He's got stage fright," the people said to each other. It was awful! Nobody could think what to do. 21 22

96

MODIFY Instruction

ESL/ELD

▲ Help children understand what *stage fright* is. Write *frightened* and *scared* on the board. Say, *Paul feels scared on the stage. He can't talk. He has stage fright.* Ask children to tell about a time that they have been scared. **(STEP-BY-STEP)**

EXTRA HELP

■ Some children may have difficulty understanding what *stage fright* is. Ask children to tell about a time when they were in front of a group of people and were so scared that they couldn't talk. Encourage them to tell how they felt. **(GUIDED QUESTIONS)**

97

Then the river lumped up and said, "Somebody is going over your bridge, Mr. Troll. They are going trip-trop, trip-trop." 23 24

97

CULTURAL CONNECTION

Stories about trolls were first told long ago in Scandinavia, the name for a part of northwest Europe. Just as in the story, it was thought that Scandinavian trolls liked to scare people. It was said they lived in castles or mountains and only came out at night, or else they'd turn into stone.

CONNECTING TO THEME

Call attention to how Jim speaks up at the right moment and says just the right thing. You might ask:

- How is Jim using his imagination?
- How does Jim help others when he uses his imagination?

SKILLS AND STRATEGIES

COMPREHENSION

Plot

TEACH/MODEL

Remind children that the plot is the plan or the series of events that the character or characters go through. Important events, problems, and solutions provide the pattern for the plot. To determine the plot:

> **read the story and think about the series of events.**

> **ask what problem the character or characters have.**

> **read to find out how the character or characters solve the problem.**

PRACTICE/APPLY

Have children review the story and recall the important events in the story. Identify the problem in the story and encourage children to predict how it will be solved. Then have children complete the story map on page **R87**.

IF children need more support with Plot,

THEN use the review lesson on page **R45**.

COMPREHENSION

25 MAKE INFERENCES

> **Paul is talking! Why do you think he finally started speaking? How do you think Paul feels about Jim now?**
(Possible answer: Paul is comfortable talking to his friend Jim, so when Jim, as the river, says something to him, Paul can answer back, as the troll. Paul probably feels very grateful to Jim for helping him.)

26 PLOT

> **How does Paul get over his stage fright? Why is this an important event in the story?**
(Jim helps Paul get over his stage fright by speaking to him. It is an important event because Jim and Paul had been fighting up until now and now they are not fighting anymore. Also, the play is able to go on after Jim helps Paul get over his stage fright and say his line.)

98

25

"Yes!" shouted Paul. "Somebody is going across my bridge and they better watch out! I'll eat them up!" Then they all did their parts perfectly. 26

98

MODIFY Instruction

ESL/ELD

▲ Ask children to begin on page 83, find a picture of Paul on every page, and describe how he is feeling. Help children tell why he's feeling the way he is. Ask, *Has Paul been happy or unhappy since the play began? How does Paul feel on this page (98)? Do you think he will be friends with Jim now?* **(PICTURE CLUES)**

GIFTED & TALENTED

✴ Challenge partners to create a dialogue between Jim and Paul. Children can discuss the boys' feelings for each other before the play and how this moment, when Jim helps Paul get over his stage fright, changed the way they were feeling. **(INNOVATE)**

99

At the end, Danny caught the troll and knocked off his ears.

ORAL LANGUAGE

Invite children to act out *The Three Billy Goats Gruff* just as the first grade did. The child playing Paul should pretend to have stage fright, and the child playing Jim should say what the river says to the troll. Remind children to speak with expression and to use their hands and other movements when speaking.

TEACHER TIP

"Props always help when children are acting out whole stories or scenes from stories. I recommend keeping a dress-up box, particularly one that contains such things as scarves and lengths of fabric with the potential to be almost anything."

SKILLS AND STRATEGIES

GENRE

Realistic Fiction

TEACH/MODEL

Help children understand that in realistic fiction, the characters, events, and settings could happen in real life.

THINK ALOUD *When I want to know if a story is realistic fiction, I think about what's real and could happen in real life.* Starring First Grade *is about a class that puts on a play. Even though the story did not actually happen, I know that it could happen in real life. That's how I know that this story is realistic fiction.*

PRACTICE/APPLY

Encourage children to participate in a conversation about what makes *Starring First Grade* realistic fiction.

COMPREHENSION

27 **SEQUENCE**

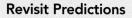

> **First, Paul can't say a thing. Next, Jim uses his imagination to say just the right thing. What happened after that? What's the last thing to happen in the story?** *(They all did their parts perfectly. Everyone cheered. The teacher pushed Jim and Paul in front for a bow.)*

28 **DRAW CONCLUSIONS**

> **Before the play started, Paul was mad at Jim. Is he still mad at Jim? How do you know how Paul's feelings have changed?** *(Paul is not still mad at Jim. They grin and grin at each other when they take their bows.)*

JOURNAL
Revisit Predictions

Ask children to look back at their predictions and record how they were or were not confirmed by the end of the story.

100

Everybody cheered for First Grade. 27

100

MODIFY Instruction

ESL/ELD

▲ Help children recall story sequence by reading the story aloud again. Before turning each page, ask children to tell you one main idea. Write key words on the board. Go through the sequence again with the board list, asking for sentences from volunteers. **(STEP-BY-STEP)**

EXTRA HELP

■ Help children understand how Paul and Jim became friends again.

- Ask children if they have ever had a problem with a friend the way that Jim and Paul did.
- Encourage them to talk about the problem and how they solved it. **(GUIDED QUESTIONS)**

101

Their teacher pushed Jim and Paul in front for a bow.
And they grinned and grinned at each other. 28

101

FAMILY READING

Suggest that families try echo-reading with the section of the story that children enjoyed the most. Families should read one page aloud and have the child read the same page back. Tell families to give guidance and support while their children read. **(10-MINUTE LITERACY BYTE)**

Description
SHARED WRITING

PREWRITE Encourage children to participate in a conversation about their favorite characters in *Starring First Grade*. Ask them to think about what each character looks like, what they like to do, how they act, and what makes them happy. Children will be writing a character description of themselves. To help them get ready, ask children to complete the character web about themselves on **Practice Book page 53.**

DAILY LANGUAGE PRACTICE

SPELLING

DAY 2: Practice Words With *s*-Blends. **See page R28.**

GRAMMAR, USAGE, MECHANICS

DAY 2: Practice Describing Words. **See page R30.**

ORAL LANGUAGE

Do not slap on the sick.
(Do not slip on the stick.)

DAY 2 WRAP-UP

READ ALOUD *Spend five to ten minutes reading from a selection of your choice.*

GUIDED READING *To extend reading, meet with the* ***red*** *and* ***blue*** *reading groups and assign Independent Center activities.* ***See pages R26–R27.***

COMPREHENSION

DAY 3 OBJECTIVES

CHILDREN WILL:

READ 30 MINUTES

- **"Mentor Profile: William Walsh," pp. 102–103**
- **Assess Comprehension**
- **Key Comprehension Skill: Sequence**
- **Daily Phonics: Digraphs *ch, wh***

WRITE 30 MINUTES

- **Respond: Write a Poster**
- **Spelling: Words with *s*-Blends**
- **Grammar, Usage, Mechanics: Describing Words**
- **Oral Language**

EXTEND SKILLS 30 MINUTES

- **Integrated Curriculum**
- **Read Aloud**
- **Guided Reading**

RESOURCES

- **Practice Book, pp. 47–49, 51, 52**
- **Spelling Resource Book, p. 103**

Preview

Ask children to read the title and study the picture.

1 SEQUENCE

> **What step do William Walsh and the children take after they decide what their mural will be about?** *(Answers should reflect children's understanding of the steps in the process of creating a mural.)*

102

MENTOR

Read Together!

William Walsh

Muralist

William Walsh uses his imagination to make murals. Murals are large paintings that tell stories.

1

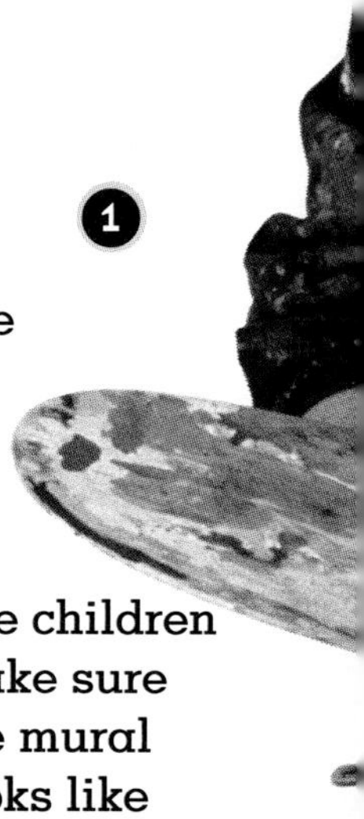

Everyone chooses the paint for the mural.

The children make sure the mural looks like their sketch.

102

MODIFY Instruction

ESL/ELD

▲ Help children read the words next to the photographs. Ask English language learners to work with a partner to match words to pictures. They can ask each other questions, for example, "*Show me a person choosing paint.*" **(PICTURE CLUES)**

EXTRA HELP

■ Before reading the profile, show the mentor video to the children again. **(MAKE CONNECTIONS)**

103

CREATIVE EXPRESSION
Everyone has stories to tell. William Walsh tells his stories using paints, brushes, and lots of imagination.
103

SKILLS AND STRATEGIES

COMPREHENSION

Captions

TEACH/MODEL

Guide children to recognize that the words near the photographs are called captions. These captions give information about the pictures.

THINK ALOUD *I can learn a lot about William Walsh by looking at the photographs on these pages. I learn even more by reading the words, or captions, near these photos.*

PRACTICE/APPLY

Ask children to read the captions aloud and describe the photographs.

Have children write notes that serve as captions for drawings and other work that is displayed in the classroom; for example, "This picture was made by Kenji."

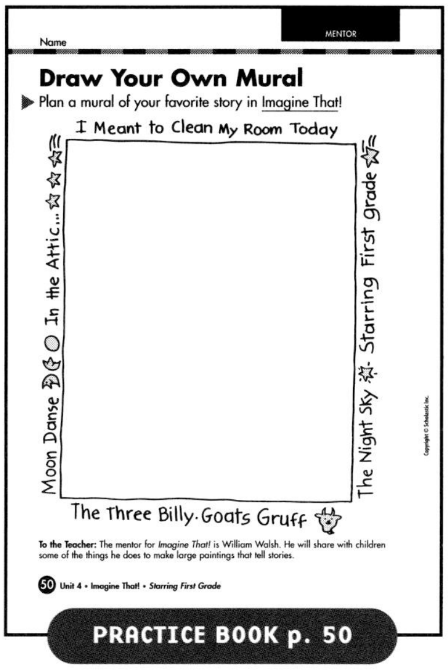
Name
MENTOR

Draw Your Own Mural

▶ Plan a mural of your favorite story in Imagine That!

I Meant to Clean My Room Today
In the Attic...
Starring First Grade
Moon Danse
The Night Sky
The Three Billy-Goats Gruff

To the Teacher: The mentor for *Imagine That!* is William Walsh. He will share with children some of the things he does to make large paintings that tell stories.

50 Unit 4 • Imagine That! • *Starring First Grade*

PRACTICE BOOK p. 50

CONNECTING TO MAGAZINES

Provide copies of children's magazines such as *Click*, and have children compare the format of magazine features with the format of this mentor profile. Discuss how pictures and captions are used in the magazine to create interest and give information.

COMPREHENSION

Think About Reading

Below are the **answers** to the *Think About Reading* questions.

1. *Everyone wants to put on* The Three Billy Goats Gruff.

2. *She wants Jim to feel special. She also wants him to stop bothering the other actors.*

3. *Jim adds a new line and helps Paul get over his stage fright.*

4. *They grin at each other because they are friends again. They are also happy that the play is over.*

5. *Both groups of children work together. Both tell a story: one in a play and the other in a painting.* **(PAIRED SELECTION)**

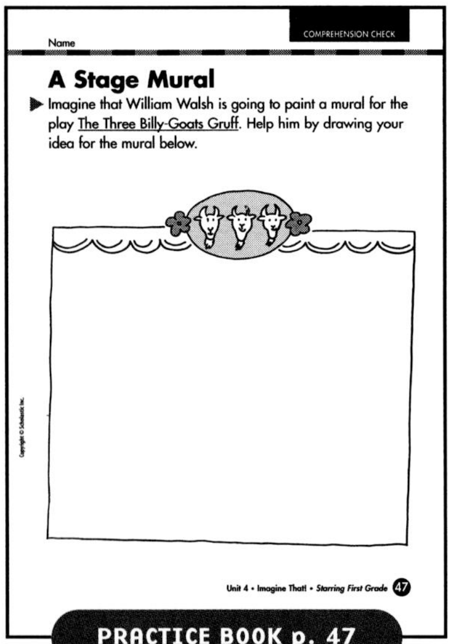
Name

COMPREHENSION CHECK

A Stage Mural

▶ Imagine that William Walsh is going to paint a mural for the play The Three Billy-Goats Gruff. Help him by drawing your idea for the mural below.

Unit 4 • Imagine That! • Starring First Grade 47

PRACTICE BOOK p. 47

104

RESPOND

Think About Reading

1. What story does First Grade want to act out?
2. Why does the teacher ask Jim to be the river?
3. How does Jim help Paul?
4. Why do Jim and Paul grin at each other?
5. How are the children who put on a play like the children who paint a mural?

104

MODIFY Instruction

ESL/ELD

▲ For the poster activity, assign children to small groups that include native speakers. Encourage the group to make decisions together and assign jobs cooperatively. **(WORK IN GROUPS)**

EXTRA HELP

■ For the writing activity, children can list the information they need for their poster. They can use the words *Who*, *What*, *When*, and *Where* to create a chart. Children can look at the illustration on page 89 to see a sample poster. **(VISUAL AIDS)**

105

Write a Poster

·st Grade wants everyone to
ne to their play! Make a poster
out their play. Tell the name of
play. Tell when and where the
ty will be, too. Add a drawing
your poster.

Literature Circle

ow do you think William
alsh would like First Grade's
ay? What do you think he
ould say to the children
er the play?

Author
Miriam Cohen

Miriam Cohen always loved to read! She read while she ate, walked, and even when she should have been doing other things. Still, she didn't start writing her own books until she had children. Many of her books are about Jim and the other children in First Grade.

More Books by
Miriam Cohen

- Lost in the Museum
- See You in Second Grade

105

TECHNOLOGY

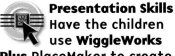

Presentation Skills Have the children use **WiggleWorks Plus** PlaceMaker to create a poster advertising the class play. It should include the name of the play, and the time and place it will be held. Encourage the children to add drawings, clip art, and descriptive words and phrases that will attract a big audience.

RESPOND

Write a Poster

Before children begin drawing or writing, have them think about these questions:

- What is the name of the play First Grade is putting on?
- What can you say about the play that will make people want to see it?
- What will you draw on the poster?

Children may want to sketch out their posters with pencil before using paint, markers, or crayons to do the actual drawing and writing.

Literature Circle

Encourage children to have a conversation about the possible responses William Walsh might have to First Grade's play. Invite children to take turns suggesting what William Walsh might say to First Grade after the play.

DAILY LANGUAGE PRACTICE

SPELLING

DAY 3: Write Words With *s*-Blends. **See page R29.**

GRAMMAR, USAGE, MECHANICS

DAY 3: Practice Describing Words. **See page R31.**

ORAL LANGUAGE

Jim is angry because he is not the sar of the play.
(Jim is angry because he is not the star of the play.)

COMPREHENSION
Sequence

SKILLS TRACE

Sequence TESTED

Introduce . . . . . pp. T210–T211
Practice . . . . p. T181
Review . . . . p. R46
Reteach . . . . p. R57

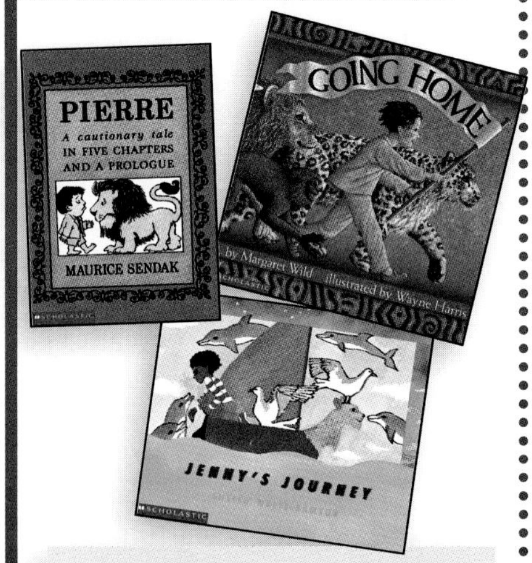
PIERRE
A cautionary tale
IN FIVE CHAPTERS
AND A PROLOGUE
MAURICE SENDAK
GOING HOME
by Margaret Wild
illustrated by Wayne Harris
JENNY'S JOURNEY

CONNECT TO THE TRADE BOOKS

Select one of the unit trade books. Read aloud the title and discuss the cover illustration.

- Have children make predictions about what might happen in the story. Record their predictions on chart paper or the chalkboard.
- Read the story a few pages at a time. Stop periodically to have children recall the story events in sequential order. Record the events in order on chart paper.
- When you have finished, review the list of events and have children summarize what happened first, next, and last in the story.

QUICKCHECK

Can children:

✔ follow the sequence of events?
✔ identify what happened first, next, last?

If YES, go on to Practice/Apply.

If NO, start at Teach/Model.

A TEACH/MODEL

USE ORAL LANGUAGE

Encourage children to discuss a routine your class follows every day. For example, you may wish to discuss getting ready to leave school. Ask children what they do first. Do they put school supplies and books away? Ask what they do next. Do they pack up their books and put on their coats? What do they do last?

The sequence of events in a story is **the order in which the important story events happen**. Signal words such as ***first, next,*** and ***last*** help show the sequence of events in a story. To determine the sequence of events:

1. Read the story and identify the important events in it.
2. Look for signal words such as ***first, next,*** and ***last*** that tell the order in which events happened.

MODIFY Instruction

ESL/ELD

▲ Have children take turns telling a sequence story about everyday life. One might tell what she does on the way home from school. Another might tell about getting ready for dinner. Encourage children to use sequence words, such as *first, next,* and *last.* **(RELATE TO REAL LIFE)**

EXTRA HELP

■ Work with children to list the order of events in *Starring First Grade*. Then analyze the list to help children discover how all the events fit into a larger three-step sequence of first choosing the play and assigning parts, next practicing the play, and last performing the play. **(DEMONSTRATE)**

LITERATURE CONNECTION

You may wish to revisit *Starring First Grade* with children to help them determine the sequence of events.

THINK ALOUD *When I read* Starring First Grade, *I think about what happens first, next, and last in the story. First the class chooses a play and everyone gets a part. But Jim is mad because he wanted to be the troll. Next, the class practices the play, and Paul gets mad because Jim tries to boss everybody. Last, the class puts on the play while Jim and Paul become friends again.*

B PRACTICE/APPLY

USE PRACTICE BOOK

Have pairs of children work together to complete **Practice Book page 48.** Have children describe what happens first, next, and last in *Starring First Grade.*

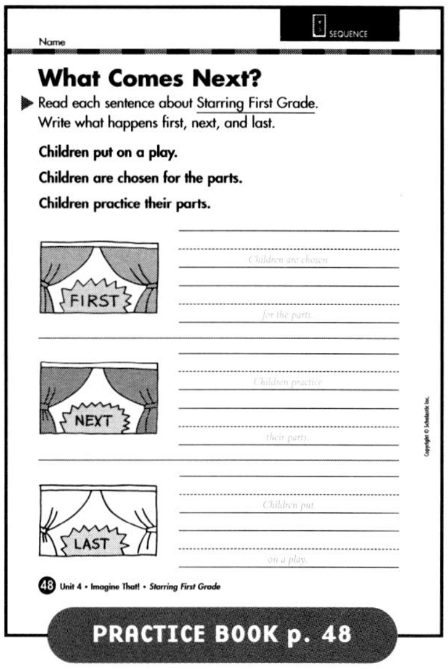
Name
SEQUENCE
What Comes Next?
▶ Read each sentence about Starring First Grade. Write what happens first, next, and last.
Children put on a play.
Children are chosen for the parts.
Children practice their parts.
FIRST
Children are chosen for the parts.
NEXT
Children practice their parts.
LAST
Children put on a play.
48 Unit 4 • Imagine That! • Starring First Grade

PRACTICE BOOK p. 48

C ASSESS

APPLY INSTRUCTIONAL ALTERNATIVES

Based on children's completion of **Practice Book page 48,** determine if they were able to recognize sequence in *Starring First Grade.* The instructional alternatives below will aid you in pinpointing children's level of proficiency. Consider the appropriate instructional alternative to promote further skill development.

To reinforce the skill, distribute **page 49** of the **Practice Book.**

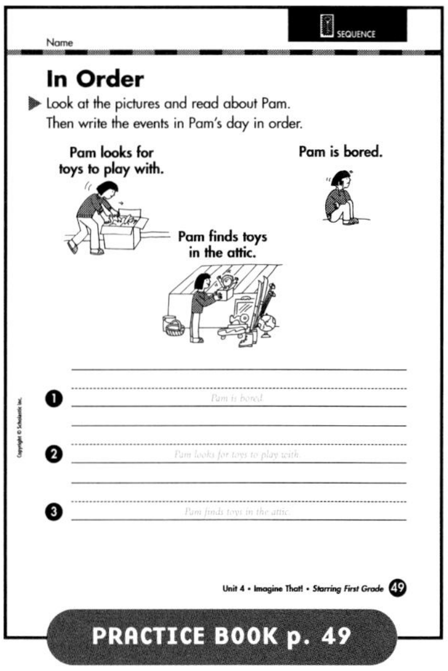
Name
SEQUENCE
In Order
▶ Look at the pictures and read about Pam. Then write the events in Pam's day in order.
Pam looks for toys to play with.
Pam is bored.
Pam finds toys in the attic.
1 Pam is bored.
2 Pam looks for toys to play with.
3 Pam finds toys in the attic.
Unit 4 • Imagine That! • Starring First Grade 49

PRACTICE BOOK p. 49

INSTRUCTIONAL ALTERNATIVES

	If the child . . .	Then
Proficient	Recognizes sequence	• Have the child apply this skill independently to a more challenging story. • Summarize a story by telling the most important events in the order in which they occurred.
Apprentice	Recalls story events but cannot identify the order in which these events happened	• Give the child the three or four major events of a familiar story. Have the child retell the events in the correct order.
Novice	Recalls random story events in incorrect order	• Retell the story with the child, identifying the major events and the order in which they happened by offering prompts such as *And then what happened?* • Use the Reteach lesson on page R57.

Starring First Grade

SELECTION WORDS With *ch, wh*

cheered	speech
marched	what
teacher	which
each	whispered

SKILLS TRACE

DIGRAPHS *ch, wh*

Introduce . . . . . . pp. T212–213
Practice . . . pp. T197, T215, T219
Review . . . . p. R53
Reteach. . . . . p. R61

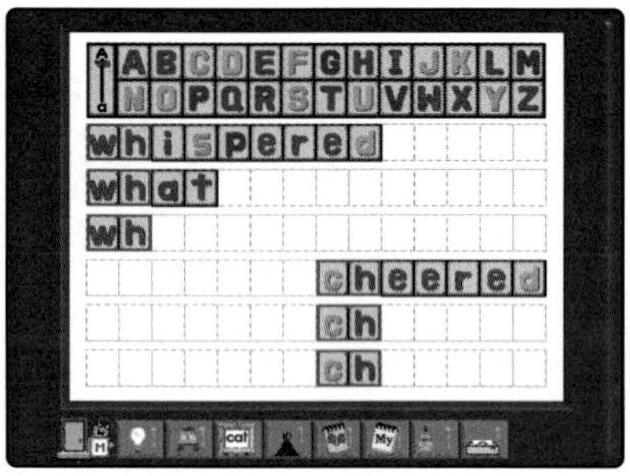
ABCDEFGHIJKLM
NOPQRSTUVWXYZ
whispered
what
wh
cheered
ch
ch

TECHNOLOGY

Have children build words with *wh* and *ch* on the **WiggleWorks Plus** Magnet Board.

- Begin with the words *whispered* and *cheered*. Have children copy *ch* and *wh* onto other lines of the Magnet Board. Then, challenge them to add letters to create new words.

DAILY PHONICS

Digraphs /ch/ch, /hw/wh

A PHONOLOGICAL AWARENESS

RHYME Sing "The Wheels on the Bus" from the *Big Book of Rhymes and Rhythms*, pages 6–7. As you sing, clap on the words with **/ch/*ch*** and **/hw/*wh***.

- On a second singing, track the print and encourage children to sing along with you, as you model appropriate movements and gestures.
- Frame ***children*** and ***wheels.*** Read each word aloud, stressing the initial sound.

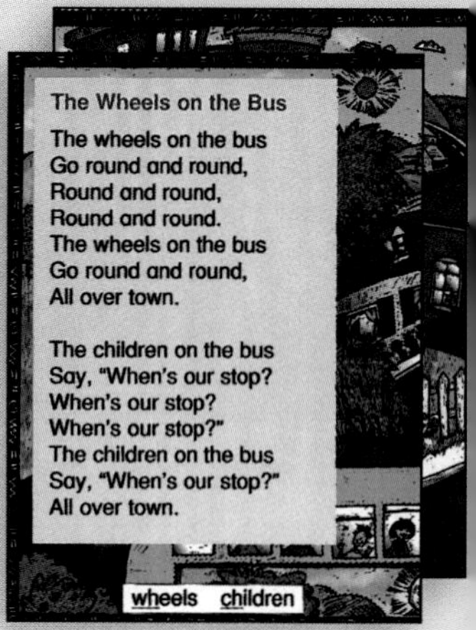
The Wheels on the Bus
The wheels on the bus
Go round and round,
Round and round,
Round and round.
The wheels on the bus
Go round and round,
All over town.
The children on the bus
Say, "When's our stop?
When's our stop?
When's our stop?"
The children on the bus
Say, "When's our stop?"
All over town.
wheels
children

***Big Book of Rhymes and Rhythms 1B*, pp. 6–7**

ORAL BLENDING Say the following word parts, and ask children to blend them. Provide corrective feedback and modeling as needed.

/ch/. . . at	**/ch/. . . op**	**/ch/. . . ase**
/hw/. . . y	**/hw/. . . en**	**/hw/. . . ale**

B CONNECT SOUND-SPELLING

INTRODUCE DIGRAPHS /ch/*ch* and /hw/*wh* Explain to children that the letters ***ch*** stand for **/ch/** as in ***chin;*** the letters ***wh*** stand for **/hw/** as in ***whale.*** Remind children that sometimes two consonants together stand for one sound. Then model blending.

THINK ALOUD *I can put the letters* **ch**, **o**, *and* **p** *together to make the word* **chop.** *Say the sounds as I move my finger under the letters. Notice that the letters* **ch** *stand for one sound,* **/ch/**.

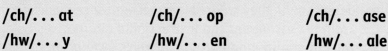

MODIFY Instruction

ESL/ELD

▲ The **/ch/** sound will be a familiar one to Spanish speakers. Ask children if they know words in any language that contain this sound and ask them to pronounce them for the class. Make a list of these words on the board. **(MAKE CONNECTIONS)**

GIFTED & TALENTED

✳ Have children make up riddles whose answers contain the spellings ***wh*** or ***ch***. Offer these examples:

- What fruit rhymes with ***beach***? *(peach)*
- What huge sea animal rhymes with ***tail***? *(whale)* **(WORD PLAY)**

Ask children to suggest other words with **/hw/*wh*** or **/ch/*ch*.** List them on chart paper and have volunteers underline the digraph in each word.

PHONICS MAINTENANCE Review the following sound-spellings: digraphs ***wh, ch;*** **/ē/*ee, ea;*** **/st/*st,*** **/sp/*sp,*** **/sn/*sn*.** Say one of these sounds. Have a volunteer write on the chalkboard the spelling or spellings that stand for the sounds. Continue with all the sounds.

C PRACTICE/APPLY

BLEND WORDS To practice using the sound-spellings and review previous sound-spellings, list the following words and sentences on the chalkboard. Have children read each chorally. Model blending as needed.

hop	chop	cat	chat
snap	when	wheel	reach

The beach has white sand.

Will a seal chase a whale?

DICTATION Dictate the following words for children to spell: ***when, chop, stand.***

BUILD WORDS Distribute the following letter cards, or have children use their own sets: ***ch, wh, ee, i, p, n, r, l.*** Give children time to build as many words as possible using the letter cards. Children can write their words on a separate sheet of paper. **(INDEPENDENT WORK)**

ch
i
n

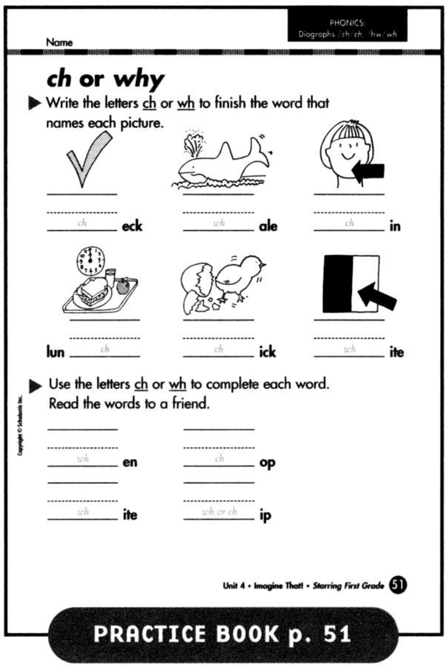
Name

PHONICS: Digraphs /ch/ch /hw/wh

ch or why

▶ Write the letters ch or wh to finish the word that names each picture.

___eck ___ale ___in

lun___ ___ick ___ite

▶ Use the letters ch or wh to complete each word. Read the words to a friend.

___en ___op

___ite ___ip

Unit 4 • Imagine That! • Starring First Grade 51

PRACTICE BOOK p. 51

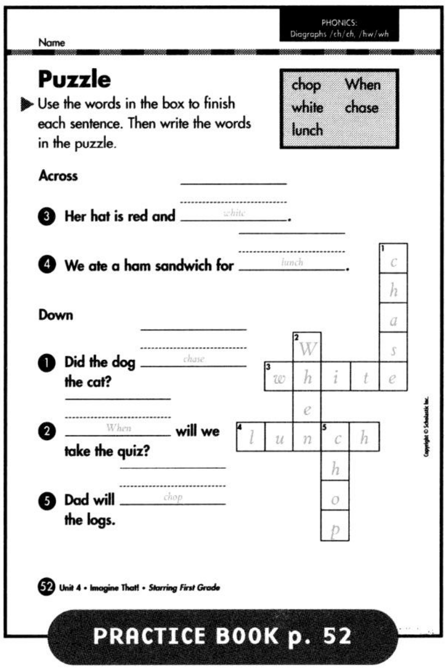
Name

PHONICS: Digraphs /ch/ch /hw/wh

Puzzle

▶ Use the words in the box to finish each sentence. Then write the words in the puzzle.

chop	When
white	chase
lunch	

Across

3 Her hat is red and ______.

4 We ate a ham sandwich for ______.

Down

1 Did the dog ______ the cat?

2 ______ will we take the quiz?

5 Dad will ______ the logs.

52 Unit 4 • Imagine That! • Starring First Grade

PRACTICE BOOK p. 52

DECODABLE TEXT

For practice reading decodable text, see ***Scholastic Decodable Readers #51 and #52.***

For additional phonics instruction and review, see ***Scholastic Phonics A, pp. 205–209.***

TOSS AND SAY

Create a cube or a die with ***wh*** on three sides and ***ch*** on the other three sides. Working with a partner, have children take turns tossing the cube and saying a word with the digraph that lands on top. The other child must use the word in a sentence.

wh
ch

Building Fluency

PHONICS READER

Guide children through a reading of **Phonics Reader #45,** *Slip Slide Baseball Jokes* or **#46** *Say It and Smile!* For a detailed lesson plan, see **Phonics Reader Teacher's Guide Part B, pages 32–35.** While children read, note how well they:

- **blend words,**
- **recognize high-frequency words,**
- **read with speed, accuracy, and expression.**

Slip Slide
Book 45
SAY IT AND SMILE!
Book 46
by Wiley Blevins
Illustrated by Tim Haggerty
SCHOLASTIC

You may wish to have children reread the story with a partner.

★ See Phonics Readers Take-Home Books 37–72 for reproducible format.

More Support Materials . . .

GOING HOME
by Margaret Wild
PIERRE
A cautionary tale IN FIVE CHAPTERS AND A PROLOGUE
MAURICE SENDAK
JENNY'S JOURNEY

TRADE BOOK LIBRARY

For additional leveled reading practice, have children read one of the following:

Going Home
CHALLENGE

Pierre
AVERAGE

Jenny's Journey
EASY

PHONICS CHAPTER BOOK 4
The Puppet Club
SCHOLASTIC

PHONICS CHAPTER BOOK

For additional practice with *s*-blends, have children read Chapter 5, "Good Stuff" in **Phonics Chapter Book 4,** *The Puppet Club.*

Slip Slide Baseball Jokes
SAY IT AND SMILE!
STILL SNORING

HOME-SCHOOL CONNECTION

Send home *Slip Slide Baseball Jokes, Say It and Smile!*, and *Still Snoring.* Have children read the books to a family member.

STILL SNORING

MY BOOK

For additional practice with high-frequency words and *s*-blends, have children read *Still Snoring.* This book is also available on **WiggleWorks Plus.**

Intervention

For children who need extra help . . .

FOCUS ON HIGH-FREQUENCY WORDS

Write the words ***which*** and ***make*** on note cards. Then follow this procedure:

- State each word aloud as children repeat it.
- Have children spell the word aloud as you point to each letter.
- Provide children with simple sentences containing each word. Help them to read the sentences. Allow ample time for them to practice reading the words and sentences before rereading *Starring First Grade*.

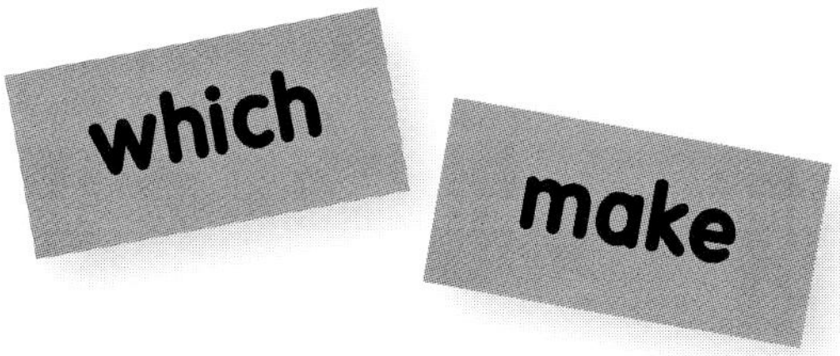
which
make

FOCUS ON PHONICS

Write the following words on index cards: ***chop, chin, check, cheer, which, what, whale, when***.

- Help children to read the word on each card.
- Then mix the cards. Have children sort the cards according to their common digraph (***ch*** or ***wh***).
- Ask children to read the words in each group.

chop

PROFESSIONAL DEVELOPMENT

GAY SU PINNELL

What's the Difference Between Consonant Blends and Digraphs?

*Consonant blends (clusters) are two consonants that appear together in a word, with each retaining its sound when blended. Consonant blends include **l**-blends **(cl, pl)**, **r**-blends **(br, tr)**, and **s**-blends **(st, spr)**.*

*Consonant digraphs are two consonants that appear together in a word and stand for one sound. The consonant digraphs are **sh, ch, th, wh, ph, gh,** and **ng.***

DAY 3 WRAP-UP

READ ALOUD *To conclude each reading session and develop children's oral vocabularies, read aloud a book of your choice. If the book contains chapters, you might choose to read only one chapter a day.*

GUIDED READING *To extend reading, meet with the **green** and **yellow** reading groups and assign Independent Center activities.* ***See pages R26–R27.***

DAY 4 OBJECTIVES

CHILDREN WILL

READ 30 MINUTES

- **Reread *Starring First Grade***

WRITE 30 MINUTES

- **Shared Writing: Description**
- **Spelling: Words With *s*-Blends**
- **Grammar, Usage, Mechanics: Describing Words**
- **Oral Language**

EXTEND SKILLS 30 MINUTES

- **Vocabulary**
- **Daily Phonics: Words With Digraphs *ch, wh***
- **Study Skills: Test-Taking Strategies**

RESOURCES

- **Practice Book, pp. 51–53**
- **Spelling Resource Book, p. 161**

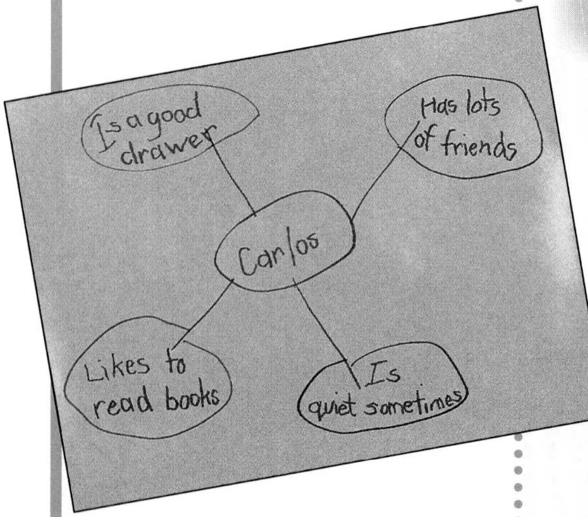
Is a good drawer
Has lots of friends
Carlos
Likes to read books
Is quiet sometimes

SHARED WRITING

Description

Starring First Grade

SELECTION CONNECTION

Using the story *Starring First Grade* as a model, children will write descriptions of real children—themselves!

THINK ABOUT WRITING

Help children understand that some stories have characters who:

- look and act like real people.
- show what makes them happy like real people.

INTRODUCE THE WRITING EVENT

Ask children to write descriptions of themselves. Encourage them to think of things to say about themselves and to think about who will read their descriptions.

TEACH/MODEL

PUT IT IN CONTEXT

Have children look back at *Starring First Grade.*

> **What did the children in the story do that reminds you of people you know?**

> **Describe one of the characters in the story.**

Model how to draw a character web and write short descriptions of yourself for it. Then ask children to draw character webs about themselves. Point out that the web and descriptions should tell:

- how they look and what they like to do.
- how they act and what makes them happy.

MODIFY Instruction

ESL/ELD

▲ Provide help to English language learners by writing several sentence-starters for them on the board:

I am a _____. I have _____ hair and _____ eyes. I like to _____. I always _____ with my friends. **(CLOZE)**

EXTRA HELP

■ If children have trouble with their character webs and descriptions, remind children of their positive character traits. Encourage children to brainstorm words and phrases that they think describe how they talk, what they like to do, how they look, and what makes them happy. **(BRAINSTORM)**

GRAMMAR CONNECTION

Have children identify the describing words in their character maps and descriptions.

WRITE

WRITE A CHARACTER DESCRIPTION

- Help children develop the ideas in their character webs to write or dictate descriptions of themselves. They can use their character webs as models for writing on sentence strips.
- Invite children to draw a picture of themselves to go with their sentences.
- Display their completed work on a class bulletin board.

ASSESS

PERFORMANCE-BASED ASSESSMENT

The following questions will help children assess their work:

✔ **Did I describe what I look like?**

✔ **Did I tell about how I act, what I like to do, and what makes me happy?**

Children may wish to carry this piece through the writing process described on **pages T278–T281.**

can read

DAILY LANGUAGE PRACTICE

SPELLING

DAY 4:

Review Words With *s*-Blends. **See page R29.**

GRAMMAR, USAGE, MECHANICS

DAY 4:

Apply Describing Words. **See page R31.**

ORAL LANGUAGE

katie likes to play sortes.

(Katie likes to play sports.)

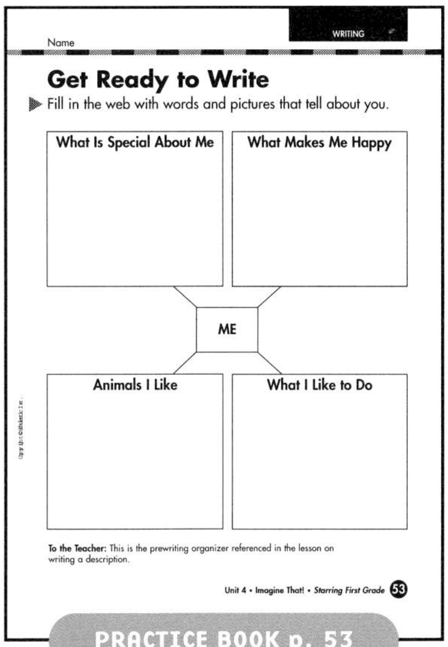

Name WRITING

Get Ready to Write

▶ Fill in the web with words and pictures that tell about you.

What Is Special About Me | What Makes Me Happy | ME | Animals I Like | What I Like to Do

To the Teacher: This is the prewriting organizer referenced in the lesson on writing a description.

Unit 4 • Imagine That! • *Starring First Grade* 53

PRACTICE BOOK p. 53

which

Which

make

Make

TEACHER TIP

Make and distribute copies of the vocabulary cards on **pages R72–R73.** Have children use these cards for additional practice.

Extend Vocabulary

Review High-Frequency Words

Write the high-frequency words ***which*** and ***make*** on note cards. For each word write a lowercase and uppercase version ***(which/Which)***. Then write the following incomplete sentences on sentence strips:

We can _____ some muffins.

_____ kind do you like best?

Read aloud each incomplete sentence, and have children place the appropriate word card in the blank space. Then help children to chorally read the sentences.

Review Story Words

Write the story words ***actors, first, story, play, troll,*** and ***goat*** on note cards. Then write the following incomplete sentences on the chalkboard:

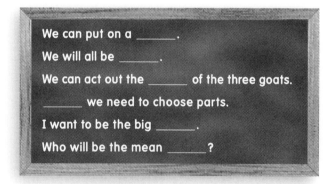

We can put on a _____.
We will all be _____.
We can act out the _____ of the three goats.
_____ we need to choose parts.
I want to be the big _____.
Who will be the mean _____?

Read aloud the incomplete sentences and have children place the appropriate note card in each blank space.

CHARACTER PORTRAITS

Have children draw the characters from *Starring First Grade,* one character per child. Then ask children to write descriptions of the characters they drew. Remind children to include in their descriptions the characters' relationships with others in the story. Have children use these descriptions and the high-frequency and story words to write a group story about another play that the First Grade might put on.

Building Fluency

Phonics Reader

Guide children through a reading of **Phonics Reader #47,** *Chuck's Lunch* or ***#48,*** *Whale of a Joke!* For a detailed lesson plan, see **Phonics Reader Teacher's Guide Part B, pp. 36–39.** While children read, note how well they:

- **blend words,**
- **recognize high-frequency words,**
- **read with speed, accuracy, and expression.**

Book 47
WHALE of a Joke!
Book 48
by Wiley Blevins
Illustrated by Jeff Moores
SCHOLASTIC

★ See Phonics Readers Take-Home Books 37–72 for reproducible format.

More Support Materials . . .

GOING HOME
PIERRE
A cautionary tale
IN FIVE CHAPTERS
AND A PROLOGUE
MAURICE SENDAK
JENNY'S JOURNEY
SCHOLASTIC

Trade Book Library

For additional leveled reading practice, have children read one of the following:

Going Home
CHALLENGE

Pierre
AVERAGE

Jenny's Journey
EASY

PHONICS
The Puppet Club

Phonics Chapter Book

For additional practice with **/ch/*ch*** and **/hw/*wh*,** have children read Chapter 6, "What's Next" in **Phonics Chapter Book 4,** *The Puppet Club.*

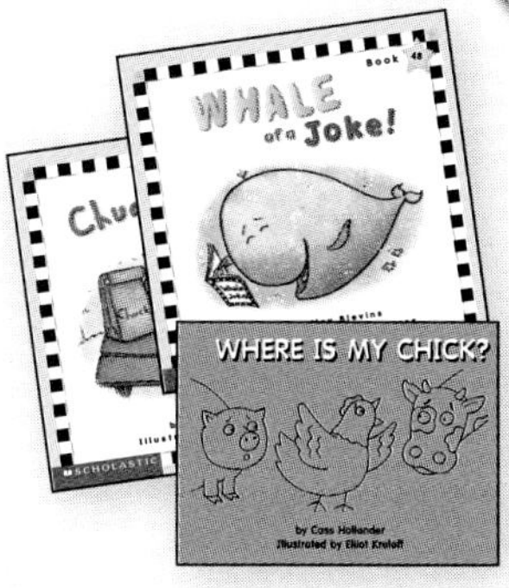
WHALE of a Joke!
WHERE IS MY CHICK?

Home-School Connection

Send home *Chuck's Lunch*, *Whale of a Joke!*, and *Where Is My Chick?* Have children read the books to a family member.

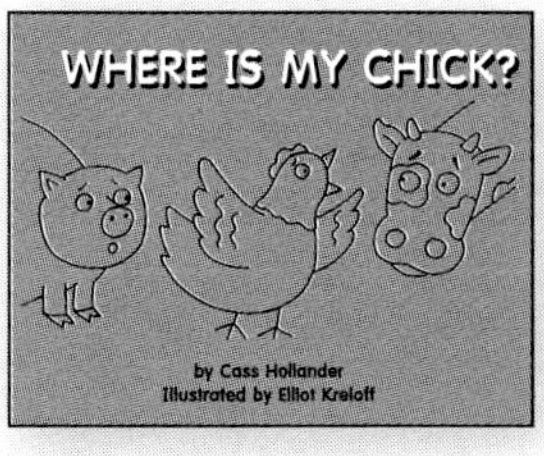
WHERE IS MY CHICK?
by Cass Hollander
Illustrated by Elliot Kreloff

My Book

For additional practice with high-frequency words and words with **/ch/*ch*** and **/hw/*wh*,** have children read *Where Is My Chick?* This book is also available on **WiggleWorks Plus.**

STUDY SKILLS

Test-Taking Strategies

A TEACH/MODEL

DEFINE STANDARDIZED TESTS

Discuss standardized tests with children. Point out that a standardized test is a test that is taken by many children. It asks questions and gives a choice of answers. Emphasize that children pick the right answer to each question.

PUT IT IN CONTEXT

Explain to children that some tests will ask them to read about a topic and then answer questions. When taking a test such as this, good strategies to remember are:

- Read the questions first. Then you will know what information to look for when you are reading.
- Read the passage carefully from beginning to end.
- Try to answer each question before you look at the answer choices.

MODEL THE SKILL

THINK ALOUD *Suppose I had to read a passage about goats. Before reading it, I would read the questions. Suppose the first question asked was: Which kind of goats usually don't have horns? Then I would know one thing to read for.*

B PRACTICE/APPLY

USING THE SKILL

Reproduce this paragraph and the question that follows for each child:

> Miriam Cohen wrote a book called *First Grade Takes a Test*. Jim, Paul, Anna Maria, and all our friends are in this book, too. They take a test. Anna Maria does very well. The other children don't. The test makes them feel bad. But the teacher says a test doesn't tell everything. She helps them feel good about all the things they know and can do.
>
> Who does very well on the test?
>
> **a.** Jim **c.** Anna Maria
>
> **b.** Paul **d.** nobody

DISCUSSING THE SAMPLE

Have children complete the sample item. Encourage them to read the question *before* they read the paragraph. Ask them if they can answer the question *before* looking at the choices. When they have completed the sample, talk about what they did.

- Was it easier to find information when you knew just what you were looking for?
- Could you answer the question before you looked at the answer?
- Did you have any trouble matching your answer to the choices given?

INFORMAL ASSESSMENT: PERFORMANCE-BASED

✔ Did children apply the test-taking strategies?

✔ Did they answer the questions correctly?

TECHNOLOGY

Test-Taking Skills Work with children to create a multiple-choice question about the story using a word processing program. For example, compose answers to the question, *Why didn't Jim want to be a tree?* Use a standard format with answers labeled ***a*** through ***d.*** Remind children to read the question first and to look for the answer while reading the story. Together, compose additional questions.

DAY 4 WRAP-UP

READ ALOUD *To develop children's ability to get information from texts, spend five to ten minutes reading from a nonfiction selection of your choice.*

GUIDED READING *To extend reading, meet with the* ***green*** *and* ***yellow*** *reading groups and assign Independent Center activities.* **See pages R26–R27.**

DAY 5 OBJECTIVES

CHILDREN WILL:

READ 30 MINUTES

- **Reading Assessment**
- **Daily Phonics: *s*-Blends, Digraphs *ch* and *wh***

WRITE 30 MINUTES

- **Writing Assessment**
- **Spelling: Words with *s*-Blends**
- **Grammar, Usage, Mechanics: Describing Words**
- **Oral Language**

EXTEND SKILLS 30 MINUTES

- **Integrated Language Arts**
- **Read Aloud**
- **Guided Reading**

RESOURCES

- **Selection Test**
- **Spelling Resource Book, p. 163**

TEACHER SELF-ASSESSMENT

✔ Did I frequently model how to blend words?

✔ Did I review high-frequency words on the Word Wall each day?

✔ Did I provide children with successful, daily reading and writing opportunities?

Reading Assessment

INFORMAL ASSESSMENT: OBSERVATION

PHONICS

Write the following ***s***-blends and digraphs on note cards: ***st, sn, sp, ch, wh.*** Display one card at a time and have the class state the sound(s) the spelling stands for. Note children who respond incorrectly or wait for classmates to respond before providing an answer.

HIGH-FREQUENCY WORDS

Write the following high-frequency words on note cards: ***which, make.*** Display one card at a time and have the class read the word. Note children who have difficulty recognizing either word.

which
make

KEY STRATEGY: SEQUENCE

Choose a trade book whose story has a clear and simple sequence. Read the story with children. Then ask children to write a sentence or draw a picture to show what happened ***first, next,*** and ***last.***

CONFERENCE

Have children reread *Starring First Grade*. As they reread, select several children to conference with. Ask them to do the following:

- read aloud a few pages of the story.
- retell the story in their own words.
- explain what they do to figure out an unfamiliar word.

Keep anecdotal records of the conferences. Place your findings in each child's assessment folder. Use the information to determine which children need additional support.

Starring First Grade

Starring First Grade

FORMAL ASSESSMENT

DECODING TEST

Make two copies of the assessment below. The assessment piece is designed to be used individually.

- Give one to the child and keep the other to record each child's errors.
- As the child reads aloud the words and sentences in the assessment boxes, record his or her attempts, corrections, errors, and passes.
- Once completed, keep each assessment piece in the child's portfolio as a running record of his or her emerging reading skills.

NAME: ______________________ **DATE:** ____________

A Have children read the following word list:

speech	**plane**	**snap**	**which**	**many**
state	**sneeze**	**when**	**make**	**soon**
each	**tree**	**clean**	**look**	**went**
white	**teacher**	**take**	**about**	**when**
chase	**peach**	**cheer**	**some**	**down**

B Have children read the following sentences.

- **Our teacher will make a speech.**
- **Which class cheered for her?**

C On a separate sheet of paper, have children write the following words and sentences.

- **stand spin fine chop**
- **Stop and sit still.**
- **We ate a peach for lunch.**

SELECTION TEST

Use the selection test to obtain a formal measure of children's mastery of the week's reading objectives.

SELF-SELECTION

Have children select one or two pieces of work from the week that they would like to place in their portfolios.

Suggest that children write a sentence telling why they chose each piece. You may also wish to select a piece that best illustrates the child's work.

Periodically review the pieces in the portfolio and remove any that no longer seem appropriate.

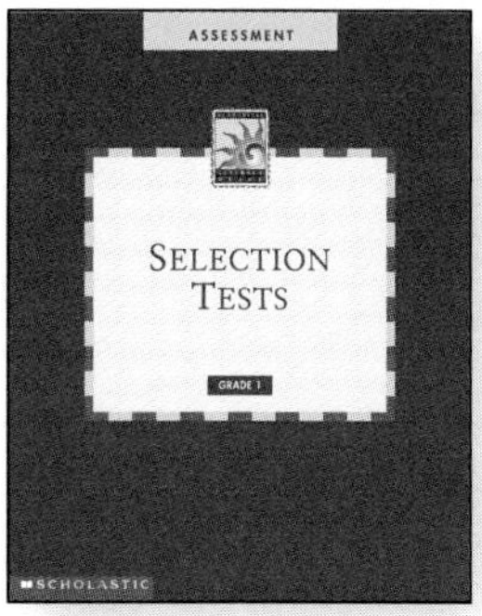
ASSESSMENT
SELECTION TESTS
GRADE 1
SCHOLASTIC

SELECTION TEST

DAILY LANGUAGE PRACTICE

Spelling

DAY 5:
Administer the Posttest for Words With *s*-Blends. **See page R29.**

Grammar, Usage, Mechanics

DAY 5:
Assess use of Describing Words. **See page R31.**

Oral Language

I have a story to tell you.
(I have a story to tell you.)

PORTFOLIO

Suggest that children add their drafts and revisions to their Literacy Portfolios.

Writing Assessment

This is a good description. It includes some details about you.
Great! Every sentence is a complete sentence.
You have some nice describing words here, too: Brown eyes and long brown hair are particularly good.
i have Brown eyes and long Brown hair.
I like to wear pants so I can play.
I like sportse. I am not big. I like to smile alot.

Proficient

Use the rubric below to assess children's writing.

CHILDREN'S WRITING RUBRIC

Proficient	• The description includes details about how the child looks and acts. • The sentences are well thought out and complete.	• Describing words are included in the writing. • The description is proofread and corrected for grammar, usage, and mechanics.
Apprentice	• The description includes some details about how the child looks and acts. • The description may not include enough describing words.	• The description may have been proofread but not completely corrected for grammar, usage, and mechanics errors.
Novice	• The description does not give details about how the child looks or acts. • The description includes few describing words and is not written in complete sentences.	• The description has not been proofread or corrected for grammar, usage, and mechanics errors.

Integrated Language Arts

WRITING

Add to the Story

MATERIALS:
Drawing paper
Crayons or markers

SUGGESTED GROUPING:
Individuals or cooperative groups

HAVE cooperative groups of children write or dictate an additional part, or sequel, to a story such as *Cinderella*, *Rapunzel*, or *Starring First Grade*. To get them started, you may wish to ask the following questions:

- Who are the characters in the story? Will they be in the sequel?
- What will these characters do in the sequel?
- Where will your sequel take place?
- What funny things might happen in this sequel?

HAVE cooperative groups talk about what they'll include in their sequels, then write or dictate sentences for them. Have children draw pictures for their stories.

Children might want to include their sequels in their Literacy Portfolios.

SPEAKING

Act Out a Play

Good For Grading

MATERIALS:
Audiocassette player and audiocassette (optional)

SUGGESTED GROUPING:
Cooperative groups

REMIND children that the first grade in *Starring First Grade* turned a familiar story into a play.

INVITE cooperative groups to make a list of characters, settings, and events in a story they want to turn into a play. Children can decide whether they'll act out the whole story or focus on a specific event.

GIVE each group an opportunity to choose roles and practice their parts before performing their play in front of the class. Encourage children to speak with expression and to use hand gestures and other movements. Children may also want to find or make props and simple costumes for their play.

HOW TO GRADE When grading a performance, look at the relationship of the original story to the play.

Play

TEACH/MODEL Share with children that a play is a story that is acted out. A scene in a play is one part of their story. Point out that in *Starring First Grade,* Danny knocks the troll's ears off in the last scene of the play.

PRACTICE/APPLY Encourage children to divide their plays into two or three parts, or scenes.

Integrated Language Arts

WRITING/VIEWING/VOCABULARY

Be a Reporter

MATERIALS: Anthology

SUGGESTED GROUPING: Individuals

Have children be reporters and choose story parts to describe. Children should use the story illustrations and their own imaginations to write their descriptions.

Ask children to dictate or draw pictures to tell more about the parts of the story they chose. Invite children to use the story words whenever possible. Encourage children to answer questions such as:

- Who is in this part of the story?
- What are they doing?
- Where are they?
- What is happening?

Encourage children to use all the picture clues to help them tell more about the story parts. Remind them that the looks on characters' faces and their body positions show whether they're happy or sad.

DAY 5 WRAP-UP

Read Aloud *Spend five to ten minutes reading from a selection of your choice.*

Guided Reading *Meet with the* ***blue*** *and* ***green*** *reading groups and assign Independent Center activities.* ***See pages R26–R27.***

SPEAKING/LISTENING

Interview a Character

MATERIALS: Audiocassette player and audiocassette (optional)

SUGGESTED GROUPING: Cooperative groups

Ask one group of children to role-play the characters in *Starring First Grade.* Then have another group interview them.

Have the second group ask the characters:

- What was your part in the play?
- What did you like about being in the play?
- What would you have changed about the play? How would you have done it differently?
- What do you like about being in first grade?
- Tell me more about some of the children in class. What are they like? What other activities would you like your class to do?

Encourage children to tape-record their interviews and listen to them before rereading the story.

TECHNOLOGY

Speaking Skills Have children use the **WiggleWorks Plus** Unit Writer to write additional interview questions. Encourage them to record responses using the Record tool. Children can also illustrate their responses using the art tools.

What was your part in the play?
What did you like about being in the play?

How to Draw a Sketch

WHY DO THIS WORKSHOP?

Pictures are one of the oldest and most fundamental ways to communicate information. Often, a single image can convey information that might take pages of words. Pictures can also be used to create narratives. Consider, for example, the immense popularity of certain movies and television series. Such picture narratives are prevalent and popular in our culture. The ability to "read" them and certainly to create them is a skill that must be learned.

For children who are just beginning to write, pictures are an important medium for giving concrete form to ideas for original narratives and stories. Sketches can help children decide what characters and settings look like. Sketching scenes is an organizational tool, helping children plan the plots of their stories. Finally, sketches can often communicate an entire story as clearly and directly as words.

GETTING STARTED

Create a Narrative

To help children focus on the task at hand, you might want to discuss the sketches reproduced on Side 1 of the Workshop Card. You might also ask any of the following questions:

> **Who is the main character in this sketch?**

> **What clues in the sketch tell you it's outside?**

Come
and

WORKSHOP OBJECTIVES

CHILDREN WILL:

- **Create a narrative**
- **Make a sketch of a setting, main character, or scene**

MATERIALS

- **Drawing paper and pencil**
- **An idea for a story**

TECHNOLOGY

Presentation Tools Guide children as they use a familiar art program to create story sketches. Children can use the drawing tools, or the clip art and stamping tools to make the sketch. Ask children to describe the story ideas as they share their sketches.

Name

WORKSHOP 2

Tell a Story

▶ Look at the picture. Then answer the questions.

1. Who is in the picture?
   A boy, a girl, and a dog
2. Where are they?
   They are outside in their yard.
3. What happened before this picture?
   They were playing.
4. What do you think will happen next?
   They will go inside.

To the Teacher: This page can be used as support for the Workshop on how to make a sketch or as a separate activity to develop skills for the Workshop.

Copyright © Scholastic Inc.

Unit 4 • Imagine That! 61

PRACTICE BOOK pp. 61, 62

Use **Practice Book pages 61** and **62** as practice for the Workshop or as a separate activity to strengthen your children's skills.

GRADE 1 CREATIVE EXPRESSION

WORKSHOP 2

How to Draw a Sketch

Artists do quick drawings called *sketches* to get their ideas on paper. This is a sketch of Clifford the Big Red Dog.

CLIFFORD
CLIFFORD
RED
You can get an idea of what Clifford looks like.
This sketch includes the setting for this story—the doghouse where Clifford lives.
Now Make Your Own

1 **PICTURE YOUR STORY**

For their story idea, children may want to use their story plan from Workshop 1, think up a new story, or even use a story they've read or heard. Once they have an idea in mind, volunteers can briefly describe their main characters.

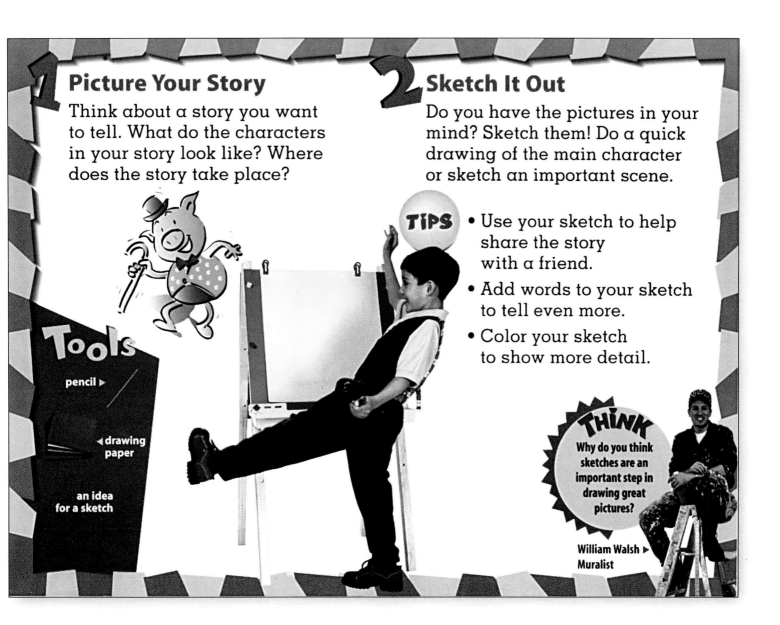

1 Picture Your Story

Think about a story you want to tell. What do the characters in your story look like? Where does the story take place?

Tools

- pencil
- drawing paper
- an idea for a sketch

2 Sketch It Out

Do you have the pictures in your mind? Sketch them! Do a quick drawing of the main character or sketch an important scene.

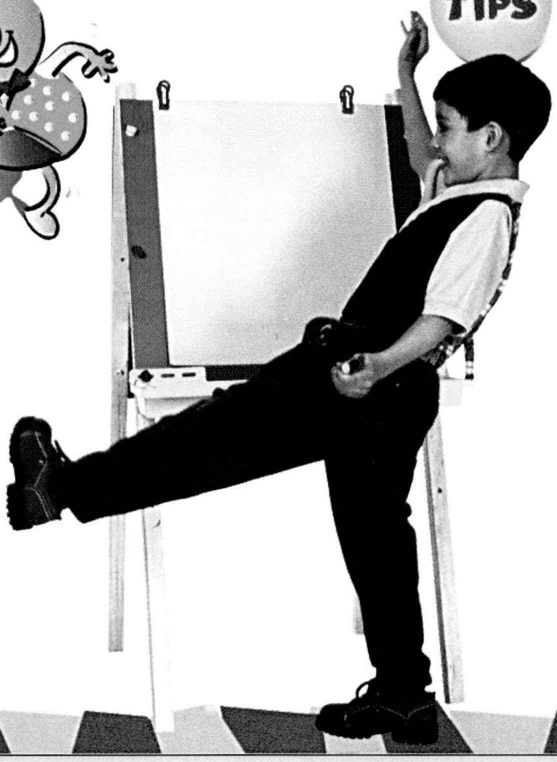

TIPS

- Use your sketch to help share the story with a friend.
- Add words to your sketch to tell even more.
- Color your sketch to show more detail.

THINK

Why do you think sketches are an important step in drawing great pictures?

William Walsh
Muralist

2 SKETCH IT OUT

Emphasize to children that although they should have their ideas well in mind before they make their sketches, they may change their ideas as they work. They can also revise their sketches if they feel the drawings don't match their ideas.

SELF-SELECTION

When children complete this Workshop, they may want to keep their sketches in their Literacy Portfolios.

Connect to Home and Community

Children can make humorous sketches of friends, family members, and places or landmarks in their community. Allow children to display their sketches in the Artist's Studio.

ASSESSMENT

INFORMAL ASSESSMENT

OBSERVATION

Review children's work. Ask yourself:

✔ Did children have a story in mind when they sketched?

✔ Did children sketch a character or an important scene?

IF NOT, TRY THIS:

Ask volunteers to give you a character description. Make a very simple stick figure drawing showing children's ideas on the chalkboard. Stress that children should not worry about all the details being perfect—the point of a sketch is to show ideas.

CHILDREN'S SELF-ASSESSMENT

> **Did I get my story idea across in the sketches I drew?**

CHILDREN'S WORKSHOP RUBRIC

Proficient	**Children can imagine a detailed story, including plot, several characters, and setting; they can make quick sketches that reflect their ideas; children can communicate story information to a friend mainly through the sketch.**
Apprentice	**Children can imagine plot, a few characters, and the setting, but can't supply many details; their sketches may not reflect their ideas satisfactorily and they must support the sketch with verbal information.**
Novice	**Children can imagine the outline of a story, but not the setting or more than one character; children have difficulty making sketches that reflect their ideas.**

The Three Billy Goats Gruff

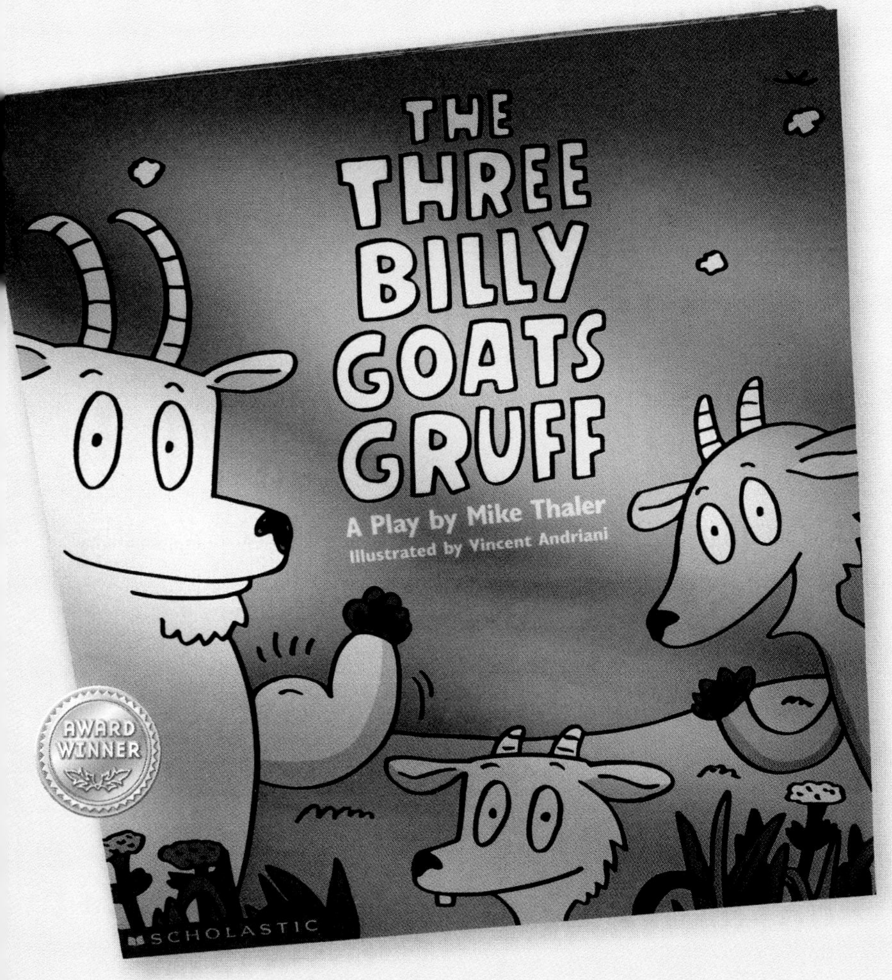
THE THREE BILLY GOATS GRUFF
A Play by Mike Thaler
Illustrated by Vincent Andriani
AWARD WINNER
SCHOLASTIC

Main Selection
Genre: Play
Award: IRA Children's Choice Award-winning author

WEEK 5 TESTED SKILLS

- **Key Comprehension Skill: Draw Conclusions**
- **Vocabulary**
- **Daily Phonics: Contractions, Plurals**
- **Spelling: Words With Contractions**
- **Grammar, Usage, Mechanics: Capitalizing Names, First Words**

Technology Connection

Build Background
Have children pretend that they must pass through a very narrow doorway to get outside to recess. Record a brainstorming session on audiocassette during which each child offers creative solutions. Play back the session and have children choose and act out their favorite plan.

Selection Summary

In this play version of the familiar folk tale *The Three Billy Goats Gruff*, the goats must cross a bridge before they can go up a mountain to munch what grows there. However, this bridge is fiercely guarded by a troll that wishes to eat the billy goats Gruff. The first two goats manage to get by the troll by promising the biggest Gruff would make the best meal. When the biggest Gruff finally reaches the bridge, he proves to be more than the mean troll can handle.

Author

MIKE THALER is also an illustrator, songwriter, and teacher. Thaler began drawing when he was a teenager. He first created cartoons for adults but soon began illustrating and writing children's literature. Another of his books is *Monkey*.

Weekly Organizer

Visit Our Web Site
www.scholastic.com

The Three Billy Goats Gruff

	DAY 1	DAY 2
READ and Introduce Skills • VOCABULARY • PHONICS • COMPREHENSION • LISTENING • SPEAKING • VIEWING 	**BUILD BACKGROUND,** p. T237 ▲ **DAILY PHONICS:** ▲ Contractions, pp. T240–T241 Practice Book, pp. 64, 65 **VOCABULARY,** p. T238 ▲ ■ Practice Book, p. 63 **PREVIEW AND PREDICT,** p. T242 **READ:** ▲ ✱ ■ *The Three Billy Goats Gruff,* pp. T242–T247 **COMPREHENSION:** Draw Conclusions, p. T245	**READ:** ▲ ■ ✱ *The Three Billy Goats Gruff,* pp. T248–T257 **DAILY PHONICS:** Contractions, p. T249 Digraphs, p. T251 Plurals, p. T255 **COMPREHENSION:** Sequence, p. T253
WRITE and Respond • GRAMMAR • USAGE • MECHANICS • SPELLING • WRITING	**SHARED WRITING,** p. T237 **JOURNAL:** High-Frequency Words, p. T239 **SPELLING:** Pretest: Contractions, p. R36 Spelling Resource Book, p. 104 **GRAMMAR, USAGE, MECHANICS:** Teach/Model: Capitalizing Names and First Words, p. R38 **ORAL LANGUAGE,** p. T247	**SHARED WRITING:** Prewrite, T257 Practice Book, p. 66 **SPELLING:** Vocabulary Practice, p. R36 Spelling Resource Book, pp. 105–107 **GRAMMAR, USAGE, MECHANICS:** Practice, p. R38 **ORAL LANGUAGE,** p. T257
EXTEND SKILLS and Apply to Literature • SKILLS • INTEGRATED LANGUAGE ARTS • INTEGRATED CURRICULUM • GUIDED READING • INDEPENDENT READING	**READ ALOUD,** p. T247 **GUIDED READING,** pp. R34–R35 **INTEGRATED CURRICULUM:** Social Studies, p. R41 **TRADE BOOKS** • ***Pierre*** • ***Jenny's Journey*** • ***Going Home*** 	**READ ALOUD,** p. T257 **GUIDED READING,** pp. R34–R35 **INTEGRATED CURRICULUM:** The Arts, p. R41 Math, p. R40 Science, p. R40

TECHNOLOGY and **REAL-WORLD SKILLS**	**WIGGLEWORKS PLUS CD-ROM** Magnet Board, pp. T238, T240 **WIGGLEWORKS PLUS CD-ROM** Speaking Skills, p. T245	**WIGGLEWORKS PLUS CD-ROM** Reading Skills, p. T257

MODIFY INSTRUCTION

● INTERVENTION ▲ ESL/ELD ■ EXTRA HELP
✳ GIFTED & TALENTED ✓ = TESTED SKILL

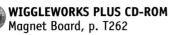

DAY 3	DAY 4	DAY 5
✓ **COMPREHENSION:** ▲ ■ Draw Conclusions, pp. T260–T261 Practice Book, pp. 67, 68 ✓ **DAILY PHONICS:** Plurals, pp. T262–T263 Practice Book, pp. 69, 70 **FOCUS ON HIGH-FREQUENCY WORDS,** p. T265 **FOCUS ON PHONICS,** p. T265	**VOCABULARY REVIEW,** p. T268 ✓ **DAILY PHONICS:** Plurals; Contractions, p. T269 **FLUENCY,** p. T269	**READING ASSESSMENT,** pp. T272–T273 Selection Test Conference Decoding Test
RESPOND: ▲ Think About Reading, p. T258 Practice Book, p. 66 **WRITE A SIGN,** p. T259 ✓ **SPELLING:** Write/Proofread, p. R37 Spelling Resource Book, p. 108 ✓ **GRAMMAR, USAGE, MECHANICS:** Practice, p. R39 **ORAL LANGUAGE,** p. T259	**SHARED WRITING** ▲ ✳ Dialogue, p. T266 Practice Book, p. 71 ✓ **SPELLING:** Study/Review, p. R37 Spelling Resource Book, p. 161 ✓ **GRAMMAR, USAGE, MECHANICS:** Apply, p. R39 **ORAL LANGUAGE,** p. T267	**WRITING ASSESSMENT,** p. T274 Child Model Children's Writing Rubric ✓ **SPELLING:** Posttest, p. R37 Spelling Practice Book, p. 163 ✓ **GRAMMAR, USAGE, MECHANICS:** Assess, p. R39 **ORAL LANGUAGE,** p. T275
READ ALOUD, p. T265 **GUIDED READING,** pp. R34–R35 **OPTIONAL MATERIALS,** p. T264 Phonics Reader #45: *Slip Slide Baseball Jokes*	**READ ALOUD,** p. T271 **GUIDED READING,** pp. R34–R35 **EXTEND VOCABULARY,** p. T268 **OPTIONAL MATERIALS,** p. T269 Phonics Reader # 46: *Say It and Smile!* **READ ALOUD:** *The Three Billy Goats Gruff,* pp. T270–T271	**READ ALOUD,** p. T276 **GUIDED READING,** pp. R34–R35 **INTEGRATED LANGUAGE ARTS:** Retell the Story, p. T275 Act Out the Play, p. T275 Draw a Comic Strip, p. T276 Create a New Story, p. T276
WIGGLEWORKS PLUS CD-ROM Presentation Skills, p. T259 **WIGGLEWORKS PLUS CD-ROM** Magnet Board, p. T262	**VIDEO** Viewing Skills, p. T271	**WIGGLEWORKS PLUS CD-ROM** Organizing Information, p. T276

Weekly Assessment

ASSESSMENT PLANNING

USE THIS CHART TO PLAN YOUR ASSESSMENT OF THE WEEKLY READING OBJECTIVES.

- **Informal Assessment is ongoing and should be used before, during and after reading.**
- **Formal assessment occurs at the end of the week on the selection test.**
- **Note that intervention activities occur throughout the lesson to support students who need extra help with skills.**

ASSESSMENT HANDBOOK

YOU MAY CHOOSE AMONG THE FOLLOWING PAGES IN THE ASSESSMENT HANDBOOK.

- **Informal Assessment**
- **Anecdotal Record**
- **Portfolio Checklist and Evaluation Forms**
- **Self-Assessment**
- **Second-Language Learners**
- **Using Technology to Assess**
- **Test Preparations**

SKILLS AND STRATEGIES

SKILLS AND STRATEGIES	Informal Assessment
COMPREHENSION Draw Conclusions	OBSERVATION **p. T245** • Did children use picture clues and story clues to draw conclusions about why the goats say hello so differently? QUICKCHECK **p. T260** • Can children use word and picture clues to draw conclusions? CHECK PRACTICE BOOK **p. 67** CONFERENCE **p. T272**
DAILY PHONICS Contractions Plurals	OBSERVATION **p. T249** • Did children recognize contractions? CHECK PRACTICE BOOK **pp. 64, 69** DICTATION **pp. T241, T263**
VOCABULARY Story Words **problem** **lunch** **bridge** **dime** **booth** **nickel** High-Frequency **were** **way**	CHECK PRACTICE BOOK **p. 63**

Formal Assessment	INTERVENTION and Instructional Alternatives	Planning Notes
SELECTION TEST • Questions 1–3 check children's mastery of the key strategy, draw conclusions. **UNIT TEST**	If children need help with drawing conclusions, then go to: • **Instructional Alternatives, p. T261** • **Review the skills lesson on pp. T260–T261**	
DECODING TEST • See p. T273. **SELECTION TEST** • Questions 4–7 check children's ability to recognize contractions and plurals. **UNIT TEST**	If children need help identifying contractions, then go to: • **Intervention, p. T265** • **Reteach, p. R61** If children need help identifying plurals, then: • **Review the skills lesson on pp. T262–T263**	
SELECTION TEST • Questions 8–10 check children's recall of high-frequency and story words. **UNIT TEST**	If children need additional practice with the vocabulary words, then go to: • **Extend Vocabulary, p. T268** • **Integrated Language Arts, p. T275**	

Technology

EXPLORING THE WIGGLEWORKS PLUS SELECTION
Children can interact with an electronic version of the literature selection in this lesson. Use this activity to direct children as they explore the WiggleWorks Plus CD-ROM.

STEP 1 Read	Be sure that children are familiar with the story by reading it once or twice on the **WiggleWorks Plus** CD-ROM.
STEP 2 Record	As children read, direct them to stop at the main points of action and record a message telling what the Troll is thinking and how the Troll is feeling at that time. Guide them to consider the action from the Troll's point of view. You might even act out those sections of the story to help children put themselves in the Troll's place.
STEP 3 Write	Now have the children use the Write area of **WiggleWorks Plus.** Ask them to use the Story Starter, "Once there were three goats who..." to begin their writing. Have them write the story from the Troll's point of view. Encourage children to illustrate their work. Print the stories and share them with the class.
STEP 4 Extend	You might extend the writing activity by having children write from a variety of perspectives. Each goat, the Troll, and even the bridge could be the narrator of the story. For more activity suggestions, see the **WiggleWorks Plus** Teaching Guide.

THE THREE BILLY GOATS GRUFF
A Play by Mike Thaler
Illustrated by Vincent Andriani
SCHOLASTIC
WiggleWorks Plus CD-ROM

Narrator: No one could use the bridge without going through his Troll booth.
Troll: I don't charge a dime. I don't charge a nickel. I'll just eat you up like a crunchy pickle.
Record
Stop
Cancel
OK
WiggleWorks Plus CD-ROM

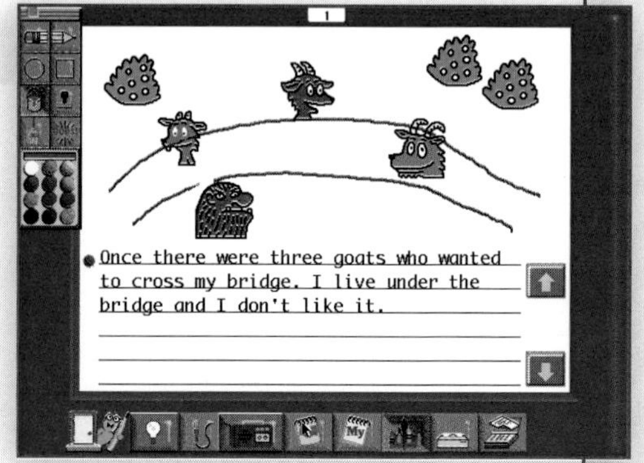
Once there were three goats who wanted to cross my bridge. I live under the bridge and I don't like it.
WiggleWorks Plus CD-ROM

Build Background

Sometimes stories and folk tales take the form of a play. Mike Thaler has rewritten this version of the folk tale The Three Billy Goats Gruff *as a play. That means that there is a cast of characters, including a narrator who helps tell the story.*

THE THREE BILLY GOATS GRUFF
A Play by Mike Thaler

Activate Prior Knowledge

DISCUSS FOLK TALES Explain to children that the story *The Three Billy Goats Gruff* is a folk tale that has been passed down from generation to generation. Point out that in this version of *The Three Billy Goats Gruff*, the author's imagination really brings the story to life!

DISCUSS USING IMAGINATION Remind children that in *Starring First Grade*, the First Grade used imagination to stage a play. Ask them to think of situations in which they had to use their own imagination.

> **How might you get across a big mud puddle that was in your way?**

SHARED WRITING *Dialogue*

INTRODUCE Ask partners to think of two characters and write what each might say about using imagination to solve problems.

DAY 1 OBJECTIVES

CHILDREN WILL:

READ 35 MINUTES
- **Build Background**
- **Vocabulary**
- **Daily Phonics: Contractions**
- ***The Three Billy Goats Gruff*, pp. 106–112**
- **Key Comprehension Skill: Draw Conclusions**
- **Genre: Play**

WRITE 25 MINUTES
- **Shared Writing: Introduce Writing a Dialogue**
- **Quickwrite: Predict**
- **Spelling: Words With Contractions**
- **Grammar, Usage, Mechanics: Capitalizing Names and First Words**
- **Oral Language**

EXTEND SKILLS 30 MINUTES
- **Integrated Curriculum**
- **Read Aloud**
- **Guided Reading**

RESOURCES
- **Practice Book, pp. 63–65**
- **Spelling Resource Book, p. 104**

MODIFY Instruction

ESL/ELD

▲ Help children preview story events and language by going through the illustrations. Ask them if they know another folk tale with a similar theme. Ask: Do these animals look real? Do you think this story will be sad or funny? Children should gather that the story will be funny. **(MAKE CONNECTIONS)**

VOCABULARY

HIGH-FREQUENCY

were way

STORY WORDS

problem lunch

bridge booth

dime nickel

VOCABULARY
High-Frequency Words

Ⓐ TEACH/MODEL

INTRODUCE HIGH-FREQUENCY WORDS Write the high-frequency words ***were*** and ***way*** in sentences on the chalkboard. Read the sentences aloud, underline the high-frequency words, and ask children if they recognize them.

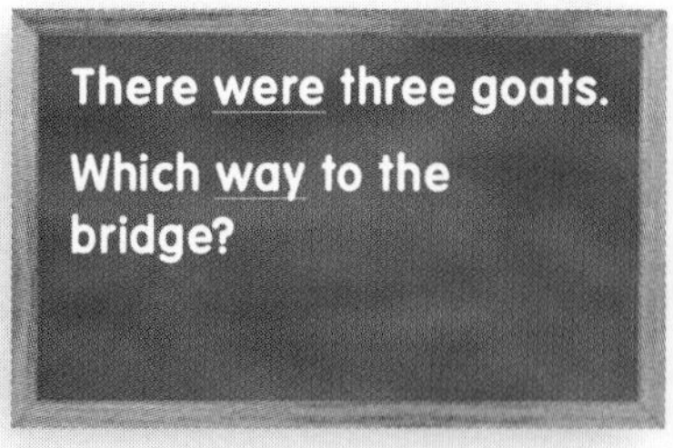
There were three goats.
Which way to the bridge?

Ask volunteers to dictate sentences using the high-frequency words. Add these to the chalkboard.

Ⓑ PRACTICE/APPLY

FOCUS ON SPELLING Write each high-frequency word on a note card. Read each word aloud. Then do the following:

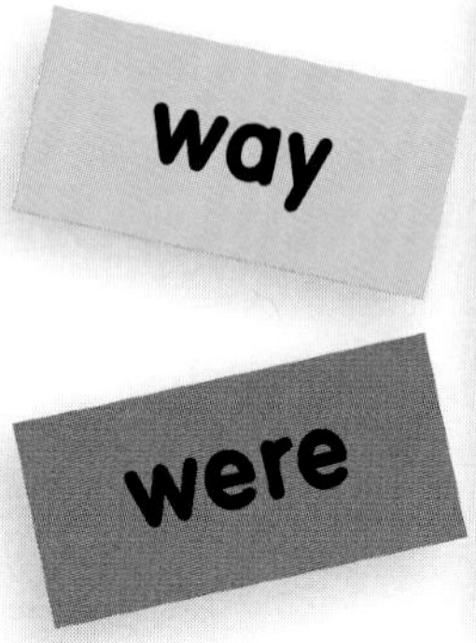
way
were

ROUTINE

1. **Display one card at a time, and ask children to state each word aloud.**
2. **Have children spell each word aloud.**
3. **Ask children to write each word in the air as they state aloud each letter. Then have them write each word on a sheet of paper or in their Journals.**

MAINTAIN VOCABULARY Add the note cards to the Word Wall. Then review the following high-frequency words on the wall: ***some, many, look, about, which, make***.

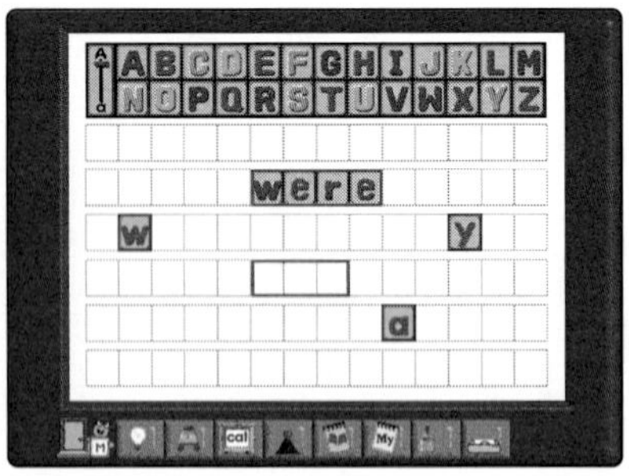
ABCDEFGHIJKLM
NOPQRSTUVWXYZ
were
w
y
a

TECHNOLOGY

Have children scramble and rebuild high-frequency words on the **WiggleWorks Plus** Magnet Board.

MODIFY Instruction

ESL/ELD

▲ Collect pictures and realia to use in introducing the story vocabulary. Play a game in which children use the real coins to buy a make-believe lunch. Make sure children understand the meaning of the high-frequency words. Use the sentences on the board to explain their meaning in context. **(USE REALIA)**

EXTRA HELP

■ Help children identify the high-frequency word ***were***. First have them find words on the Word Wall that begin with the letter ***w***. Next have them find words in which the letter ***w*** is followed by an ***e***. If children cannot identify the word ***were***, give them the next letter. Repeat a similar procedure for the word ***way***. **(STEP-BY-STEP)**

Story Words

Ⓐ TEACH/APPLY

INTRODUCE STORY WORDS

The story also contains the following Story Words: ***problem, lunch, bridge, booth, dime, nickel.***

- Write these words on the chalkboard, read them aloud, and discuss their meanings if necessary.
- Point out previously taught sound-spelling correspondences such as final *e*, and *r*-blends.
- Have children list words that are related in some way. For example, a dime and a nickel are both coins; a bridge and a booth can both be found on a toll road.

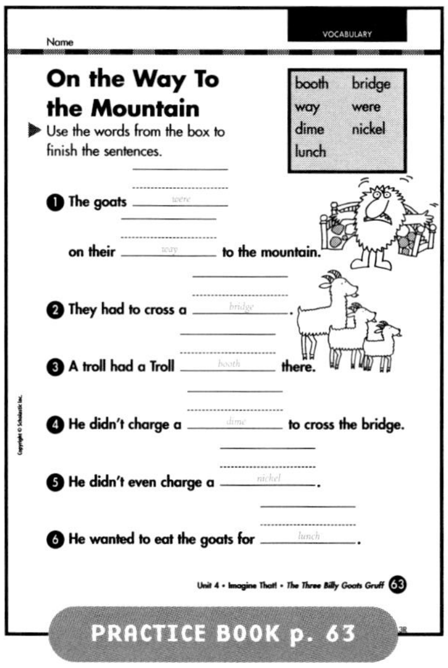

Name VOCABULARY

On the Way To the Mountain

▶ Use the words from the box to finish the sentences.

booth	bridge
way	were
dime	nickel
lunch	

1. The goats ____ on their ____ to the mountain.
2. They had to cross a ____.
3. A troll had a Troll ____ there.
4. He didn't charge a ____ to cross the bridge.
5. He didn't even charge a ____.
6. He wanted to eat the goats for ____.

Unit 4 • Imagine That! • The Three Billy Goats Gruff 63

PRACTICE BOOK p. 63

Ⓑ PRACTICE/APPLY

BUILD STORY BACKGROUND

Point out to children that a toll is something you pay when you drive across certain bridges or get onto highways called toll roads. The toll is paid at a booth.

- Have children who have seen a tollbooth describe it.
- Invite children to close their eyes and imagine a toll booth.
- Ask them to imagine giving the person at the booth a coin and then crossing the bridge or getting onto the highway.
- Ask children to draw a picture of this scene.

I gave the man in the booth a dime.
TOLL

WRITE TO READ

- When completed, have children write a sentence about their picture using one or more of the Story Words.

I'M THINKING OF . . .

Model a game that uses story words. Tell children that you are thinking of a word that begins with ***d*** and ends with ***e***. Give an incomplete sentence in which the word fits as an example: *I spent a ____ at the store*. Ask children if they can guess the word. ***(dime)*** Invite partners or small groups of children to continue the game with other story words.

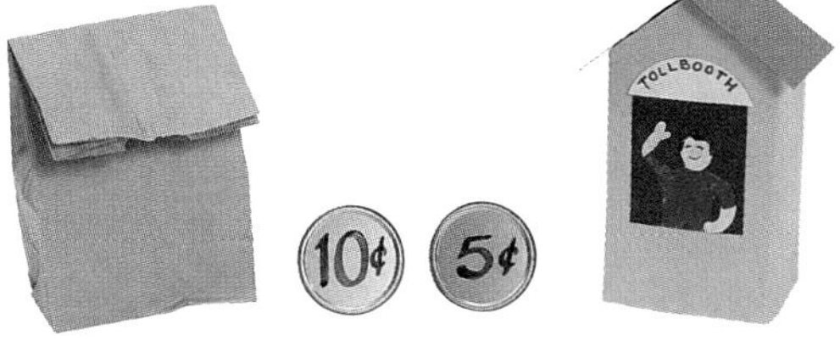
TOLLBOOTH
10¢
5¢

JOURNAL

Ask children to write a sentence using each **high-frequency word** in their Journals. You might suggest the following sentence starters:

The goats were ____.

Which way ____.

THE
THREE
BILLY
GOATS
GRUFF

SELECTION WORDS: Contractions

don't	it's
I'll	who's
I'm	you'll
I've	

SKILLS TRACE

CONTRACTIONS TESTED

Introduce. . . . . . pp. T240–T241
Practice. . . . pp. T249, T264–T265
Reteach. . . . . p. R61

ABCDEFGHIJKLM
NOPQRSTUVWXYZ
do not
don't
I will
who is

TECHNOLOGY

Have children build contractions on the **WiggleWorks Plus** Magnet Board.

- Begin with the word pairs *do/not, I/will,* and *who/is.* Have children combine the words to form contractions.
- Have children search for contractions in classroom books and add them to the list.

DAILY PHONICS

Contractions

A TEACH/MODEL

LISTEN FOR CONTRACTIONS Write the song on chart paper and sing it aloud. Point to the contractions as you sing.

- Have children sing the song and clap every time they sing the words *I've* and *don't.*

I've been working on the railroad
All the livelong day.
I've been working on the railroad
Just to pass the time away.
Don't you hear the whistle blowing?
Rise up so early in the dawn.
Don't you hear the captain shouting,
"Dinah, blow your horn"?

INTRODUCE CONTRACTIONS Write the word ***don't*** on the chalkboard. Explain to children that a contraction is two words that are shortened into one, such as ***don't.***

THINK ALOUD *When I see the word **don't,** I know it is a contraction. The special mark called an apostrophe shows me that **do** and **not** were put together to form the contraction **don't.** The apostrophe replaces the letter **o.***

- On the chalkboard, write: ***Who's that? It's only me.***
- Read aloud the sentences and ask volunteers to frame the contractions ***who's*** and ***it's.*** Ask what two words could be used in place of each contraction.

Who's that?	Who is that?
It's only me.	It is only me.

- Have children read the sentences again and substitute the words for the contractions.

MODIFY Instruction

ESL/ELD

▲ Make a chart with the contractions in the story. First help children understand the words. Then write, for example, *do not* and *don't.* Use colored chalk to x out the *o* in *not* and to circle the apostrophe that replaces it in *don't.* Say each word pair aloud and have children repeat. Then do the same with the new contraction. **(COLOR CODE)**

PHONICS MAINTENANCE Review the following sound-spellings: ***st, sp, sn, ch, wh.*** Say one of these sounds. Have a volunteer write on the chalkboard the spelling that stands for the sound(s). Continue with all the sounds.

B PRACTICE/APPLY

BLEND WORDS To practice reading contractions and review previous sound-spellings, list the following words and sentences on the chalkboard. Have children read each chorally. Model blending as needed.

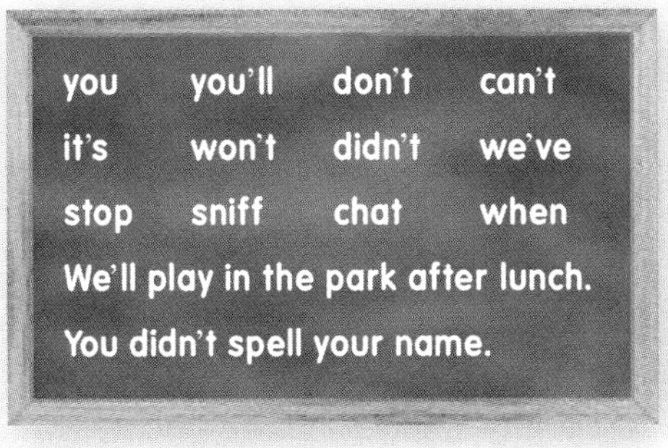
you you'll don't can't
it's won't didn't we've
stop sniff chat when
We'll play in the park after lunch.
You didn't spell your name.

DICTATION Dictate the following words for children to spell: ***I'm, don't, spot, chin.***

BUILD CONTRACTIONS Write the following words on index cards: ***not, will, is, can, did, do, is, it, you.*** Have children select two words that can be combined to form a contraction. Ask a volunteer to write the contraction on the chalkboard. Continue with other words.

CONTRACTION TELEPHONE

Have children work in threes. Ask one child to think of a sentence with a contraction and whisper the sentence to a second child. Ask the second child to whisper the sentence to a third child, using the words that make up the contraction. Have the third child say the sentence aloud. Children can check to see if the sentences match. Have them switch roles and play again.

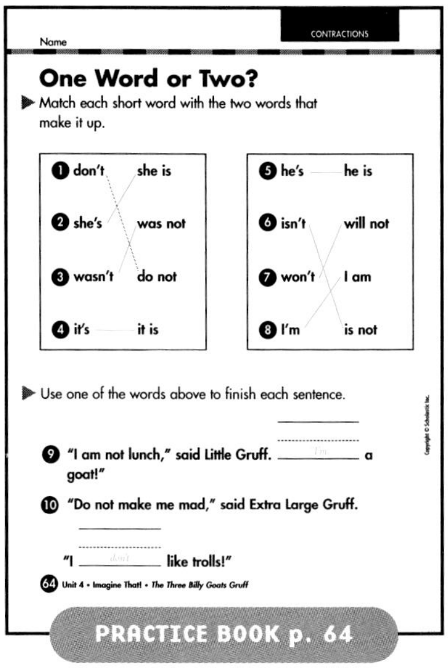

Name CONTRACTIONS

One Word or Two?

▶ Match each short word with the two words that make it up.

1 don't	she is	5 he's	he is
2 she's	was not	6 isn't	will not
3 wasn't	do not	7 won't	I am
4 it's	it is	8 I'm	is not

▶ Use one of the words above to finish each sentence.

9 "I am not lunch," said Little Gruff. "________ a goat!"

10 "Do not make me mad," said Extra Large Gruff. "I ________ like trolls!"

64 Unit 4 • Imagine That! • *The Three Billy Goats Gruff*

PRACTICE BOOK p. 64

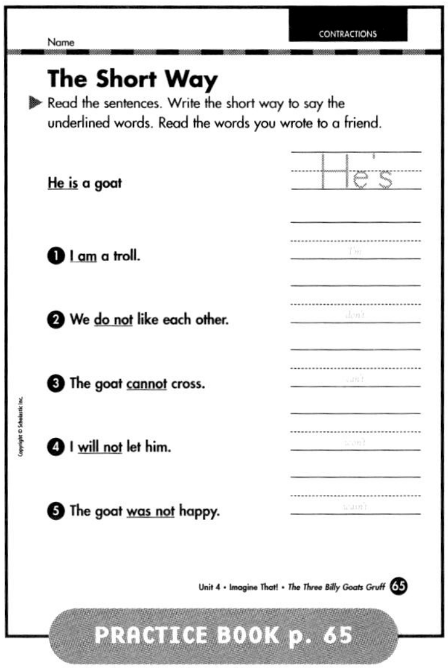

Name CONTRACTIONS

The Short Way

▶ Read the sentences. Write the short way to say the underlined words. Read the words you wrote to a friend.

He is a goat — He's

1 I am a troll.

2 We do not like each other.

3 The goat cannot cross.

4 I will not let him.

5 The goat was not happy.

Unit 4 • Imagine That! • *The Three Billy Goats Gruff* 65

PRACTICE BOOK p. 65

DECODABLE TEXT

For practice reading decodable text, see ***Scholastic Decodable Reader #53.***

For additional phonics instruction and review, see ***Scholastic Phonics A, p. 217.***

COMPREHENSION

Preview and Predict

Tell children that *The Three Billy Goats Gruff* is a play based on the folk tale by the same name. Ask children to look at the page that introduces the cast of characters.

> **Why do you think the writer wrote about each character before starting the play?**

> **How do you think it will help you read the play?**

Help children make predictions before they read by asking a question:

> **How do you think reading a play will be different from reading a story?**

JOURNAL

Make Predictions

Ask children to write their predictions in their journals. Encourage them to write about how a play is different from a story and how they are alike.

Set a Purpose

Discuss with children a purpose for reading. They may want to find out how this play is different from the play in *Starring First Grade*. Then have them read page 107.

106

PLAY

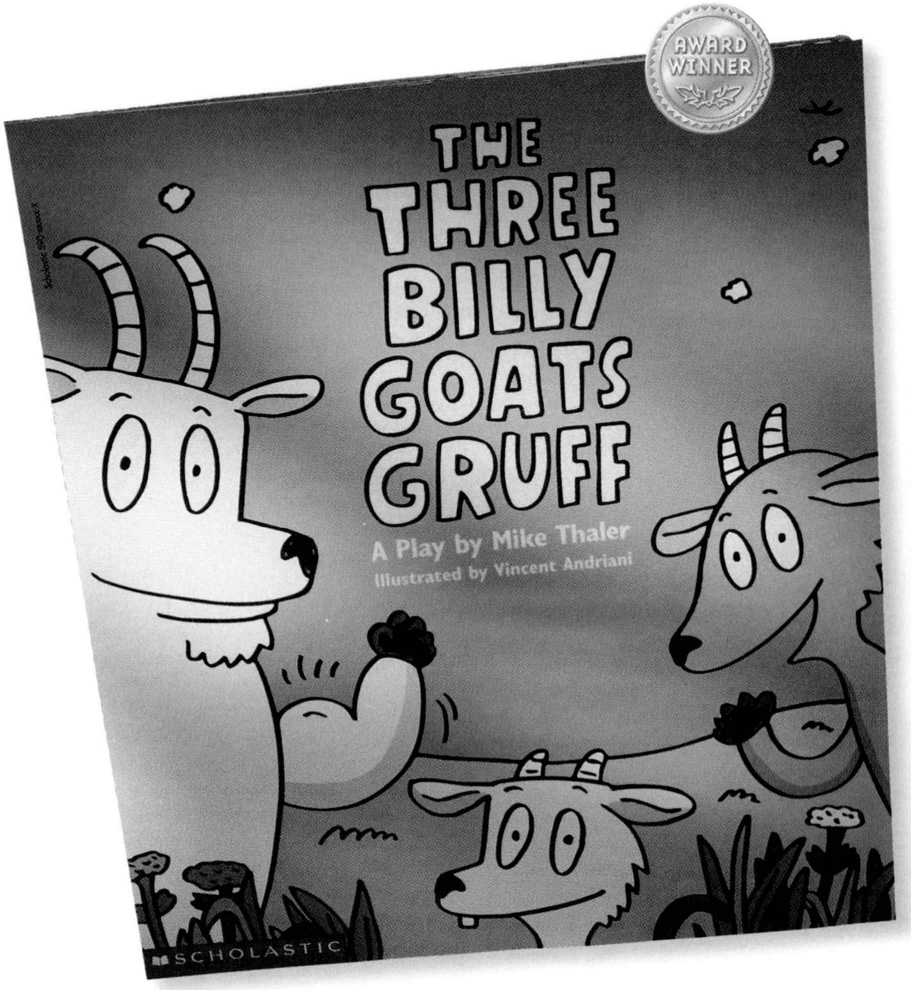
AWARD WINNER
THE THREE BILLY GOATS GRUFF
A Play by Mike Thaler
Illustrated by Vincent Andriani
SCHOLASTIC

106

CLASSROOM Management

WHOLE CLASS

On-Level Use the questions, think alouds, and skills and strategies lessons to guide children through a reading of the play.

Below-Level Read the play aloud, using different voices for the characters. Next, have children read along with you. The audiocassette may be used to preview this selection.

COOPERATIVE

Above-Level You might choose to have a group of above-level children read the play together. Children can tape record a dramatic reading of the story or record it on the computer. When completed, have these children rejoin the group to participate in the story discussion.

107

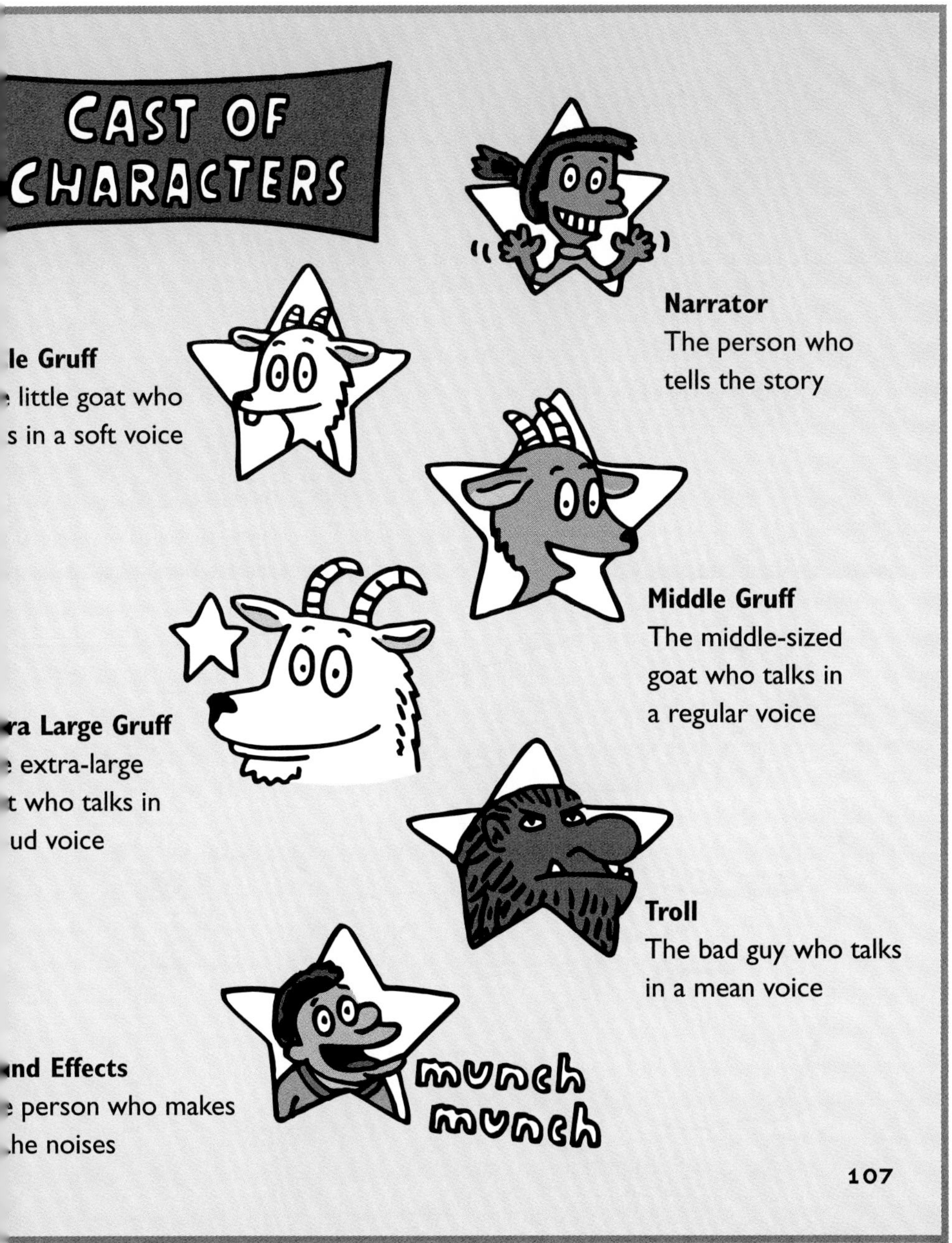
CAST OF CHARACTERS

Narrator
The person who tells the story

le Gruff
little goat who s in a soft voice

Middle Gruff
The middle-sized goat who talks in a regular voice

ra Large Gruff
extra-large t who talks in ud voice

Troll
The bad guy who talks in a mean voice

nd Effects
person who makes he noises

munch munch

107

SKILLS AND STRATEGIES

Revisit the selection for skills instruction.

✓ = Tested Skill

LITERARY GENRE

Play

TEACH/MODEL
Help children recognize the features of a play.

THINK ALOUD *I knew this story was turned into a play because it had a cast of characters, sound effects, and a description of where the story took place. It was easy to follow the story by reading what each character said, and I had fun reading the different parts and changing my voice for Little Gruff, Middle Gruff, Extra Large Gruff, and Troll.*

PRACTICE/APPLY
Invite children to act out their favorite part of the play. Then have them write a note to a classmate telling him or her which was their favorite part.

SMALL GROUP TO WHOLE CLASS

ESL/ELD Have children who need extra help or who are acquiring English listen to the story on the audiocassette prior to the class reading. This will help them to become familiar with the story sequence and vocabulary. Have children do the pre- and post-listening activities. **(USE AUDIO)**

COMPREHENSION

1 DRAW CONCLUSIONS

> **Where does this story take place? How can you tell?** *(It is set in the country. The picture shows open land, flowers, bushes, trees, a stream, and no buildings.)*

INTERVENTION TIP

Using Type for Emphasis

To help children with intonation and emphasis, remind them that Extra Large Gruff speaks in a deep, extra-loud voice. Point out that everything he says is set in all capital letters to remind the reader that he says it in a deep, extra-loud voice. Invite children to find other places where type is used to show emphasis.

108

Narrator: Once upon a time there were three billy goats Gruff. Little Gruff...

Little Gruff: Hi.

Narrator: Middle Gruff...

Middle Gruff: Hi, hi.

Narrator: And Extra Large Gruff...

Extra Large Gruff: HI, HI, HI!

Narrator: One day they decided to go up the mountain to munch the wonderful things that were growing there.

108

MODIFY Instruction

ESL/ELD

▲ Model *soft, regular, loud,* and *mean* voices. Remind children about the characters they saw as they first looked through the story. Explain that the type gives clues on how to speak. Ask: *Which character will have a mean voice?* Have them try speaking in the tone of voice of each character. **(KINESTHETIC)**

EXTRA HELP

■ Help children understand how to read and follow a play. Explain that each character says what is written after his or her name. Sometimes there are instructions about how to say the words. For example, on page 119, the troll is supposed to mumble his lines. **(LITERARY STYLE/KEY POINTS)**

109

1

Little Gruff: Yum.

Middle Gruff: Yum, yum.

Extra Large Gruff: YUM, YUM, YUM!

Narrator: But to get there they had to cross a bridge.

Little Gruff: No problem.

Middle Gruff: No problem.

Extra Large Gruff: NO PROBLEM!

Narrator: But under the bridge lived a mean and hungry Troll.

109

SOCIAL STUDIES

Ask children to complete the **Map the Play** activity on **page R41** where they will make a simple map of the play's events and use it to retell the play's story line. The activity will help children learn how to make and use a map.

TECHNOLOGY

Speaking Skills While working in small groups of four, use Read Aloud in **WiggleWorks Plus** to listen to the story. Remind children to listen for how the words are said by the narrator. Now, have each child play the part of a different character and record the story dialogue in Read.

SKILLS AND STRATEGIES

COMPREHENSION

Draw Conclusions

TEACH/MODEL

Point out to children that writers do not always explain everything. They give the readers enough information so the readers can figure out some things by themselves.

THINK ALOUD *I can use picture clues and story clues to help me conclude where this story takes place. I see flowers, trees, a stream and no buildings in the picture. I learn from the story that the goats are going up a mountain to eat. I can draw conclusions from these clues that the story takes place in the country.*

PRACTICE/APPLY

Ask children to give their own explanations as to why Little Gruff says "Hi," Middle Gruff says "Hi, Hi," and Extra Large Gruff says "HI! HI! HI!"

INFORMAL ASSESSMENT
OBSERVATION

Did children:

- ✔ use picture clues and story clues to draw conclusions about why the goats say hello so differently?
- ✔ apply what they know about *The Three Billy Goats Gruff* to draw conclusions?

See pages T260–T261 for a full skills lesson on Draw Conclusions.

COMPREHENSION

2 Author's Craft

> **How would a tollbooth be like this "troll booth"? How would it be different?** *(At both booths, travelers pay something before crossing the bridge. Travelers give money to tollbooth operators. But the Gruffs had to pay by being lunch for Troll.)*

3 Critical Thinking: Analyze

> **Why do you think Troll chose to hide under this bridge?** *(Possible answer: He knows travelers cross the bridge and he wants to surprise them from where he hides.)*

SELF-MONITORING STRATEGY

Word Attack

Think Aloud *Follow along as I read what Troll says: "I don't charge a dime, I don't charge a noodle." That doesn't make sense. What would the troll charge to cross the bridge? He says he won't charge a dime. Let's name some other coins; there are quarters, pennies and nickels. Nickel starts with an n.*

> **Does nickel make sense in the sentence?**

OPTION You may end the first day's reading here or have children continue reading the selection.

110

STOMP
STAMP
STEP

Little Gruff: Oh!

Middle Gruff: Oh, oh!

Extra Large Gruff: NO PROBLEM!

Narrator: No one could use the bridge without going through his Troll booth. 2

Troll: I don't charge a dime.
I don't charge a nickel.
I'll just eat you up
like a crunchy pickle.

110

MODIFY Instruction

ESL/ELD

▲ Make sure English language learners are clear about the concept of paying a toll. Play a "pay toll" game, in which children make a pretend bridge out of chairs and take turns playing the part of the tollbooth operator and the customer. Model appropriate language. **(ROLE-PLAY)**

EXTRA HELP

■ Have partners dictate or write a description of Troll. Encourage them to use the picture on page 111. Ask them to include details about Troll's facial expression, his teeth, and his red gym shoes. **(WORK IN PAIRS)**

111

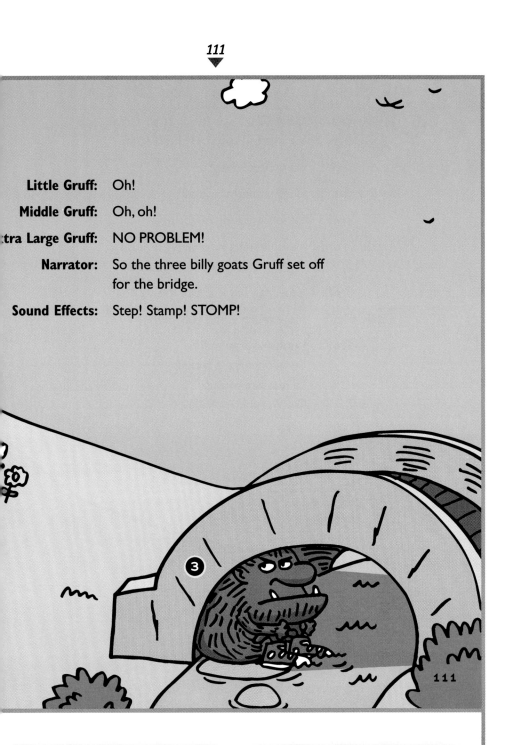

Little Gruff:	Oh!
Middle Gruff:	Oh, oh!
tra Large Gruff:	NO PROBLEM!
Narrator:	So the three billy goats Gruff set off for the bridge.
Sound Effects:	Step! Stamp! STOMP!

3
111

MENTOR CONNECTION

Discuss how William Walsh might use his imagination and creativity to retell *The Three Billy Goats Gruff.*

VISUAL LITERACY

Point out the words *STEP! STAMP! STOMP!* in the picture. Tell children that the words stand for the sounds that the goats make as they walk. Have them say the words aloud. Discuss how the words reflect the size of each goat. Then ask children to suggest other words for walking sounds.

Quickwrite

PREDICT
Ask children to write about what the goats might do next in the story. They may also wish to refine the predictions they made before reading.

DAILY LANGUAGE PRACTICE

SPELLING
DAY 1:
Administer the Pretest for Contractions. **See page R36.**

GRAMMAR, USAGE, MECHANICS
DAY 1:
Teach and Model Capitalizing Names and First Words. **See page R38.**

ORAL LANGUAGE
the three billy goat gruff dont like troll.
(The three billy goats Gruff don't like troll.)

DAY 1 WRAP-UP

READ ALOUD *To develop children's oral vocabularies, spend five to ten minutes reading from a selection of your choice.*

GUIDED READING *To extend reading, meet with the* **red** *and* **blue** *reading groups and assign Independent Center activities.* ***See pages R34–R35.***

COMPREHENSION

DAY 2 OBJECTIVES

CHILDREN WILL:

READ 40 MINUTES

- ***The Three Billy Goats Gruff*, pp. 112–121**
- **Daily Phonics: Contractions**
- **Words With Digraphs *ch, wh***
- **Plurals**

WRITE 20 MINUTES

- **Shared Writing: Prewrite a Dialogue**
- **Spelling: Words With Contractions**
- **Grammar, Usage, Mechanics: Capitalizing Names and First Words**
- **Oral Language**

EXTEND SKILLS 30 MINUTES

- **Integrated Curriculum**
- **Read Aloud**
- **Guided Reading**

RESOURCES

- **Practice Book, pp. 73–74**
- **Spelling Resource Book, pp. 105–107**

Reread

You may wish to have children independently reread the first part of the story before beginning Day 2 reading.

4 SUMMARIZE

> **Where are the three goats going? Why?** *(They're going to the mountain to munch.)*

5 DRAW CONCLUSIONS

> **Why do you think Little Gruff thinks Troll will like his brother better?** *(Middle Gruff is bigger.)*

112

Narrator: Little Gruff was the first to arrive. **4**
He started to cross the bridge.

Sound Effects: Step! Step! Step!

Narrator: Out jumped the Troll!

Troll: Who's crossing my bridge?

Little Gruff: It's only me, Little Gruff. I'm on
my way to munch the mountain.

Troll: Well, you have to pay the toll!

Little Gruff: How much is the toll?

Troll: I don't charge a dime.
I don't charge a nickel.
I'll just eat you up
like a crunchy pickle.

5

STAMP
STAMP

112

MODIFY Instruction

ESL/ELD

▲ Ask multi-level questions to help children summarize: *Point to Little Gruff. Show me Troll. Are there three goats or four goats? Are they going to the mountain or the sea? What do they have to cross? Who is under the bridge?* **(MULTI-LEVEL QUESTIONS)**

EXTRA HELP

■ Children may need help summarizing what has happened so far. Encourage them to use the pictures to retell the story using their own words. **(USE VISUALS)**

113

le Gruff: Oh, don't eat me!
My big brother's coming.
And I have a hunch,
you'll like him better for your lunch.

Troll: Well, okay. I'll wait and eat him.

113

THE ARTS

Have children complete the **Make Troll and Goat Masks** activity on **page R41** where they will make paper-bag masks of the characters in the play. Children will learn to describe and model details of the characters faces.

TEACHER TIP

"Children love to hear and use rhymes. When reading this story, I had my class find the rhyming words in Troll's dialogue. After writing those words on the board, I challenged the children to use the words in rhymes of their own."

DAILY PHONICS

Contractions

TEACH/MODEL

Remind children that a contraction is a shortened form of two words that are combined, such as ***don't***.

THINK ALOUD *I see the word* ***don't*** *on page 113. I know that it might be a contraction because it has an apostrophe. In a contraction, the apostrophe tells me that two words were combined and some of the letters were left out. As I look at* ***don't*** *and the words around it, I can figure out that it is made from the words* ***do*** *and* ***not.***

PRACTICE/APPLY

Have children use this graphic organizer to help them identify other contractions in the play, such as ***I'll*** and ***you'll*** on page 115.

APOSTROPHE
↓
WORD + WORD
↑
TAKE OUT LETTER(S)

> **How can you tell that the word is a contraction?**

> **What words were combined to make the contraction?**

INFORMAL ASSESSMENT
OBSERVATION

Did children:

✔ recognize contractions?

✔ understand how contractions are formed?

✔ understand the function of the apostrophe?

COMPREHENSION

6 SEQUENCE

> **The three goats are going over the bridge one at a time. Which goat goes first? Which goat do you think will go next?** *(Little Gruff went first. Middle Gruff will go next and then Extra Large Gruff.)*

7 DRAW CONCLUSIONS

> **Think about how Troll acts when Little Gruff and Middle Gruff try to cross the bridge. What do you think will happen when Large Gruff tries to cross? Why?** *(Possible answer: Troll will try to stop Large Gruff because Troll has been waiting for him.)*

114

6
Narrator: Middle Gruff was the next to arr
He started to cross the bridge.
Sound Effects: Stamp! Stamp! Stamp!
Troll: Who's crossing my bridge?
Middle Gruff: It's only me, Middle Gruff.
I'm on my way to munch
the mountain.
STOMP
STOMP
STAMP
STAMP
114

MODIFY Instruction

ESL/ELD

▲ Show children that the order in which the goats cross the bridge matches their size order. Practice ordinal numbers before asking children to work in pairs to look for other examples of order in the story. For example: *first, next, last/Little, Middle, Extra Large/step, stamp, stomp.* **(SEQUENCE)**

EXTRA HELP

■ Use a two-column chart to help children focus on how the scenes are alike. Reread pages 112–115 aloud, and have children guide you in writing what Little Gruff does in the first column and what Middle Gruff does in the second. **(GRAPHIC DEVICE)**

115

Troll: Well, you have to pay the toll!

Middle Gruff: How much is the toll?

Troll: I don't charge a dime.
I don't charge a nickel.
I'll just eat you up
like a crunchy pickle.

Middle Gruff: Oh, don't eat me!
My big brother's coming. 7
And I'm much thinner.
You'll like him better for your dinner.

Troll: Well, okay. I'll wait and eat him.

STEP STEP
115

CONNECTING TO THEME

Discuss with children how the author uses his imagination in *The Three Billy Goats Gruff*. Children should mention the illustrations and the humorous dialogue.

FAMILY RESOURCES

Families can help support children's literacy by logging onto the American Library Association web site at **www.ala.org/parentspage/** Families will find hints for promoting reading, as well as booklists for children.

DAILY PHONICS

Digraphs *ch, wh*

TEACH/MODEL

Review with children that the letters ***ch*** can stand for **/ch/** as in ***chair,*** and that the letters ***wh*** can stand for **/hw/** as in ***wheel.*** Write the words ***chair, bunch***, and ***wheel*** on the chalkboard. Read the words with children. Then have volunteers underline the digraph ***ch*** or ***wh*** and say the sound that each stands for.

PRACTICE/APPLY

Apply the lesson to words in the play.

- Ask children to find words with ***ch*** and ***wh***.
- Write these and other words with **/ch/** and **/hw/** on index cards, one word per card, and place them in a bag.
- Ask volunteers to draw a card from the bag, read aloud the word, and state another word that begins with the same sound.

wheel
chair

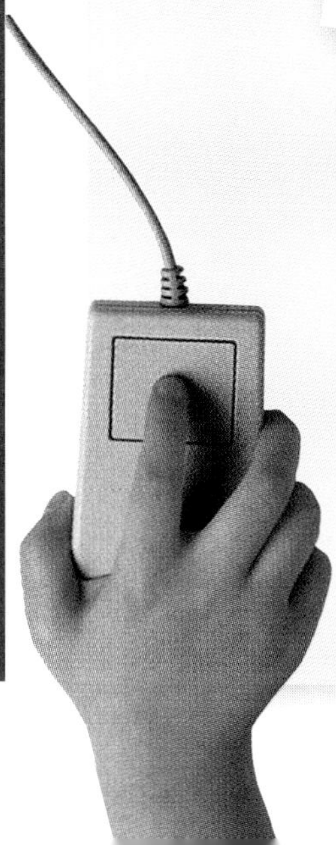

COMPREHENSION

8 SEQUENCE

> **Which goat comes to the bridge last? Did you notice anything about the order in which the goats cross the bridge?** *(Extra Large Gruff is last. The goats cross the bridge in size order, from smallest to biggest.)*

9 MAKE INFERENCES

> **How do you think Extra Large Gruff knows that Troll's name is Nosey?** *(Possible answer: Troll has a large nose. He also acts nosey when he asks who's crossing his bridge.)*

10 DRAW CONCLUSIONS

> **Do you think Extra Large Gruff will get across the bridge? Why or why not?** *(Possible answer: Extra Large Gruff will get across the bridge because he is the biggest of the three goats; he is strong and he practices martial arts.)*

INTERVENTION TIP

Build Background Information

Some children may not know what Extra Large Gruff means when he says he knows kung fu, karate, and *goat jujitsu*. Tell children that kung fu is a fighting style from China, karate comes from Japan, and jujitsu comes from China and Japan.

116

Narrator: Extra Large Gruff was the last to arrive. He started to cross the bridge. 8

Sound Effects: STOMP! STOMP! STOMP!

Troll: Who's crossing my bridge?

Extra Large Gruff: It's me, Extra Large Gruff. I'm on my way to munch the mountain. What's it to you?

Troll: Well, you have to pay the toll!

Extra Large Gruff: No way, Nosey.

Troll: How did you know my name was Nosey?

Extra Large Gruff: Listen Nosey, I've got muscles,
and my muscles got muscles.
And I know kung fu, karate, and
goat jitsu.

Troll: Well, you have to pay the toll anyway.

9

STOMP!

116

MODIFY Instruction

ESL/ELD

▲ Have children point to the appropriate art and then "make a muscle" to show they understand what muscles are. Ask: *Do you think Extra Large Gruff is stronger than the Troll? Why? How many think Extra Large will get across the bridge? How many think the Troll will stop him?* **(PREDICT)**

EXTRA HELP

■ Ask children to imagine that Extra Large Gruff is not strong and bold. Have partners act out what might happen when he meets Troll. Remind children that Extra Large Gruff has no big brother to help him out. What could he do? **(ROLE-PLAY)**

117

Extra Large Gruff: Just for laughs, what is the toll?
Troll: I don't charge a dime.
I don't charge a nickel.
I'll just eat you up
like a crunchy pickle.
10
117

MATH

Ask children to complete the **Solve Money Problems** activity on **page R40.** Have children do math problems based on the troll's tolls in *The Three Billy Goats Gruff*.

CULTURAL CONNECTION

Explain that goats are valued for their coats, milk, and meat. In China, Europe, and North America, goats are raised for their milk, which is used to make cheese. Encourage children to share what they know about animals in different cultures.

SKILLS AND STRATEGIES

COMPREHENSION

Sequence

TEACH/MODEL

Remind children that when they put events in order they should think about what happened first, next, then, and last.

THINK ALOUD *When I put things in order, I ask myself: "What happened first? What happened next? What happened last?" When I know the answers, I can put everything in order.*

PRACTICE/APPLY

Help children fold a piece of paper into four equal parts. They can write the words ***first, next, then,*** or ***last*** in each box. Then have children draw a picture in each box to show the order of events in the play. When they have finished reading the play, children can draw a picture in the last box to show the last event in the story.

> **What are the three important events that have happened so far?**

> **Describe the events using the words *first, next,* and *then.***

COMPREHENSION

11 COMPARE/CONTRAST

> **What does Extra Large Gruff do to get across the bridge and past Troll? How is this different from what Little Gruff does to get across the bridge and past Troll?** *(Possible answer: Extra Large Gruff uses his muscles and skill to get past Troll. Little Gruff tricks Troll in order to cross the bridge.)*

12 GENRE: PLAY

> **Who says *Whack! Whomp! Wrap!* on page 119? If you were that person, how would you say the words? Why would you say them that way?** *(The sound effects person says the words. The words should be said in a loud and forceful way because they represent the sounds of a fight.)*

118

Extra Large Gruff: Cool it, Bridge Breath. If you get in my way,
I'll wrap your feet around your nose,
and you'll spend your days sniffing your smelly toes.

Troll: Now you've got my goat!
I'M COMING UP RIGHT NOW TO EAT YOU UP!

118

MODIFY Instruction

ESL/ELD

▲ Children may be confused by the idiom *got my goat*. Have them look at the art to answer. Ask: *Does Troll look happy? Does he look mad or sad? How does Troll look? How do you think he feels?* Ask volunteers to offer other ways to say "You've got my goat." (You make me mad.) **(KEY WORDS)**

GIFTED & TALENTED

✳ Help children prepare a list of the onomatopoetic words, such as ***whack*** and ***wham*** in the play. Then ask volunteers to act out the words. The child who guesses the sound can perform next. **(ACT IT OUT)**

119

WHOMP!
WHACK!
WRAP!

Narrator: So up came the Troll.

Sound Effects: Whack! Whomp! Wrap! 12

Narrator: And Extra Large Gruff did just what he said he would do. 11

Troll: (mumbling) Unwrap me. Phew! Do my feet smell bad!

119

SCIENCE

Have children complete the **Learn About Goats** activity on **page R40.** Children will collect information about goat resource materials in your Artist's Studio or library.

CONNECTING TO THEME

Point out to children that the author of this play uses his imagination to create the characters and make them come to life. Each character has his own look and style, yet all three goats are somewhat alike. Have children list ways in which the three Gruffs are alike and ways in which they are different.

DAILY PHONICS

Plurals

TEACH/MODEL
Remind children that plural words tell about more than one. Talk about how an ***s*** added to the end of a word often shows that the word means more than one.

THINK ALOUD *When I look at the word **toes,** I see the **s** on the end of it. I know that this means there is more than one toe. Whenever I see an **s** added to the end of a word, I think about whether that word means more than one of something.*

PRACTICE/APPLY
You may wish to write the graphic organizer below on the chalkboard or on chart paper. Have children identify and write plurals from *The Three Billy Goats Gruff* to complete the graph.

Word	Plural
goat	goats
thing	
muscle	

After children have completed the graph, ask:

- How did you write plural words?
- How can you recognize plural words in what you read?

Ask children to identify classroom objects on sticky notes using plurals.

INFORMAL ASSESSMENT
Did children:

✔ recognize and read plurals?

See pages T62–T63 for a full phonics lesson on Plurals.

COMPREHENSION

13 SUMMARIZE

> **What were the most important parts of this play? How would you retell it for someone who has not read it?**
> *(Answers should reflect an understanding of summarizing and sequence of events.)*

JOURNAL

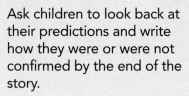

Revisit Predictions

Ask children to look back at their predictions and write how they were or were not confirmed by the end of the story.

120

Narrator: And then Extra Large Gruff happily wen[t] up the mountain to join his brothers for months and months of merry munc[h]
Sound Effects: Munch! Munch! MUNCH!
All: Snip, snap, snout.
This tale's told out. 13
120

MODIFY Instruction

ESL/ELD

▲ Help children summarize by posing yes/no questions. Model or rephrase a full sentence after each yes/no answer, and have children repeat. For example: *Were the Gruffs going to visit Troll? No, the three Goats were going to the mountain. Did Troll try to stop them? Yes, Troll wanted to eat them!* **(PARAPHRASE)**

EXTRA HELP

■ Help children understand the sentence ***This tale's told out.*** Point out that a tale is another word for a story or a play. Guide children to understand that this is the end of the story and that everything that needs to be told has been told. **(STEP-BY-STEP)**

121

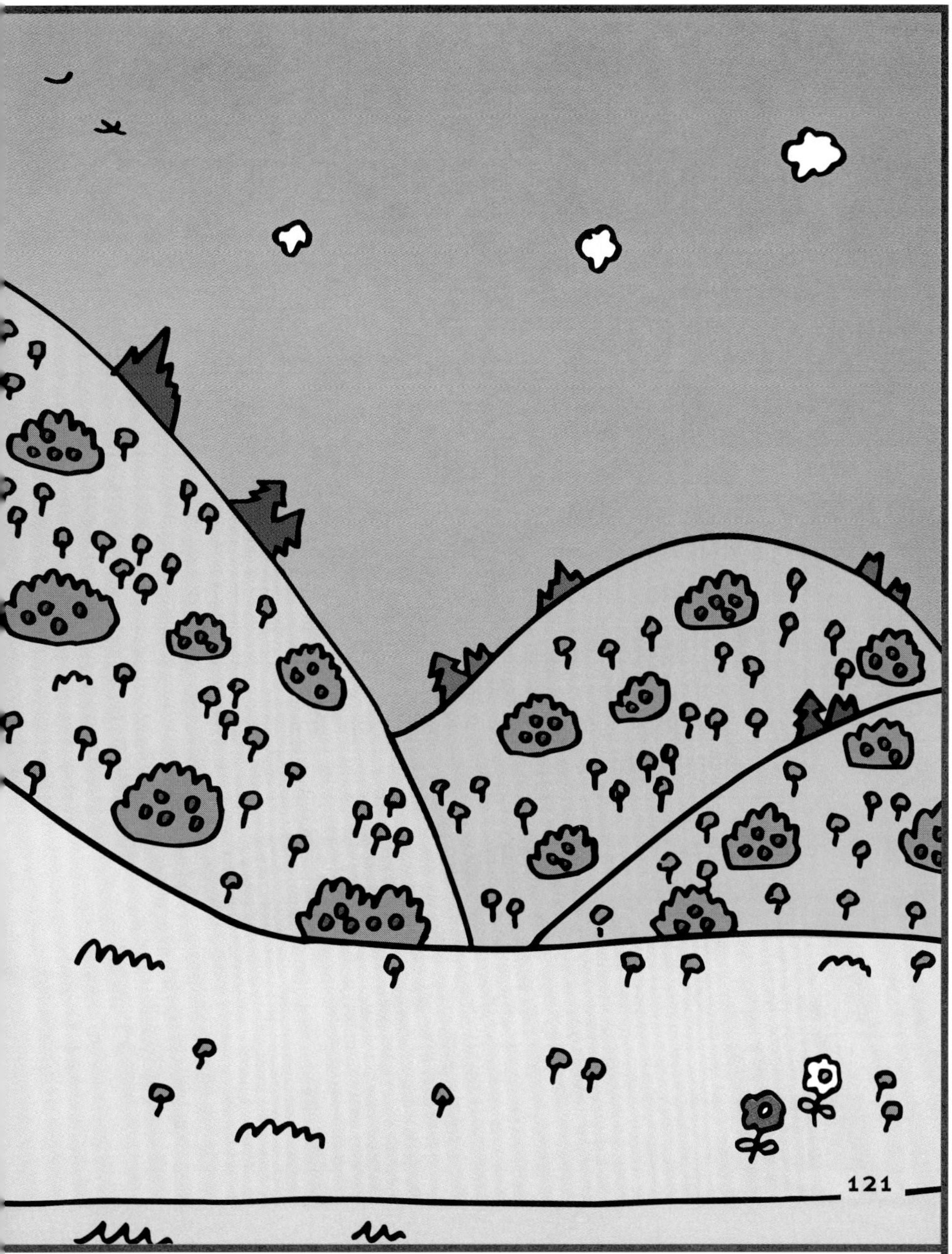
121

TECHNOLOGY

READING SKILLS Have children read the story in **WiggleWorks Plus**, and find five words from the story that name a person, place, or a thing. Ask them to put the words on the My Words list. Have children copy the words onto the Magnet Board and make them plural by adding the letter *s*.

WORD STUDY

Point out that ***whack*** and ***wham*** are words that sound like sounds. Ask children to find other words for sounds in this play. Invite them to say the onomatopoetic words aloud.

Whack wham

Dialogue

SHARED WRITING

PREWRITE Using *The Three Billy Goats Gruff* as a model, discuss dialogue. Point out that dialogue is what the characters say aloud. Tell children that they will be writing dialogue for the goats and Troll. Help them think of things that the goats and Troll might say to one another and begin the prewriting organizer.

Use **Practice Book, p. 64.**

DAILY LANGUAGE PRACTICE

SPELLING

DAY 2:
Practice the Spelling Words with Contractions. **See page R36.**

GRAMMAR, USAGE, MECHANICS

DAY 2:
Practice Capitalizing Names and First Words. **See page R38.**

ORAL LANGUAGE

"Ill wait and eat him," said troll.
("I'll wait and eat him," said Troll.)

DAY 2 WRAP-UP

READ ALOUD *Spend five to ten minutes reading from a selection of your choice.*

GUIDED READING *To extend reading, meet with the* ***green*** *and* ***yellow*** *reading groups and assign Independent Center Activities.* ***See pages R34–R35.***

COMPREHENSION

DAY 3 OBJECTIVES

CHILDREN WILL:

READ 25 MINUTES

- **Assess Comprehension**
- **Key Comprehension Skill: Draw Conclusions**
- **Daily Phonics: Plurals**

WRITE 35 MINUTES

- **Respond: Write Signs**
- **Spelling: Words With Contractions**
- **Grammar, Usage, Mechanics: Capitalizing Names and First Words**
- **Oral Language**

EXTEND SKILLS 30 MINUTES

- **Integrated Curriculum**
- **Read Aloud**
- **Guided Reading**

RESOURCES

- **Practice Book, pp. 66–70**
- **Spelling Resource Book, p. 108**

Think About Reading

Below are the **answers** to the story map *Think About Reading* questions.

1. *Little Gruff, Middle Gruff, and Extra Large Gruff.*
2. *A mean Troll lives under the bridge.*
3. *They want to cross Troll's bridge.*
4. *They tell him to wait for their big brother.*
5. *He wraps Troll's feet around his nose.*

122

RESPOND

THINK ABOUT READING

Answer the questions in the story map on another piece of paper.

CHARACTERS

1. What are the names of the three goats?
2. Who lives under the bridge?

PROBLEM

3. What do the three goats want to do?
4. What do Little Gruff and Middle Gruff tell Troll?

ENDING

5. How does Extra Large Gruff keep Troll from eating him?

STAMP
STAMP

122

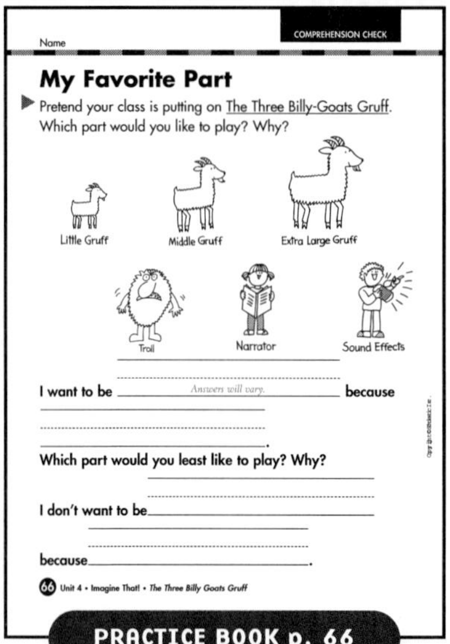
Name COMPREHENSION CHECK

My Favorite Part

Pretend your class is putting on The Three Billy-Goats Gruff. Which part would you like to play? Why?

Little Gruff Middle Gruff Extra Large Gruff

Troll Narrator Sound Effects

I want to be *Answers will vary.* because

Which part would you least like to play? Why?

I don't want to be

because

66 Unit 4 • Imagine That! • The Three Billy Goats Gruff

PRACTICE BOOK p. 66

MODIFY Instruction

ESL/ELD

▲ Brainstorm words that can warn people (*Look out; be careful; danger ahead*) and write them on the board. Model a sign (*Watch out for the Troll!*) Have children work in pairs to draw their own "Troll Bridges" with warning signs for a bulletin board. **(MODEL)**

123

WRITE A SIGN

What should everyone know about the troll under the bridge? Write a warning sign to put on the bridge. Tell about the mean and hungry troll. Tell about the Troll booth.

LITERATURE CIRCLE

How did the Gruffs feel at the beginning of the play? How did Troll feel? How did they all feel at the end of the play? Talk about your ideas.

STEP

AUTHOR MIKE THALER

Mike Thaler likes to laugh and make other people laugh. That's why he enjoys writing funny stories for children. He also creates cartoons and draws pictures, visits schools, and helps children tell their own funny stories.

More Books by Mike Thaler

- My Cat is Going to the Dogs
- The Librarian From the Black Lagoon
- Moving to Mars

123

ORAL LANGUAGE

Have children work in groups of three. Ask them to role-play the three Gruffs as they talk about their experience with Troll. Encourage children to look back at the Cast of Characters on page 107 to determine the voice that they should use for each character.

TECHNOLOGY

Presentation Skills Invite children to use **WiggleWorks Plus** PlaceMaker to create the troll warning sign for the bridge. Children can use either the banner or poster formats to produce a message complete with graphics. Brainstorm what type of information should be on a warning sign.

RESPOND

Write Signs

Before children begin to write, have them think about these questions:

- **How do you know that the troll is mean and hungry?**
- **Do signs have a lot of words or only a few?**
- **How are words written on signs?**

Children may wish to write their signs on construction paper and display them.

Literature Circle

Encourage children to participate in a conversation about why Little Gruff and Middle Gruff felt worried about Troll, while Extra Large Gruff felt there would be no problem.

DAILY LANGUAGE PRACTICE

SPELLING
DAY 3:
Write Contractions. **See page R37.**

GRAMMAR, USAGE, MECHANICS
DAY 3:
Practice Capitalizing Names and First Words. **See page R39.**

ORAL LANGUAGE
all the gruffs were happy. troll wasnt.
(All the Gruffs were happy. Troll wasn't.)

DAY 3

COMPREHENSION
Draw Conclusions

SKILLS TRACE

DRAW CONCLUSIONS TESTED

Introduce . . . . . pp. T260–T261
Practice . . . . p. T245

PIERRE
A cautionary tale in five chapters and a prologue
MAURICE SENDAK
GOING HOME
by Margaret Wild
illustrated by Wayne Harris
JENNY'S JOURNEY

CONNECT TO TRADE BOOKS

Select one of the unit trade books. Read aloud the title and discuss the cover illustration.

- Have children make predictions about what might happen in the story. Record their predictions on chart paper or on the chalkboard.
- Read a few pages at a time. Stop and have children draw conclusions about what you have read.
- Encourage children to draw some final conclusions at the end of the story and explain how they came to those conclusions.

QUICKCHECK

Can children:

✔ use word and picture clues to draw conclusions?

✔ use their prior knowledge to draw conclusions?

If YES, go on to Practice/Apply.

If NO, start at Teach/Model.

A TEACH/MODEL

USE ORAL LANGUAGE

Ask children to imagine they saw a family packing their car with suitcases and then locking up their house. What might be happening? Discuss the clues.

Explain to children that drawing conclusions is **making decisions about a story and its characters.** The events in a story and what children already know help them to draw conclusions about it. To draw conclusions:

- Read the text and look at pictures to find important details about characters and setting.
- Use the clues from the text and pictures as well as their own experiences to draw conclusions about the story.
- Check the story or play to see if their conclusions make sense, and change them if necessary.

MODIFY Instruction

ESL/ELD

▲ Have English language learners go back to look at pages 120 and 121 of the story. Ask: *Why are the two goats on the mountain laughing? What did the Extra Large Gruff do to Troll? Where will Troll go now?* Help them draw the conclusion that the Goats have won. **(GUIDED QUESTIONS)**

EXTRA HELP

■ Before children begin pages 62 and 63 in the Practice Book, help them recall conclusions that they drew when reading *The Three Billy Goats Gruff*. Help children apply the steps above to review how they came to each conclusion. **(RECALL)**

LITERATURE CONNECTION

THINK ALOUD *As I read about Extra Large Gruff, I learned that he was strong and tough. He looked big, talked in a loud voice, and he stomped. I know people who are big and loud and stomp. They would not let a troll get in their way. Based on the pictures of Extra Large Gruff, the text of the play, and what I already know, I drew the conclusion that this goat would make it past the troll and over the bridge.*

B PRACTICE/APPLY

USE PRACTICE BOOK

Have children practice what they learned about drawing conclusions by completing **Practice Book page 67. (INDIVIDUALS)**

C ASSESS

APPLY INSTRUCTIONAL ALTERNATIVES

Based on children's completion of **Practice Book page 67**, determine their ability to draw conclusions. The instructional alternatives below will aid you in pinpointing children's level of proficiency. Consider the appropriate instructional alternatives to promote further skill development.

To reinforce the skill, distribute **Practice Book page 68.**

INSTRUCTIONAL ALTERNATIVES

	If the child . . .	Then
Proficient	Draws a valid conclusion	• Have the child apply this skill independently to a more challenging story. • Present the beginning of a new story. Have the child draw possible conclusions and provide a rationale for them. Then present the rest of the story. Give the child the opportunity to revise his or her conclusions.
Apprentice	Draws conclusions but cannot provide rationale for them based on text, picture clues, or prior knowledge	• Have the child work with others to brainstorm conclusions. Children should then identify clues in the text and pictures as well as the prior knowledge that supports or negates the conclusions.
Novice	Draws a conclusion that does not fit the situation and the conclusion is not based on a rationale of text, picture clues, and prior knowledge	• Provide the child with details of a scenario and work with the child to select a set of possible conclusions. • Guide the child in identifying the text, picture clues, and prior knowledge that might help him or her to draw conclusions in any given situation or story.

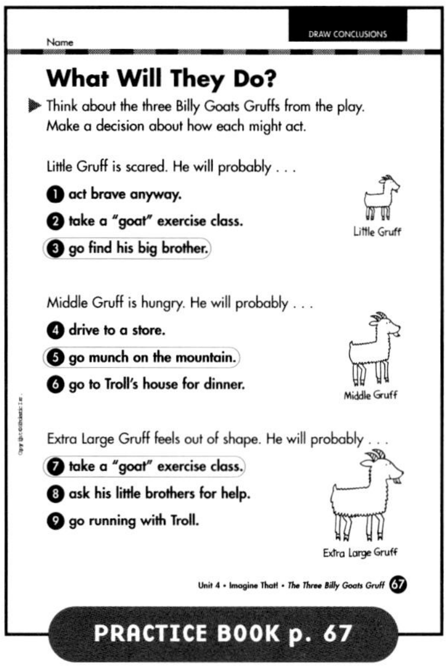
Name
DRAW CONCLUSIONS

What Will They Do?

Think about the three Billy Goats Gruffs from the play. Make a decision about how each might act.

Little Gruff is scared. He will probably . . .
1 act brave anyway.
2 take a "goat" exercise class.
3 go find his big brother.

Middle Gruff is hungry. He will probably . . .
4 drive to a store.
5 go munch on the mountain.
6 go to Troll's house for dinner.

Extra Large Gruff feels out of shape. He will probably . . .
7 take a "goat" exercise class.
8 ask his little brothers for help.
9 go running with Troll.

Little Gruff
Middle Gruff
Extra Large Gruff

Unit 4 • Imagine That! • The Three Billy Goats Gruff 67

PRACTICE BOOK p. 67

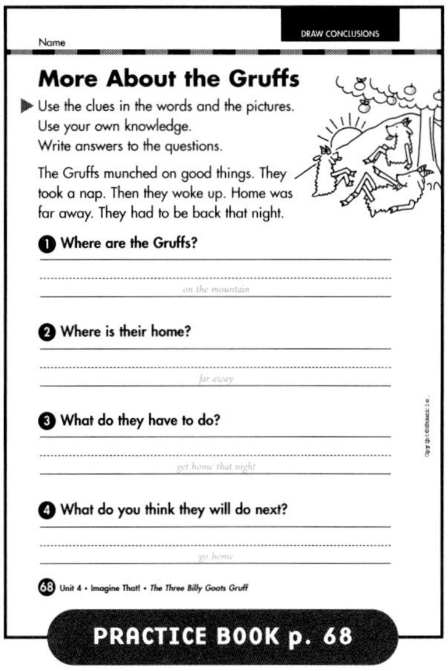
Name
DRAW CONCLUSIONS

More About the Gruffs

Use the clues in the words and the pictures. Use your own knowledge. Write answers to the questions.

The Gruffs munched on good things. They took a nap. Then they woke up. Home was far away. They had to be back that night.

1 Where are the Gruffs?
on the mountain

2 Where is their home?
far away

3 What do they have to do?
get home that night

4 What do you think they will do next?
go home

68 Unit 4 • Imagine That! • The Three Billy Goats Gruff

PRACTICE BOOK p. 68

THE THREE BILLY GOATS GRUFF

SELECTION WORDS: Plurals

brothers, goats, laughs, months, muscles, things, toes

SKILLS TRACE

PLURALS TESTED

Introduce . . . .pp. T262–263
Practice . . . . .p. T255
Review . . . . .p. T269
Reteach . . . . .p. R62

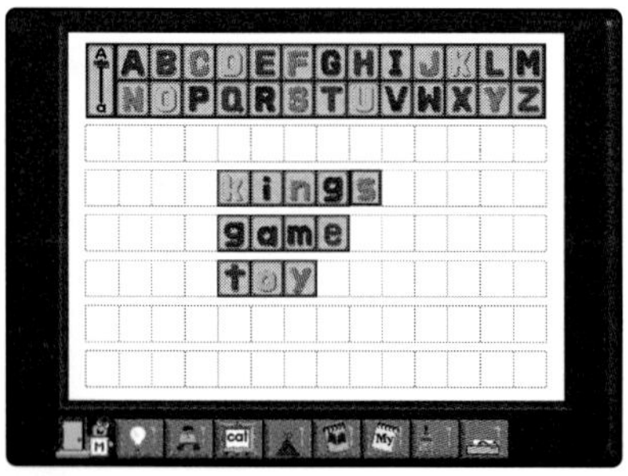
ABCDEFGHIJKLM
NOPQRSTUVWXYZ
kings
game
toy

TECHNOLOGY

Have children write plurals on the **WiggleWorks Plus** Magnet Board.

- Begin with the words ***king, game,*** and ***toy.*** Have children add an ***s*** to each word to make it mean more than one.
- Have children search for plurals in classroom books and add them to the list.

DAILY PHONICS

Plurals

A TEACH/MODEL

LISTEN FOR PLURALS Write the following nursery rhyme on chart paper and read it aloud. Point to the words ***bells, shells,*** and ***maids*** as you read.

- After reading aloud the rhyme several times, have children say it with you.
- Have children clap when they say the words ***bells, shells,*** and ***maids.***

> **Mary, Mary, quite contrary,**
>
> **How does your garden grow?**
>
> **With silver bells and cockle shells,**
>
> **And pretty maids all in a row.**

INTRODUCE PLURALS Tell children that plurals are words that mean more than one. Remind them that when they see an ***s*** at the end of a word, it often means that the word means more than one and is a plural. Then write the word ***goats*** on the chalkboard.

THINK ALOUD *When I want to know if there is more than one of something, I look at the ending of a word. The word* **goats** *has an* **s** *on the end of it. This tells me that there is more than one goat.*

- Have children list on the chalkboard other plurals. You might suggest that they begin with the plurals of classroom objects such as books and pencils.

PHONICS MAINTENANCE Review the following sound-spellings: ***st, sp, sn, ch, wh.*** Say one of these sounds. Have a volunteer write on the chalkboard the spelling that stands for the sound(s). Continue with all the sounds.

MODIFY Instruction

ESL/ELD

▲ Write these words on the board: *goat, mountain, brother, toll, dime.* Point to each word and say, *How many?* Write the number "1" in front of each word. Then write the number 2 on the board. Let children take turns choosing a word and writing its plural next to the number "2." **(LINGUISTIC CLUES)**

EXTRA HELP

■ Write singular and plural nouns on the chalkboard. Point to each word as you read it aloud. Have children raise their hands when they hear a word that is a plural. **(MULTISENSORY TECHNIQUES)**

B PRACTICE/APPLY

BLEND WORDS To practice reading plurals and review previous sound-spellings, list the following words and sentences on the chalkboard. Have children read each chorally. Model blending as needed.

dog	dogs	goat	goats
snake	snakes	bike	bikes
spell	stick	which	chop

The three goats ran into the shed.

I need some pens, pencils, and chalk.

DICTATION Dictate the following words for children to spell: ***cats, sticks, whales, chips.***

BUILD PLURALS Write the following words on index cards: ***bag, cat, dime, step, whale, check, snack.*** Also write ***s*** on one card. Have children combine a word card with the ***s*** card to form a plural. Write the plurals on the chalkboard.

bag cat dime

step whale check snack

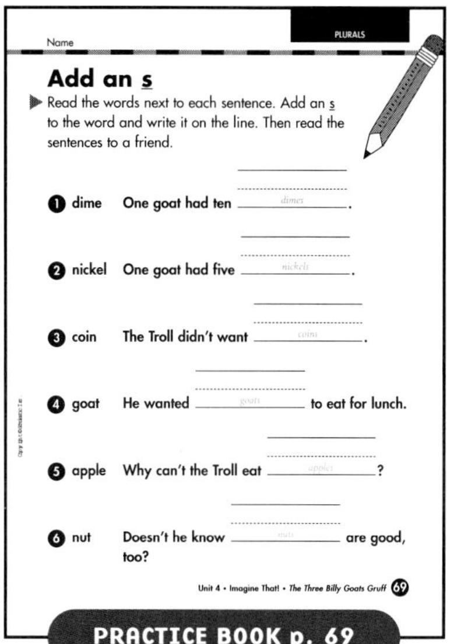
Name PLURALS

Add an s

Read the words next to each sentence. Add an s to the word and write it on the line. Then read the sentences to a friend.

1. dime — One goat had ten dimes.
2. nickel — One goat had five nickels.
3. coin — The Troll didn't want coins.
4. goat — He wanted goats to eat for lunch.
5. apple — Why can't the Troll eat apples?
6. nut — Doesn't he know nuts are good, too?

Unit 4 • Imagine That! • The Three Billy Goats Gruff 69

PRACTICE BOOK p. 69

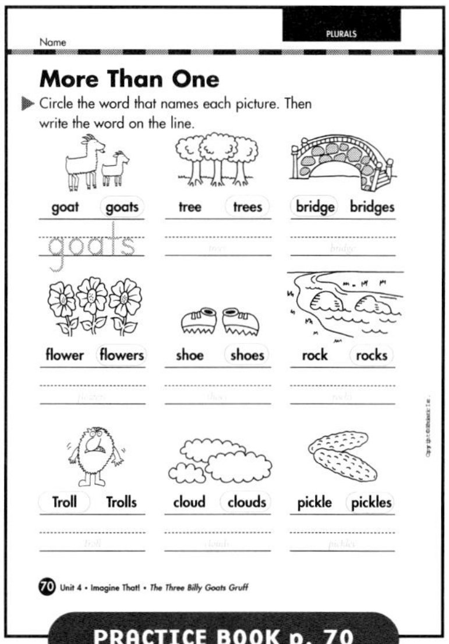
Name PLURALS

More Than One

Circle the word that names each picture. Then write the word on the line.

goat goats — goats | tree trees | bridge bridges
flower flowers | shoe shoes | rock rocks
Troll Trolls | cloud clouds | pickle pickles

70 Unit 4 • Imagine That! • The Three Billy Goats Gruff

PRACTICE BOOK p. 70

DECODABLE TEXT

For practice reading decodable text, see ***Scholastic Decodable Reader #54.***

For additional phonics instruction and review, see ***Scholastic Phonics A, pp. 204, 233.***

PLURAL BOUNCE

Have children stand in a circle. Give one child a ball to bounce. Have the child bounce the ball once, say a singular word, and toss the ball to a second child. That child must catch the ball and say the plural of the word. The second child then bounces the ball once, says another singular word, and tosses the ball to another child who says a plural. Continue until each child has participated.

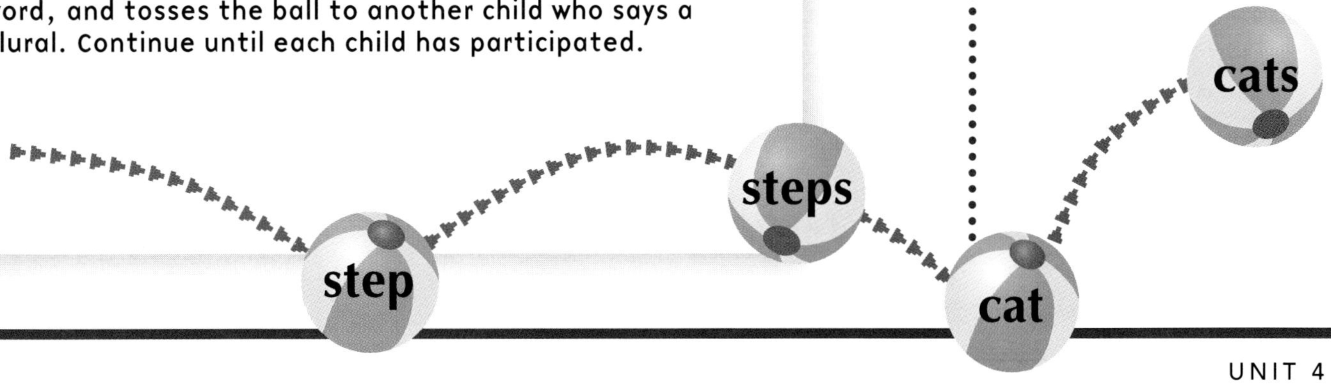
step
steps
cat
cats

Building Fluency

Phonics Reader

Slip Slide Baseball Jokes
Book 45
by Gail Tuchman
Illustrated by Tony Griego
SCHOLASTIC

Guide children through a reading of **Phonics Reader #45,** *Slip Slide Baseball Jokes.* For a detailed lesson plan, see **Phonics Reader Teacher's Guide Part B, pages 32–33.** While children read, note how well they:

- **blend words,**
- **recognize high-frequency words,**
- **read with speed, accuracy, and expression.**

You may wish to have children reread the story with a partner.

★ See Phonics Readers Take-Home Books 37–72 for reproducible format.

More Support Materials . . .

GOING HOME
PIERRE
A cautionary tale IN FIVE CHAPTERS AND A PROLOGUE
JENNY'S JOURNEY
SCHOLASTIC

Trade Book Library

For additional leveled reading practice, have children read one of the following:

Going Home
CHALLENGE

Pierre
AVERAGE

Jenny's Journey
EASY

Phonics and Word Building Kit

Have children form contractions using the word building cards. The Phonics and Word Building Kit Teacher's Guide also contains additional phonics and structural analysis activities.

Home-School Connection

Slip Slide Baseball Jokes
DON'T BE AFRAID

Send home *Slip Slide Baseball Jokes* and *Don't Be Afraid.* Have children read the books to a family member.

My Book

DON'T BE AFRAID

For additional practice with high-frequency words and contractions, have children read *Don't Be Afraid.* The My Book is also available on **WiggleWorks Plus.**

Intervention

For children who need extra help . . .

FOCUS ON HIGH-FREQUENCY WORDS

Write the following sentences on sentence strips. Each sentence focuses on one or more of the high-frequency words from this unit.

We were very happy.

Which dog is bigger?

Which way should I go?

We have many books.

- Read aloud each sentence. Help children find or draw a picture to match each sentence. Attach the pictures to index cards.
- Then have children chorally read each sentence and match the sentence to the picture card.
- Continue by mixing the cards and strips for children to practice reading and matching.

FOCUS ON PHONICS

Provide time for children to play with the words that they encountered in the story, such as ***I'm, I'll, it's, goats,*** and ***things.***

- Make each word using magnetic letters or letter cards as children observe.
- Have children trace the letters in each word with their fingers as you say the sound for which each stands.
- Mix the letters and have children reform the words.
- Model blending as needed.

g oa t s

PROFESSIONAL DEVELOPMENT

JOHN SHEFELBINE

Dictating Words With Multiple Spellings

*Many sounds, particularly vowels, have more than one spelling. For example, common spellings for long **e** include **e, ee, ea,** and **y**. When asking children to spell a word such as **feet**, ask them, "Do you know which **e** to use?" If the children don't know, tell them and help them think of a way of remembering the spelling for that particular word. An association with a familiar word is one strategy (i.e., I see my feet.).*

DAY 3 WRAP-UP

READ ALOUD *To conclude each reading session and develop children's oral vocabularies, read aloud a book of your choice. If the book contains chapters, you might choose to read only one chapter a day.*

GUIDED READING *To extend reading, meet with the **red** and **blue** reading groups and assign Independent Center activities.* ***See pages R34–R35.***

DAY 4 OBJECTIVES

CHILDREN WILL:

READ 25 MINUTES

- **Reread *The Three Billy Goats Gruff***

WRITE 45 MINUTES

- **Shared Writing: Dialogue**
- **Spelling: Words With Contractions**
- **Grammar, Usage, Mechanics: Capitalizing Names and First Words**
- **Oral Language**

EXTEND SKILLS 20 MINUTES

- **Vocabulary**
- **Daily Phonics: Plurals**
- **Read Aloud**

RESOURCES

- **Practice Book, p. 71**
- **Spelling Resource Book, p. 161**

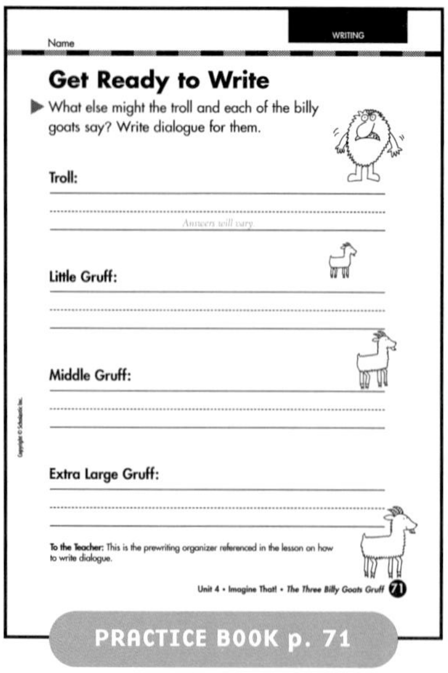

Name WRITING

Get Ready to Write

▶ What else might the troll and each of the billy goats say? Write dialogue for them.

Troll:

Answers will vary

Little Gruff:

Middle Gruff:

Extra Large Gruff:

To the Teacher: This is the prewriting organizer referenced in the lesson on how to write dialogue.

Unit 4 • Imagine That! • The Three Billy Goats Gruff 71

PRACTICE BOOK p. 71

SHARED WRITING

Dialogue

THE THREE BILLY GOATS GRUFF

SELECTION CONNECTION

Using dialogue in *The Three Billy Goats Gruff* as a model, children will write their own dialogue for the play.

THINK ABOUT WRITING

Encourage children to talk about favorite plays they've seen, read, or performed. Ask who the characters were and what they said to each other. Help children understand that dialogue in a play:

- is what the characters say to one another,
- helps the audience understand the story,
- may rhyme.

INTRODUCE THE WRITING EVENT

Explain to children that they will work together to develop their own dialogue for the characters in *The Three Billy Goats Gruff*. Ask them to think about how their dialogue will help the audience understand the play.

TEACH/MODEL

PUT IT IN CONTEXT

Ask children to look at the beginning of *The Three Billy Goats Gruff*. Point out the characters in the play. Go over the first two or three pages of dialogue with children.

> **How does the dialogue help you understand the characters?**

> **How does the dialogue help you understand what is happening in the play?**

MODIFY Instruction

ESL/ELD

▲ Prepare children for the Shared Writing activity by having them act out the dialogue in the story between the goats and Troll. Make sure they understand the meaning of the words each character says. Model pronunciation as necessary. **(ROLE-PLAY)**

GIFTED & TALENTED

✳ Challenge proficient writers to write their dialogue in rhyme. You may wish to have children work with a partner to complete this rhyming dialogue. **(RHYME)**

Have children brainstorm what they would have the characters say.

- Have children write or dictate their ideas on the chalkboard.
- Encourage children to write or dictate the characters' names before their dialogue.

GRAMMAR CONNECTION

- Have children check their dialogue to be sure they have capitalized names and first words.

WRITE

WRITE DIALOGUE

- Have children pick a scene from *The Three Billy Goats Gruff* and write or dictate new dialogue.
- Encourage children to identify each of the characters speaking.
- Remind children that they may also include a narrator and sound effects in their scene.

ASSESS

PERFORMANCE-BASED ASSESSMENT

The following questions will help children assess their work.

✔ **Have we created new dialogue for the characters?**

✔ **Does our dialogue follow the pattern of *The Three Billy Goats Gruff*, with the character's names coming before their words?**

✔ **Does the dialogue tell what is happening in the story?**

Children may wish to carry this piece through the writing process described on pages T290–T293.

DAILY LANGUAGE PRACTICE

SPELLING

DAY 4:
Review Contractions.

Have children proofread sentences. **See page R37.**

GRAMMAR, USAGE, MECHANICS

DAY 4:
Apply Capitalizing Names and First Words. **See page R39.**

ORAL LANGUAGE

billy goat dont like trolls.
(Billy goats don't like trolls.)

TEACHER TIP

"I have children in my class record their dialogue on tape. Then we play it back to hear how it sounds. You can also have children act out the dialogue and video tape it for viewing!"

Extend Vocabulary

Review High-Frequency Words

Write the high-frequency words ***were*** and ***way*** on note cards. Then write the following incomplete sentences on the chalkboard:

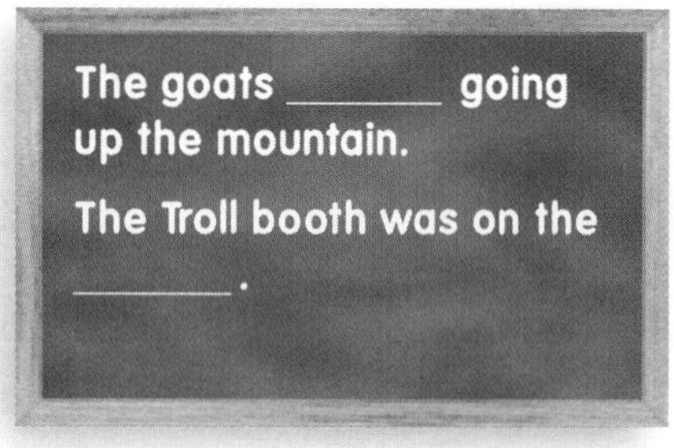
The goats ______ going up the mountain.
The Troll booth was on the ______.

Read aloud the incomplete sentences, and have children place the appropriate high-frequency word in the correct blank space. Then help children chorally read the sentences.

Review Story Words

Write the story words ***problem, lunch, bridge, booth, dime,*** and ***nickel*** on note cards. Then write the following incomplete sentences on sentence strips:

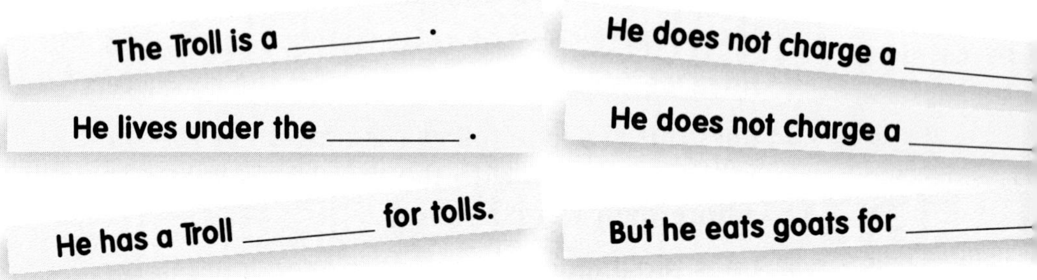
The Troll is a ______.
He lives under the ______.
He has a Troll ______ for tolls.
He does not charge a ______
He does not charge a ______
But he eats goats for ______

Read aloud the incomplete sentences and have children place the appropriate story word note card in the blank space. Then help them to chorally read the sentences.

TEACHER TIP

Make and distribute copies of the vocabulary cards on pp. R74–R75. Have children use these cards for additional practice.

MORE DIALOGUE

Write each of the high-frequency words and story words on chart paper. As a group, decide how to use each word in a line of dialogue from one character in the play. You might begin by using the word *way* in the following example: *"The goat is coming my way," the Troll said.*

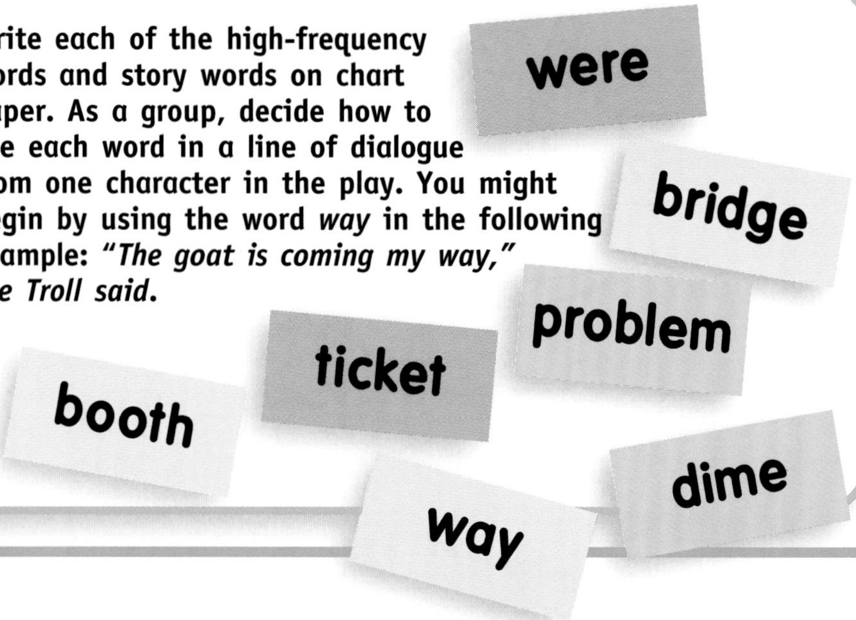
were
bridge
problem
ticket
booth
dime
way

Building Fluency

Phonics Reader

Guide children through a reading of **Phonics Reader #46,** *Say It and Smile!* For a detailed lesson plan, see **Phonics Reader Teacher's Guide Part B, pp. 34–35.** While children read, note how well they:

- **blend words,**
- **recognize high-frequency words,**
- **read with speed, accuracy, and expression.**

SAY IT AND SMILE!
Book 46
by Wiley Blevins
Illustrated by Tim Haggerty
SCHOLASTIC

You may wish to have children reread the story with a partner.

★ See Phonics Readers Take-Home Books 37–72 for reproducible format.

More Support Materials . . .

GOING HOME
PIERRE
A cautionary tale
IN FIVE CHAPTERS
AND A PROLOGUE
JENNY'S JOURNEY
SCHOLASTIC

Trade Book Library

For additional leveled reading practice, have children read one of the following:

Going Home
CHALLENGE

Pierre
AVERAGE

Jenny's Journey
EASY

PHONICS
The
Puppet Club
SCHOLASTIC

Phonics Chapter Book

For additional practice with plurals and contractions, have children reread **Phonics Chapter Book 4,** *The Puppet Club.*

Home-School Connection

SAY IT AND SMILE!
LOTS OF ORANGES

Send home *Say It and Smile!* and *Lots of Oranges.* Have children read the books to a family member.

LOTS OF ORANGES
by Cass Hollander
Illustrated by Vincent Andriani
SCHOLASTIC

My Book

For additional practice with high-frequency words and plurals, have children read *Lots of Oranges.* The My Book is also available on **WiggleWorks Plus.**

Listen to the Read Aloud

THE
THREE
BILLY
GOATS
GRUFF
A Play by Mike Thaler
SCHOLASTIC

READ ALOUD BOOK
The Three Billy Goats Gruff

Introduce the Read Aloud

CREATE INTEREST

Ask children to name three stories they know that have the word *three* in their titles. You may wish to suggest *Goldilocks and the Three Bears, The Three Little Pigs,* and *The Three Billy Goats Gruff.* Ask children to talk about the three animals in each story. Then tell children that today's Read Aloud is one of those stories: *The Three Billy Goats Gruff.*

Share the Read Aloud

MAKE PREDICTIONS

Show children the cover of the book. Read the title and the name of the illustrator. Point out that *The Three Billy Goats Gruff* is a folk tale that comes from Norway.

Read aloud the story. As children become familiar with the particular language patterns of this retelling, encourage them to join in when you read the troll's challenges and the goats' responses. When you have finished the story, invite volunteers to offer their ideas about the three goats and the troll.

The number three recurs often in European folk tales, but may appear less often in folk tales from other cultures. As you introduce the Read Aloud, you may want to ask children to think of animal stories they know, without placing emphasis on the number three.
(CULTURAL DISTINCTIONS)

Think About the Read Aloud

DISCUSSION

Give children a moment to share their thoughts and opinions about the story. These questions may help:

> **What do you think of this story?**

> **How did the Troll change from the beginning to the end of the story? What do you think Troll learned from the goats?**

> **As you listened to this story, which were your favorite parts?**

Focus on Language

Talk with children about onomatopoeia, repetition, and dialogue in *The Three Billy Goats Gruff.*

> **What words sound like sounds?**

> **Why do you think the author put those words in the story? How did they make the story come alive?**

> **What parts of this story are repeated? Why do you think they are repeated?**

Ask children to recall dialogue between characters in the story. Help them draw conclusions about the personalities of the characters based on what they say.

ACTIVITY: ACT OUT THE STORY

Have groups take turns acting out the story. Let each group decide if they want you to read the story while they act it out and create sound effects, or if they want to make up lines and act out the story without narration. Remind children to use hand gestures and other movements as they speak to make the story more interesting.

Make Connections

ORAL LANGUAGE

To Children's Lives

DISCUSSION In *The Three Billy Goats Gruff,* the three goats work together to trick the troll. Invite children to tell about times when they worked together with friends or family to plan or do something.

To *The Three Billy Goats Gruff*

DISCUSSION Invite children to compare the two versions of *The Three Billy Goats Gruff.* How are the two folk tales different?

LISTEN TO NARRATIVE

TEACH/MODEL Talk with children about how listening to narrative text helps them to enjoy it and learn important story details.

THINK ALOUD *When I listen to folk tales, I pay attention so I don't miss any important details. In* The Three Billy Goats Gruff, *I liked listening to the "TRIP, TRAP," and the troll's shouts of "What's that tripping over my bridge?" When I tell this story, I will include these parts.*

PRACTICE/APPLY Have children listen as volunteers retell parts of the story in their own words.

TECHNOLOGY

Viewing Skills
Videotape children dramatizing the story. Discuss how this story can be understood while using very few props or costumes. Have children brainstorm ways to portray each character using gestures, voices, and sound effects rather than costumes. Also plan how to have students become the bridge and the mountain.

DAY 4 WRAP-UP

READ ALOUD *Spend five to ten minutes reading from a selection of your choice.*

GUIDED READING *To extend reading, meet with the* ***green*** *and* ***yellow*** *reading groups and assign Independent Center activities.* ***See pages R34–R35.***

Reading Assessment

DAY 5 OBJECTIVES

CHILDREN WILL:

READ 30 MINUTES

- **Reading Assessment**
- **Daily Phonics: Contractions, Plurals**

WRITE 30 MINUTES

- **Writing Assessment**
- **Spelling: Words With Contractions**
- **Grammar, Usage, Mechanics: Capitalize Names and First Words**
- **Oral Language**

EXTEND SKILLS 30 MINUTES

- **Integrated Language Arts**
- **Read Aloud**
- **Guided Reading**

RESOURCES

- **Selection Test**
- **Spelling Resource Book p. 163**

REGROUPING TIP

- Assess and regroup children for leveled reading every six weeks.
- Use the results of your informal and formal assessments to regroup children as necessary.
- Be sure all children are involved in whole class and small group instruction throughout each day.

INFORMAL ASSESSMENT: OBSERVATION

PHONICS

Write the following words on note cards: ***I'll, it's, goats, don't, brothers, you'll, things.*** Display one card at a time and have children read the words. If the word is a contraction, have children state the two words from which it is formed. If it is a plural, have children name the singular form. Note children who respond incorrectly or wait for classmates to respond before providing an answer.

HIGH-FREQUENCY WORDS

Write the following words on note cards: ***were, way.*** Display one card at a time and have the class read the word. Note children who have difficulty recognizing either word.

KEY STRATEGY: DRAW CONCLUSIONS

Have children read a few pages of a book they haven't read yet. Help them draw conclusions about the story or its characters based on clues from text and pictures as well as their own experiences. Have children name elements from the story that validate their conclusions.

CONFERENCE

Have children reread *The Three Billy Goats Gruff.* As they reread, select several children to conference with. Ask them to do the following:

- **read aloud a few pages of the play.**
- **retell the play in their own words.**
- **explain what they do to figure out an unfamiliar word.**

Keep anecdotal records of the conferences. Place your findings in each child's assessment folder. Use the information to determine which children need additional support.

THE THREE BILLY GOATS GRUFF

The Three Billy Goats Gruff

FORMAL ASSESSMENT

DECODING TEST

Make two copies of the assessment below. The assessment piece is designed to be used individually.

- Give one to the child and keep the other to record each child's errors.
- As the child reads aloud the words and sentences in the assessment boxes, record his or her attempts, corrections, errors, and passes.
- Once completed, keep each assessment piece in the child's portfolio as a running record of his or her emerging reading skills.

NAME: ______________________________ **DATE:** ____________

A Have children read the following word list:

can't	**time**	**green**	**were**	**way**
wheels	**date**	**mine**	**which**	**make**
chips	**jumping**	**read**	**look**	**about**
clean	**I'll**	**clap**	**some**	**soon**
frog	**lunch**	**falling**	**many**	**went**

B Have children read the following word sentences.

- **Were the goats sleeping?**
- **We didn't read those books.**

C On a separate sheet of paper, have children write the following words and sentences.

- **can't homes chin when**
- **Which goats didn't run?**
- **Did he stomp his feet?**

SELECTION TEST

Use the selection test to obtain a formal measure of children's mastery of the week's reading objectives.

SELF-SELECTION

Have children select one or two pieces of work from the week that they would like to place in their portfolios.

Suggest that children write a sentence telling why they chose each piece. You may also wish to select a piece that best illustrates the child's work.

Periodically review the pieces in the portfolio and remove any that no longer seem appropriate.

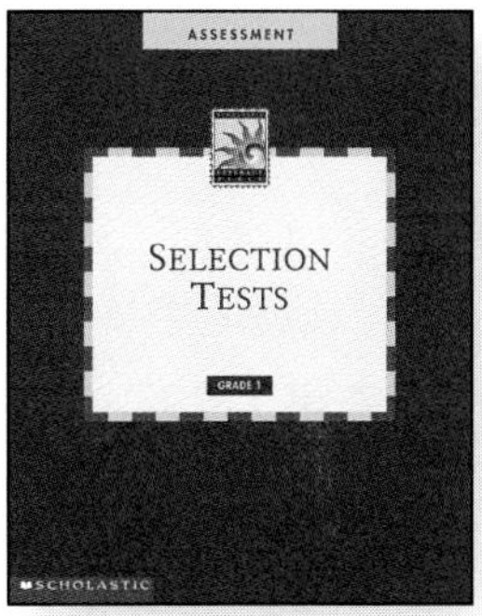
ASSESSMENT
SELECTION TESTS

SELECTION TEST

DAILY LANGUAGE PRACTICE

SPELLING

DAY 5:
Administer the Posttest for Contractions. **See page R37**.

GRAMMAR, USAGE, MECHANICS

DAY 5:
Assess Capitalizing Names and First Words. **See page R39**.

DAILY LANGUAGE PRACTICE

"im coming to eat you," said troll.
(I'm coming to eat you," said Troll.)

PORTFOLIO

Suggest that children add their drafts and revisions to their Literacy Portfolios.

Writing Assessment

It looks like you proofread your writing, but did you correct it for errors?
Good! Your dialogue is original!
Why don't you work on this more: I'm not sure what is happening here.
I am little Gruff I am hungry. I need my lunch
I am going up the hill to munch.
Out jumped the green troll
who's that walking on my roof
I hear the noise of a little hoof
HAY PIG
PAY

Apprentice

Use the rubric below to assess children's writing.

CHILDREN'S WRITING RUBRIC

Proficient	• The dialogue is original and rhymes. • The dialogue clearly tells the audience what is happening.	• The dialogue is proofread and corrected for grammar, usage, and mechanics errors.
Apprentice	• The dialogue may be original but may or may not rhyme. • The dialogue may or may not clearly tell the audience what is happening.	• The dialogue may be proofread, but not completely corrected for grammar, usage, and mechanics errors.
Novice	• The dialogue is not original and does not rhyme. • The dialogue does not clearly tell what is happening.	• The dialogue has not been proofread or corrected for errors.

Integrated Language Arts

ORAL LANGUAGE

Retell the Story

MATERIALS: Anthology

SUGGESTED GROUPING: Whole class and cooperative groups

Ask cooperative groups of children to retell *The Three Billy Goats Gruff* from the troll's point of view. How would the troll change the story to make himself look good?

Provide time for children to meet in groups and talk about how the story might change. Have them plan their retellings.

Invite the groups to take turns acting out and retelling their versions of the story. Children playing the part of the troll may want to change their voices and gestures.

WRITING/VIEWING

Act Out the Play

MATERIALS: Anthology

SUGGESTED GROUPING: Whole class and cooperative groups

Challenge the whole class to work together to act out this play. Children might take on any of these roles:

- actor
- director, stage manager, or prompter
- costume, prop, or mask maker
- writer of program

Provide an opportunity for children to choose roles, rehearse, and perform the play. Have them invite another class or children's family members to watch the performance.

Encourage children to write and decorate invitations to give to people they would like to have at the performance.

Invitation

Teach/Model Talk about how an invitation is a way of asking someone if they'd like to participate in an event. Point out that when writing an invitation, it is important to include what the event is and when it will occur.

Apply Have children include the name of the play and when it will be performed in their invitations.

Integrated Language Arts

WRITING

Draw a Comic Strip

MATERIALS: Anthology

SUGGESTED GROUPING: Partners or cooperative groups

CHALLENGE partners or cooperative groups to draw, write, or dictate comic strips showing events in the play. Suggest they create a comic strip with three or four frames.

HELP children get started by explaining what a comic strip is. Draw a picture of its shape, showing three or four frames. Explain that each frame contains a picture. Often, each frame also contains words. Each frame shows one event or action, and one frame leads to another.

GIVE children time to create their comic strips, to draw pictures for them, and to write or dictate words for the characters shown.

ENCOURAGE children to use speech balloons to write any dialogue they include in their comic strips.

Children can use the Paint Tools to create their cartoons in the WiggleWorks writing area.

WRITING/SPEAKING

Create a New Story

Good For Grading

MATERIALS: Anthology

SUGGESTED GROUPING: Individuals

ASK children to think about what might happen if the three little pigs or the three bears met up with the troll. How would the story change?

CHILDREN can choose any part of the story they wish; substitute new characters, events, or settings; and tell a whole new (and probably very funny) story. Nothing is too silly—as long as children can tell or draw it.

PROVIDE opportunities for children to share their new stories with friends, in cooperative groups, or with the whole class. Children who are listening might like to suggest additional innovations.

HOW TO GRADE When grading these new stories, look for imagination and an understanding of the story plot.

TECHNOLOGY

Organizing Information Guide children to use **WiggleWorks Plus** PlaceMaker to create a story map for a new version of the play starring either the three bears or the three pigs. Use the art tools to draw either circles or boxes. Fill in the areas to show connected thoughts and themes. Have children explain the sequence and main ideas of their stories.

DAY 5 WRAP-UP

READ ALOUD *Spend five to ten minutes reading from a selection of your choice.*

GUIDED READING *Meet with the **red** and **blue** reading groups and assign Independent Center activities.* ***See pages R34–R35.***

Unit 4 Wrap-Up

Children demonstrate independence and make meaningful connections to the real world.

WEEK 6 OBJECTIVES

WRITING PROCESS
Story With Dialogue
- write a story in which two characters talk with each other

TRADE BOOK LIBRARY
- demonstrate independence

PROJECT
Make a Story Mural
- create a story and make a mural showing the story

PRESENTATION SKILL
Speak to Inform
- tell the story orally while showing the mural

HOME INVOLVEMENT
- plan a family literacy night

TECHNOLOGY
- use **WiggleWorks Plus** CD-ROM to record story ideas and then write and illustrate a story

END OF UNIT ASSESSMENT
- follow-up on the baseline assessment and conduct formal and informal assessment

WEEKLY ORGANIZER

DAY 1	DAY 2	DAY 3	DAY 4	DAY 5
• WRITING PROCESS • TRADE BOOK LIBRARY • TECHNOLOGY	• WRITING PROCESS • TRADE BOOK LIBRARY • TECHNOLOGY	• WRITING PROCESS • TRADE BOOK LIBRARY • PROJECT	• TRADE BOOK LIBRARY • PROJECT • HOME INVOLVEMENT	• TRADE BOOK LIBRARY • PRESENTATION SKILL • END OF UNIT ASSESSMENT

WRAP-UP

WEEK 6 WRITING OBJECTIVES

CHILDREN WILL:

- **write an original story with dialogue**
- **use dialogue between two characters to tell the story action**
- **capitalize character names and the first word in a sentence**

MATERIALS

- **Anthology pp. 106–122**
- **Practice Book p. 71**

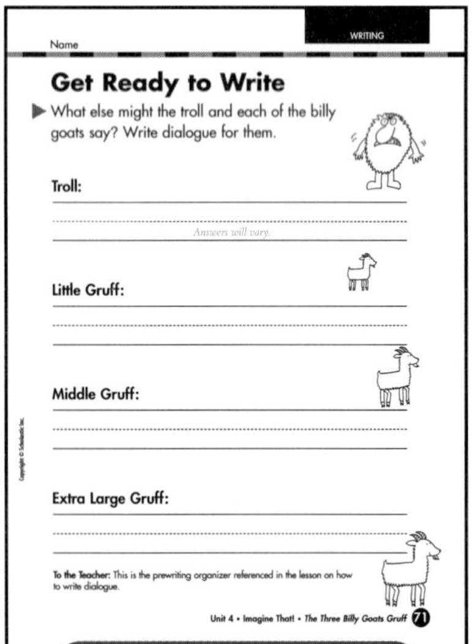
Name WRITING

Get Ready to Write

▶ What else might the troll and each of the billy goats say? Write dialogue for them.

Troll:

Answers will vary.

Little Gruff:

Middle Gruff:

Extra Large Gruff:

To the Teacher: This is the prewriting organizer referenced in the lesson on how to write dialogue.

Unit 4 • Imagine That! • *The Three Billy Goats Gruff* 71

PRACTICE BOOK p. 71

STORY WITH DIALOGUE

THINK ABOUT WRITING

Tell children that characters in stories may speak to each other, giving information and asking questions.

- Have a child name a favorite story or book and choose two of its characters.
- Invite children to think of something these two characters might say to each other.
- Record the information in a chart similar to the one below.

Story Character	What the Character Says
Little Red Riding Hood	"Grandmother, what big eyes you have!"
The Wolf	"The better to see you with my dear."

LITERATURE CONNECTION

Invite children to recall words the troll and three billy goats said to each other in the play *The Three Billy Goats Gruff*. Write these on the chalkboard. Enclose the words with quotation marks. Include clue words such as ***said, says, ask,*** or ***asked*** that help readers know that a character is speaking. Divide children into character parts. Have children read aloud the words of their assigned characters as you point to children. Say the narrator's part together.

PREWRITE

COMPLETE A PREWRITING ORGANIZER

Children can do this activity as a whole class or in pairs. Make three columns on the chalkboard or have children fold lined paper into thirds. You may wish to take this opportunity to discuss the distinguishing features of a paragraph, such as indenting the first line.

- Have children brainstorm characters who might talk with each other in a story. Write suggestions in column one.

Remind children that they may want to write a realistic story with the characters being people, such as two friends, or children may want to write a make-believe story in which animals talk or a person and an animal talk.

- Invite children to brainstorm a list of places where the characters might be. Write these ideas in column two.
- Suggest that children brainstorm things the characters might say. List these sentences in column three.

Point to a pair of characters, a place, and a saying. Have a child orally begin a story. Remind children that the story beginning should tell who and where the characters are and what they say. Repeat this.

Using the character, place, and saying lists, have children complete **Practice Book page 71** independently. On this page, they will begin planning for their story. In the top box, children draw the two characters who will be in the story and the setting. Below the picture, children write ideas for what the characters might say.

DRAFT

WRITE

Based on their decisions in Prewrite, have children begin a draft. Encourage them to tell who and where the characters are in the first sentences and then to include dialogue. Here is an example:

AT THE TOY STORE

Mike and Kim went to a toy store. ❶ Mike said, "I will get something for my brother." "What does he like to play with?" asked Kim. "He likes cars and trucks," said Mike. ❷ Kim and Mike like to play ball. ❸	❶ Two characters and the setting are named. ❷ This part of the draft is good because the two characters are talking to each other. ❸ This sentence is out of place; it is a new topic.

UNITED STATES
WORLD MAP

TING PROCESS

TECHNOLOGY

Writing Skills Have children use a familiar word processor to compose their stories. Show them how to format the characters' dialogue using boldface, italics, and underlining to make it stand out from the rest of the text. Suggest that they use different colored type for different characters.

TEACHER TIP

"Encourage children to reread their dialogues aloud, using a different voice for the words each character speaks. As children read, have them check that they have identified who is speaking in their writing. If they have not, they can revise to make the writing more clear."

PROOFREADING MARKS

◯	Check spelling
∧	Add
——	Cross out

REVISE/PROOFREAD

REVISE Remind children that revising gives them a chance to make their writing better. Children can ask classmates to read their stories and make suggestions or ask questions about anything that is unclear. Children can also ask for feedback from the teacher. Encourage children to read their stories and ask themselves these questions:

- Are there two characters?
- Does each character say something?
- Did I use words such as ***say*** or ***said*** to help a reader know who is speaking?

PROOFREAD Have children proofread their revisions. You may want to ask children the following questions:

- Did you circle any words you don't know how to spell or think you may have misspelled?
- Did you check the spellings of high-frequency words on the Word Wall?
- Did you write in complete sentences?
- Did you begin each sentence with a capital letter?
- Did you begin each character's name with a capital letter?

After making their own corrections, children may also want to have a peer edit their story.

PUBLISH

ACT IT OUT Group children by threes. Invite the groups to do dramatic readings and act out the stories. One child can take the role of the narrator and the other two children can read what the characters say.

PUPPET SHOW Have children read the dialogue they wrote to each other. Then have children make puppets of the characters. Children can present the puppets saying the dialogue.

WRI

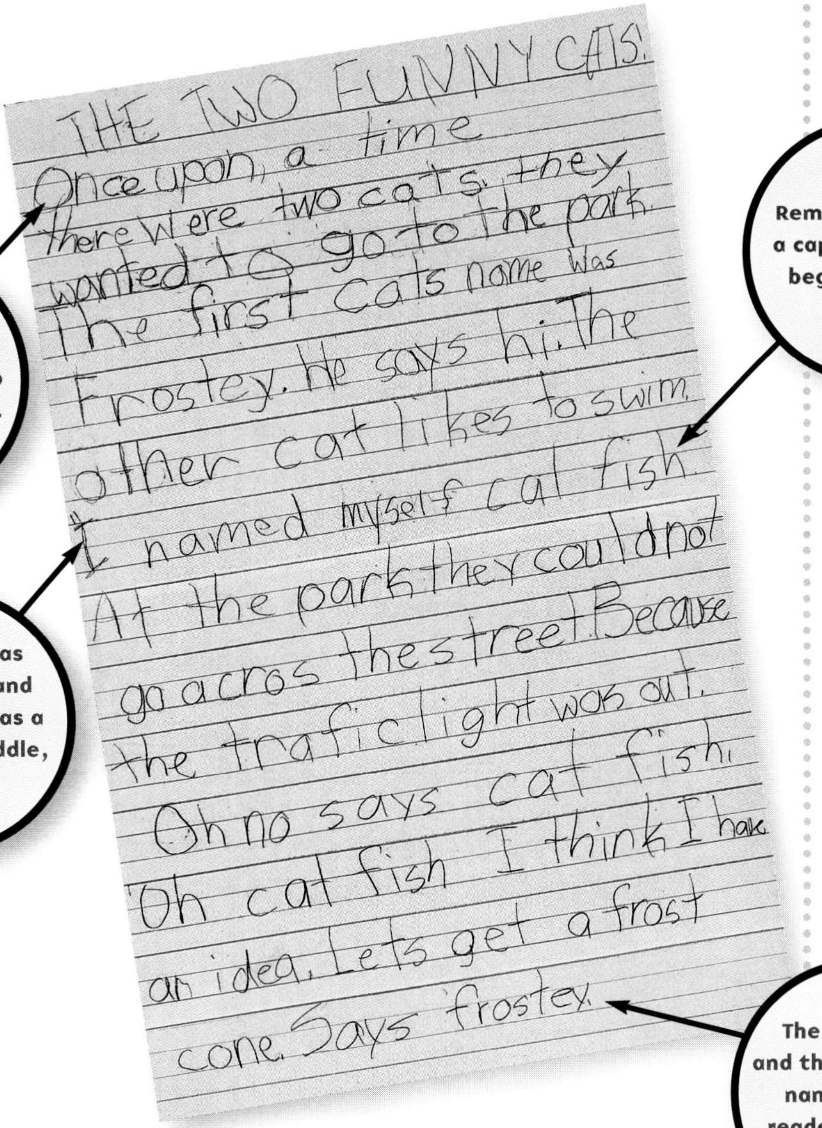
THE TWO FUNNY CATS!
Once upon a time
There were two cats. they
wanted to go to the park.
The first Cats name was
Frostey. He says hi. The
other cat likes to swim.
I named myself cat fish.
At the park they could not
go acros the street Because
the traficlight was out.
Oh no says cat fish.
Oh cat fish I think I have
an idea. Lets get a frost
cone Says frostey.

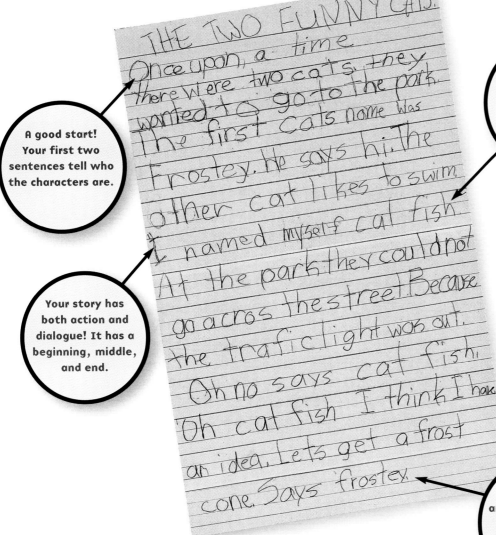

A good start! Your first two sentences tell who the characters are.

Remember to use a capital letter to begin the cats' names.

Your story has both action and dialogue! It has a beginning, middle, and end.

The word *says* and the character's name help the reader know who is speaking.

Apprentice

Use the rubric below to assess children's writing.

CHILDREN'S WRITING RUBRIC

Proficient	• Dialogue is original and clearly tells the audience what is happening. • Dialogue clearly indicates who is speaking. Words spoken may be in quotation marks.	• The child effectively tells the story with both dialogue and action. • The dialogue is proofread and corrected for grammar, usage, and mechanics.
Apprentice	• The dialogue may be original but may or may not tell the audience what is happening. • It may sometimes be hard to know who is speaking.	• The story may have dialogue or action that doesn't relate to the main idea. • The dialogue has been proofread, but not completely corrected for errors.
Novice	• Dialogue is not used or it is hard to figure out where the dialogue begins and ends. • The character that is speaking is not identified.	• The dialogue doesn't make sense. • The story has not been proofread or corrected for errors.

TEACHER TIP

"Ask children to read sentences in their stories that tell what characters say. Have children point out the words that tell which characters are speaking. Brainstorm with children other action words that could replace **says** *or* **said.***"*

Trade Book Library

Book Guide
JENNY'S JOURNEY
SHEILA WHITE SAMTON
SCHOLASTIC

Challenge
Average
▶ Easy

DECODABLE TEXT
For practice reading decodable text, see ***Scholastic Decodable Readers #55–57.***

LITERARY Connection

CHARACTER In *Jenny's Journey* and *In the Attic,* the main characters use their imaginations. Have children compare Jenny and the boy in the attic by exploring questions such as these:

> **What is the same about how Jenny and the boy in the attic use their imaginations?**

> **Where do each go? Are these places real or imaginary? How do you know?**

> **Why do Jenny and the boy begin to imagine things? What are some of the things each imagines?**

Have children use a Venn diagram similar to the one shown below. In the circle marked "Jenny" have children write words or phrases to tell some of the things that Jenny imagined. In the circle marked "Boy in the Attic" have children write words or phrases to tell some of the things the boy imagined. Where the circles join, have children write how Jenny and the boy in the attic are alike.

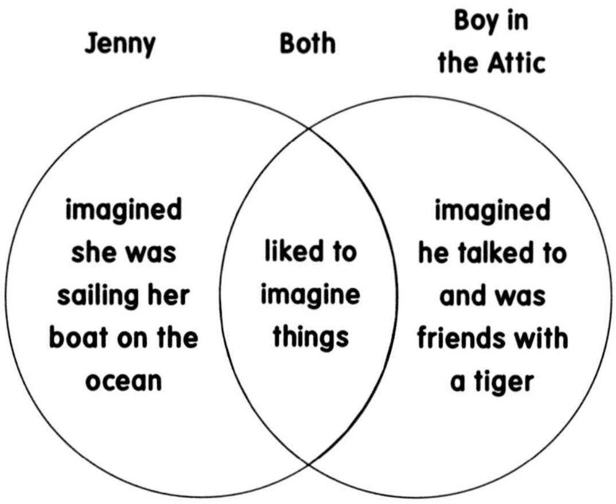
Jenny
Both
Boy in the Attic
imagined she was sailing her boat on the ocean
liked to imagine things
imagined he talked to and was friends with a tiger

TRADE

AUTHOR Connection

Point out that Margaret Wild, the author of *Going Home,* has written a fantasy, although parts of the story are realistic or true. On the other hand, Alice Pernick, the author of *The Night Sky,* writes about things that are fact. Invite children to use the chart below to compare and contrast true and make-believe elements in each story. In the box "This Is Make-Believe" for *The Night Sky,* children may write that nothing is make-believe in the story.

	GOING HOME	THE NIGHT SKY
This Is True	Hugo was in the hospital. His mother and sister came to visit.	The moon is the brightest light in the night sky.
This Is Make-Believe	Hugo went with an elephant to the African grasslands.	Nothing is make-believe.

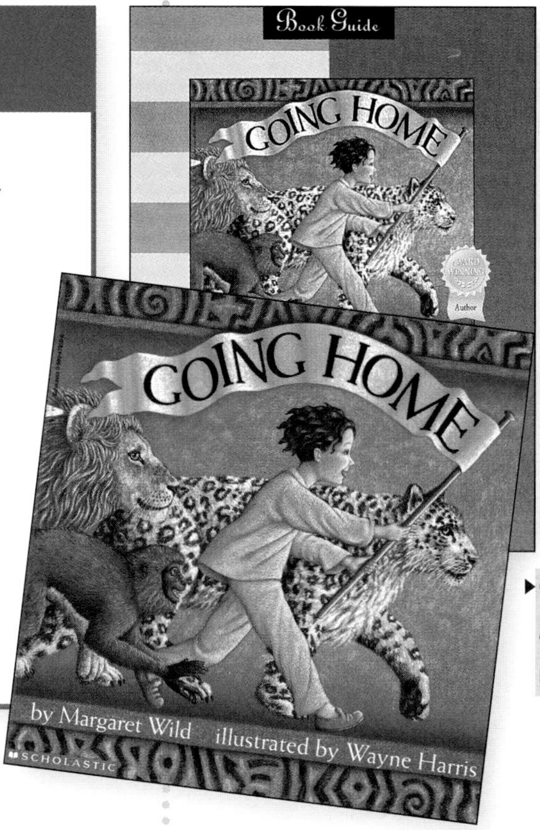
Book Guide
GOING HOME
by Margaret Wild
illustrated by Wayne Harris
SCHOLASTIC

▶ Challenge
Average
Easy

KEY SKILL Connection

Draw Conclusions Help children focus on drawing conclusions by imagining that Pierre met the troll and three billy goats. Have children answer the questions below and give reasons for their conclusions. You may want to divide children into pairs or small groups and have them act out their responses.

> **How might Pierre react to the troll in *The Three Billy Goats Gruff*? Why do you think so?**

> **Imagine that the three billy goats and Pierre meet each other. What might they say?**

Book Guide
PIERRE
A cautionary tale
IN FIVE CHAPTERS
AND A PROLOGUE
MAURICE SENDAK
SCHOLASTIC

Challenge
▶ Average
Easy

BOOKS

PROJECT OBJECTIVES

CHILDREN WILL:
- create a story
- make a mural showing their story

MATERIALS
- Pencils
- Markers
- Mural paper
- Paint
- Brushes

MODIFY Instruction

EXTRA HELP

Although making a mural to tell a story is natural for first graders, you may want to help them divide into groups to work on different scenes from the story. Help children apply the story planning and sketching skills they practiced in the Workshops as they create their murals. **(WORK IN GROUPS)**

TECHNOLOGY

Organizing Information Have children use the story starters in **WiggleWorks Plus** Unit Writer to organize their ideas. For example: "In my story mural I will show..." Add story starters to the list, or use the Record tool to record suggestions.

MAKE A STORY MURAL

GETTING STARTED

Use Pictures to Tell a Story

To focus children on the Project, spend some time discussing the information about murals and the art on Side 1 of the Project Card. You could also ask the following questions:

> **What do you think a mural is?**

> **What story does the mural in the picture tell?**

Home Involvement

Find out where there are murals in your community. Possible places include public buildings on both outside and inside walls, parks, subway stations, and museums. Family members can take children to see the murals firsthand. Children can talk about the murals with family members and report back to the class about the murals they saw, whether they told a story, and what story they told.

Children may also be interested in seeing other examples of public art in your community, such as statues and sculptures that decorate a site or pay homage to an important person or event.

Troubleshooting

Once cooperative groups have planned their murals, they should think about what each group member will do. Each individual could be responsible for completing a whole scene or drawing a single character in all the scenes. Or, one group member could sketch, others outline and paint, and others add words in speech balloons.

Make sure children ask permission from the appropriate people to display the murals in the school.

PRO

GRADE 1 CREATIVE EXPRESSION

PROJECT

How to Make a Story Mural

Murals are pictures that tell a story. People who make murals want to share a story they have imagined. They first decide where the story takes place and who is in the story.

Many murals are found on walls outside. This way everyone can enjoy the artist's work.
Pictures on murals are big so people can see them.

Now Make Your Own

1 Plan a Mural

Tell a story in your mural.

Think about how you can show:

- where and when the story takes place.
- who is in the story.
- what happens in the story.

2 Make a Mural

Use a pencil to make a sketch on mural paper.

Then trace over your pencil lines, and color them in with markers or paint.

Remember, murals are big, so you can include a lot.

TIPS

- Add words with speech balloons or labels.
- Hang your mural in the classroom, the cafeteria, the library, or the hallway.

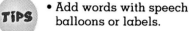

Tools
pencil
mural paper
markers or crayons
paint and brushes
CONGRATULATIONS
Now you know how to share your imagination through stories and pictures.
William Walsh
Muralist

1 Plan a Mural

Discuss what must be planned before children begin their murals. First, each group must choose a story to tell. The story could be one they planned in Workshop 1, a new story, or one they've read. Then group members should think about how to show the items listed on the card: where and when the story takes place, who's in the story, and what happens. Finally, they should decide which scenes they'll represent on their murals. Emphasize that the scenes they choose should make the story clear to someone who doesn't know it.

Have children work in cooperative groups to choose the story and plan how to present it. Children can use the Project Planner on **Practice Book pages 75** and **76** to organize their ideas for the mural.

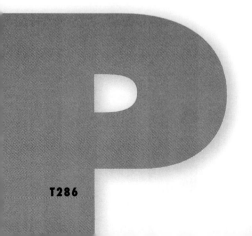

PRO

2 Make a Mural

Have children begin by dividing their mural paper into sections, one section for each scene they've planned. Then they can sketch each scene. Encourage them to make each character recognizable from one scene to the next.

CHILDREN'S PRESENTATIONS Use the Presentation Skill Lesson on pages T288–T289 to support children in giving and viewing their presentations. The lesson will help children show and tell about their story murals.

ASSESSMENT

INFORMAL ASSESSMENT

OBSERVATION

When children have finished making their murals, review their work and answer any questions they might have. Ask yourself:

✔ Did children plan their murals?

✔ Did children's murals tell a story?

✔ How did children organize the story on their murals?

CHILDREN'S SELF-ASSESSMENT

> **Does my mural tell a story? What story does my mural tell?**

Use the rubric below to assess children's understanding of the project.

CHILDREN'S PROJECT RUBRIC

Proficient	**Children work well with group members in choosing stories for murals; children show ability to visualize and prioritize in planning scenes to depict and in sketching murals.**
Apprentice	**Children make positive contributions in choosing stories; children may not always suggest the most appropriate scenes for telling the stories; children rely on trial and error in sketching murals.**
Novice	**Children hardly contribute in choosing the story; they may sketch individual scenes, but have trouble planning the whole story.**

SELF-SELECTION

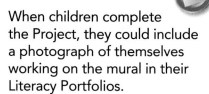

When children complete the Project, they could include a photograph of themselves working on the mural in their Literacy Portfolios.

Alternatively, they might want to write a short paragraph or draw a picture about what they did.

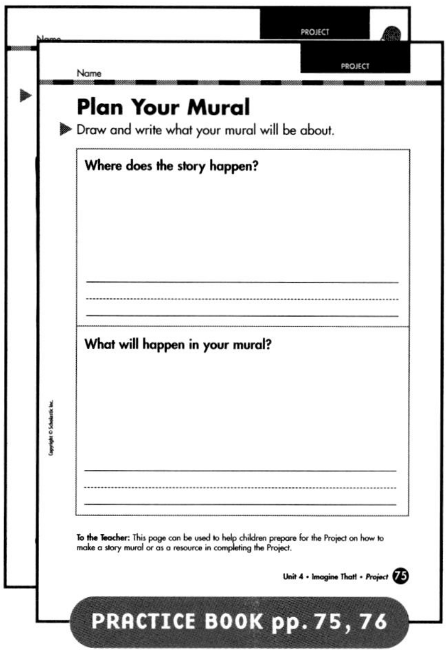
PROJECT

Name

Plan Your Mural

▶ Draw and write what your mural will be about.

Where does the story happen?

What will happen in your mural?

To the Teacher: This page can be used to help children prepare for the Project on how to make a story mural or as a resource in completing the Project.

Unit 4 • Imagine That! • Project 75

PRACTICE BOOK pp. 75, 76

Practice Book pages 75 and 76 can help children plan their mural and illustrate their favorite activity.

PRESENTATION SKILL OBJECTIVE

CHILDREN WILL:

- **make an oral presentation of their mural**

MATERIALS

- **Children's murals**
- **Audiocassette recorder (optional)**

TECHNOLOGY

Speaking Skills Videotape the children making their oral presentations. Then review the tapes with them. Ask them if they would do anything differently after seeing their presentations. Would they speak louder or more slowly? Did they remember to say everything that they wanted to mention?

PRESENT A MURAL

A TEACH/MODEL

PUT IT IN CONTEXT From magazines, cut out a few pictures that show action, or find pictures of a scene from a picture book. Hold up one picture at a time and invite children to create a story about it. Put the following questions on the chalkboard to guide them:

> **Who is in the picture?**

> **Where are they?**

> **What are they doing now?**

> **What do you imagine will happen next?**

Suggest that groups of children use these questions to help them create stories about their murals.

Remind children that when telling the stories about their murals, it is important to talk clearly and loudly enough for the audience to hear them. Encourage children to use expression in their voices. You might demonstrate talking too slowly, too fast, without expression, or without looking at the audience.

PRO

B PRACTICE/APPLY

SHOW AND TELL Suggest that children work in their cooperative groups and use the questions written on the chalkboard (Teach/Model) to help them think about what they might say in an oral presentation about their murals. Point out to children that telling an interesting story will make their murals come alive for the audience.

Have children decide what each child in their group will talk about when their group makes its oral presentation. Different children might point out things in the mural, name and describe the characters and setting, tell what is happening in the mural, or tell what might happen next.

If the mural has several scenes, children might choose to take turns talking about scenes. Have children practice their parts of the presentation and then take turns presenting their mural to the rest of the class.

As another option, children can apply the skill of show-and-tell by making a video of their presentations. Children might want to invite other classes to view the video. Children may also enjoy taking photographs of their murals for a class memory book.

C ASSESS

INFORMAL ASSESSMENT: OBSERVATION When children have finished their oral presentations, ask yourself:

✔ Did children's oral narratives tell the story of their murals?

✔ Did children speak clearly and so that they could be heard?

CHILDREN'S SELF-ASSESSMENT

✔ Does telling about the mural make it better? How so?

MODIFY Instruction

ESL/ELD

▲ Work in a small group with children acquiring English. Write what children plan to say for the presentation on sentence strips. Have children practice reading each sentence aloud. Encourage children to record and listen to their readings a few times until they feel prepared to present them to the group. **(READ ALOUD)**

EXTRA HELP

■ As you review children's murals with the whole class, write children's main ideas on sentence strips. Children who need help to prepare their oral presentations can use these sentence strips as idea starters. **(USE SENTENCE STRIPS)**

JECT

Home Involvement

Family Literacy Night

Your classroom Artist's Studio can become the focus of a Literacy Event during which children share with family members their work completed during the *Imagine That!* unit. You may use the following options for planning, organizing, and setting up the event.

- **ANNOUNCEMENTS** Children can use watercolor paints to color the background for a mini-poster. When the paint dries have them write *Come to our Artist's Studio for an* Imagine That! *Event* and add the date, time, and place. They can give their posters to family members.
- **HOME/COMMUNITY** In the Home learning station, children may choose to do any of the following:
  - act out the play "The Three Billy Goats Gruff"
  - read the poems or sing the song found in the unit
  - make the recipe for lemonade and serve it to visitors
  - show the video on mural artist William Walsh

Learning Stations

In the Artist's Studio, display children's writing, drawings and murals done during the *Imagine That!* unit. Invite children to take their family on a tour of the Artist's Studio. In addition, have children help you set up active learning stations such as the following:

- ***IMAGINE THAT!* MURAL** Tape a long strip of paper to the wall and set out a variety of art materials. Label the mural "Imagine That!" Write ideas for unusual things to draw (a boy riding a fish; an elephant putting out a fire). Invite all to draw an idea on the mural.
- **STORY CENTER** Place the trade books and other fantasy books in this area for family members to read together.
- **WRITING CENTER** Draw a ladder and above it put the following sign: *Imagine that! I climbed the ladder and found. . .* Invite children or family members to write answers. Post the writings around the ladder. You might want to put the book *In the Attic* in this center to inspire creative possibilities!

Interactive Writing

Children can use Unit Writer on the **WiggleWorks Plus** CD-ROM to compose a story from one of the included Story Starters. Use the children's illustrated and published stories to expand on the Creative Expression theme.

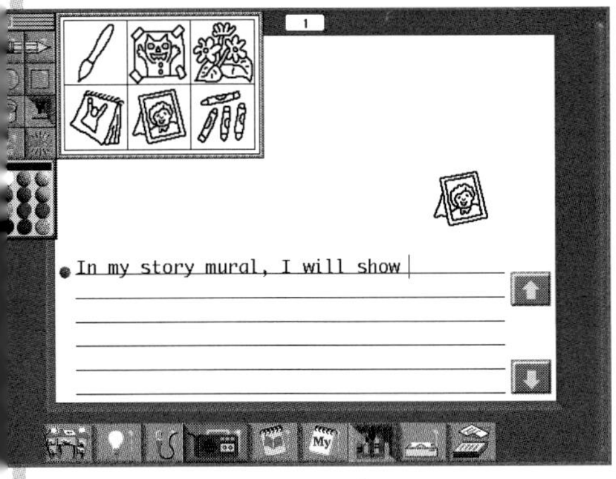
In my story mural, I will show

WiggleWorks Plus CD-ROM

- **RECORD** Ask children to imagine what they would create if they were an artist. Then, have them use the Record Tool to capture themselves describing how they would create their artwork.

- **ILLUSTRATE** Have children play back their recordings and draw pictures to illustrate what their voices are describing. Encourage them to use as many Paint Tools as possible.

- **WRITE** Now, ask children to write text to accompany their stories, listening to the recordings and looking at their illustrations for guidance. Children can click the Read button to hear their stories read aloud by the computer.

- **EXTEND** Print out the stories for children to share with their families. Encourage children to interview family members, asking them what they would create if they were an artist and why.

For more activity suggestions, see the **WiggleWorks Plus** Teaching Guide.

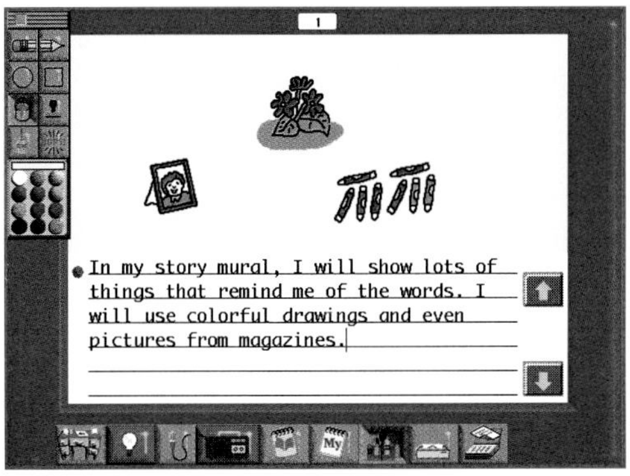
In my story mural, I will show lots of things that remind me of the words. I will use colorful drawings and even pictures from magazines.

WiggleWorks Plus CD-ROM

Scholastic Solutions

Remember to visit the Scholastic Solutions area on www.scholastic.com to learn more about the variety of Scholastic's resources for teachers. Here you can find trade books, leveled libraries, phonics resources, magazines, videos, CD-ROMs, and professional books correlated to your content needs.

WEEK 6 ASSESSMENT

SEE THE ASSESSMENT HANDBOOK FOR:

- Guidelines for Assessment Planning
- Methods of Assessment including Observation and Portfolio
- Tools for Assessment including Literacy Record and Literacy Log
- Oral Reading Assessment
- Rubrics for Evaluation
- Grading Guidelines

Children's Assessment

FOLLOW-UP ON BASELINE ASSESSMENT

The Baseline Assessment established the conceptual level at which each child began the unit. By repeating this task, children will demonstrate the growth they've experienced over the course of this unit.

Have children think up a story and repeat the rest of the Baseline Assessment exercise. Compare their pictures and explanations with those they completed before you taught the unit. Refer to the unit concepts for *Imagine That!* and ask yourself whether the child's present work reflects a greater understanding of the concepts.

As a check on your evaluation, ask children questions that will reveal whether the unit concepts have become a part of their thinking. For example, ask *What would this classroom look like if you were an ant?*

K-W-L

Refer to the K-W-L chart you have been working on throughout this unit. Finish filling in the "What Did We Learn?" section. Have children write what they still want to learn about how imagination helps us to look at things in new ways.

CHILDREN'S SELF-ASSESSMENT

Have children look back at the Unit Planner pages from the Practice Book. Then they should complete the "What Did I Learn?" page in the Practice Book. Did they meet the goals they set for themselves?

ASSES

OBSERVATIONAL CHECKLIST

Use the Individual and Class Unit Checklists for *Imagine That!* in the Classroom Management Forms to record your end of unit evaluations and observations of each child in your class. You can then complete and send home the Family Literacy Newsletter.

INFORMAL ASSESSMENT

Consider using Workshops, Projects, and writing activities as opportunities to assess what children have learned about creative expression. You can make use of the rubrics noted in the Teacher's Edition, and child self-assessment pieces.

PORTFOLIO

Allow children time to sort through the material they've saved for their Literacy Portfolios. Distribute the Portfolio Checklist in the Assessment Handbook to help children decide what to keep in their *Imagine That!* Portfolio.

FORMAL TESTING

- ✔ **See the Spelling Test Form in the Spelling Resource Book.**
- ✔ **To prepare children for the *Imagine That!* Unit Test, see the Teacher's Test Manual.**
- ✔ **Forms A and B of the test and directions for administering, scoring, and using the tests are in the Teacher's Test Manual.**

SPELLING RESOURCE BOOK
LITERACY PLACE
gate
late
bake
rake
SCHOLASTIC

Spelling Resource Book

TEACHER'S TEST MANUAL
LITERACY PLACE
SCHOLASTIC

Teacher's Test Manual

Unit Test Form A

Unit Test Form B

TEACHER SELF-ASSESSMENT

Spend some time critiquing your own teaching:

- ✔ Which parts of the unit did not catch my children's interest? How can I teach these parts differently?
- ✔ What activities appealed most to the children? Which did I enjoy teaching?
- ✔ Did I communicate to children the many ways to express oneself creatively?

Glossary

GLOSSARY

You will find all your vocabulary words in ABC order in the Glossary. This page shows you how to use it.

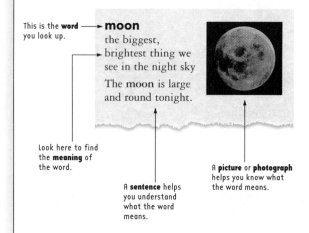

This is the **word** you look up. → **moon**

Look here to find the **meaning** of the word. → the biggest, brightest thing we see in the night sky

A **sentence** helps you understand what the word means. → The **moon** is large and round tonight.

A **picture** or **photograph** helps you know what the word means.

actors
people in a play, movie, or TV show
We met the **actors** after the play.

attic
the space or room below the roof of a house
We put old clothes and pictures in our **attic**.

booth
a small enclosed place
Dad paid the man in the ticket **booth** before we saw the movie.

bored
to be tired of or not interested in something
Ben was **bored** with checkers after playing five games.

bridge
something built for people and animals so they can cross over water, roads, and spaces
Cars go over the **bridge** to get over the river.

cake
a sweet, baked food made with flour, butter, eggs, and sugar
Put a candle on the **cake**.

cave
a large hole underground or in the side of a hill
The bear hid her cubs in a **cave**.

dime
a coin that is worth 10 cents
A **dime** is worth the same as two nickels.

first
coming before second
January is the **first** month of the year.

bridge

game
an activity with rules that can be played by one or more people
Our team won the soccer **game**.

goat
an animal with horns, hooves, and a beard
Farmer Brown's **goat** lives in a pen with sheep.

king
a man who rules a country or group of people
The **king** works hard to make the country a better place.

ladder
a set of steps used for climbing
We used the **ladder** to help us hang the pictures.

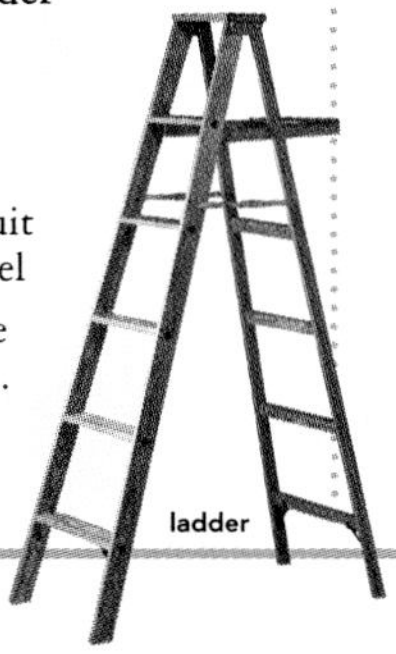
ladder

lemon
a sour-tasting fruit with a yellow peel
Squeeze the juice from this **lemon**.

light
brightness, or something that gives off brightness
I read by the **light** of my lamp.

lunch
the meal you eat in the middle of the day
Jill and Sandra eat sandwiches for **lunch** at noon.

moon
the biggest, brightest thing we see in the night sky
The **moon** is large and round tonight.

moon

nickel
a coin that is worth five cents
Five pennies equal one **nickel**.

night
the time between sunset and sunrise, when it is dark
Night is the opposite of day.

planets
the nine big, round objects that move around the sun
Earth is one of the nine **planets**.

play
a story that is acted, often on a stage or in a theater
Jack got the part of the hero in our school **play**.

problem
something that is hard to deal with or understand
When I have a **problem**, I ask for help.

shine
to give off light
The moon and the stars **shine** at night.

sky
the area of space high above us
Rain falls from clouds in the **sky**.

stars
faraway points of light that shine in the night sky
We can see **stars** only when it's dark.

story
a tale made up for people to enjoy
My grandfather reads me a **story**.

sun
the big hot ball of gas that gives us light and heat in the sky
The **sun** gives us light and keeps us warm.

talk
to say words
I **talk** to my friends at school.

toys
things to play with
Amber's dolls are her favorite **toys**.

troll
a mean creature in a folk tale who often lives under a bridge
The prince saved the village from the evil **troll**.

SARY

Additional Support

GROUPING AND REGROUPING

- Assess and regroup children for guided reading every six weeks.
- Children progress at different rates, so ongoing assessment is essential. Use the results of your informal and formal assessments to regroup children as necessary. Remember, grouping should be dynamic. It should change according to children's needs.
- Form guided reading groups composed of children who are reading approximately the same level of text.
- Be sure that children are in many different groups throughout the day. Children benefit from interactions with classmates at different levels. So both homogeneous small groups for guided reading and other small and large groups for literacy activities throughout the day are critical.

CONDUCTING GUIDED READING GROUPS

Meet with at least two reading groups each day. Select a book on each group's instructional reading level from the *Scholastic Guided Reading Library* or a book in your classroom library. For more information on conducting guided reading groups, see *Scholastic Guided Reading Library,* Teacher's Guide.

SETTING UP INDEPENDENT CENTERS

While meeting with each reading group, have the rest of the class work in the Independent Centers listed below. Place the appropriate center cards in a pocket chart for student reference. Rotate the cards each day. Children may also use this time to do the following:

- revise or complete writing assignments,
- complete Practice Book pages,
- write in their Journals,
- read independently.

SAMPLE MANAGEMENT PLAN FOR CENTERS

RED GROUP	BLUE GROUP	GREEN GROUP	YELLOW GROUP
ABC Center	Listening	Independent	Art Center
Art Center	ABC Center	Listening	Independent
Independent	Art Center	ABC Center	Listening

MID-YEAR CHECKLIST

[ ] I have a well-organized, leveled set of books for guided reading sessions.

[ ] I have a guided reading area with ample materials (dry-erase board, paper, pocket chart, letter cards, etc.).

[ ] Children work productively in centers while I meet with guided reading groups.

[ ] I have grouped children according to reading level and strategy use. Groups are flexible, and I reassess groups at least every six weeks.

[ ] My lessons include an introduction to the book, a reading of the entire text by all children, and follow-up work.

GAY SU PINNELL

Independent Centers

Children can work in these centers while you meet with guided reading groups.

ABC CENTER

Place several word and alphabet games in the ABC Center. Select games that review this and previous weeks' phonics skills. The games should be fun, instructional, and challenging yet not beyond the class's current ability. Have children play the games with a partner or in a group. Tell children to follow the rules and play fairly.

INDEPENDENT READING

Select several books for each reading group and place them in the appropriate Browsing Box. The books you choose can be ones that the children have read during guided reading, or they might be titles you have identified as suitable for each group's independent reading level. Tell children to select a book and read it softly to themselves. You may need to establish guidelines to help children self-select appropriate books. Afterward, children can gather in a small group and talk about the books they read.

GOING HOME
PIERRE
A cautionary tale
IN FIVE CHAPTERS
AND A PROLOGUE
MAURICE SENDAK
JENNY'S JOURNEY

ART CENTER

Ask children to draw a picture about *Chicken Pedro and the Falling Sky* or another story that they like. The pictures they draw should capture their responses to the story. Children can, if they wish, draw a picture of their favorite part of the story or show themselves playing a role in the story.

LISTENING

Place three stories on tape, including the audiocassette version of *Chicken Pedro and the Falling Sky,* in the Listening Center. Ask children to select one story and follow along in the book as it is read aloud. To close the activity, suggest that children retell the story in their own words to a friend.

Scholastic Cass
Scholastic Cassettes

Spelling

WEEK 1 RESOURCES

SPELLING RESOURCE BOOK

- **Word Sort,** p. 84
- **Extra Help,** p. 85
- **Vocabulary Practice,** p. 86
- **Challenge,** p. 87
- **Proofread,** p. 88
- **Student Test Form,** p. 161
- **Individual Progress Chart,** p. 162
- **Class Progress Chart,** p. 163
- **Word Sort Chart,** p. 164
- **My Words to Learn,** p. 165
- **Spelling Award Form,** p. 166
- **Family Newsletter,** p. 170*

ADDITIONAL RESOURCES

- **Spelling Strategy Poster**
- **Proofreading Marks Poster**

*You may wish to send home the Unit 4 Family Newsletter.

SPELLING LIST

Words With Final *e*

bake late
rake gate
lake

High-Frequency

soon went

DAY 1 PRETEST/SELF-CHECK

ADMINISTER THE PRETEST

1. Did you lock the **gate**?
2. I like to swim in the **lake**.
3. We will **bake** a cake for Mom.
4. Will you help me **rake** the leaves?
5. I was **late** to school this morning.
6. We **went** to the park.
7. **Soon** we will go to the store.

SPELLING CONCEPT

Teach the spelling concept and present the spelling words. Point out the long *a* spelling patterns.

WORD SORT

On the chalkboard, draw the word sort circles. Ask children to sort the spelling words on the circles. *(**ake:** lake, bake, rake; **ate:** gate, late)*

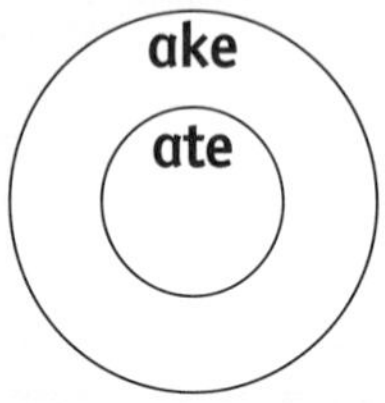
ake
ate

Have children complete **Spelling Resource Book, page 84.**

Word Sort

Name

Word Sort

1. Write a spelling word in each box.
2. Cut on the ------ lines.
3. Sort the words.

Spelling Words	
bake	gate
lake	late
rake	soon
went	

SPELLING RESOURCE BOOK p. 84

DAY 2 VOCABULARY PRACTICE

BUILD VOCABULARY: CONTEXT CLUES

- Review how context clues can help readers figure out new words. Write on the chalkboard: *I used a* <u>*rake*</u> *to collect the leaves.* Ask children which words are clues to the meaning of *rake.* *(to collect the leaves)*
- Continue with other spelling words and sentences.

WORD STUDY: WORD FAMILIES

- Write *bake* on the chalkboard. Say the word, erase the *b,* and say the word family *ake.* Write the letter *l* in front of *ake.* Have children blend *l* with *ake* to say the new word.
- Write on the chalkboard: *I closed the* <u>*late*</u> *to keep the dog in the yard.* Ask children to replace the underlined word with a spelling word that is from the same word family and makes sense in the sentence.

Have children complete **Spelling Resource Book, page 85, 86,** or **87.**

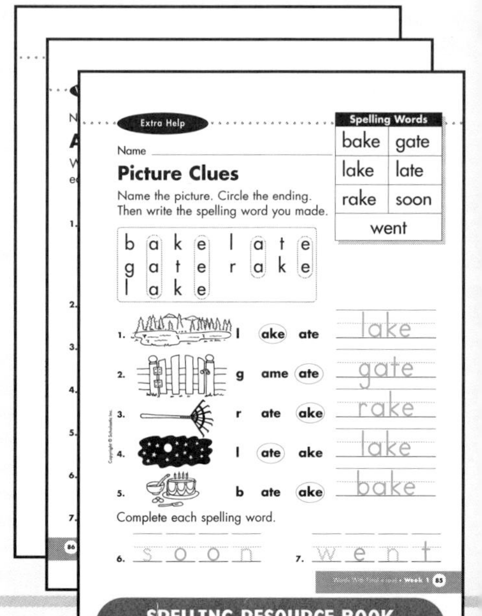
Extra Help

Name

Picture Clues

Name the picture. Circle the ending. Then write the spelling word you made.

Spelling Words	
bake	gate
lake	late
rake	soon
went	

1. l ake ate lake
2. g ame ate gate
3. r ate ake rake
4. l ate ake lake
5. b ate ake bake

Complete each spelling word.

6. soon 7. went

SPELLING RESOURCE BOOK pp. 85, 86, 87

DAY 3 WRITE/PROOFREAD

WRITE

- Tell children that they will write about what animals might say if they could talk. Encourage children to use at least two spelling words in their writing.
- Using a graphic organizer will help children get started.

Animal: → **Who it would speak to:** → **What it might say:**

Children may:

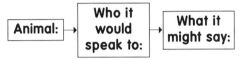

- draw a picture of their animals and write what they say in their speech balloons.
- act out their written animal dialogue.

PROOFREAD

PROOFREADING MARKS

Mark	Meaning
(oval)	Check spelling
∧	Add
——	Cross out

- Review the proofreading marks, using the class Proofreading Chart for reference.
- Use the following sentence for proofreading practice:

  Will you help bake
  ~~You will~~ (hlp) me (bak) a cake?

Have children complete **Spelling Resource Book, page 88.**

DAY 4 STUDY/REVIEW

ABC ORDER

- Review the letters of the alphabet with children by naming two letters and asking children to tell which appears first in the alphabet.
- Write the following word groupings on the chalkboard. Ask children to put the words within each grouping in ABC order and to check their work by circling the first letter in each word.

gate	*bake*	**rake**	*cave*
bake	*came*	**late**	*late*
lake	*gate*	**cave**	*rake*
came	*lake*		

TEST YOURSELF

- Review the Spelling Strategy.
- Partners can take turns dictating a spelling word and spelling it using magnetic letters or a dry-erase board.
- Children can choose three spelling words and write them in scrambled order. Then partners can unscramble each other's words.

Children may practice for their spelling tests using the **Student Test Form, page 161.**

DAY 5 POSTTEST/SELF-CHECK

ADMINISTER THE POSTTEST

For the Posttest, read aloud the sentences from Day 1. Have children write each spelling word.

Then have children:

- self-check.
- record the results of their Posttest on the **Individual Progress Chart.**
- keep a list of their misspelled words in their spelling journals.

ASSESSMENT

Record the results of children's Posttests on the **Class Progress Chart, Spelling Resource Book, page 163.**

See **Handwriting Practice, page 20** for practice writing the letters *S* and *U*.

Write and Proofread
Name
Fun with Mom
Circle three more words that are spelled wrong. Write them correctly above the lines. Add the missing period.
mom is late. I help her
paint the gat. We raek
the leaves. Then we bak
cookies. Can we take
them to the lack?
PROOFREADING MARKS

SPELLING RESOURCE BOOK p. 88

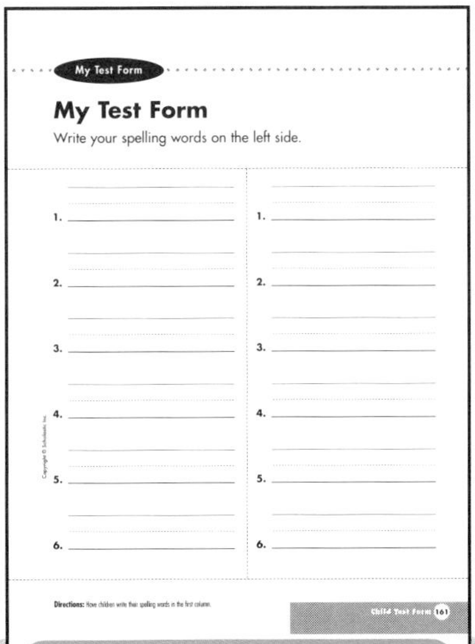
My Test Form
My Test Form
Write your spelling words on the left side.
1.
2.
3.
4.
5.
6.

SPELLING RESOURCE BOOK p. 161

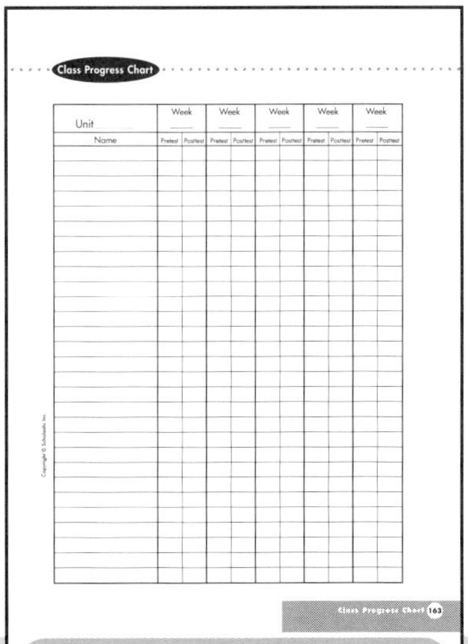
Class Progress Chart
Unit
Name
Week

SPELLING RESOURCE BOOK p. 163

WEEK 1 Word Order

Grammar, Usage, Mechanics

OBJECTIVES

Children will explore the word order in sentences in *Chicken Pedro and the Falling Sky* and in their writing.

RESOURCES

Practice Book, p. 14
Grammar, Usage, Mechanics Resource Book, pp. 64–67

Word Order

Words that are in order say something that makes sense.

Words that are out of order do not make sense.

A sentence is made up of words in a certain order.

MODIFY Instruction

ESL/ELD

▲ Make sentence strips with key sentences from the story in scrambled word order. For example, *gate Chicken opened garden the Pedro.* Work together to cut up the strips and reorder the words correctly. Let children compare their sentences to the words in the book. **(USE SENTENCE STRIPS)**

DAY 1 TEACH/MODEL

SELECTION LINK

- Write the following sentence from **Anthology page 9** on the chalkboard. Under it write the words out of order.

  I am going for a walk.

  Going I walk for am a

  Point out that the correct word order helps a sentence makes sense. It tells what the sentence is about and what is happening. Ask children which group of words makes sense. Share this hint: A sentence always begins with a capital letter and ends with a period.
- Write these mixed-up sentences on the chalkboard and ask children to look for the capitalized word. Then have children say the words in an order that makes sense. Read each aloud, pointing to the ending punctuation.

  the opened He gate.

  morning! What nice a

  are Where you going?

- Using the graphic organizer, have children put these sentences from **Anthology page 11** in the correct order.

  falling. The is sky

  tell King. I the must

  sun me. The hit

Capital	Words in Order	Period

DAY 2 PRACTICE

REVIEW

- Review with children how the word order in a sentence helps the sentence make sense. Remind children that complete sentences start with a capital letter and end with a period, question mark, or exclamation mark.
- Write the words from each of these short sentences on index cards. Display one group at a time. Ask volunteers to place them in an order that makes sense. Encourage children to move the cards around and say the words aloud until the word order makes sense.

the | out | Watch | for | fox!

sun | Did | the | fall?

animals | The | like | lemonade.

- Have each child write one short sentence that ends with a period on a sheet of paper. On the back, have each child write the sentence out of order but include the capital letter and the period. Have children exchange papers with a partner. Allow time for each partner to write the words in an order that makes sense. Have partners check their answer against the original sentence.

DAY 3 PRACTICE

RETEACH

- Review with children that sentences are made up of words that have a certain order. Remind children that a sentence always begins with a capital letter and ends with a period, question mark, or exclamation mark.
- Write the following mixed-up sentences on the chalkboard. Provide the correct ending punctuation. Have children put each sentence in order by saying the words aloud. Ask children to point out where the capitalized word and ending punctuation go.

Why Chicken Pedro was sad ?
was the A cave by fox .
lemon on A him fell !

Have children complete **Practice Book, page 14.**

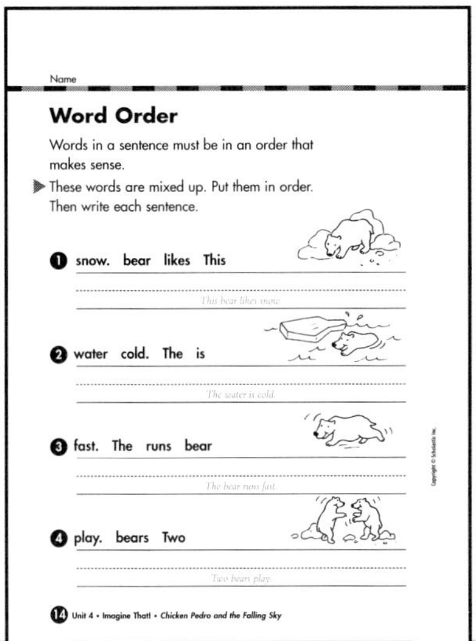

Name

Word Order

Words in a sentence must be in an order that makes sense.

▶ These words are mixed up. Put them in order. Then write each sentence.

1. snow. bear likes This
2. water cold. The is
3. fast. The runs bear
4. play. bears Two

14 Unit 4 • Imagine That! • Chicken Pedro and the Falling Sky

PRACTICE BOOK p. 14

DAY 4 APPLY

WRITING CONNECTION

- Review with children that complete sentences have a certain word order that makes sense. Remind them that complete sentences begin with a capital letter and end with a period, question mark, or exclamation mark.
- Write the following chart on the chalkboard.

WHO OR WHAT	WORD ORDER	ENDING
The king	sat under the	umbrella.

Point out how each part of the sentence fits in the chart. Encourage volunteers to create sentences about the king or queen and write them on their own charts. Have children share these with the class.

REVISE/PROOFREAD

- After children have proofread their animal story, have them find two complete sentences about an animal and place them on the chart.

Is
my
?
this
cat

DAY 5 ASSESS

QUICKCHECK

- Ask children to write a complete sentence about one of the animals in *Chicken Pedro and the Falling Sky*.
- Write the following sentence on the chalkboard and have children identify the errors.

the animals drank cake and ate lemonade

(The animals drank lemonade and ate cake.)

INFORMAL ASSESSMENT
OBSERVATION

✔ Did children begin the sentence with a capital letter?

✔ Did children place the words in an order that makes sense?

✔ Did children use a period, question mark, or exclamation mark at the end of the sentence?

If children need additional support, use the **Reteach** lesson on **page R63**.

MATH

Add It Up

OBJECTIVE: Use diagrams and illustrations.

MATERIALS: None

Activity

Children make up number stories about Chicken Pedro and his friends.

Connect to the Anthology

Many friends joined Chicken Pedro on his way to see the King. Ask children to make up number stories about Chicken Pedro and his friends.

Make New Discoveries

- Ask children to look at the pictures in the story again. When Maria the Hen joins Chicken Pedro on **page 16** of the story, how many characters in all are traveling to the palace? How many glasses of lemonade do the King and Queen serve at the end of the story?
- Have children draw pictures to make other number stories. Ask them to write number sentences to go with their pictures.

How to Assess

Were children able to make up number stories?

2+1=3

SCIENCE

Find Out About the Sun

OBJECTIVE: Collect data.

MATERIALS: Age-appropriate reference materials that include information about the sun

Activity

Children collect facts about the sun, for example, how big it is, and share what they learn with their classmates.

Connect to the Anthology

Chicken Pedro does not know very much about the sky or the sun. When a lemon hits him on the head, he thinks it is the sun.

Make New Discoveries

- The sun may seem small to children, and perhaps may even seem flat. Help children find books that tell about the sun. Encourage children to collect as many facts and pictures as they can about the sun.
- Discuss the size of the sun by comparing it to known objects.
- On a piece of chart paper, record information that children collect about the sun. For example:

  The sun is a giant ball of hot gases.
  The sun heats the earth.

How to Assess

Were children able to collect and share information about the sun?

SOCIAL STUDIES

Spreading the News

OBJECTIVE:
Use diagrams and illustrations.

MATERIALS:
Poster board
Construction paper
Markers
Crayons

ACTIVITY

Children make a display that shows how people communicate news today. **(VISUAL LITERACY)**

CONNECT TO THE ANTHOLOGY

Remind children that Chicken Pedro had to walk to the Palace to tell the King the news about the falling sky. Today we have many different ways of sending news to all parts of the world.

MAKE NEW DISCOVERIES

- Children brainstorm the different ways we communicate news today.
- Groups of children choose a form of communication, such as newspapers, magazines, telephone, radio, television, Internet.
- Each group draws a picture or makes a poster to illustrate their communication method. Have children make a display of their work in a corner of the classroom and label it *Spreading the News.*
- Children can add to the display by bringing newspapers, magazines, and other items from home.

HOW TO ASSESS

Were children able to describe and illustrate many forms of communication?

THE ARTS

Make Paintings of the Sky

OBJECTIVE:
Use observation.

MATERIALS:
Paint
Paintbrushes
Crayons
Paper

ACTIVITY

Children make drawings of the sky as it looks at different times of day and night.

CONNECT TO THE ANTHOLOGY

Chicken Pedro thought the sky was falling, but did he ever look at the sky to see if he was right?

MAKE NEW DISCOVERIES

- Have children observe the sky at different times of the day. Remind them to watch the sky as the sun sets at night.
- Discuss children's observations of how the sky changes.
- Encourage children to make drawings or paintings of the sky as it looks at different times of the day or night.

HOW TO ASSESS

Were children able to describe their observations of the sky and make drawings or paintings of what they observed?

ASSESSMENT

Select two children in each guided reading group to observe. Keep anecdotal records on each child's reading performance. Consider the following questions:

- ✔ **What cues does the child use to figure out words and make meaning while reading?**
- ✔ **How well does the child use strategies to solve reading problems?**
- ✔ **What sound-spellings or high-frequency words are causing the child difficulty?**

When completed, add the anecdotal records to the child's literacy folder for future use when grading or conferencing.

Conducting Guided Reading Groups

Meet with at least two reading groups each day. Select a book on each group's instructional reading level from the *Scholastic Guided Reading Library* or a book in your classroom library. For more information on conducting guided reading groups, see *Scholastic Guided Reading Library,* Teacher's Guide.

Setting Up Independent Centers

While meeting with each reading group, have the rest of the class work in the Independent Centers listed below. Place the appropriate center cards in a pocket chart for student reference. Rotate the cards each day. Children may also use this time to do the following:

- revise or complete writing assignments,
- complete Practice Book pages,
- write in their Journals,
- read independently.

SAMPLE MANAGEMENT PLAN FOR CENTERS

RED GROUP	BLUE GROUP	GREEN GROUP	YELLOW GROUP
Overhead Projector	Independent	ABC Center	Technology
Technology	Overhead Projector	Independent	ABC Center
ABC Center	Technology	Overhead Projector	Independent

TEACHER TIP

While children are reading, be sure they are:

- checking that the text makes sense.
- making, confirming, and revising predictions based on the text.
- problem-solving words on the spot.
- confirming word solving by rereading text.
- using knowledge of phonics, sentence structure, and word meanings to word solve and make meaning from text.

GAY SU PINNELL

Independent Centers

Children can work in these centers while you meet with guided reading groups.

OVERHEAD PROJECTOR

Select several poems and stories, including examples of children's writing, and reproduce them on plastic transparencies. Safely secure the overhead projector in front of a white paper screen, and have children project and read them. Children can take turns pointing to the words on the transparency while their partners read.

ABC CENTER

Have children go to the ABC Center and work on activities centered on building words. Tasks can include making words from a small set of letters, building words using this week's phonics skills, or forming related words such as word families. Children can use magnetic, tile, or foam letters for these activities.

mine
shine
bone
cone

TECHNOLOGY

The Night Sky is a **WiggleWorks Plus** selection. Each day have two children from each group sit together at a word processor and reread the selection using **WiggleWorks Plus.** When they have finished, ask children to go to the Write area and write a short summary of the story.

INDEPENDENT READING

Put several books in the Browsing Box for each reading group. These books can include books previously read during guided reading or books on each group's independent reading level. Tell children to choose a book to read or reread independently. After they have finished reading their books, have children draw a picture of their favorite part of the story.

JENNY'S JOURNEY
SCHOLASTIC
GOING HOME
by Margaret Wild
illustrated by Wayne Harris
SCHOLASTIC
PIERRE
A cautionary tale
IN FIVE CHAPTERS
AND A PROLOGUE
MAURICE SENDAK

WEEK 2 Words With Final *e* (*o-e, i-e*)

Spelling

WEEK 2 RESOURCES

SPELLING RESOURCE BOOK

- **Word Sort,** p. 89
- **Extra Help,** p. 90
- **Vocabulary Practice,** p. 91
- **Challenge,** p. 92
- **Proofread,** p. 93
- **Student Test Form,** p. 161
- **Individual Progress Chart,** p. 162
- **Class Progress Chart,** p. 163
- **Word Sort Chart,** p. 164
- **My Words to Learn,** p. 165
- **Spelling Award Form,** p. 166

ADDITIONAL RESOURCES

- **Spelling Strategy Poster**
- **Proofreading Marks Poster**

SPELLING LIST

Words With Final *e*

shine bone
fine cone
mine

High-Frequency

some many

DAY 1 PRETEST/SELF-CHECK

ADMINISTER THE PRETEST

1. The stars **shine** at night.
2. I was sick, but now I feel **fine.**
3. Is that book **mine** or yours?
4. The dog buried the **bone.**
5. I like ice cream in a **cone.**
6. I need **some** new crayons.
7. I have **many** books.

SPELLING CONCEPT

Teach the spelling concept and present the spelling words. Point out the long *i* and *o* spelling patterns.

WORD SORT

On the chalkboard, draw the word sort chart. Ask children to sort the spelling words in the boxes. *(**o_e:** bone, cone; **i_e:** shine, fine, mine)*

Long o o_e	Long i i_e

Have children complete **Spelling Resource Book, page 89.**

DAY 2 VOCABULARY PRACTICE

BUILD VOCABULARY: WORD-PICTURE ASSOCIATION

- Discuss how pictures can often give clues to a word's meaning. Then draw a star on the chalkboard. Ask children which spelling word they think of when they look at the star. *(shine)*
- Children can draw, or cut out of magazines, pictures of items they associate with one of the spelling words. *(dog—bone; ice cream—cone)*

WORD STUDY: RHYMING WORDS

- Write on the chalkboard: *I gave the dog a lone.* Ask children to replace the underlined word with a spelling word that rhymes and makes sense in the sentence.
- Write the following words in a column on the chalkboard: *shine, cone, mine.* In a second column write these words: *bone, fine, line.* Ask children to match a word in the first column with a rhyming word in the second column.

Have children complete **Spelling Resource Book, page 90, 91,** or **92.**

Word Sort

Name

Word Sort

1. Write a spelling word in each box.
2. Cut on the -------- lines.
3. Sort the words.

Spelling Words	
fine	bone
mine	cone
shine	some
many	

SPELLING RESOURCE BOOK p. 89

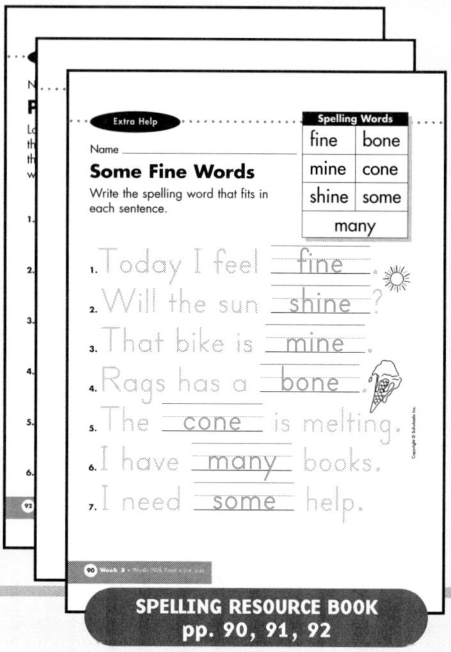

Extra Help

Name

Some Fine Words

Write the spelling word that fits in each sentence.

Spelling Words	
fine	bone
mine	cone
shine	some
many	

1. Today I feel fine.
2. Will the sun shine?
3. That bike is mine.
4. Rags has a bone.
5. The cone is melting.
6. I have many books.
7. I need some help.

SPELLING RESOURCE BOOK pp. 90, 91, 92

DAY 3 WRITE/PROOFREAD

WRITE

- Tell children that they will write a description of what they might see in the night sky.
- Children might brainstorm a list of descriptive words before they begin writing. A graphic organizer will help them get started.

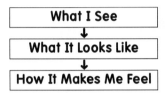

What I See
↓
What It Looks Like
↓
How It Makes Me Feel

Children may:

- write a description of the sky during the daytime and compare it to their description of the night sky.
- draw side-by-side pictures of their descriptions.

PROOFREAD

- Review the proofreading marks, using the class Proofreading Chart for reference.
- Use the following sentence for proofreading practice:

S B an cone
sam brown ate ice-cream con.

Have children complete **Spelling Resource Book, page 93.**

DAY 4 STUDY/REVIEW

GLOSSARY

- Review that a glossary gives information about the meanings of words in a book.
- Write the words and definitions below on the chalkboard. Ask children to write each spelling word next to its definition.

shine fine mine bone cone

_____ **belonging to me**
_____ **well, good**
_____ **a favorite treat for a dog**
_____ **a triangular-shaped food that holds ice cream**
_____ **to glow brightly**

TEST YOURSELF

- Review the Spelling Strategy.
- Children can choose three spelling words and write them, leaving out one or two letters. Then partners can switch papers and fill in the blanks to complete the words.
- Partners can take turns dictating a sentence that contains a spelling word and writing the word.

Children may practice for their spelling tests using the **Student Test Form, page 161.**

DAY 5 POSTTEST/SELF-CHECK

ADMINISTER THE POSTTEST

For the Posttest, read aloud the sentences from Day 1. Have children write each spelling word.

Then have children:

- self-check.
- record the results of their Posttest on the **Individual Progress Chart.**
- keep a list of their misspelled words in their spelling journals.

ASSESSMENT

Record the results of children's Posttests on the **Class Progress Chart, Spelling Resource Book, page 163.**

See **Handwriting Practice, page 21** for practice writing the letters *I* and *H*.

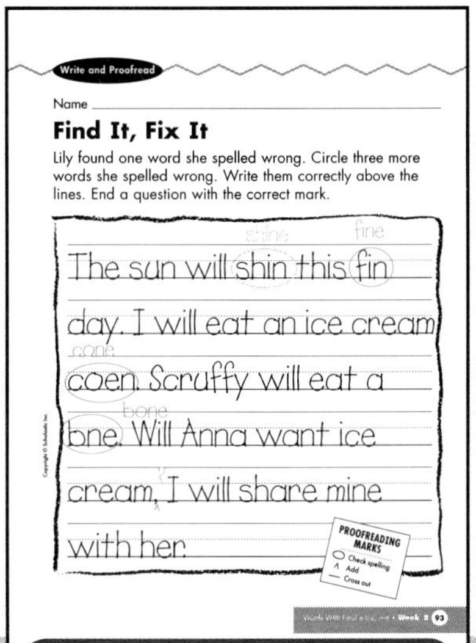
Write and Proofread
Name
Find It, Fix It
Lily found one word she spelled wrong. Circle three more words she spelled wrong. Write them correctly above the lines. End a question with the correct mark.
The sun will shin this fin day. I will eat an ice cream coen. Scruffy will eat a bne. Will Anna want ice cream, I will share mine with her.
PROOFREADING MARKS

SPELLING RESOURCE BOOK p. 93

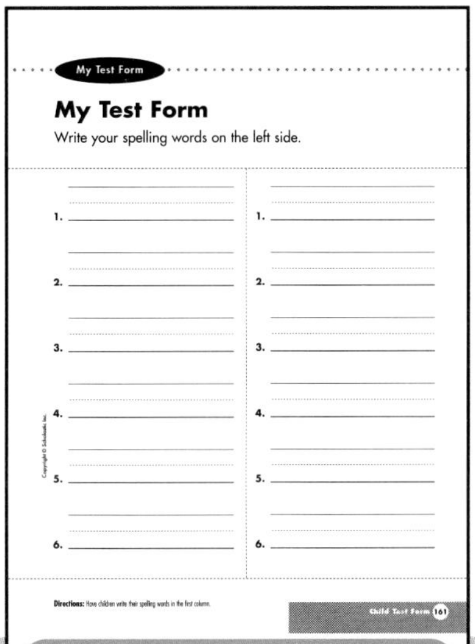
My Test Form
My Test Form
Write your spelling words on the left side.
1. 2. 3. 4. 5. 6.

SPELLING RESOURCE BOOK p. 161

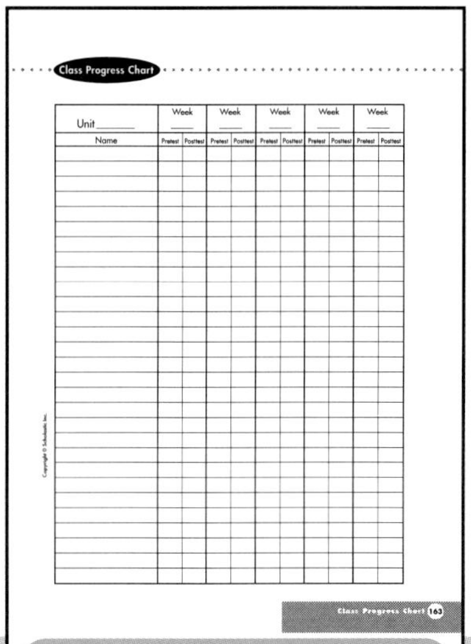
Class Progress Chart
Unit
Name
Week

SPELLING RESOURCE BOOK p. 163

WEEK 2 Capitalizing Titles

Grammar, Usage, Mechanics

OBJECTIVES

Children will explore capitalizing titles in *The Night Sky* and in their writing.

RESOURCES

Practice Book, p. 24
Grammar, Usage, Mechanics Resource Book, pp. 68–71

Capitalizing Titles

Important words in a title are capitalized.

Words such as *and, of, to,* and *by* are usually not capitalized.

The first word in a title is always capitalized.

MODIFY Instruction

ESL/ELD

▲ Gather several of children's favorite books. Read the title aloud. Tell children that all the words in a title need a capital letter except short words such as *and* or *to*. Ask one child to come up and point to each capital letter as you read the titles again. **(MULTISENSORY TECHNIQUES)**

DAY 1 TEACH/MODEL

SELECTION LINK

- Write the following selection title on the chalkboard.

  The Night Sky

  Circle each of the capital letters. Point out how each word in the title is capitalized.

- Then write:

  Looking at the Night Sky

  Ask volunteers to underline the words that are capitalized. Elicit from children how the first word and all the important words are capitalized. Explain why the words *at* and *the* are not capitalized in this title, and *Looking, Night* and *Sky* are—*Looking* is the first word; *Night* and *Sky* are important words.

- Then have children look at the song, "Twinkle, Twinkle, Little Star," following the selection. Ask children to write the title with capital letters on a chart. Then ask children to write a new title, using capital letters where appropriate, and place it on the chart.

The song's title: *Twinkle, Twinkle Little Star*

A new title: *The Twinkle of a Star*

DAY 2 PRACTICE

REVIEW

- Review with children that important words in a title are capitalized.
- Write the following title on the chalkboard and have volunteers identify which words need to be capitalized.

  planets in the sky

  Ask children to explain why *planets* and *sky* start with a capital letter, and *in* and *the* do not.

- Ask children to name some of their favorite stories. Write several titles in all lowercase letters on the chalkboard. Have children choose one to write correctly. Remind them to capitalize the first word and all the important words in the title.

the three little pigs
mary had a little lamb
hansel and gretel
little red riding hood

Have pairs of children exchange papers and check that the appropriate words in the title are capitalized.

DAY 3 PRACTICE

RETEACH

- Review with children that important words in a title are capitalized.
- Ask children to work with a partner and create a new title for the story, *The Night Sky*. Ask pairs to write this title on sentence strips using correct capitalization. Remind children to capitalize all the important words. Have children display these in two areas. In one area have all the titles that have all capitals, and in the other area have titles that have one or more words with lowercase letters.
- Share the titles, having volunteers read the titles aloud.

Have children complete **Practice Book, page 24.**

DAY 4 APPLY

WRITING CONNECTION

- Review with children that important words in a title are capitalized.
- Write the following titles on the chalkboard and ask children to identify which of the words will need to be capitalized in each title.

the little dipper
(The Little Dipper)

looking at the moon
(Looking at the Moon)

stars and me
(Stars and Me)

REVISE/PROOFREAD

- After children have proofread their list of tips, have children choose one title they could use for their list and write it above the list.

DAY 5 ASSESS

QUICKCHECK

- Ask children to write a title for a story about the stars, the moon, or a planet.
- Write the following title on the chalkboard and have children tell what the error is.

Look at The Sky

(Look at the Sky.)

INFORMAL ASSESSMENT
OBSERVATION

✔ Did children begin the first word of the title with a capital letter?

✔ Are all the important words in capital letters?

If children need additional support, use the **Reteach** lesson on **page R64.**

Name

Capitalizing Titles

Most words in a book title begin with a capital letter.

▶ Write each book title correctly on the book.

1. harry's house
2. stone soup
3. the snowy day
4. what's inside?

24 Unit 4 • Imagine That! • The Night Sky

PRACTICE BOOK p. 24

MATH

Count the Days

OBJECTIVE: Use charts, graphs, and visual displays.

MATERIALS: Copy of current month's calendar showing phases of the moon (for each child)

Activity

In *The Night Sky,* children discovered that the moon looks different at various times of the month. Using a calendar, they will quantify this knowledge. **(VISUAL LITERACY)**

Connect to the Anthology

Have children compare the two pictures of the moon on **Anthology pages 30** and **31.** Ask why the moon looks different in the two pictures.

Make New Discoveries

- Give each child a copy of this month's calendar. Tell children to look at the shapes of the moon on it. Ask them questions that can be answered by counting days on their calendars. For example: *How many days are there between a new moon and a full moon?*

How to Assess

Were children able to count the number of days between any two phases of the moon?

SCIENCE

Model Sun, Earth, and Moon

OBJECTIVE: Use observation.

MATERIALS: None

Activity

Children role-play the relative positions and motions of the sun, Earth, and moon.

Connect to the Anthology

Have children look at the picture of the full moon on **Anthology page 30.** Ask them: Do you think the moon and Earth move?

Make New Discoveries

- Ask three children to play the roles of the sun, Earth, and moon. The sun child stands still in the middle of the room.
- The Earth child stands about eight feet away from the sun and spins around slowly, imitating the rotation of Earth. The spinning Earth moves around the sun in a circle.
- The moon child moves around Earth in a circle while Earth orbits the sun. The moon, however, doesn't spin as it orbits.

How to Assess

Were children able to transfer their observations of the model to the real moon and Earth?

SOCIAL STUDIES

Retell Moon Tales

OBJECTIVE: Synthesize information.

MATERIALS: Moon stories from a variety of cultures

Activity

Children hone their storytelling skills and their ability to distinguish between reality and fantasy as they share stories about the moon.

Connect to the Anthology

Ask if anyone has a story or poem about the moon to share.

Make New Discoveries

- Tell children that groups of people around the world tell different moon stories. For example, a Chinese story tells about a rabbit that lives on the moon and grinds materials with a stone, trying to find the secret that will allow people to live longer. Help children find moon stories in the school or classroom library.
- Children choose one story to retell. After each retelling, discuss what is real in the story and what is make-believe.

How to Assess

Were children able to retell main ideas and some supporting details? Were they able to distinguish between fact and fantasy?

THE ARTS

Make a Space Mobile

OBJECTIVE: Use observation.

MATERIALS: Aluminum foil String Coat hangers

Activity

Children build mobiles that show the relative positions of the moon and stars.

Connect to the Anthology

Have children look at the pictures of the moon in *The Night Sky*. Ask them which they think is closer to Earth, the moon or the stars.

Make New Discoveries

- Groups of five children work together. Each child crumples a piece of foil into a ball. Help children tie the strings to a hanger.
- Have the group lie on the floor, heads close together. Hold the hanger so that the mobile is just a few inches above the children. Point out the moon (the ball on the long string), and tell them that the moon is smaller than a star. Why do the stars look smaller than the moon? (They're farther away.)

How to Assess

Can children draw conclusions from the model?

ASSESSMENT

Select two children in each guided reading group to observe. Keep anecdotal records on each child's reading performance. Consider the following questions:

- ✔ **What cues does the child use to figure out words and make meaning while reading?**
- ✔ **How well does the child retell the story?**
- ✔ **What sound-spellings or high-frequency words are causing the child difficulty?**

When completed, add the anecdotal records to the child's literacy folder for future use when grading or conferencing.

CONDUCTING GUIDED READING GROUPS

Meet with at least two reading groups each day. Select a book on each group's instructional reading level from the *Scholastic Guided Reading Library* or a book in your classroom library. For more information on conducting guided reading groups, see *Scholastic Guided Reading Library*, Teacher's Guide.

SETTING UP INDEPENDENT CENTERS

While meeting with each reading group, have the rest of the class work in the Independent Centers listed below. Place the appropriate center cards in a pocket chart for student reference. Rotate the cards each day. Children may also use this time to do the following:

- revise or complete writing assignments,
- complete Practice Book pages,
- write in their Journals,
- read independently.

SAMPLE MANAGEMENT PLAN FOR CENTERS

RED GROUP	BLUE GROUP	GREEN GROUP	YELLOW GROUP
Paired Reading	ABC Center	Independent	Poem Box
Poem Box	Paired Reading	ABC Center	Independent
Independent	Poem Box	Paired Reading	ABC Center

TEACHER TIP

During guided reading sessions, keep in mind these goals:

- Lessons are fast-paced.
- Children are engaged throughout the lesson.
- Children talk about the meaning of the story and about specific aspects of the print.
- The selected texts are appropriate for the strategies children are using and appropriate for their reading level.
- Powerful teaching points are chosen to illustrate the reading process and word-solving strategies.

GAY SU PINNELL

Independent Centers

Children can work in these centers while you meet with guided reading groups.

PAIRED READING

Have partners select and read a book together. Suggest that partners take turns reading the book to each other, or they can alternate reading one page at a time. If a child cannot find a partner, he or she can read the selection into a tape recorder and play it back.

PIERRE
A cautionary tale
IN FIVE CHAPTERS
AND A PROLOGUE
MAURICE SENDAK

GOING HOME
by Margaret Wild illustrated by Wayne Harris

INDEPENDENT READING

Have children choose a book from the Browsing Box to read independently. The books can be titles that children have read during guided reading or ones that correspond to their independent reading level. Ask children to read or reread the books softly to themselves. Afterward, each child can go to the Writing Center and write a summary of the book.

JENNY'S JOURNEY

POEM BOX

Collect poems for the class Poem Box. The poems can be ones that you have read to the children and that they can read on their own. Decodable poems are available in *Scholastic Phonics A*. You can paste copies of the poems on tagboard. Have children select a poem they like and read it softly to themselves. Then have them read the poem to a classmate. Suggest that they draw a picture that shows how they feel about the poem.

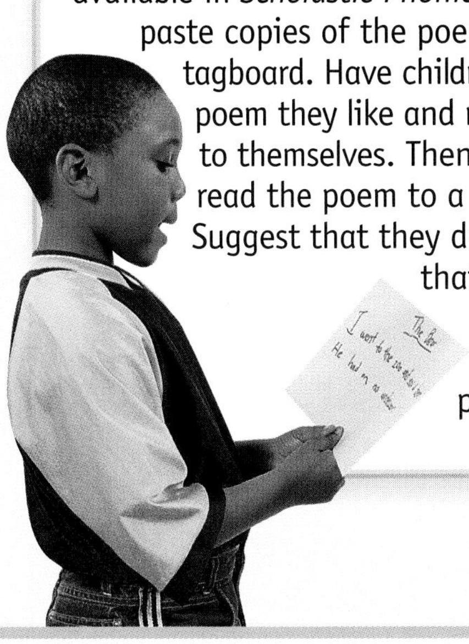

ABC CENTER

Have children go to the ABC Center to work on activities centered on making words. Tasks can include making words from a small set of letters, or words with *r*-blend and *l*-blends. Children can use magnetic, tile, or foam letters for these activities. You might have children work with partners. They can search this week's stories for words to build for their partner to read.

WEEK 3 Words With *l*-Blends

Spelling

WEEK 3 RESOURCES

SPELLING RESOURCE BOOK
- **Word Sort,** p. 94
- **Extra Help,** p. 95
- **Vocabulary Practice,** p. 96
- **Challenge,** p. 97
- **Proofread,** p. 98
- **Student Test Form,** p. 161
- **Individual Progress Chart,** p. 162
- **Class Progress Chart,** p. 163
- **Word Sort Chart,** p. 164
- **My Words to Learn,** p. 165
- **Spelling Award Form,** p. 166

ADDITIONAL RESOURCES
- **Spelling Strategy Poster**
- **Proofreading Marks Poster**

SPELLING LIST

Words With *l*-Blends

place	black
plant	block
plane	

High-Frequency

about	look

DAY 1 PRETEST/SELF-CHECK

ADMINISTER THE PRETEST

1. My room is my favorite **place.**
2. I need to water that **plant.**
3. Did you ever fly in a **plane**?
4. My little **black** dog got lost.
5. Do not **block** the doorway with toys.
6. **Look** at the moon.
7. What is that book **about**?

SPELLING CONCEPT

Teach the spelling concept and present the spelling words. Point out and model how to pronounce the *l*-blend in each word.

WORD SORT

On the chalkboard, draw the word sort graphic organizer. Ask children to sort the spelling words on the triangles. *(**pl:** plane, plant, place; **bl:** black, block)*

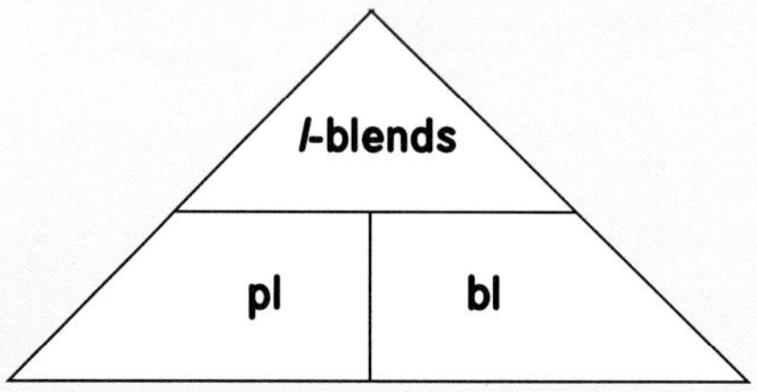

l-blends
pl
bl

Have children complete **Spelling Resource Book, page 94.**

Word Sort
Spelling Words
place black
plant block
plane look
about
Name
Word Sort
1. Write a spelling word in each box.
2. Cut on the -------- lines.
3. Sort the words.

SPELLING RESOURCE BOOK p. 94

DAY 2 VOCABULARY PRACTICE

BUILD VOCABULARY: COMPOUND WORDS

- Write *someplace* on the chalkboard. Read the word aloud and tell children that it is a compound word made up of a spelling word and another word. Ask children to name the two words and to identify the spelling word.
- Write the words below in two columns on the chalkboard. Have children match a word in column one to a word in column two to form a compound word. Then ask them to write the new word and circle the spelling word.

place	**block**
air	**berry**
black	**mat**
sun	**plane**

WORD STUDY: BUILD WORDS

- Write *back* on the chalkboard. Say the word. Then write the letter *l* after the *b* and blend the *b* and *l* together to say the new word.
- Write these words on the chalkboard with the letters widely spaced: *pant, back, pace*. Ask children to add an *l* to each word to form a spelling word.

Have children complete **Spelling Resource Book, pages 95, 96,** or **97.**

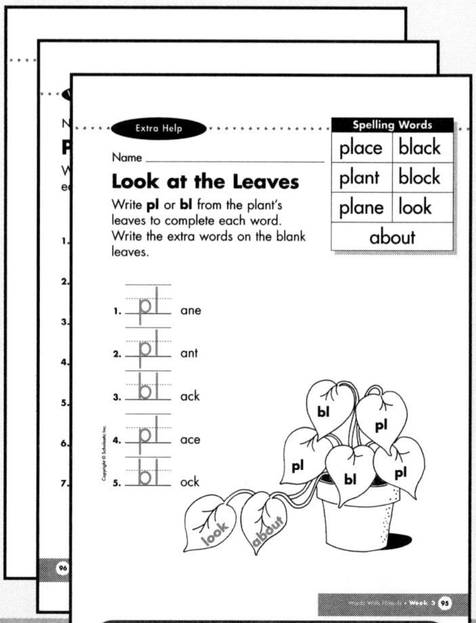

Extra Help
Spelling Words
place black
plant block
plane look
about
Name
Look at the Leaves
Write pl or bl from the plant's leaves to complete each word. Write the extra words on the blank leaves.
1. pl ane
2. pl ant
3. bl ack
4. pl ace
5. bl ock
bl
pl
pl
bl
pl
look
about

SPELLING RESOURCE BOOK pp. 95, 96, 97

DAY 3 WRITE/PROOFREAD

WRITE

- Tell children that they will write about an imaginary place. They can describe what the place looks like and what makes it special.
- A graphic organizer such as the one below might help children organize their ideas before they begin writing.

Where it is:

↓

How it looks:

↓

Why it's special:

Children may:

- give their imaginary place a name.
- draw a picture of themselves in their imaginary place.

PROOFREAD

- Review the proofreading marks, using the class Proofreading Chart for reference.
- Use the following sentence for proofreading practice:

The flowers on that pant is pretty. (plant are)

Have children complete **Spelling Resource Book, page 98.**

DAY 4 STUDY/REVIEW

ABC ORDER

- Review the letters of the alphabet by writing the following sequences of letters on the chalkboard. Invite children to write the missing letters in the blanks.

__ fghi **lmn __ p**
jk __ mn **__ uvwx**

- Write the following groups of words on the board. Ask children to write a spelling word that could come between the two words in ABC order.

apple, _____, cake *(black; block)*
kite, _____, run *(place; plant; plane)*
man, _____, toy *(place; plant; plane)*

TEST YOURSELF

- Review the Spelling Strategy.
- Partners can take turns dictating a spelling word and spelling it using magnetic letters or a dry-erase board.
- Children can take turns dictating incomplete sentences and writing the spelling word that completes each sentence.

Children may practice for their spelling tests using the **Student Test Form, page 161.**

DAY 5 POSTTEST/SELF-CHECK

ADMINISTER THE POSTTEST

For the Posttest, read aloud the sentences from Day 1. Have children write each spelling word.

Then have children:

- self-check.
- record the results of their Posttest on the **Individual Progress Chart.**
- keep a list of their misspelled words in their spelling journals.

ASSESSMENT

Record the results of children's Posttests on the **Class Progress Chart, Spelling Resource Book, page 163.**

See **Handwriting Practice, page 22** for practice writing the letters *E* and *F*.

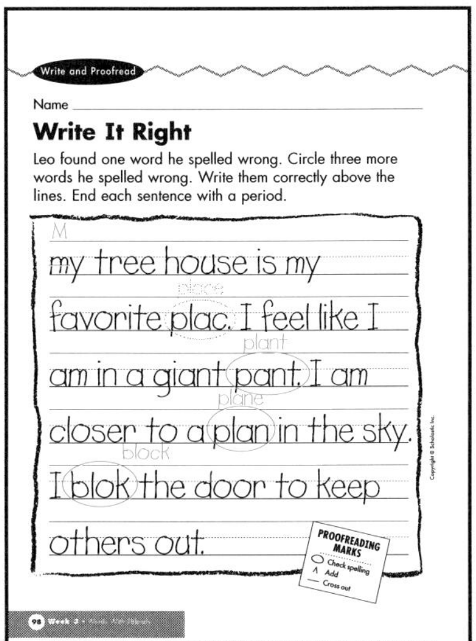
Write and Proofread

Name

Write It Right

Leo found one word he spelled wrong. Circle three more words he spelled wrong. Write them correctly above the lines. End each sentence with a period.

my tree house is my favorite plac. I feel like I am in a giant pant. I am closer to a plan in the sky. I blok the door to keep others out.

PROOFREADING MARKS

SPELLING RESOURCE BOOK p. 98

My Test Form

My Test Form

Write your spelling words on the left side.

1. 2. 3. 4. 5. 6.

1. 2. 3. 4. 5. 6.

SPELLING RESOURCE BOOK p. 161

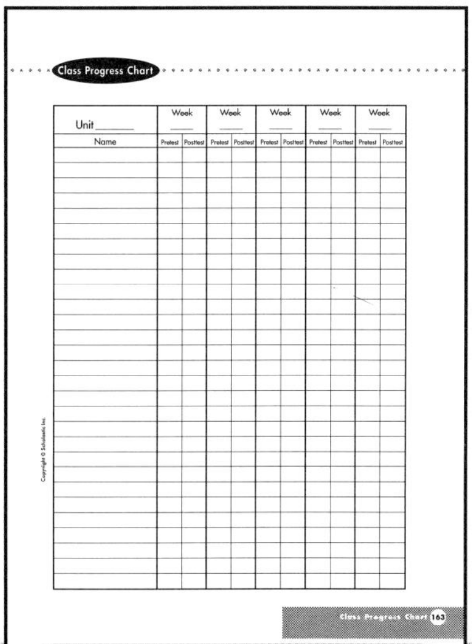
Class Progress Chart

Unit ____ Name | Week | Week | Week | Week | Week (Pretest / Posttest)

SPELLING RESOURCE BOOK p. 163

WEEK 3 Irregular Verbs

Grammar, Usage, Mechanics

OBJECTIVES

Children will explore the irregular verbs *have* and *be* in *In the Attic* and in their writing.

RESOURCES

Practice Book, p. 37
Grammar, Usage, Mechanics Resource Book, pp. 72–75

Irregular Verbs

The irregular verbs *be* and *have* change in special ways.

- *is* and *has* tell about now.
- *was* and *had* tell about the past.

MODIFY Instruction

ESL/ELD

▲ Give children extra practice with time clues. Start a T-chart with the headings Present and Past. Write "Today" under Present and "Yesterday" under Past. Help children add other words to each category. Then write simple sentences with *is/was, has/had*, including time clues, on the chalkboard. Underline the verb in each sentence. Ask children to identify it as past or present. **(CATEGORIZE)**

DAY 1 TEACH/MODEL

SELECTION LINK

- Write the following sentences on the chalkboard. (The first sentence is from **Anthology page 4.**)

  He had a million toys, but he was bored.

  He has a million toys, but he is bored.

  Elicit from children which sentence is telling about now, or the present, and which is telling about the past.

  Point out that some verbs tell about the past and some verbs tell about the present. Underline the verbs in both sentences. Elicit from children how the underlined verbs changed from the past to the present.
- Write these sentences on the chalkboard:

  The boy was alone.

  He is in a flying machine.

  He had played with a spider.

  The spider has a web.

  Underline the irregular verb in each sentence. Ask children to identify if the verb takes place now or in the past and place the answer on a chart.

Now	Past
is	*was*
has	*had*

- Have pairs of children look in the story to find examples of *was* and *had*. Have them write one of the sentences, and circle the word.

DAY 2 PRACTICE

REVIEW

- Review with children that irregular verbs change in a special way. Remind children how the word *is* in the present becomes *was* in the past, and *has* in the present becomes *had* in the past.
- Write these sentences on the chalkboard and have children identify which word fits in the sentence.

  Now he (*is, was*) eating dinner.

  Yesterday he (*is, was*) in the attic.
- Write these sentences on the chalkboard and have children identify which word fits in the sentence.

  Last week the boy (*has, had*) lots of toys.

  Today the boy (*has, had*) a fire truck.

  Ask volunteers to identify which sentence in each set is happening now and which happened in the past.
- Have children write one sentence using the word *was* and another using the word *had*. Remind children that these are special verbs and take place in the past.

DAY 3 PRACTICE

RETEACH

- Review with children that irregular verbs change in a special way. Remind children how the word *is* in the present becomes *was* in the past, and *has* in the present becomes *had* in the past.
- Write the following sentence stems on index cards: *Today, he...; Yesterday, she...; Last week, he...; The other day, she...; Last year, he...; Now, she...; This minute, he...; Right now, she....*

  Give pairs of children a card. Ask pairs to use *is, was, has,* or *had* in a sentence beginning with one of the sentence stems. Have children share their sentences and explain which sentences tell about now and which tell about the past.

Have children complete **Practice Book, page 37**.

Name

Irregular Verbs

The verbs is and has tell about now. The verbs was and had tell about the past.

▶ Read the words in the chart. Then write the correct word in the sentences below.

Now	In the Past
is	was
has	had

1. Today it ______ hot out.
2. Last week it ______ cold out.
3. Today Lee ______ shorts on.
4. Last week Lee ______ a coat on.

Copyright © Scholastic Inc.

Unit 4 • Imagine That! • *In the Attic* 37

PRACTICE BOOK p. 37

DAY 4 APPLY

WRITING CONNECTION

- Review with children that irregular verbs change in a special way. Remind children how the word *is* in the present becomes *was* in the past, and *has* in the present becomes *had* in the past.
- Write the words *is, was, has,* and *had* on the chalkboard. Divide children into groups of four, and have each child write one sentence using one of the words so that all four words are distributed among each group. Then have each group member share his or her sentence with the group. Encourage the other group members to evaluate the correct use of the irregular verb.

REVISE/PROOFREAD

- After children have proofread their fantasy stories, have them find sentences where they used *had, has, is,* or *was.* Ask children to write one of those sentences on the chart.

Now:	______________________
	______________________
Then:	______________________
	______________________

DAY 5 ASSESS

QUICKCHECK

- Ask children to write a sentence about something that happened either today or yesterday using one of the irregular verbs *is, was, has,* or *had.*
- Write the following sentence on the chalkboard and have children identify the error.

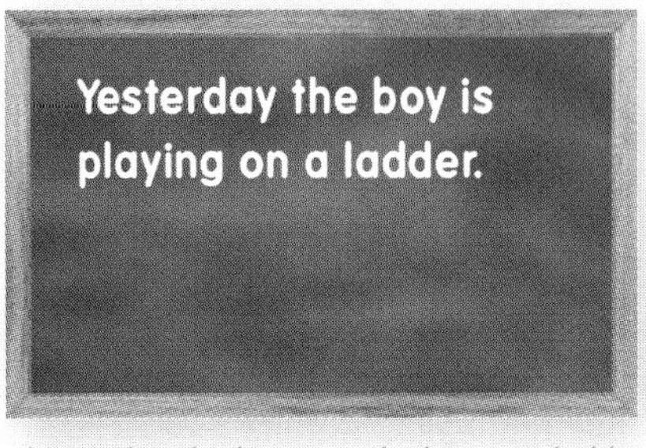
Yesterday the boy is playing on a ladder.

(Yesterday the boy was playing on a ladder.)

INFORMAL ASSESSMENT
OBSERVATION

✔ Did the sentence have the correct verb tense?

✔ Did the sentence start with a capital letter?

✔ Did the sentence end with the correct punctuation?

If children need additional support, use the **Reteach** lesson on **page R64.**

MATH

Solve Picture Problems

OBJECTIVE:
Note relevant details.

MATERIALS:
None

Activity

Children use illustrations as the basis for simple math problems. **(VISUAL LITERACY)**

Connect to the Anthology

Refer children to the picture of the mouse family in the attic.

Make New Discoveries

- Ask questions about the mouse family's imaginary activities that can be answered with a number. For example: How many mice are riding on the roller skate? How many are sitting near the boy? How many mice are there altogether?
- Invite volunteers to explain how they arrived at their answers.
- Use other illustrations in the selection in the same way.

How to Assess

Were children able to use mathematical reasoning as they described their computations?

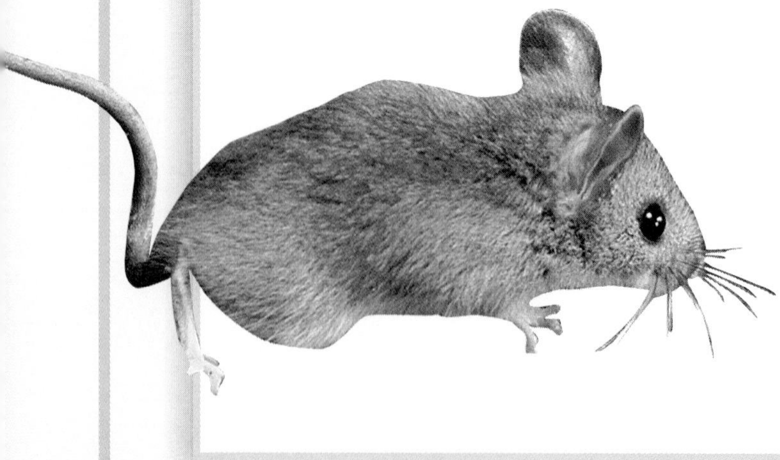

SCIENCE

Explore Structures

OBJECTIVE:
Note relevant details.

MATERIALS:
Drinking straws
Paper clips
Pipe cleaners
Paper
Tape
Scissors

Activity

Children build models of ladders and compare them.

Connect to the Anthology

Have children look at the illustrations on **Anthology pages 48** and **49.** Direct their attention to the tall ladder. Ask how ladders are alike.

Make New Discoveries

- Partners choose building materials. Encourage them to be imaginative in their designs; their ladders don't have to conform to the standard model.
- Partners make their ladder as tall as possible, given the limitations of their materials and first-grade fingers.
- Display the ladders and have children discuss how they're alike and different.

How to Assess

Were children able to compare and contrast their model ladders?

SOCIAL STUDIES

What's Real and What's Not?

OBJECTIVE: Note relevant details.

MATERIALS:
Paper
Pencils
Crayons

Activity

Children identify real-world objects and events in an imaginary world. **(VISUAL LITERACY)**

Connect to the Anthology

Ask children to look at the illustration in *In the Attic* showing the boy making a web with the spider. Discuss what is imaginary and what is real in the picture.

Make New Discoveries

- Point out that sometimes stories can have both real and imaginary things in them. Invite children to draw a picture that shows them doing something. Encourage them to show things that can be real and things that aren't real.
- Children can display their pictures. Lead a class discussion in which children identify the real and imaginary things in each one.

How to Assess

Did children's pictures indicate an awareness of the real world?

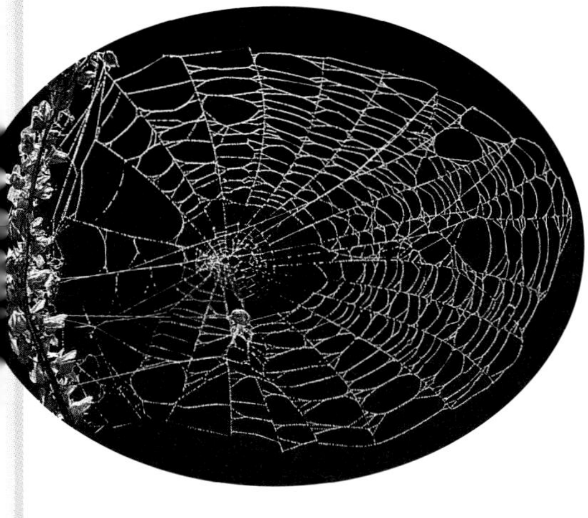

THE ARTS

What Do You Get When . . .

OBJECTIVE: Note relevant details.

MATERIALS:
Paper
Pencils
Crayons

Activity

Children create an imaginary creature by combining two animals. **(VISUAL LITERACY)**

Connect to the Anthology

Let children tell about some of the imaginary friends the boy in the story had. What would you do if you had an imaginary animal friend?

Make New Discoveries

- Partners work together to create an imaginary creature by mixing two animals. Each child thinks of a favorite animal. Partners then decide how they can combine their two favorite animals to draw one creature.
- Partners display their imaginary creature. Other children can try to identify the animals that were combined to create them.

How to Assess

Were children able to combine relevant details to create an imaginary animal by combining two animals?

ASSESSMENT

Select two children in each guided reading group to observe. Keep anecdotal records on each child's reading performance. Consider the following questions:

- ✔ **What cues does the child use to figure out words and make meaning while reading?**
- ✔ **How well does the child retell the story?**
- ✔ **What sound-spellings or high-frequency words are causing the child difficulty?**

When completed, add the anecdotal records to the child's literacy folder for future use when grading or conferencing.

Conducting Guided Reading Groups

Meet with at least two reading groups each day. Select a book on each group's instructional reading level from the *Scholastic Guided Reading Library* or a book in your classroom library. For more information on conducting guided reading groups, see *Scholastic Guided Reading Library*, Teacher's Guide.

Setting Up Independent Centers

While meeting with each reading group, have the rest of the class work in the Independent Centers listed below. Place the appropriate center cards in a pocket chart for student reference. Rotate the cards each day. Children may also use this time to do the following:

- revise or complete writing assignments,
- complete Practice Book pages,
- write in their Journals,
- read independently.

SAMPLE MANAGEMENT PLAN FOR CENTERS

RED GROUP	BLUE GROUP	GREEN GROUP	YELLOW GROUP
ABC Center	Listening	Writing	Independent
Independent	ABC Center	Listening	Writing
Writing	Independent	ABC Center	Listening

TEACHER TIP

During guided reading sessions, assess children's comprehension by:

- looking for a high rate of accuracy.
- noting whether children readily use phonics, meaning, and syntax cues.
- observing whether children search for meaning through repeated attempts.
- assessing fluency and phrasing.
- asking questions, having children retell the story, or listening closely as children share their responses to the story.

GAY SU PINNELL

Independent Centers

Children can work in these centers while you meet with guided reading groups.

ABC CENTER

Have children spend time in the ABC Center. Prepare sets of word cards for children to sort into categories. Categories can include words that begin with the same initial letter or final letter, words that rhyme, and words that have the same vowel sound. Children can work independently or with partners. Encourage children to share their word categories with other classmates.

WRITING CENTER

Have children go to the Writing Center to write a story about something they like to do. Suggest that they use the pronoun *I* in telling their story. Children can draw pictures to go with their stories. Allow class time for children to share their stories with classmates.

I like to run.
I am happy.
I Can Sing.

INDEPENDENT READING

Collect several books to place in the Browsing Box for each reading group. Select books the children have read during guided reading or that match each group's independent reading level. Tell children to choose a book and read it independently. Afterward, children can retell the story to a classmate.

JENNY'S JOURNEY
PIERRE
A cautionary tale
IN FIVE CHAPTERS
AND A PROLOGUE
MAURICE SENDAK
GOING HOME
Margaret Wild
illustrated by Wayne Harris

LISTENING

Place three stories on tape in the Listening Center. One tape should be the audiocassette version of *Starring First Grade*. Ask children to select one tape and follow along in the book as the story is read aloud. After listening, children can gather in a group to tell what they like about the stories.

Scholastic Cassettes

WEEK 4 Words with *s*-Blends

Spelling

WEEK 4 RESOURCES

SPELLING RESOURCE BOOK
- **Word Sort,** p. 99
- **Extra Help,** p. 100
- **Vocabulary Practice,** p. 101
- **Challenge,** p. 102
- **Proofread,** p. 103
- **Student Test Form,** p. 161
- **Individual Progress Chart,** p. 162
- **Class Progress Chart,** p. 163
- **Word Sort Chart,** p. 164
- **My Words to Learn,** p. 165
- **Spelling Award Form,** p. 166

ADDITIONAL RESOURCES
- **Spelling Strategy Poster**
- **Proofreading Marks Poster**

SPELLING LIST

Words With *s*-Blends

sniff	stand
snap	stage
step	

High-Frequency

make	which

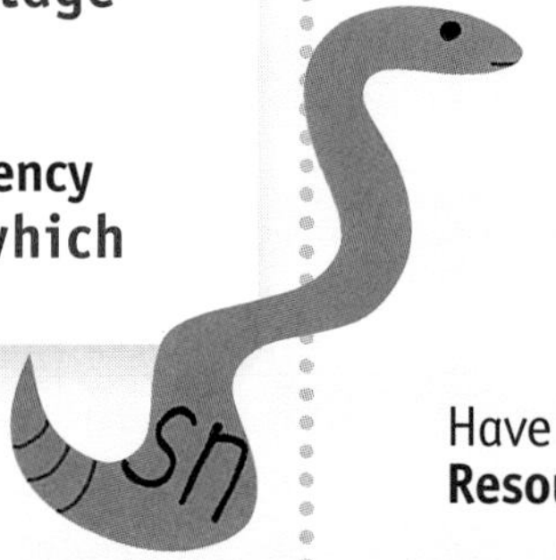
sn

DAY 1 PRETEST/SELF-CHECK

ADMINISTER THE PRETEST

1. Do not **step** in the puddle.
2. I bent down to **sniff** the flower.
3. Can you **snap** your fingers?
4. Go **stand** next to Sara.
5. We stood on **stage** to sing the song.
6. I can **make** a puppet.
7. **Which** hat should I wear?

SPELLING CONCEPT

Teach the spelling concept and present the spelling words. Point out and model how to pronounce the *s*-blend in each word.

WORD SORT

On the chalkboard, draw the graphic organizer for the word sort. Ask children to sort the spelling words in the snake and the star. (**sn:** *sniff, snap;* **st:** *step, stand, stage)*

St

Have children complete the **Spelling Resource Book, page 99.**

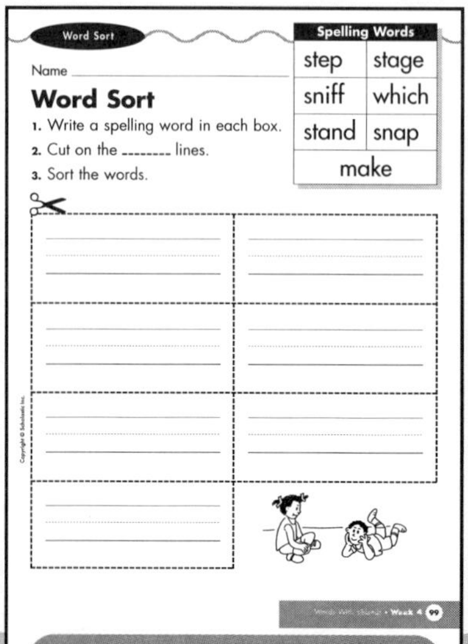
Word Sort
Spelling Words

step	stage
sniff	which
stand	snap
make	

Name ____

Word Sort

1. Write a spelling word in each box.
2. Cut on the ------- lines.
3. Sort the words.

SPELLING RESOURCE BOOK p. 99

DAY 2 VOCABULARY PRACTICE

BUILD VOCABULARY: CONTEXT CLUES

- Review how context clues can help readers figure out an unfamiliar word. Then write the following sentence on the chalkboard and ask children to supply a spelling word that makes sense: *Can you ____ your fingers to the music?* (snap)
- Provide the sentences below and read them aloud. Ask children to use context clues to supply the missing words.

I tripped because I did not watch my ________. *(step)*

I like to ________ flowers because they smell good. *(sniff)*

WORD STUDY: ALLITERATION

- Write the following sentence on the chalkboard: *Sandy said to sniff the sunflower.* Underline the first letter in each word that begins with *s*. Explain that this is an example of alliteration.
- Write on the chalkboard: *Can Sam cand and sing?* Ask children to replace the underlined letter with an *s*-blend to create a word that makes sense in the sentence.

Have children complete **Spelling Resource Book, page 100, 101,** or **102.**

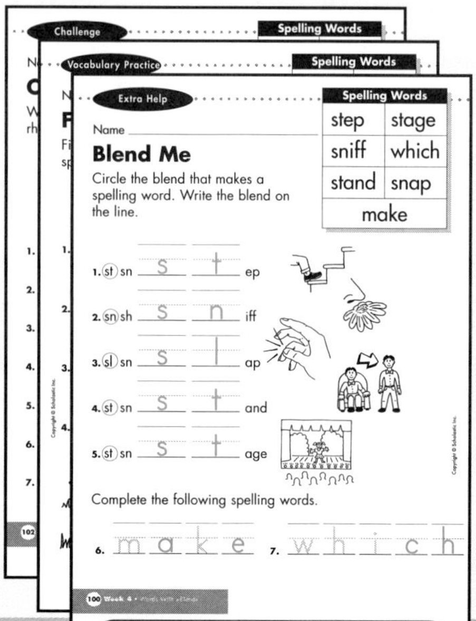
Challenge — Spelling Words
Vocabulary Practice — Spelling Words
Extra Help — Spelling Words

step	stage
sniff	which
stand	snap
make	

Name ____

Blend Me

Circle the blend that makes a spelling word. Write the blend on the line.

1. st sn — s t — ep
2. sn sh — s n — iff
3. sl sn — s l — ap
4. st sn — s t — and
5. st sn — s t — age

Complete the following spelling words.

6. make 7. which

SPELLING RESOURCE BOOK pp. 100, 101, 102

DAY 3 VOCABULARY PRACTICE

WRITE

- Tell children that they will write a silly tongue twister. Explain that they should write a sentence that includes as many words that begin with the same sound as they can.
- Using a graphic organizer will help children get started.

Beginning sound: → **Words that begin with that sound:**

Children may:

- make their tongue twisters into rebus sentences by replacing some of the words with drawings or pictures cut from magazines.
- challenge classmates to recite their tongue twisters as fast as they can.

PROOFREAD

- Review the proofreading marks, using the class Proofreading Chart for reference.
- Use the following sentence for proofreading practice:

the stage

Walk slowly across stag.

Have children complete **Spelling Resource Book, page 103.**

DAY 4 STUDY/REVIEW

GLOSSARY/ABC ORDER

- Review that a glossary lists words and their meanings in ABC order.
- Write the following words and definitions on the chalkboard. Ask children to write the word that belongs with each definition.

sniff	**snap**	**stage**
step	**stand**	

to move forward with your foot ________

a place to perform ________

to smell ________

a quick, sharp sound, as made by your fingers ________

to remain on your feet; to not sit ________

TEST YOURSELF

- Review the Spelling Strategy.
- Partners can make flash cards for the spelling words and take turns reading and then spelling the words.
- Children can choose three spelling words and write them in scrambled order. Then partners can unscramble each other's words.

Children may practice for their spelling tests using the **Student Test Form, page 161.**

DAY 5 POSTTEST/SELF-CHECK

ADMINISTER THE POSTTEST

For the Posttest, read aloud the sentences from Day 1. Have children write each spelling word.

Then have children:

- self-check.
- record the results of their Posttest on the **Individual Progress Chart.**
- keep a list of their misspelled words in their spelling journals.

ASSESSMENT

Record the results of children's Posttests on the **Class Progress Chart, Spelling Resource Book, page 163.**

See **Handwriting Practice, page 23** for practice writing the letters *P* and *B*.

Write and Proofread

Name

Mark It Up

Marcos found one word he spelled wrong.
Circle two other words he spelled wrong.
Write them correctly above the lines.
Write *I* as a capital letter.

What a day! i did not watch my steep. I fell off the staige. Everyone tried to help. Then mom helped mak things better. She gave me a hug!

PROOFREADING MARKS

SPELLING RESOURCE BOOK p. 103

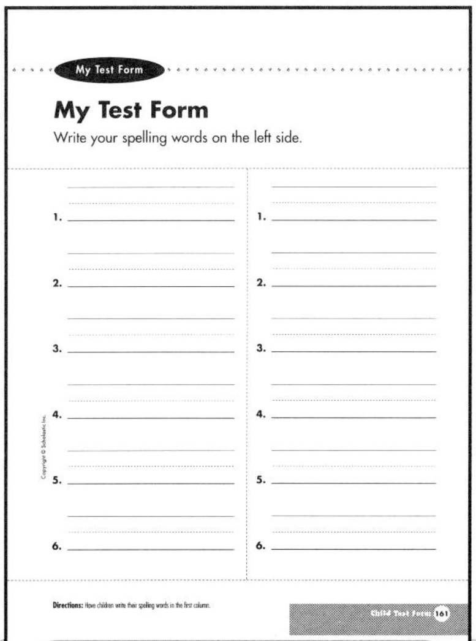
My Test Form

My Test Form

Write your spelling words on the left side.

1. 2. 3. 4. 5. 6.

SPELLING RESOURCE BOOK p. 161

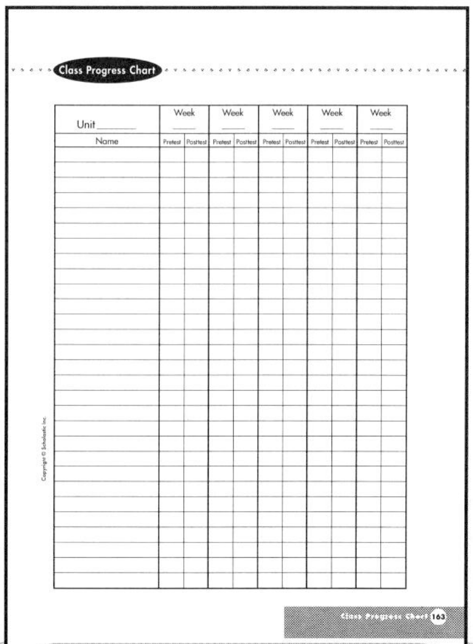
Class Progress Chart

Unit | Name | Week | Week | Week | Week | Week

SPELLING RESOURCE BOOK p. 163

WEEK 4 Describing Words

Grammar, Usage, Mechanics

OBJECTIVES

Children will explore the describing words in *Starring First Grade* and in their writing.

RESOURCES

Practice Book, p. 54
Grammar, Usage, Mechanics Resource Book, pp. 76–79

Describing Words

Words that describe people, places, or things are called adjectives.

These tell us more about people, places, and things.

MODIFY Instruction

ESL/ELD

▲ Help English language learners with describing words by playing a guessing game. Give them clues, using words that tell what a classroom object looks like, and have students guess what it is. Model the procedure with a fluent speaker. Teacher: *I am looking at a sweater. It is* ***green.*** *It has* ***five*** *buttons.* Student: *Is it Carla's sweater?* Children take turns leading the game. **(KEY WORDS)**

DAY 1 TEACH/MODEL

SELECTION LINK

- Write the following story-related sentences on the chalkboard.

  Danny was the biggest goat.

  The teacher picked two of her goats.

  Underline *biggest* and *two* in the sentences. Point out that those words tell how many goats there are and the size of the goat. Explain that *biggest* and *two* are *describing words.*
- Write the following sentences on the chalkboard:

  I see a little tree.

  The tree is green.

  There were three trees in the show.

  Have children read each sentence, looking for the describing word that is telling more about the tree or trees. Ask a volunteer to underline the describing word in each sentence.
- Ask pairs of children to find words in the story that describe goats, girl, and grade and place them on the chart. Examples may be found on **Anthology pages 77–78.**

Describing Word

1. ____________________ **goats**
   (two)
2. ____________________ **girl**
   (little)
3. ____________________ **grade**
   (first)

DAY 2 PRACTICE

REVIEW

- Review with children that describing words tell more about people, places, and things. They help us paint a picture in our mind. Tell children that some describing words tell the size, color, shape, or number of another word.
- Place children in groups of four and give each group a copy of these four sentences:

  A white snowflake twirled.

  A big troll wants to cross.

  They were happy.

  Ask groups to circle the describing words and tell who or what each is describing. Have groups share their answers.
- Ask children to look at the last picture of the story on **Anthology page 101.** Then ask each child to write a sentence with a describing word about the picture. Have children share their sentences with the class.

DAY 3 PRACTICE

RETEACH

- Review with children that describing words tell more about people, places, and things.
- Write the following describing words and sentences on the chalkboard and have children complete the blank with one of the *describing words.*

good	**tiny**	**blue**	**ugly**

The troll was _______. *(ugly)*

The river was _______. *(blue)*

A _______ leaf fell. *(tiny)*

It was a _______ play. *(good)*

Have children complete **Practice Book, page 54.**

DAY 4 APPLY

WRITING CONNECTION

- Review with children that describing words tell more about people, places, and things.
- Write the word *bridge* on the chalkboard. Have children write one sentence using a describing word that tells about the bridge. Encourage children to describe what the bridge looks like. Remind them they may tell about its color, size, or shape.
- Have children share their sentences with a partner. Have partners circle the describing words.

REVISE/PROOFREAD

- After children have proofread their description, have them look for describing words and place them on the chart.

How It Looks	
What It's Like	

DAY 5 ASSESS

QUICKCHECK

- Ask children to write a sentence that describes a goat—for example, using words that describe what color it is or how it looks, acts, or moves. Have volunteers share their completed sentences. Classmates can identify the describing words.
- Write the following sentence on the chalkboard and have children identify the describing word.

The goats crossed a wooden bridge.

(wooden)

INFORMAL ASSESSMENT
OBSERVATION

✔ Did the sentence have a describing word?

If children need additional support, use the **Reteach** lesson on **page R65.**

Name

Describing Words

Describing words tell more about people, places, and things.

▶ **A.** Look at each picture. Circle the two words that describe it. Then write them on the lines.

1. **long shiny bug**
   long **snake**
   shiny **snake**
2. **eat big pink**
   big **pig**
   pink **pig**

▶ **B.** Look at the giraffe. Write two words that describe it on the lines.

3. *Make sure children have written an adjective to describe the giraffe.* **giraffe**
4. *Make sure children have written an adjective to describe the giraffe.* **giraffe**

54 Unit 4 • Imagine That! • *Starring First Grade*

Copyright © Scholastic Inc.

PRACTICE BOOK p. 54

MATH

Count Characters

OBJECTIVE:
Collect data.

MATERIALS:
None

Activity

Children do computations using the characters in the first-grade play. **(VISUAL LITERACY)**

Connect to the Anthology

Remind children that in *Starring First Grade,* the teacher adds characters so that everyone can have a role in *The Three Billy Goats Gruff.*

Make New Discoveries

- Ask children how many characters were in the story to begin with.
- Ask how they can figure out how many roles the teacher added.
- Ask how many characters would have to be added to the story so that everyone in your own class could have a role in the play. Have children describe how they arrived at their answers.

How to Assess

Were children able to use mathematical reasoning in making their calculations?

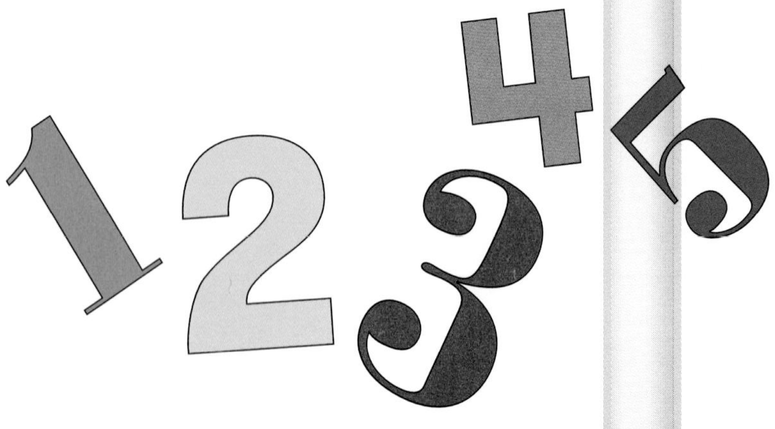

SCIENCE

Build Model Bridges

OBJECTIVE:
Field test.

MATERIALS:
Modeling clay
Cardboard
Building blocks
Construction paper
Straws
Pipe cleaners

Activity

Children experiment with different materials to build model bridges that can support a small amount of weight.

Connect to the Anthology

Have children look at the picture of the bridge on **Anthology page 95.** Invite volunteers to try to identify the materials used in building it.

Make New Discoveries

- Let children work in the Artist's Studio in small groups to build model bridges.
- They can test their bridges' ability to hold weight by putting small balls of clay on them.

How to Assess

Did children build and test their models? Did they adjust and retest their models if they failed?

SOCIAL STUDIES

Cooperation!

OBJECTIVE:
Make a plan.

MATERIALS:
None

Activity

The class works together to make a cooperative plan for choosing the role each child will play.

Connect to the Anthology

Remind children that in *Starring First Grade,* the teacher decides which roles the children will play in *The Three Billy Goats Gruff.*

Make New Discoveries

- Explain that every child must have a role in the play. If two or more children want the same role, a fair way must be worked out to decide who will play the role.
- Ask children to think of different ways to assign roles in a play. Can children come up with a plan for letting everyone choose a role he or she wants? What if two or more people want the same role?

How to Assess

Were children able to work together to make a reasonable plan?

THE ARTS

Design a Set

OBJECTIVE:
Brainstorm multiple approaches.

MATERIALS:
Modeling clay
Cardboard
Building blocks
Construction paper
Straws
Pipe cleaners

Activity

Children design and build miniature stage sets based on the selection's illustrations.

Connect to the Anthology

Review the illustrations in *Starring First Grade* that show different parts of the stage set.

Make New Discoveries

- Using the bridges they built in the science option as a starting point, groups make other miniature components for model stage sets for *The Three Billy Goats Gruff* as illustrated in *Starring First Grade.*
- Children can make small paper figures of themselves to add to the final stage sets. Each child can show himself or herself in costume for the role each was assigned in the social studies option.

How to Assess

Did children work together to design and build their model stage sets?

ASSESSMENT

Select two children in each guided reading group to observe. Keep anecdotal records on each child's reading performance. Consider the following questions:

- ✔ **What cues does the child use to figure out words and make meaning while reading?**
- ✔ **How well does the child retell the story?**
- ✔ **What sound-spellings or high-frequency words are causing the child difficulty?**

When completed, add the anecdotal records to the child's literacy folder for future use when grading or conferencing.

Conducting Guided Reading Groups

Meet with at least two reading groups each day. Select a book on each group's instructional reading level from the *Scholastic Guided Reading Library* or a book in your classroom library. For more information on conducting guided reading groups, see *Scholastic Guided Reading Library,* Teacher's Guide.

Setting Up Independent Centers

While meeting with each reading group, have the rest of the class work in the Independent Centers listed below. Place the appropriate center cards in a pocket chart for student reference. Rotate the cards each day. Children may also use this time to do the following:

- revise or complete writing assignments,
- complete Practice Book pages,
- write in their Journals,
- read independently.

SAMPLE MANAGEMENT PLAN FOR CENTERS

RED GROUP	BLUE GROUP	GREEN GROUP	YELLOW GROUP
Drama	ABC Center	Independent	Technology
Technology	Drama	ABC Center	Independent
Independent	Technology	Drama	ABC Center

TEACHER TIP

To make sure that the Independent Centers continue to meet the children's needs,

- monitor each center for a few moments at a time as often as you can.
- confirm that children are following the correct routines and using each area independently.
- verify that each center has materials that encourage children to explore and work independently.
- reorganize materials and prepare new labels for the centers on a regular basis.
- check that all equipment, such as computers, audiotape systems, and the overhead projector, is in proper working order.

GAY SU PINNELL

Independent Centers

Children can work in these centers while you meet with guided reading groups.

DRAMA

Have children practice performing the play *The Three Billy Goats Gruff* or write a skit for another story they enjoy. Children can make masks in the Art Center, or they can use finger puppets to act out the story. If time permits, invite children to present their dramatic version of the story to the class.

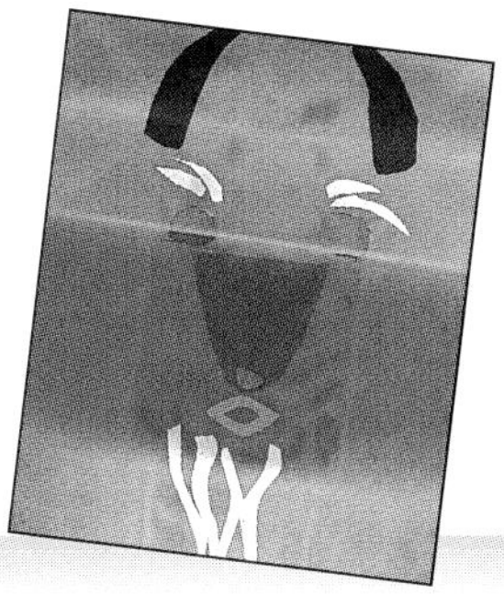

INDEPENDENT READING

Choose several books for each reading group, and place them in the appropriate Browsing Box. The books can be a mix of previously read titles and ones that correspond to each group's independent reading level. Have children choose a book to read or reread independently. Afterward, children may enjoy drawing a picture of their favorite part of the story.

PIERRE
A cautionary tale
IN FIVE CHAPTERS
AND A PROLOGUE
MAURICE SENDAK
JENNY'S JOURNEY
GOING HOME
by Margaret Wild illustrated by Wayne Harris
SCHOLASTIC

TECHNOLOGY

Each day, ask two children from each group to use the **WiggleWorks Plus** version of *The Three Billy Goats Gruff.* Have children reread the selection together. When they have worked through the selection, ask them to visit the Write area and write a brief summary of the story.

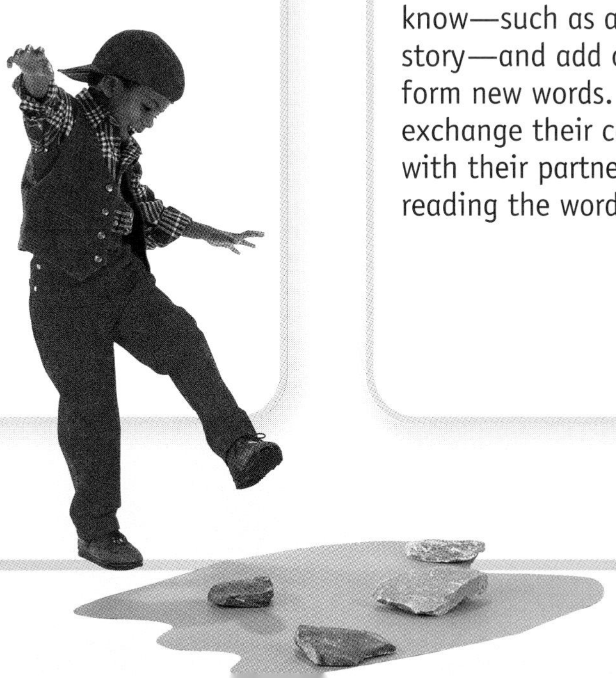

ABC CENTER

Have children spend time in the ABC Center building word ladders. Children can work with magnetic letters or letter tiles to construct a ladder of words. Tell children to begin with a word they know—such as a word from this week's story—and add or remove letters to form new words. Ask children to exchange their completed word ladders with their partners and take turns reading the words aloud.

WEEK 5 Contractions

Spelling

WEEK 5 RESOURCES

SPELLING RESOURCE BOOK

- **Word Sort,** p. 104
- **Extra Help,** p. 105
- **Vocabulary Practice,** p. 106
- **Challenge,** p. 107
- **Proofread,** p. 108
- **Student Test Form,** p. 161
- **Individual Progress Chart,** p. 162
- **Class Progress Chart,** p. 163
- **Word Sort Chart,** p. 164
- **My Words to Learn,** p. 165
- **Spelling Award Form,** p. 166

ADDITIONAL RESOURCES

- **Spelling Strategy Poster**
- **Proofreading Marks Poster**

SPELLING LIST

Contractions

I'll	she's
he'll	it's
you'll	

High-Frequency

way	were

DAY 1 PRETEST/SELF-CHECK

ADMINISTER THE PRETEST

1. **I'll** call you later.
2. **It's** hot outside today.
3. Hurry or **you'll** be late.
4. Dad said **he'll** help me.
5. **She's** the fastest runner in school.
6. That is the **way** to school.
7. We **were** having fun!

SPELLING CONCEPT

Teach the spelling concept and present the spelling words. Point out that a contraction is a shortened form of two words that are put together. Help children name the two words that make up each spelling word.

WORD SORT

On the chalkboard, draw the word sort chart. Ask children to sort the spelling words in the boxes. *(__ **will:** I'll, you'll, he'll; __ **is:** It's, she's)*

Contractions	
__ will	__ is

Have children complete **Spelling Resource Book, page 104.**

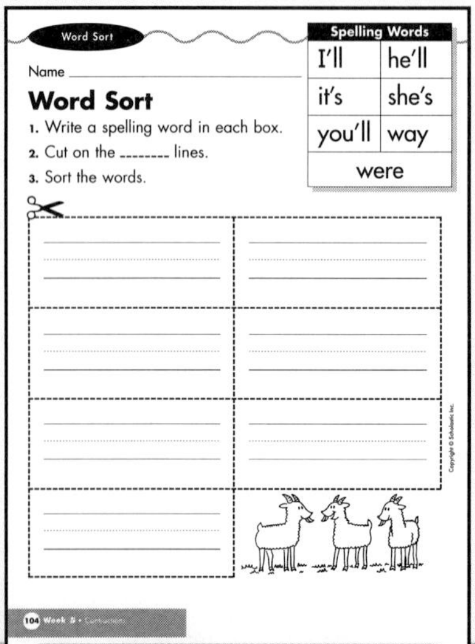
Word Sort
Spelling Words
I'll he'll
it's she's
you'll way
were
Name
Word Sort
1. Write a spelling word in each box.
2. Cut on the -------- lines.
3. Sort the words.
104 Week 5 • Contractions

SPELLING RESOURCE BOOK p.104

DAY 2 VOCABULARY PRACTICE

BUILD VOCABULARY: CONTRACTIONS

- Review that contractions are short words formed by two words put together.
- Write the following sentence on the chalkboard. Ask children to circle the two words that can be replaced with a contraction. Then ask them to write the contraction on the line.

Carlos said he will be late. ______

WORD STUDY: CONTRACTIONS

- Write *I'll* on the chalkboard and ask children which two words form the contraction. *(I will)* Write *I will* on the chalkboard. Point out that the *w* and *i* are replaced by an apostrophe.
- Write the following words in two columns. Ask children to match each contraction in the first column with the two words that form it in the second column.

I'll	**it is**
he'll	**you will**
it's	**she is**
she's	**I will**
you'll	**he will**

Have children complete **Spelling Resource Book, page 105, 106,** or **107.**

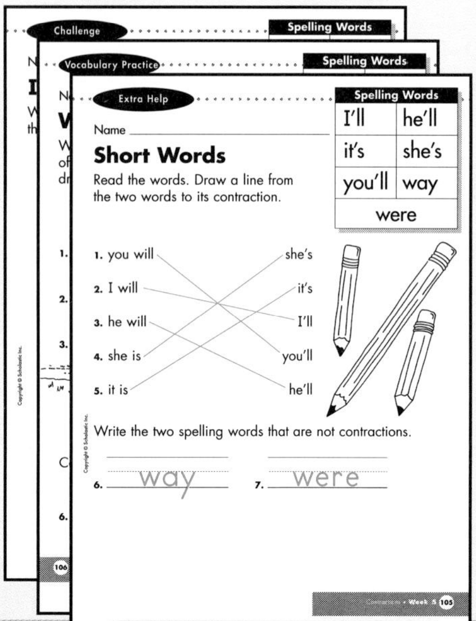
Challenge
Spelling Words
Vocabulary Practice
Spelling Words
Extra Help
Spelling Words
I'll he'll
it's she's
you'll way
were
Name
Short Words
Read the words. Draw a line from the two words to its contraction.
1. you will
2. I will
3. he will
4. she is
5. it is
she's
it's
I'll
you'll
he'll
Write the two spelling words that are not contractions.
6. way
7. were
Contractions • Week 5 105

SPELLING RESOURCE BOOK pp. 105, 106, 107

DAY 3 WRITE/PROOFREAD

WRITE

- Tell children that they will write about what they would say or do if they met a troll.
- Using a graphic organizer will help children get started.

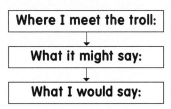

Where I meet the troll:
↓
What it might say:
↓
What I would say:

Children may:

- draw a picture of their encounter with the troll and include speech balloons to show the dialogue.
- act out their story with classmates.

PROOFREAD

- Review the proofreading marks, using the class Proofreading Chart for reference.
- Use the following sentence for proofreading practice:

M G she'll
ms. gonzales said sh'ell be here soon? .

Have children complete **Spelling Resource Book, page 108.**

DAY 4 STUDY/REVIEW

ABC ORDER

- Review the letters of the alphabet by writing the following sequences of letters on the chalkboard. Invite children to write the missing letters in the blanks.

__ **hi** **l** __ **n** **qr** __

p __ **r** __ **wx** **cd** __

- Write the following word groupings on the board. Ask children to put the words within each grouping in ABC order and to check their work by circling the first letter in each word.

I'll	*he'll*	**you'll**	*it's*
he'll	*I'll*	**it's**	*she's*
you'll	*you'll*	**she's**	*you'll*

TEST YOURSELF

- Review the Spelling Strategy.
- Partners can take turns dictating a spelling word and spelling it using magnetic letters or a dry-erase board.
- Children can choose three spelling words and write the two words that form those contractions. Then partners can write the contraction for each pair of words.

Children may practice for their spelling tests using the **Student Test Form, page 161.**

DAY 5 POSTTEST/SELF-CHECK

ADMINISTER THE POSTTEST

For the Posttest, read aloud the sentences from Day 1. Have children write each spelling word.

Then have children:

- self-check.
- record the results of their Posttest on the **Individual Progress Chart.**
- keep a list of their misspelled words in their spelling journals.

ASSESSMENT

Record the results of children's Posttests on the **Class Progress Chart, Spelling Resource Book, page 163.**

See **Handwriting Practice, pages 24–25** for practice writing the letters *M, N, A,* and *R.*

Write and Proofread
Name
Mark It Up
Carla found one word she spelled wrong. Circle two more words she spelled wrong. Write them correctly above the lines. Begin each sentence with a capital letter.
my best friend is moving. Its going to be lonely without her. Mom said I'wll make a new best friend. maybe shei's right!
PROOFREADING MARKS

SPELLING RESOURCE BOOK p.108

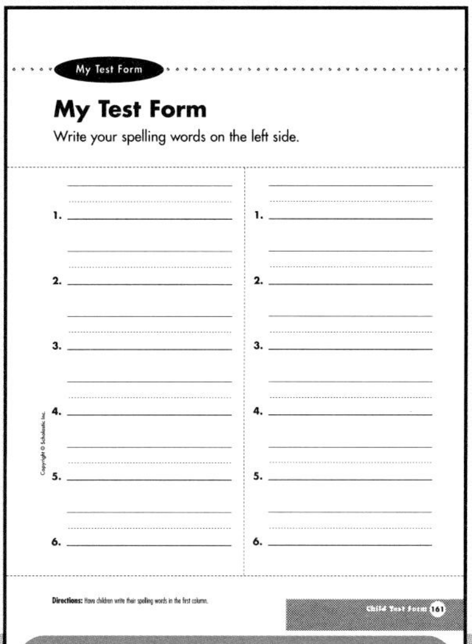
My Test Form
My Test Form
Write your spelling words on the left side.
1. 2. 3. 4. 5. 6.

SPELLING RESOURCE BOOK p.161

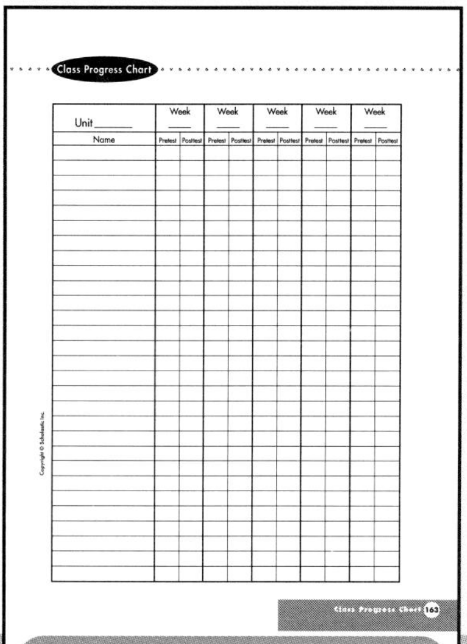
Class Progress Chart
Unit Name Week Week Week Week Week

SPELLING RESOURCE BOOK p.163

WEEK 5 Capitalizing Names and First Words

Grammar, Usage, Mechanics

OBJECTIVES

Children will explore the capitalization of names and first words in sentences in *The Three Billy Goats Gruff* and in their writing.

RESOURCES

Practice Book, p. 72
Grammar, Usage, Mechanics Resource Book, pp. 80–83

Some words need to be capitalized.

The first word in a sentence starts with a capital letter.
Words that name a particular person, place, or thing are capitalized.

MODIFY Instruction

ESL/ELD

▲ Ask children to draw names of people and things from the story and write them on the board, all with lowercase letters. Point out that names of people and places must begin with a capital letter. Go over the words, and for each one ask: *Is this a name? Capital or no capital?* When children respond correctly, ask a volunteer to come up to the chalkboard to copy the word, underlining any capitalized letters. **(CATEGORIZE)**

DAY 1 TEACH/MODEL

SELECTION LINK

- Write the following sentence from **Anthology page 118** on the chalkboard:

  It's only me, Little Gruff.

  Underline the capital letters in *Little Gruff*. Point out that this is a name of a character. Names are capitalized. Say the first and last names of several children in the class and explain that all first and last names are capitalized. Then point out that the sentence also begins with a capital letter.
- Have children look at the cast of characters on **Anthology page 107.** Elicit from children which letters are capitalized.
- Write the following sentence on the chalkboard:

  The second goat to meet Troll was Middle Gruff.

  Ask volunteers to underline the capital letters in this sentence. Ask why each is capitalized. Review that names and the beginnings of sentences are capitalized.
- Have children work with a partner and find names that begin with a capital letter on **Anthology page 116.** You may wish to display the capitalized words on a chart.

Names
Nosey
Extra Large Gruff

DAY 2 PRACTICE

REVIEW

- Review with children that the first word in a sentence starts with a capital letter. Also remind children that names of specific people, places, or things are capitalized.
- Write this sentence on the chalkboard and have children tell which words are capitalized.

  He did not like it when Extra Large Gruff called him Nosey. *(He, Extra Large Gruff, Nosey)*

  Ask children to identify why each word is capitalized.
- Have children work in coach/writer pairs. Have each writer write a sentence using one of the character's names. Ask the coach to check that his or her partner is placing capital letters where they belong. Then have children switch roles.

DAY 3 PRACTICE

RETEACH

- Review with children that the first word in a sentence and the names of specific people, places, or things are capitalized.
- Write the following sentences on the chalkboard and ask volunteers to underline the capitalized words.

  The monster's name was Troll.

  He let Little Gruff go up the mountain.

  Then ask children which words are names for people, places, or things. *(Troll, Little Gruff)*
- Ask children to name particular places, people, and things that need capital letters and list them on the chalkboard.

Have children complete **Practice Book, page 72.**

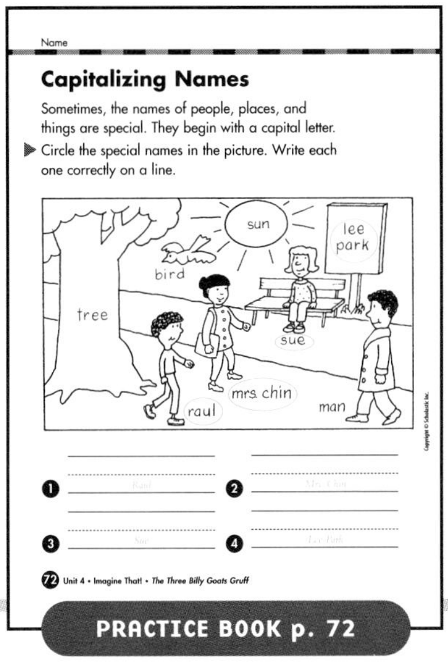
Name

Capitalizing Names

Sometimes, the names of people, places, and things are special. They begin with a capital letter.

▶ Circle the special names in the picture. Write each one correctly on a line.

sun
lee park
bird
tree
sue
mrs. chin
raul
man

1 ____ 2 ____

3 ____ 4 ____

72 Unit 4 • Imagine That! • *The Three Billy Goats Gruff*

Copyright © Scholastic Inc.

PRACTICE BOOK p. 72

DAY 4 APPLY

WRITING CONNECTION

- Review that the first word in a sentence and names of specific people, places, or things are capitalized.
- Write these word groups on the chalkboard.

  goat, Middle Gruff

  monster, Troll

  bridge, Golden Gate Bridge

  Ask children to tell why some words in each group begin with a capital letter and some do not.
- Write these word groups and have children choose the word that should begin with a capital letter. Ask children to write a sentence using each word.

  nickname, nosey *(Nosey)*

  middle gruff, brother *(Middle Gruff)*

  Have children exchange papers to check for capital letters.

REVISE/PROOFREAD

- After children have proofread their dialogue, have them look for capital letters they used. Remind them to check for words that need to be capitalized. Draw two circles on the chalkboard and have children place one of the capitalized words they used in each circle.

Beginning Capitals **Names**

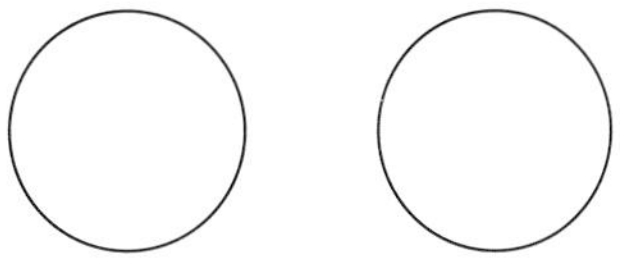

DAY 5 ASSESS

QUICKCHECK

- Ask children to write a sentence using their first and last name. When completed, have children trade papers with a partner and confirm that each other's names begin with capital letters.
- Write the following sentence on the chalkboard and have children identify the errors.

we saw bob read
about troll.

(We saw Bob read about Troll.)

INFORMAL ASSESSMENT
OBSERVATION

✔ Did children begin the sentence with a capital letter?

✔ Did children capitalize names?

If children need additional support, use the **Reteach** lesson on **page R65.**

MATH

Solve Money Problems

OBJECTIVE: Analyze information.

MATERIALS: None

ACTIVITY

Children do computations based on the troll's tolls.

CONNECT TO THE ANTHOLOGY

Ask a volunteer to read the rhyme the troll recites when he's asked how much the toll is.

MAKE NEW DISCOVERIES

- Ask children to figure out how much each goat would have to pay if the troll really did charge a dime and a nickel. Volunteers can explain how they figured it out.
- Here's another one: Pretend that each of the three goats paid the troll a dime and a nickel to cross the bridge. How much money did the troll collect in all? Again, let children explain how they got the answer.
- As time permits, let children create other math problems based on *The Three Billy Goats Gruff.*

HOW TO ASSESS

Were children able to describe their mathematical reasoning?

SCIENCE

Learn About Goats

OBJECTIVE: Collect data.

MATERIALS: Reference materials that include information about goats

ACTIVITY

Children collect information about real goats from resource materials.

CONNECT TO THE ANTHOLOGY

Have children look at the picture on **Anthology page 120.** What are the three billy goats eating? Do goats really eat grass? Invite volunteers to tell what they know about goats.

MAKE NEW DISCOVERIES

- Ask children what questions they have about goats. You may want to write their questions on the chalkboard.
- Suggest that children find out the answers to their questions by looking in reference materials.
- Show children how they can use reference materials to collect information. You may need to help children use the index and table of contents to locate information.
- Allow time for children to share what they find out. Ask how real goats are different from those in the story.

HOW TO ASSESS

Were children able to collect data about goats from various resource materials?

SOCIAL STUDIES

Map the Play

OBJECTIVE: Use diagrams and illustrations.

MATERIALS: Chart paper Markers

ACTIVITY

Children make a simple map of the play's events and use it to retell the story line. **(VISUAL LITERACY)**

CONNECT TO THE ANTHOLOGY

Reread the narrator's last line on **Anthology page 108** concerning the goat's destination. Ask children where they think the goats were at the beginning of the story.

MAKE NEW DISCOVERIES

- Go through the script a page at a time, asking children to identify important places (the mountain, the bridge, the troll's tollbooth, the river, and so on).
- As a group, decide on a symbol for each place. Work with children to put the symbols in logical places on chart paper.
- Let children use the map as a guide in retelling the story without using the script.

HOW TO ASSESS

Were children able to use the map to retell the story?

THE ARTS

Make Troll and Goat Masks

OBJECTIVE: Interpret information.

MATERIALS: Paper bags Scissors Markers or crayons Construction paper Glue

ACTIVITY

Children make paper-bag masks to represent the characters in the play *The Three Billy Goats Gruff*.

CONNECT TO THE ANTHOLOGY

Have children look at the pictures of the goats and the troll on the "Cast of Characters" page. Ask them to describe each character's features.

MAKE NEW DISCOVERIES

- Help children cut eyeholes in their paper bags. Show them how to cut out details such as horns, teeth, and ears from construction paper.
- Children may want to use the masks to perform the play.

HOW TO ASSESS

Were children able to describe and show details of the characters' faces?

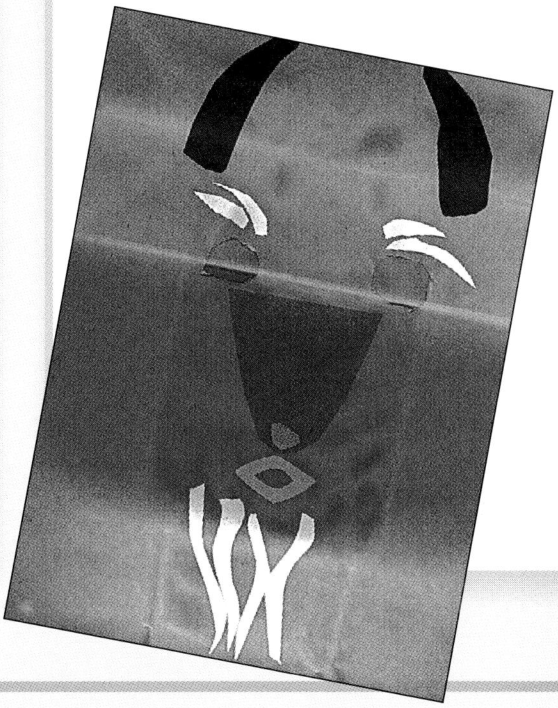

AKE INFERENCES

OBJECTIVE

- Children review making inferences.

MATERIALS

- Anthology, pp. 46–70
- Practice Book, p. 39

SUGGESTED GROUPING

- Small group or individuals

SKILLS TRACE

Make Inferences — TESTED

- Introduce, p. T44
- Practice, p. T27
- Review, p. R43
- Reteach, p. R56

1 REVIEW

Tell children that when the words of a story do not directly state information about feelings, actions, or places, readers can use story clues and their own experiences to figure out the missing information.

Read the following to children and have them use this method to figure out information that is not stated directly.

Mary looked everywhere for her lost dog. She sat on her porch and thought, "I have no one to play with. No one greets me with a wagging tail when I come home."

Ask the following:

> **How does Mary feel? How do you know?**

> **How would you describe Mary's dog?**

2 PRACTICE/APPLY

PUT IT IN CONTEXT Have children revisit *In the Attic* and review the plot of the story by looking through the pictures. When children are finished, have them work in cooperative groups. Encourage children to discuss and write down answers to the following two questions:

> **Why did the boy want to share what he found in the attic? Why would you want to share such wonderful things with someone else?**

> **Was the boy frightened when he found the tiger in the attic? Why do you think this?**

Have children support their inferences with information from the story and their own experiences.

3 ASSESS

DID CHILDREN:

✔ understand that an inference is an informed guess?

✔ make inferences from story clues and their own experiences?

IF NOT, TRY THIS:

See the **Reteach** lesson on **page R56.**

CHILDREN'S SELF-ASSESSMENT:

✔ Do I use clues from the story and what I know to make inferences?

For additional support, see **Practice Book page 39.**

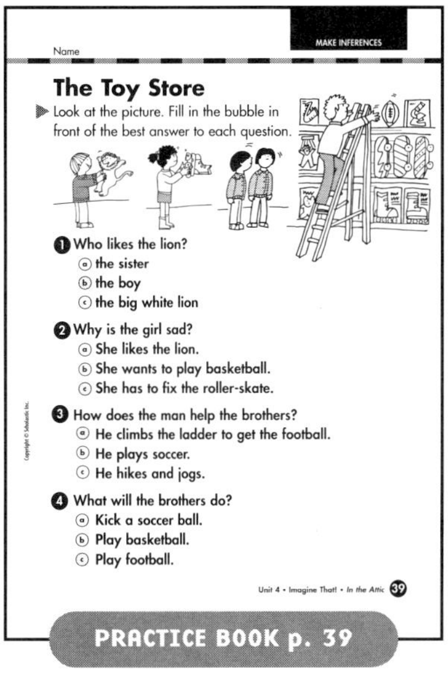
Name

MAKE INFERENCES

The Toy Store

Look at the picture. Fill in the bubble in front of the best answer to each question.

1. Who likes the lion?
   - (a) the sister
   - (b) the boy
   - (c) the big white lion
2. Why is the girl sad?
   - (a) She likes the lion.
   - (b) She wants to play basketball.
   - (c) She has to fix the roller-skate.
3. How does the man help the brothers?
   - (a) He climbs the ladder to get the football.
   - (b) He plays soccer.
   - (c) He hikes and jogs.
4. What will the brothers do?
   - (a) Kick a soccer ball.
   - (b) Play basketball.
   - (c) Play football.

Unit 4 • Imagine That! • *In the Attic* 39

Copyright © Scholastic Inc.

PRACTICE BOOK p. 39

Categorize Information

OBJECTIVE
- Children review how to categorize information.

MATERIALS
- Anthology, pp. 46–70
- Practice Book, p. 40

SUGGESTED GROUPING
- Small group or individuals

SKILLS TRACE

Categorize Information TESTED
- Introduce, p. T90
- Practice, p. T75
- Review, p. R44

1 REVIEW

Tell children that categorizing, or sorting things into groups, can help them remember and understand the details of a reading selection. Remind them that in order to categorize things, children should first find ways in which those things are alike. Children can then sort the things into groups.

Assemble classroom objects such as pencils, crayons, and pens. Work with children to categorize the objects in several different ways, such as by color, by function, or by shape.

2 PRACTICE/APPLY

PUT IT IN CONTEXT Have children look at the picture of the boy on pages 54–55 of *In the Attic.* Help children notice that the boy is resting on his back, looking up at many different things. Ask children to look carefully at the objects and name two categories for them. Guide children to recognize that some of the objects are plants and others are insects. Create a chart such as the following. Help children sort the objects in the picture into the category *Plants* or *Insects.*

PLANTS	INSECTS
tulips	butterfly
yellow flowers	moth
grass	beetles
vines	grasshopper
tiny trees	caterpillars

3 ASSESS

DID CHILDREN:

✔ understand the concept of grouping items together according to a common element?

✔ understand categorizing as a way of ordering story information?

IF NOT, TRY THIS:

Look for opportunities in the unit trade books and upcoming selections for children to categorize information.

CHILDREN'S SELF-ASSESSMENT:

✔ Can I find ways that objects are alike?

✔ Can I name categories into which to sort things?

For additional support, see **Practice Book page 40.**

Name
CATEGORIZE INFORMATION
Real or Make Believe?
Categorize the pictures.
Write R below the picture if it is real.
Write M below the picture if it is make believe.
M
1 F
2 R
3 R
4 M
5 M
6 R
7 R
8 M
40 Unit 4 • Imagine That! • In the Attic

PRACTICE BOOK p. 40

PLOT

OBJECTIVE
- Children review plot.

MATERIALS
- Anthology, pp. 74–101
- Practice Book, p. 55

SUGGESTED GROUPING
- Small groups or individuals

SKILLS TRACE
Plot TESTED
- Introduce, p. T150
- Practice, p. T125
- Review, p. R45
- Reteach, p. R56

1 REVIEW

Remind children that plot is an author's plan for a story. Many times the author will organize the events of a story around a problem and how a character solves it. A reader knows that if the problem is solved, there will usually be a happy ending.

2 PRACTICE/APPLY

PUT IT IN CONTEXT Have children revisit *Starring First Grade*. Draw a large problem/solution chart on the chalkboard. After children have reviewed the story, have them dictate a problem that one of the characters had, the steps the character took to solve it, and the final solution to that problem. Children may copy the chart and illustrate the sentences on it.

Problem/Solution Chart
Problem: Jim wants to be the troll.
Steps taken: ________
Solution: ________

3 ASSESS

DID CHILDREN:

✔ understand plot as the author's plan for a story?

✔ identify the problem and solution, main characters, and setting in a story?

✔ follow a sequence of events leading to a solution of a problem?

IF NOT, TRY THIS:

See the **Reteach** lesson on **page R56.**

CHILDREN'S SELF-ASSESSMENT:

✔ Do I understand a character's problem and the things he or she does to solve it?

✔ Do I understand whether the problem is solved at the end of a story?

For additional support, see **Practice Book page 55.**

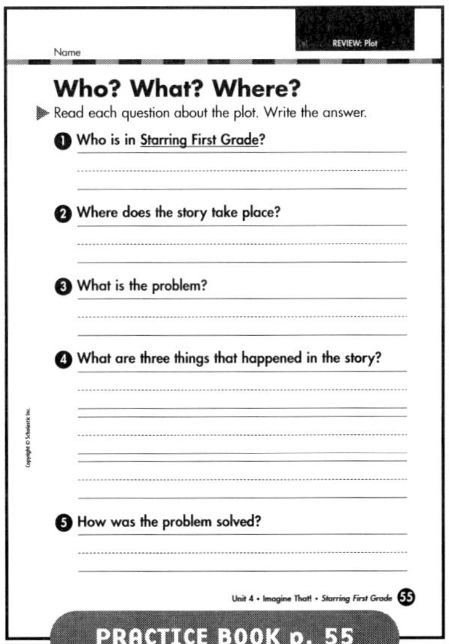
Name REVIEW: Plot

Who? What? Where?

▶ Read each question about the plot. Write the answer.

1. Who is in Starring First Grade?
2. Where does the story take place?
3. What is the problem?
4. What are three things that happened in the story?
5. How was the problem solved?

Unit 4 • Imagine That! • Starring First Grade 55

PRACTICE BOOK p. 55

SEQUENCE

OBJECTIVE

- Children review sequence.

MATERIALS

- Anthology, pp. 106–121
- Practice Book, p. 73

SUGGESTED GROUPING

- Small group or individuals

SKILLS TRACE

Sequence TESTED

- Introduce, p. T210
- Practice, p. T181
- Review, p. R46
- Reteach, p. R57

1 REVIEW

Remind children that in a story, events happen in a certain order. Tell children that there are things they can do to remember this order. Write these steps on the chalkboard or on chart paper. Read these steps aloud several times:

1. **Ask: What happened first, next, and last in the story?**
2. **Retell the story in your own words.**
3. **Ask: Does the order of events make sense?**

Write the following sentences on the chalkboard and read them aloud:

Tiffany and Bill decided to play baseball.

They got their bat and ball.

They went to the park to play.

Help children recognize that only this order makes sense. The children made a decision, got what they needed, and went where they could play baseball.

2 PRACTICE/APPLY

PUT IT IN CONTEXT Set up a sequence chart on the chalkboard with the headings *First, Next, Then,* and *Last.* Ask children to list events from *The Three Billy Goats Gruff* that correspond to these headings. Then encourage children to use the chart to retell the story events in chronological order.

First:	The three billy goats Gruff decide to go up the mountain.
Next:	
Then:	
Last:	

3 ASSESS

DID CHILDREN:

✔ understand the importance of figuring out what happened first, next, and last in a story?

✔ state the sequence of events in a story?

IF NOT, TRY THIS:

See the **Reteach** lesson on **page R57.**

CHILDREN'S SELF-ASSESSMENT:

✔ Can I remember and tell what happens first, next, and last in a story?

For additional support, see **Practice Book page 73.**

Name

SEQUENCE

First, Next, Last

▶ Draw a circle around the best answer to each question.

1. What do the goats do first?
   They go down the mountain.
   They go up the mountain.
   They munch good things.
2. What do they do next?
   They munch good things.
   They take a nap.
   They talk to Troll.
3. What do they do last?
   They play a game.
   They go down the mountain.
   They take a nap.

Unit 4 • Imagine That! • *The Three Billy Goats Gruff* 73

PRACTICE BOOK p. 73

PHONICS: FINAL *e* (*a-e*)

OBJECTIVE

- Children review final *e* (*a-e*).

MATERIALS

- Index cards
- Practice Book, p. 41

SUGGESTED GROUPING

- Small groups or individuals

SKILLS TRACE

Final *e* (*a-e*) TESTED

- Introduce, p. T22
- Practice, pp. T29, T48, T49, T53
- Review, p. R47
- Reteach, p. R57

❶ REVIEW

Say these words: ***make, cake, bake.*** Ask children to repeat the words, elongating the vowel sound /ā/ as they do so. Then isolate the vowel sound and ask children to say it several times after you. Write the words on the chalkboard and point out the final ***e*** in each word. Explain that the letter is often called the ***e***-marker because it signals that the first vowel sound is long.

❷ PRACTICE/APPLY

PUT IT IN CONTEXT Write the following sentences on the chalkboard and read them with children:

The boy found a <u>place</u> to rest.

He <u>made</u> a flying machine.

He found a <u>game</u> that could go on forever.

Have volunteers underline the word in each sentence that has the long ***a*** sound. Then have them frame the final ***e*** in each word. Next, write long and short ***a*** words on index cards. Read the words with children and have them sort the cards into two piles: words with long vowel ***a*** and words with short vowel ***a.*** Use words such as: ***mad, made, cap, cape, pan, pane, can, cane, man, mane, tap, tape, van, vane.***

When the words are sorted, ask children to name other words with /ā/. Have them write the words on index cards and add them to the long ***a*** pile. Point out those that have final ***e.***

❸ ASSESS

DID CHILDREN:

✔ recognize the ***e***-marker and connect the long ***a*** sound with the letters ***a-e***?

✔ distinguish between long and short vowel ***a*** sounds?

✔ generate words with final ***e*** (***a-e***)?

IF NOT, TRY THIS:

See the **Reteach** lesson on **page R57.**

CHILDREN'S SELF-ASSESSMENT:

✔ Do I know that final ***e*** signals that the vowel sound is long?

✔ Can I name some words that have the long ***a*** sound?

For additional support, see **Practice Book page 41.**

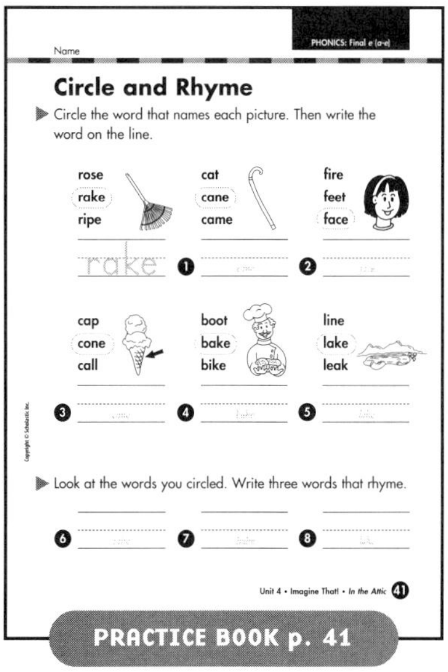
Name

PHONICS: Final e (a-e)

Circle and Rhyme

▶ Circle the word that names each picture. Then write the word on the line.

rose, rake, ripe — rake

❶ cat, cane, came

❷ fire, feet, face

❸ cap, cone, call

❹ boot, bake, bike

❺ line, lake, leak

▶ Look at the words you circled. Write three words that rhyme.

❻ ❼ ❽

Unit 4 • Imagine That! • In the Attic 41

PRACTICE BOOK p. 41

PHONICS: INFLECTIONAL ENDING *-ing*

OBJECTIVES

- Children review inflectional ending *-ing*.

MATERIALS

- Self-sticking notes
- Chart paper
- Practice Book, p. 42

SUGGESTED GROUPING

- Small group or individuals

SKILLS TRACE

Inflectional Ending *-ing* TESTED

- Introduce, p. T46
- Practice, p. T33
- Review, p. R48
- Reteach, p. R58

1 REVIEW

Remind children that some verbs, or action words, end in the letters ***-ing.*** Write the following sentences on the chalkboard and read them with children:

The boy played a game with the tiger.

The boy is playing a game with the tiger.

Ask children which sentence tells about an action that is happening now. Have a volunteer draw a line under the letters ***-ing*** in that sentence. Point out that when the ending ***-ing*** is added to a verb, it often signals that the action is happening now.

Write the following words on the chalkboard and read them with children: ***flying, eating, worked, thinking, opening, climbed, reading.*** Have children name the words that describe actions that are happening now. Call on volunteers to draw a line under the letters ***-ing*** in those words.

2 PRACTICE/APPLY

PUT IT IN CONTEXT Write the following words on the chalkboard: ***rest, talk, look, play.*** Ask children to copy each word onto a self-sticking note and add the ending ***-ing*** to it. Then write the following incomplete sentences on chart paper. Have children complete each sentence by sticking one of their notes in the blank.

I am _____ for someone to play with.

I like _____ to my new friend.

We are _____ a game together.

Now we are _____ in a cool place.

3 ASSESS

DID CHILDREN:

✔ recognize the inflectional ending ***-ing***?

✔ understand that adding ***-ing*** to a word can change the tense of that word?

✔ generate and write words that have the ending ***-ing***?

IF NOT, TRY THIS:

See the **Reteach** lesson on **page R58.**

CHILDREN'S SELF-ASSESSMENT:

✔ Do I know how the ending ***-ing*** changes a word?

✔ Can I use words with ***-ing*** in sentences that tell about now?

For additional support, see **Practice Book page 42.**

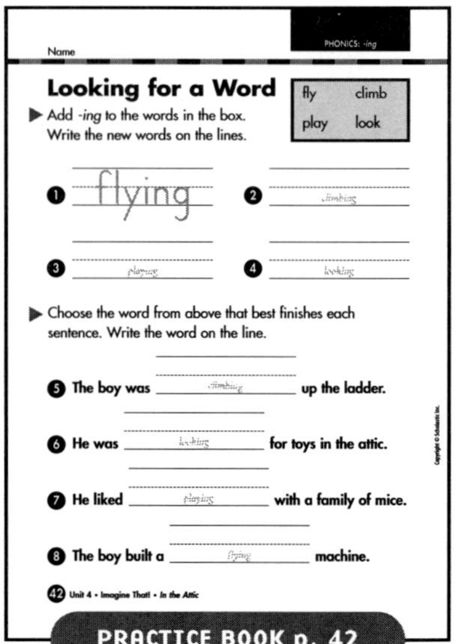

Name

PHONICS: -ing

Looking for a Word

fly climb play look

▶ Add *-ing* to the words in the box. Write the new words on the lines.

1 flying 2 climbing

3 playing 4 looking

▶ Choose the word from above that best finishes each sentence. Write the word on the line.

5 The boy was climbing up the ladder.

6 He was looking for toys in the attic.

7 He liked playing with a family of mice.

8 The boy built a flying machine.

42 Unit 4 • Imagine That! • In the Attic

PRACTICE BOOK p. 42

Phonics: Final *e* (*e-e*, *i-e*, *o-e*, *u-e*)

OBJECTIVE

- Children review final *e* (*e-e*, *i-e*, *o-e*, *u-e*).

MATERIALS

- Practice Book, p. 57

SUGGESTED GROUPING

- Small groups or individuals

SKILLS TRACE

Final *e* TESTED

- Introduce, p. T70
- Practice, pp. T77, T94, T95
- Review, p. R49
- Reteach, p. R58

1 REVIEW

Say these words: ***hide, ride, side.*** Ask children to repeat the words, elongating the vowel sound /ī/ as they do so. Then isolate the vowel sound and ask children to say it several times after you. Write the words on the chalkboard and point out the final ***e*** in each word. Remind children that the letter is called the ***e***-marker because it signals that the first vowel sound is long. Follow the same procedure with the following sets of words:

Eve	**bone**	**cute**
Pete	**hope**	**cube**
these	**hole**	**huge**

2 PRACTICE/APPLY

PUT IT IN CONTEXT Write the headings *Short Vowels* and *Long Vowels* on the chalkboard. Display the following list of words: ***mad, made, place, tan, ate, pan, drop, home, rope, hop, hope, spot, dim, dime, kite, ride, it, cut, cute, but, use, mule, hut, step, Steve.*** Ask children to put each word into the appropriate category.

Then write the following sentences on the chalkboard and read them with children. Have children use a long vowel word to complete each sentence.

The children are in first ____. *(grade)*

They act out a play on ____. *(stage)*

Jim ____ under a blue cloth. *(hides)*

Paul and Jim don't talk for a ____ week. *(whole)*

3 ASSESS

DID CHILDREN:

✔ recognize words with an ***e***-marker?

✔ understand the function of the ***e***-marker?

✔ distinguish between long and short vowel sounds?

IF NOT, TRY THIS:

See the **Reteach** lesson on **page R58.**

CHILDREN'S SELF-ASSESSMENT:

✔ Do I know what an ***e***-marker does in a word?

✔ Can I name words with an ***e***-marker?

For additional support, see **Practice Book page 57.**

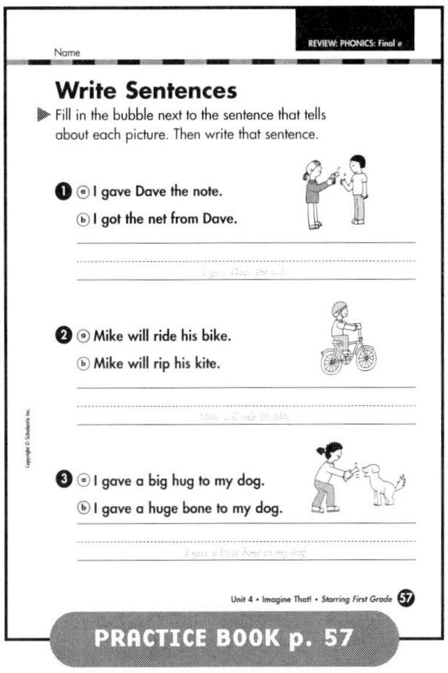
Name
REVIEW: PHONICS: Final *e*

Write Sentences

▶ Fill in the bubble next to the sentence that tells about each picture. Then write that sentence.

1 ⓐ I gave Dave the note.
ⓑ I got the net from Dave.

2 ⓐ Mike will ride his bike.
ⓑ Mike will rip his kite.

3 ⓐ I gave a big hug to my dog.
ⓑ I gave a huge bone to my dog.

Copyright © Scholastic Inc.

Unit 4 • Imagine That! • *Starring First Grade* 57

PRACTICE BOOK p. 57

Phonics: Vowel /ē/*ea, ee*

OBJECTIVE

- Children review vowel /ē/*ea, ee*.

MATERIALS

- Practice Book, p. 56

SUGGESTED GROUPING

- Small groups or individuals

SKILLS TRACE

Vowel /ē/*ea, ee* TESTED

- Introduce, p. T92
- Practice, pp. T81, T99
- Review, p. R50
- Reteach, p. R59

1 REVIEW

Ask children to listen for the vowel sound as you say the following words: ***meat, team, need, seat.*** Isolate the **/ē/** sound and have children repeat it after you. Help children identify the sound as the long ***e*** sound. Then ask children to raise their hands when they hear words with **/ē/.** Recite words such as the following: ***dream, met, feed, deep, clean, sleep, pet, mean.***

On the chalkboard, write the long ***e*** words you recited. Read the words with children. Then point to the letters ***ea*** in ***dream.*** Explain that the letters ***ea*** can stand for **/ē/**—the long ***e*** sound. Point to the vowel letters in ***deep*** and explain that the letters ***ee*** can also stand for **/ē/**. Have volunteers underline the letters that stand for the long ***e*** sound in the remaining words.

2 PRACTICE/APPLY

PUT IT IN CONTEXT Have children construct word ladders for words with ***ee*** and ***ea.*** Ask them to write the words ***lean*** and ***feed.*** Show them how to make new words by changing the initial or final consonant. Suggest some ***ea*** and ***ee*** words for children who need extra help.

Then have children complete the following sentences with long ***e*** words.

_____ person in class had a part in the play. ***(Each)***

The _____ picked Paul to be the troll. ***(teacher)***

Danny was one of the _____ billy goats. ***(three)***

The audience _____ at the end of the play. ***(cheered)***

3 ASSESS

DID CHILDREN:

✔ recognize the **/ē/** sound?

✔ connect the sound **/ē/** with the letters ***ea*** and ***ee***?

✔ read words with **/ē/*ea, ee***?

IF NOT, TRY THIS:

See the **Reteach** lesson on **page R59.**

CHILDREN'S SELF-ASSESSMENT:

✔ Do I know what letters stand for the **/ē/** sound in ***need*** and ***lean***?

For additional support, see **Practice Book page 56.**

REVIEW: PHONICS: Vowel /ē/ ea, ee

Name

Pick the Best Word

▶ Fill in the bubble next to the word that best finishes each sentence. Write the word on the line.

1. We see the _____ as it sits on the rock on the shore.
   (a) step (b) seal (c) seem
2. He has _____ socks on his feet.
   (a) green (b) grab (c) greet
3. See that big dog? It's _____.
   (a) met (b) meet (c) mean
4. He set the _____ out for us to sit on.
   (a) sea (b) sleep (c) seat
5. I will _____ my meal in my lunch bag.
   (a) read (b) teach (c) keep

Copyright © Scholastic Inc.

56 Unit 4 • Imagine That! • *Starring First Grade*

PRACTICE BOOK p. 56

PHONICS: *l*-BLENDS

OBJECTIVE
- Children review *l*-blends.

MATERIALS
- Index cards
- Practice Book, p. 58

SUGGESTED GROUPING
- Small groups or individuals

SKILLS TRACE

l-Blends TESTED
- Introduce, p. T120
- Practice, pp. T131, T154
- Review, p. R51
- Reteach, p. R59

1 REVIEW

Say the words ***block, blade,*** and ***black.*** Ask children to name the two sounds they hear at the beginning of each word. Help them identify the sounds **/bl/**. Repeat with the words ***clock, close, cloud; flap, flag, flame;*** and ***play, please, plane.*** Guide children to recognize the sounds **/kl/**, **/fl/**, and **/pl/**.

Remind children that some words begin with a consonant letter plus the letter ***l.*** Write the words you recited on the chalkboard and read them with children. Draw a line under the *l*-blend in each word as you read it aloud. Help children recognize that the letters ***bl*** stand for the sounds **/bl/**, and the letters ***cl, fl,*** and ***pl*** stand for the sounds **/kl/**, **/fl/**, and **/pl/**.

2 PRACTICE/APPLY

PUT IT IN CONTEXT Write the following sentences on the chalkboard and read them with children. Ask children to name the words in each sentence that begin with an *l*-blend. Have volunteers draw a line under each of those words.

The <u>class</u> put on a <u>play</u>.

The <u>players</u> took their <u>places</u> on the <u>floor</u>.

Anna was a <u>playful</u> <u>flake</u> of snow.

Jim hid under a <u>blue</u> <u>blanket</u>.

The audience <u>clapped</u>.

Ask partners to write the words from the sentences on index cards. Then have children mix up their cards and sort the words according to the initial *l*-blend.

3 ASSESS

DID CHILDREN:

✔ identify the sounds of *l*-blends?

✔ connect the letters ***bl, cl, fl,*** and ***pl*** to the sounds **/bl/**, **/kl/**, **/fl/**, and **/pl/**?

✔ read words with **/bl/*bl***, **/kl/*cl***, **/fl/*fl***, and **/pl/*pl***?

IF NOT, TRY THIS:

See the **Reteach** lesson on **page R59.**

CHILDREN'S SELF-ASSESSMENT:

✔ Do I know what letters stand for the sounds **/bl/**, **/kl/**, **/fl/**, and **/pl/**?

For additional support, see **Practice Book page 58.**

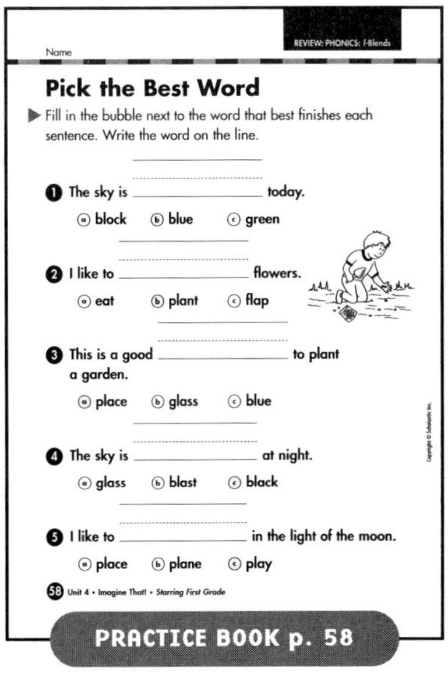
Name REVIEW: PHONICS: *l*-Blends

Pick the Best Word

▶ Fill in the bubble next to the word that best finishes each sentence. Write the word on the line.

1. The sky is ________ today.
   (a) block (b) blue (c) green
2. I like to ________ flowers.
   (a) eat (b) plant (c) flap
3. This is a good ________ to plant a garden.
   (a) place (b) glass (c) blue
4. The sky is ________ at night.
   (a) glass (b) blast (c) black
5. I like to ________ in the light of the moon.
   (a) place (b) plane (c) play

58 Unit 4 • Imagine That! • *Starring First Grade*

Copyright © Scholastic Inc.

PRACTICE BOOK p. 58

PHONICS: *r*-BLENDS

OBJECTIVE
- Children review *r*-blends.

MATERIALS
- Index cards
- Practice Book, p. 59

SUGGESTED GROUPING
- Small groups or individuals

SKILLS TRACE

r-Blends TESTED
- Introduce, p. T152
- Practice, pp. T141, T159
- Review, p. R52
- Reteach, p. R60

1 REVIEW

Say the following sentence and ask children to name the two beginning sounds they hear most often in the words: ***Brian's brother made bread for breakfast.*** Help children identify the sounds /**br**/. Repeat with the following sentences, helping children identify the sounds /**kr**/, /**fr**/, /**gr**/, and /**tr**/:

A crowd of crazy crows crossed the creek.

On Friday my friend found a frisky frog.

Grandpa grinned as he greased the griddle.

Trin packed a trunk for his train trip.

Then write the words ***bread, creek, frog, grin,*** and ***trip*** on the chalkboard. Draw a line under the *r*-blend in each word as you read it aloud. Help children identify the two letters that stand for the *r*-blend at the beginning of each word.

2 PRACTICE/APPLY

PUT IT IN CONTEXT Write the following sentences on the chalkboard and read them with children. Ask children to name the words in each sentence that begin with an *r*-blend. Have volunteers draw a line under each of those words.

A troll lived under a bridge.

A group of trees grew nearby.

The frightened goats crossed the bridge.

The troll frowned and growled at them.

Ask children to write words with *r*-blends on index cards. Have groups of children combine their cards and then sort the words according to the initial *r*-blend.

3 ASSESS

DID CHILDREN:

✔ identify the sounds of *r*-blends?

✔ connect the letters ***br, cr, fr, gr,*** and ***tr*** to the sounds /**br**/, /**kr**/, /**fr**/, /**gr**/, and /**tr**/?

✔ read words with /**br**/***br***, /**kr**/***cr***, /**fr**/***fr***, /**gr**/***gr***, and /**tr**/***tr***?

IF NOT, TRY THIS:

See the **Reteach** lesson on **page R60.**

CHILDREN'S SELF-ASSESSMENT:

✔ Do I know what letters stand for the sounds /**br**/, /**kr**/, /**fr**/, /**gr**/, and /**tr**/?

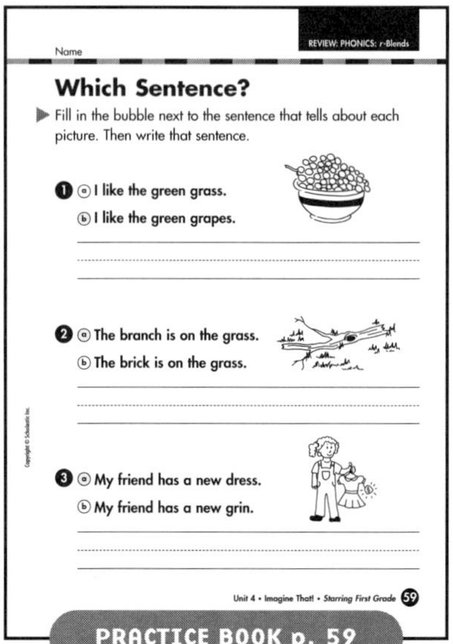
REVIEW: PHONICS: r-Blends
Name
Which Sentence?
Fill in the bubble next to the sentence that tells about each picture. Then write that sentence.
1 ⓐ I like the green grass.
ⓑ I like the green grapes.
2 ⓐ The branch is on the grass.
ⓑ The brick is on the grass.
3 ⓐ My friend has a new dress.
ⓑ My friend has a new grin.
Unit 4 • Imagine That! • Starring First Grade 59

PRACTICE BOOK p. 59

PHONICS: DIGRAPHS /ch/*ch*, /hw/*wh*

OBJECTIVE

- Children review digraphs /ch/*ch*, /hw/*wh*.

MATERIALS

- Practice Book, p. 74

SUGGESTED GROUPING

- Small groups or individuals

SKILLS TRACE

Digraphs /ch/*ch*, /hw/*wh* TESTED

- Introduce, p. T212
- Practice, pp. T197, T215, T219
- Review, p. R53
- Reteach, p. R61

1 REVIEW

Write the words ***chase, cheer,*** and ***much*** on the chalkboard. Read the words as you underline the letters ***ch*** in each. Have children repeat the words after you. Follow the same procedure with ***what, whale,*** and ***why.*** Remind children that sometimes two letters stand for one sound. The letters ***ch*** stand for the beginning sound in ***chase*** and the ending sound in ***much.*** The letters ***wh*** stand for the beginning sound in ***what.***

2 PRACTICE/APPLY

PUT IT IN CONTEXT Draw a Venn diagram on the chalkboard and have children supply words that have the target sounds. Then challenge them to think of a word that has both sounds. Write that word in the intersection. *(which)*

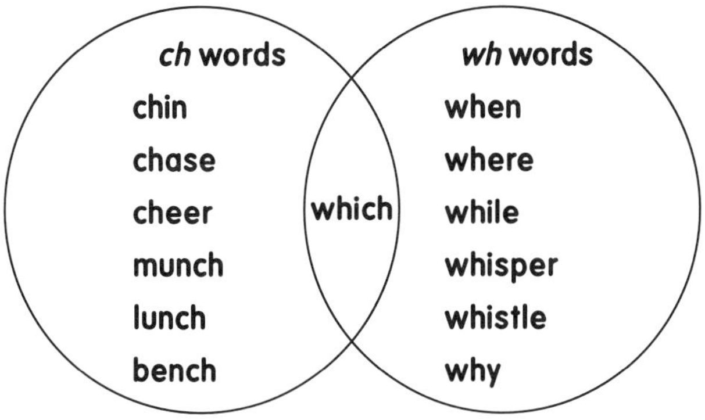
ch words
chin
chase
cheer
munch
lunch
bench
which
wh words
when
where
while
whisper
whistle
why

Ask children to use words from the diagram in sentences about the story *The Three Billy Goats Gruff.* Challenge children to select one word from the ***ch*** group and one from the ***wh*** group to use in the same sentence.

3 ASSESS

DID CHILDREN:

✔ recognize the sounds represented by the letters ***ch*** and ***wh***?

✔ connect the sounds **/ch/** and **/hw/** to the letters ***ch*** and ***wh***?

IF NOT, TRY THIS:

See the **Reteach** lesson on **page R61.**

CHILDREN'S SELF-ASSESSMENT:

✔ What sound do I hear at the beginning of the word ***chair*** and the end of the word ***lunch****?* What letters stand for that sound?

✔ What sound do I hear at the beginning of the words ***what*** *and* ***where***? What letters stand for that sound?

For additional support, see **Practice Book page 74.**

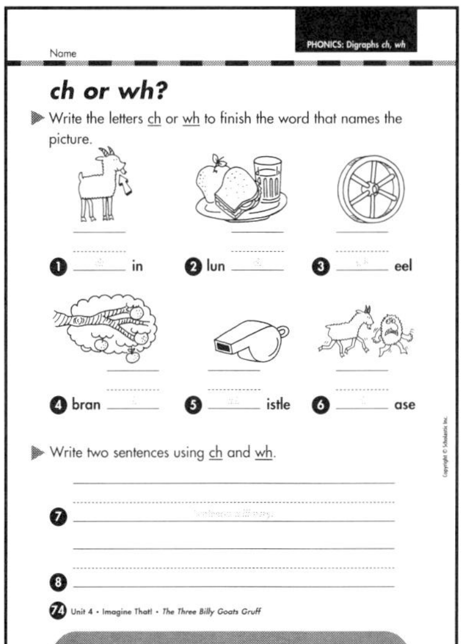
Name
PHONICS: Digraphs ch, wh
ch or wh?
Write the letters ch or wh to finish the word that names the picture.
1 in
2 lun
3 eel
4 bran
5 istle
6 ase
Write two sentences using ch and wh.
7
8
74 Unit 4 • Imagine That! • The Three Billy Goats Gruff

PRACTICE BOOK p. 74

Study Skills: Sort/Organize Information

OBJECTIVE

- Children review how to sort and organize information.

MATERIALS

- Workshop 1
- Practice Book, p. 43

SUGGESTED GROUPING

- Small groups or individuals

SKILLS TRACE

Sort/Organize Information TESTED

- Introduce, p. T100
- Practice, p. T101
- Review, p. R54
- Reteach, p. R62

1 REVIEW

Remind children what they did to create a Story Plan in Workshop 1. Encourage them to recall how they identified characters, settings, and plots in their stories. Ask questions such as:

> **What steps did you go through in making your plan?**

> **Did you think about the whole story at once, or did you work on one part at a time? Which parts did you work on?**

2 PRACTICE/APPLY

PUT IT IN CONTEXT Have children review their story plans. Did each group make a story plan before beginning a mural? Which groups did not? Encourage children to share their experiences. How did creating story plans ahead of time help make the work easier? Did having plans make the work more interesting as well as easier? How do children think that not creating story plans might have affected their work?

Ask children to imagine another story mural they might like to make. Encourage them to work in cooperative groups to make story plans for that mural. As a starting point, suggest that the whole class review their experience with making story plans. What are some good ways to make these plans? Which ways didn't seem to work? Let each group make a new plan, taking advantage of the collective experience of the class.

3 ASSESS

DID CHILDREN:

✔ explain why it's useful to sort and organize information into a story plan before writing?

✔ explain what steps they used to make story plans?

✔ evaluate which ways of making plans worked and which did not?

IF NOT, TRY THIS:

See the **Reteach** lesson on **page R62.**

CHILDREN'S SELF-ASSESSMENT:

✔ When I want to write a story, do I sort and organize information so that I can write the best story possible?

For additional support, see **Practice Book page 43.**

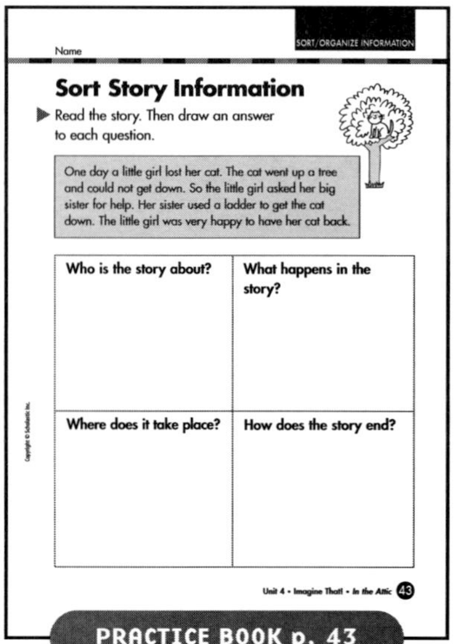

Name SORT/ORGANIZE INFORMATION

Sort Story Information

▶ Read the story. Then draw an answer to each question.

One day a little girl lost her cat. The cat went up a tree and could not get down. So the little girl asked her big sister for help. Her sister used a ladder to get the cat down. The little girl was very happy to have her cat back.

Who is the story about?	What happens in the story?
Where does it take place?	How does the story end?

Unit 4 • Imagine That! • In the Attic 43

PRACTICE BOOK p. 43

Study Skills: Graphic Aids: Pictures

OBJECTIVE

- Children review how to use pictures to acquire information.

MATERIALS

- Workshops 1 and 2
- Practice Book, p. 60

SUGGESTED GROUPING

- Small groups or individuals

SKILLS TRACE

Graphic Aids: Pictures TESTED

- Introduce, p. T160
- Practice, p. T161
- Review, p. R55
- Reteach, p. R63

1 REVIEW

Remind children of how they sketched out part of a story in Workshop 2. Ask them to recall how they compared their own drawings to the picture of Clifford. Then ask them to tell some of the things you can learn from pictures, and some of the things an artist can show or communicate through pictures. Encourage children to also give examples of other situations in which they can get information from pictures rather than words.

> **When is it better to get information from pictures?**

> **What kinds of clues should you look for if you want to find out more?**

2 PRACTICE/APPLY

PUT IT IN CONTEXT Have children review their story mural projects. What kinds of information did they try to communicate through those pictures? What kinds of information were they able to find in murals that other groups made? Encourage groups to look at each other's murals and give feedback about them.

Ask children: *What information do the viewers get from the pictures? Is this the information that the artists intended to convey?* Ask the artists to look at their own murals as if for the first time. Ask them: *What information would you get? What information might be missing or misleading?* Suggest that groups revise their murals using their own and each other's feedback.

3 ASSESS

DID CHILDREN:

✔ explain what kinds of information pictures can provide?

✔ identify information in each other's story murals?

✔ evaluate the information in their own story murals?

IF NOT, TRY THIS:

See the **Reteach** lesson on **page R63.**

CHILDREN'S SELF-ASSESSMENT:

✔ What kinds of clues can I find in pictures that will help me get information?

For additional support, see **Practice Book page 60.**

Name
REVIEW: STUDY SKILLS

Pictures That Tell Stories

▶ Circle the sentence that tells about each picture.

1
The dog is sniffing the cat.
The dog is running away.
The cat is in the hat.

2
The girl and boy fly kites.
The boy plays ball with a friend.
The boy and girl read a book.

3
He can walk.
He can sing.
He can jog.

4
They will fly kites.
They will play basketball.
They will plant vegetables.

60 Unit 4 • Imagine That! • Starring First Grade

PRACTICE BOOK p. 60

Reteach

Make Inferences

1 CONSTRUCT

You walk into the kitchen and there's a carton of milk lying on its side on the kitchen table. The cat is sitting on the table, drinking the spilled milk. What do you think happened? How can you tell?

2 CONNECT

When you figured out that the cat probably knocked over the milk, you made an inference. You put together things that you saw (the cat on the table; the spilled milk) with things that you already knew (cats can jump up on tables; they like to drink milk). When you read, you also see and read about clues, put them together with what you already know, and come up with ideas about what you've read. That way, you can understand more about what you're reading.

Now would be a wonderful time to read with children, making inferences together. The unit trade books can provide you with many opportunities to practice making inferences.

3 CONFIRM

Suppose a friend said, "I don't know how to make inferences!" How would you help your friend realize that he or she makes inferences all the time?

When does it help you to be able to figure out things, the way you figured out how the milk got spilled?

Plot

1 CONSTRUCT

You have an important part in a play. You've tried and tried, but you can't seem to remember your lines. You decide to ask a friend to help you, but he just jokes around and isn't any help at all! Then you ask your aunt who has acted in plays before. She reads through the lines with you. She explains what she does when she studies lines in a play. Suddenly it all comes together. You can remember your lines and read them with feeling! What was your problem? What did you do to try to solve it? What was the solution?

2 CONNECT

Thinking about one of your own problems and how you solved it is just like thinking about the plot of a story. For example, when you read you'll notice that a main character has a problem. He or she will try different ways to solve that problem. Usually the character will succeed in finding a solution. You can enjoy and understand stories more when you notice what is happening in the plot.

This would be a great time to read with children, identifying plots in other stories or books. The unit trade books can be a useful resource for your class.

3 CONFIRM

If a friend asked you for help in figuring out the plot of a story, what would you tell your friend?

How could you explain to your friend the importance of plot in a story?

Sequence

1 CONSTRUCT

You're getting ready to go roller-skating. First, you get dressed. Next, you put on your roller skates. Last, you go outside and start skating. Can you tell what things you did, in the order in which you did them? What would have happened if you had done one of the steps out of order?

2 CONNECT

When you remembered the order of things you did to get ready to go roller-skating, you were noticing and remembering sequence, the order in which events take place. If you notice sequence when you read, you'll understand and remember the story better. Words like *first, next, then,* and *last* can help you notice sequence.

This would be a great time to read with children, identifying the sequence of events as you read. The unit trade books offer many opportunities for this.

3 CONFIRM

Suppose a friend says, "I don't see what difference it makes to have events happen in a certain order. Why can't we start with the last event and end with the first one?" How would you explain sequence to this friend?

When might it help to know the order of events?

Final *e (a-e)*

1 CONSTRUCT

Say the words ***mad*** **and** ***made,*** emphasizing the vowel sound in each word. Ask children which word has /ā/—the long ***a*** sound. Then ask children to write an ***a*** in the air each time they hear a word with the long ***a*** sound. Say words such as ***came, date, bag, game, bat, lake, dad, fan, name, sale, lap,*** and ***wade.***

2 CONNECT

On the chalkboard, write the long ***a*** words you recited. Guide children to see that the final ***e*** signals a long vowel sound. Give each child a blank card and have children write the letter ***e*** on their card. Say short and long ***a*** words such as the following: ***late, cat, save, sat, base, mat, rake, rat,*** and ***gaze.*** Ask children to hold up their card if the word has a final ***e*** marker.

3 CONFIRM

Write the following words on the chalkboard: ***cap, mad, rat, van.*** Ask children to say and write each word. Then have them write each word again, adding a final ***e*** marker to each one. Listen for the long vowel sound as children say each new word.

Inflectional Ending *-ing*

❶ CONSTRUCT

Write the following sentences on the chalkboard and read them with children. Ask children which sentence tells about an action that is happening now.

The children acted in a play.
The children are acting in a play.

Underline the ending ***-ing*** in the word ***acting.*** Remind children that when the ending ***-ing*** is added to a verb, it often signals that an action is happening now.

❷ CONNECT

Write the following sentences on the chalkboard and read them with children. Have children tell if each sentence tells about something happening now or something that happened in the past.

A boy is turning on the lights.
We looked at the stage.
We are waiting for the play to start.
Two boys walked on stage.
We watched them sing and dance.

Draw a line under the sentences that tell about actions that happened in the past. Have children tell you how to change the sentences to make them tell about the present.

❸ CONFIRM

Write the following verbs on the chalkboard: ***cook, play, brush, plant.*** Ask children to write each word, add -***ing,*** and use the word in a sentence that tells about an action that is happening now.

Final *e*

❶ CONSTRUCT

Say the words ***made, bike, note,*** and ***cute*** and have children repeat the words after you. Ask them to name the vowel sound they hear in each word. Help them recognize that each word has a long vowel sound. Then ask children to raise their hands each time they hear a word with a long vowel sound. Say words such as ***cone, lake, sit, mine, rope, hot, kite, use, mule, same,*** and ***can.***

❷ CONNECT

On the chalkboard, write the words with long vowels that you recited. Guide children to see that the final ***e*** signals a long vowel sound. Give each child a blank card and have children write the letter ***e*** on their card. Say words such as the following: ***date, fan, bit, fine, pop, bone, fun,*** and ***cute.*** Ask children to hold up their card if the word has a final ***e*** marker.

❸ CONFIRM

Write the following words on the chalkboard: ***tap, pin, hop, cub.*** Ask children to say and write each word. Then have them write each word again with a final ***e*** marker. Listen for the long vowel sound as children say each new word.

Vowel /ē/ea, ee

❶ CONSTRUCT

Say the following words aloud, emphasizing the long ***e*** sound in each word: ***bean, read, sleep, knee.*** Then ask children to gently slap their knee each time they hear a word with **/ē/**—the same long vowel sound they hear in ***knee.*** Say words such as ***team, cheap, set, deep, help, pen,*** and ***heat.***

❷ CONNECT

Write the long ***e*** words you recited on the chalkboard. Provide index cards and ask children to write ***ea*** on one card and ***ee*** on the other. Have volunteers circle the letters that stand for the long ***e*** sound in each word. Say each word aloud again. Ask children to hold up the card that shows which letters stand for the long ***e*** sound.

❸ CONFIRM

Write ***meat*** and ***feet*** on the chalkboard. Ask children to build words by changing the initial or final consonant in each of the words you wrote. Have children circle the letters in each new word that stand for the long ***e*** sound.

l-Blends

❶ CONSTRUCT

Write the words ***block, clap, flat,*** and ***plane*** on the chalkboard. Read the words aloud, emphasizing the sound of the initial *l*-blend in each. Have children repeat the words after you. Ask them to identify the beginning sounds in each word. Then say the following groups of words. Have children clap when they hear three words in a row that begin with the same two sounds.

black, blink, blue
clap, cat, quit
fly, flame, flip
pan, plane, dime
cloud, clown, clip
blank, bike, pin
phone, face, flake
plan, place, please

❷ CONNECT

Have children write the letters ***bl, cl, fl,*** and ***pl*** on index cards. Say words that begin with the sounds ***/bl/, /kl/, /fl/,*** and ***/pl/.*** Have children hold up a card to show the letters that stand for the two sounds at the beginning of each word.

❸ CONFIRM

Have children number a sheet of paper from 1 to 10. Say the words ***blink, clean, flag, clear, plow, flew, plane, blow, flap,*** and ***class.*** Have children write the two letters that stand for the sounds that they hear at the beginning of each word.

Reteach

r-Blends

❶ CONSTRUCT

Recite the following words and have children repeat the words after you: ***break, creek, free, grin, treat.*** Then write the words on the chalkboard and draw a line under the initial blend in each.

break creek free grin treat

Say the following words and have children take turns going to the chalkboard and pointing to the word that begins with the same two sounds: ***broom, tree, grow, cross, frog, train, bread, frown, crate, ground.***

❷ CONNECT

Have children write the letters ***br, cr, fr, gr,*** and ***tr*** on craft sticks. Say *r*-blend words such as ***crawl, breeze, trick, grin, from, brick, cream, friend, great,*** and ***trap.*** Have children hold up the appropriate *r*-blend stick to indicate the letters that stand for the beginning sounds in each word.

❸ CONFIRM

Have children number a sheet of paper from 1 to 10. Say ten words that begin with the *r*-blends ***br, cr, fr, gr,*** and ***tr.*** Have children write the two letters that stand for the sounds that they hear at the beginning of each word.

s-Blends

❶ CONSTRUCT

Slowly say the words ***spin, spot,*** and ***spine,*** emphasizing the sounds for the consonant blend ***sp.*** Ask children to listen for the sounds at the beginning of each word. Say words such as the following: ***sit, spoon, pen, spaghetti, spider,*** and ***sun.*** Have children spin when they hear words that have ***/sp/***—the same beginning consonant blend as ***spin.***

Repeat with ***sn,*** asking children to snap their fingers when they hear words with the ***/sn/*** sounds. Then repeat for ***st,*** asking children to stomp their feet when they hear the sounds ***/st/.***

❷ CONNECT

Write ***spin, snap,*** and ***stomp*** on the chalkboard. Say the words aloud and guide children to recognize the two letters that stand for the initial sounds in each word. Then provide blank cards and ask children to write the letters ***s, p, n,*** and ***t*** on separate cards. As you say words beginning with ***sp, sn,*** or ***st,*** ask children to hold up the two letters that make up the beginning sounds they hear.

❸ CONFIRM

Write the following word endings on the chalkboard: ***ack, ill, ub.*** Ask children to build words using these endings and their ***s, p, n,*** and ***t*** cards.

Digraphs /ch/*ch*, /hw/*wh*

❶ CONSTRUCT

Write the words ***chin*** and ***lunch*** on the chalkboard. Read the words aloud, stressing the sound ***/ch/*** in each word. Have children repeat the words after you. Then say the following words and ask children to point to their chin whenever they hear a word that begins or ends with the sound ***/ch/*** as in ***chin: chair, cot, beach, chip, both, chill, teach, car, much.***

Repeat for the consonant digraph ***/hw/wh*** by asking children to whisper ***yes*** each time they hear a word with the ***/hw/*** sound as in ***whisper.*** Say words such as ***whale, hen, what, wheat, heat, whip, whiz, chain,*** and ***when.***

❷ CONNECT

Give children two blank index cards. Ask them to write ***ch*** on one card and ***wh*** on the other. Say words that have the sound ***/ch/*** or ***/hw/*** in them. Ask children to hold up the appropriate card to show which sound they hear.

❸ CONFIRM

Have children work in pairs. Ask one child to write a list of digraph ***ch*** words. Remind that child that the words can begin or end with the letters ***ch.*** Ask the other child to make a list of digraph ***wh*** words. Have children read aloud each other's list of words. Then encourage children to create sentences using words from both lists.

Contractions

❶ CONSTRUCT

Write the following sentences on the chalkboard and read them aloud:

Maria is not here today.
She's sick.

Look at the second sentence, "She's sick." Can you think of another way to write this sentence? What two words mean the same thing as *she's?*

❷ CONNECT

The word *she's* is a contraction. A contraction is a way of combining two small words into one word. The apostrophe shows that one or more letters were left out when the words were put together. When you read and write, look for an apostrophe. It may tell you that the word is a contraction.

Take this opportunity to look for contractions in materials you are reading with children. The unit trade books provide outside reading possibilities.

❸ CONFIRM

How do you form contractions? When do you use contractions?

How does knowing how to form contractions help you when you read and write?

Plurals

1 CONSTRUCT

You and a friend are walking your dogs together. Suddenly the dogs see a squirrel. The dogs take off together, pulling their leashes out of your hands. "We'd better go after them," your friend says. "You know what will happen if they get into Mrs. Pittman's garden!" Before your friend can say anything else, you hear Mrs. Pittman's voice. "Whose dogs are these?" she yells. Do you think she has spotted just your dog, or are both of the dogs in the garden? What makes you think so?

2 CONNECT

When you heard Mrs. Pittman ask about the dogs, you knew that both you and your friend were in trouble! The *s* at the end of the naming word *dog* signaled that the word was naming more than one. When you read, you'll often notice naming words that end with an *s*. These naming words stand for more than one person, place, or thing.

Take this opportunity to look for other plurals as you read with children. The unit trade books provide a good resource for additional reading materials.

3 CONFIRM

You want to change a naming word to make it mean more than one. How can you change the word?

How do you use plurals in your everyday conversations with friends?

Sort/Organize Information

1 CONSTRUCT

You just had an exciting experience. While you were riding home on your bike, you noticed a cat stuck in a tree. You tried to coax it down, but it wouldn't budge. A neighbor saw what was happening and called the fire department. As you watched, a fire truck arrived and a firefighter climbed up into the tree to rescue the frightened cat. You rush home to tell your mother all the details, but she's about to leave to take your sister to the dentist. You have to talk fast! How can you sort out what to tell your mom?

2 CONNECT

When you figured out what to tell your mom about your experience, you were sorting and organizing information. You can do the same thing when you read and write stories, sorting out people (the character), places (the setting), and the things that happened (the plot).

This is a good time to focus on sorting and organizing as you read with children. The unit trade books provide great opportunities for children to practice this skill.

3 CONFIRM

Suppose something exciting happens to a friend, but your friend doesn't know how to tell about it in a clear and interesting way. What advice would you give your friend?

Why is it useful to know how to sort and organize information?

Graphic Aids/ Pictures

1 CONSTRUCT

Imagine that someone has given you a comic book in a foreign language. You can't read any of the words, but you can look at the pictures. You leaf through the book and discover that you can actually follow the story! A villain is trying to steal something, but a hero appears. The villain tries to get away, but the hero stops him. How did you know what was happening?

2 CONNECT

When you saw the pictures in the comic book, you used the clues you found in them to figure out the story. For example, maybe you could tell who was the hero and who was the villain by the expressions on their faces, the clothes they wore, or the way other people looked at them. In the same way, you can also use pictures to give you clues about other things you read.

Now would be a wonderful time to read with children, looking at illustrations and identifying picture clues. The unit trade books can be an excellent resource.

3 CONFIRM

What if you had a friend who always looked at the words and never looked at the pictures? How would you tell your friend what he or she was missing?

When is it important to get clues from pictures?

Word Order

RETEACH

The words in a sentence are in order. The order of the words makes sense.

PRACTICE

Write a sentence for each group of words. Begin each sentence with a capital letter. End each sentence with a period.

1. **the dog a bone has**
2. **eats lunch the boy**
3. **likes peanuts elephant the**
4. **cat the mouse the chases**
5. **ball play the girls**

Capitalizing Titles

A title begins with a capital letter. Some titles end with a period.

PRACTICE
Write each title correctly.

1. ms _____ Jones works at the zoo.
2. dr _____ Sanchez works there, too.
3. Our teacher mr _____ Ramon took us to see the animals.
4. We saw a chimp named mrs _____ Banana.
5. We saw a seal named miss _____ Flipper.

Irregular Verbs

The words *have* and *has* are helping words. They are used with *run, come, seen, gone, done,* and *given.*

They are not used with *ran, came, saw, went, did,* and *gave.* These words tell about the past.

PRACTICE
Write the correct word for each sentence.

1. I _____ an elephant jump a fence. (saw, seen)
2. I _____ him some peanuts. (gave, given)
3. Maybe you have _____ that elephant, too. (saw, seen)
4. I know he has _____ back to my house. (come, came)
5. I have _____ to look for him. (gone, went)

Adjectives

RETEACH

A word that tells how something looks is an adjective.

PRACTICE

Tell about a monster.
Use the following adjectives or use others you know.

Size: big, teeny, small, giant-sized
Shape: round, fat, square, cone, box
Color: green, purple, blue, pink, yellow
Feel: rough, scaly, smooth

1. I saw a _____ monster. (size)
2. It had _____ toes. (how many)
3. It was _____ and _____. (colors)

Capitalizing Names and First Words

RETEACH

A sentence begins with a capital letter.
A proper name begins with a capital letter.

PRACTICE

Find the errors in each sentence. Write each sentence correctly.

1. our dog is brown and black.
2. his name is spot.
3. we have a cat named fluffy, too.
4. she likes to run in my friend tom's yard.
5. fluffy and spot do not like to play together.

Name

WEEK 1

lemon	sun
sky	king
cave	cake

Copyright © Scholastic Inc.

Teacher Note: The words above are story words. You may use the blank cards to add additional words.

Name

TEACHER RESOURCES

WEEK 1

soon	went

Copyright © Scholastic Inc.

Teacher Note: The words above are high-frequency words.
You may use the blank cards to add additional words.

Name

WEEK 2

stars	planets
night	shine
moon	light

Copyright © Scholastic Inc.

Teacher Note: The words above are story words. You may use the blank cards to add additional words.

Name

WEEK 2

some

many

Copyright © Scholastic Inc.

Teacher Note: The words above are high-frequency words. You may use the blank cards to add additional words.

Name

WEEK 3

bored	attic
toys	game
talk	ladder

Copyright © Scholastic Inc.

Teacher Note: The words above are story words. You may use the blank cards to add additional words.

Name

WEEK 3

look	about

Copyright © Scholastic Inc.

Teacher Note: The words above are high-frequency words. You may use the blank cards to add additional words.

Name

WEEK 4

actors	first
story	play
troll	goat

Copyright © Scholastic Inc.

Teacher Note: The words above are story words. You may use the blank cards to add additional words.

Name

WEEK 4

which

make

Copyright © Scholastic Inc.

Teacher Note: The words above are high-frequency words. You may use the blank cards to add additional words.

Name

WEEK 5

problem	lunch
bridge	booth
dime	nickel

Copyright © Scholastic Inc.

Teacher Note: The words above are story words. You may use the blank cards to add additional words.

Name

WEEK 5

were

way

Copyright © Scholastic Inc.

Teacher Note: The words above are high-frequency words. You may use the blank cards to add additional words.

Name

A	B	C	D
E	F	G	H
I	J	K	L
M	N	O	P

Copyright © Scholastic Inc.

Name

TEACHER RESOURCES

Q	R	S	T
U	V	W	X
Y	Z	a	e
i	o	u	CAPITAL LETTERS

Copyright © Scholastic Inc.

Name

a	b	c	d
e	f	g	h
i	j	k	l
m	n	o	p

Copyright © Scholastic Inc.

Name

q	r	s	t
u	v	w	x
y	z	a	e
i	o	u	small letters

Copyright © Scholastic Inc.

Name

WHAT DO YOU HEAR?

Copyright © Scholastic Inc.

Name

Copyright © Scholastic Inc.

Teacher Note: The above picture cards are: bat, bee, bus, cat, coat, cup, dog, duck, fan, fish, fox, leaf, lip, log, man, moon.

Name

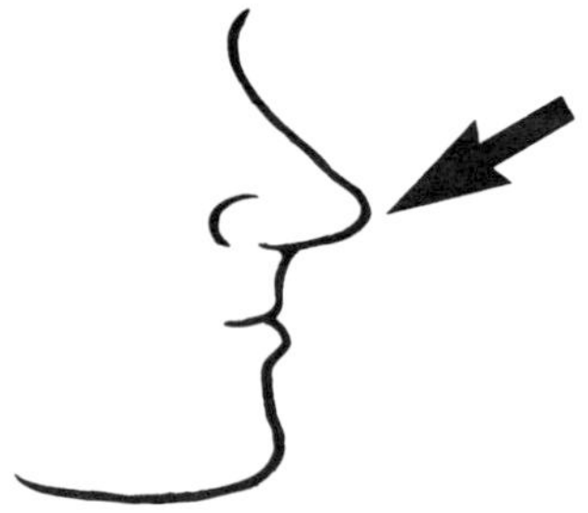

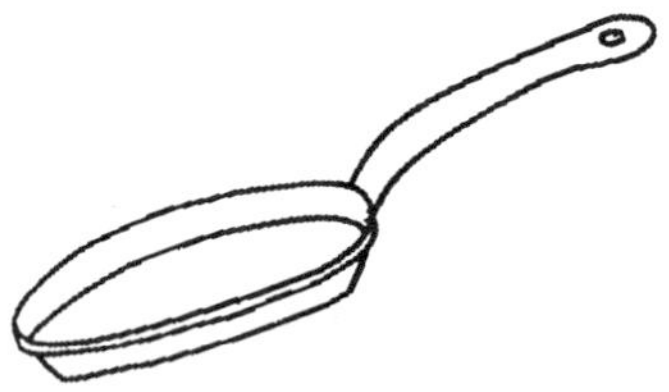

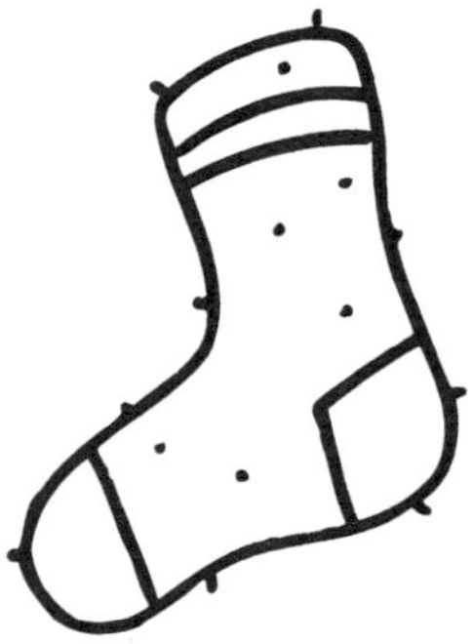

Copyright © Scholastic Inc.

Teacher Note: The above picture cards are: mop, nest, nose, nut, pan, pen, pig, ring, rock, run, six, sock, sun, ten, tie, top.

Name

TEACHER RESOURCES

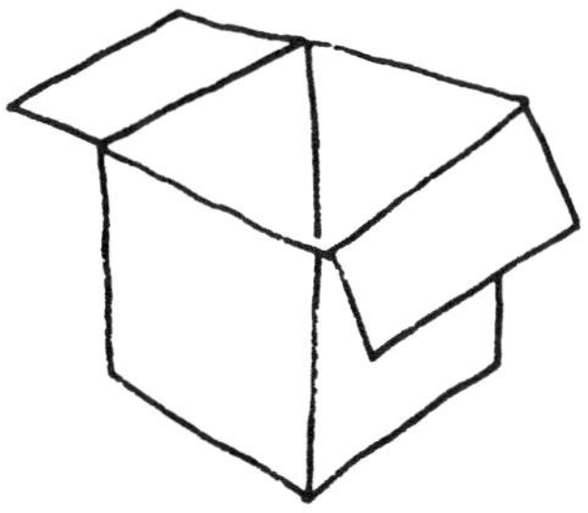
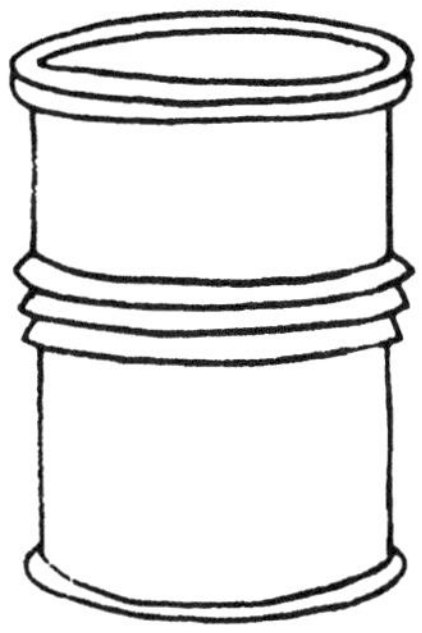
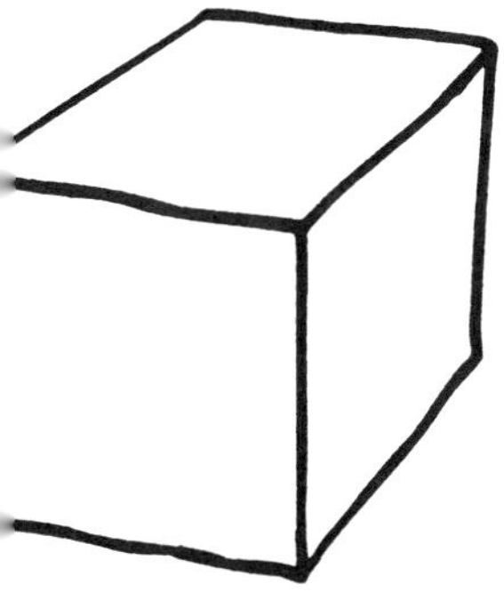

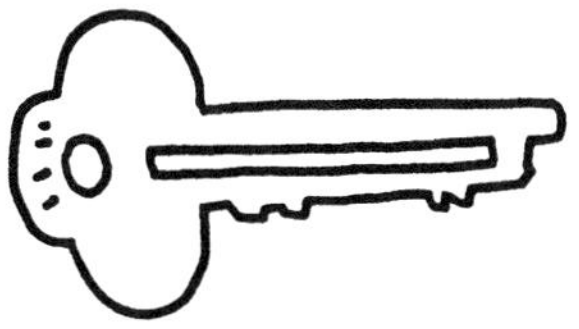

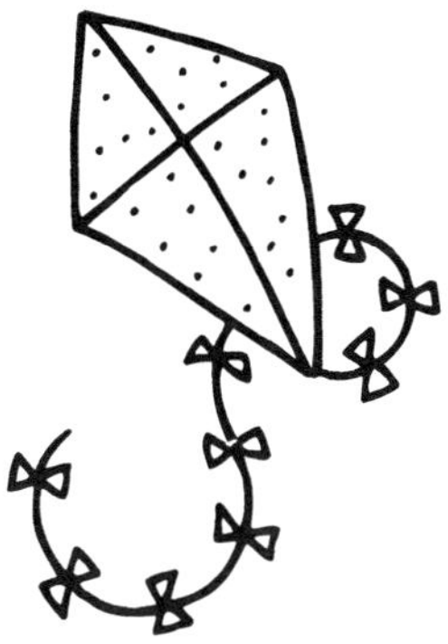
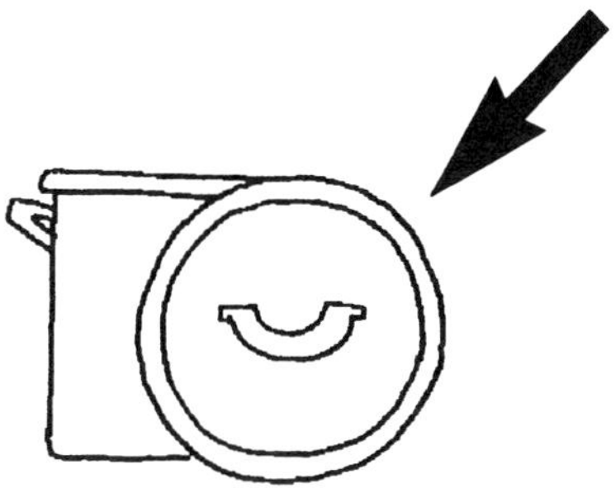

Copyright © Scholastic Inc.

Teacher Note: The above picture cards are: bike, boat, box, can, cube, five, game, goat, hat, house, jump, key, king, kite, lid, light.

Name

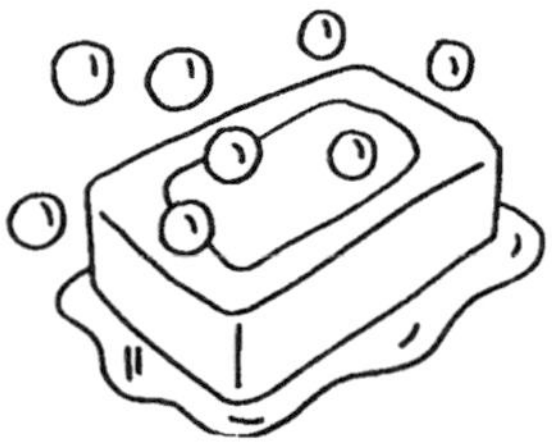

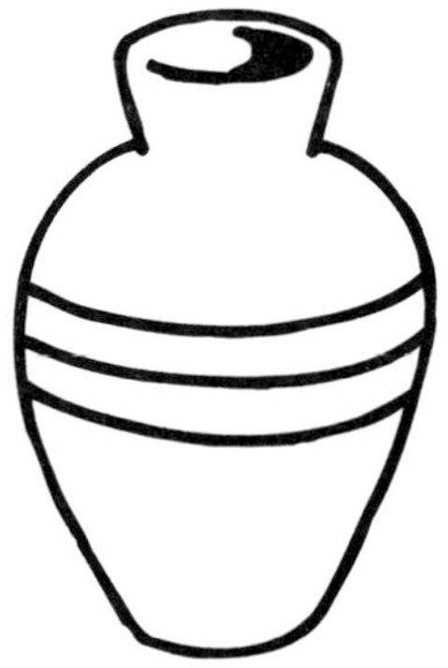

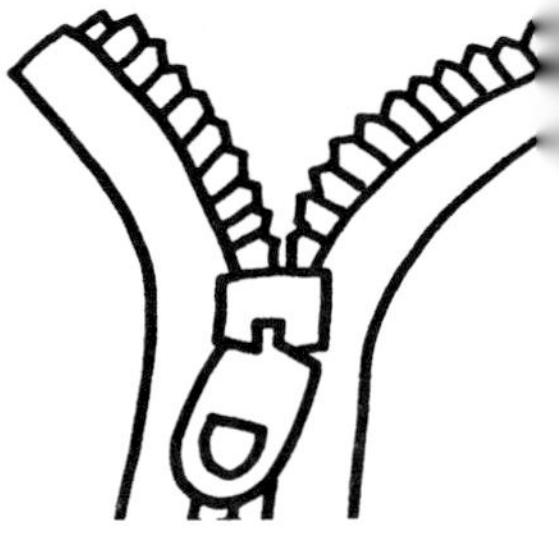

Copyright © Scholastic Inc.

Teacher Note: The above picture cards are: map, mice, nail, net, rain, rake, rose, sit, soap, turtle, vase, vest, web, wig, yarn, zipper.

Name

Book Report

Book Title ____________________

I like this book because ____________________

____

____

____

This picture shows what I like best about the book.

Copyright © Scholastic Inc.

Name

STORYBOARD

Story Title ______________________________

Write or draw the story's events in the order in which they happened.

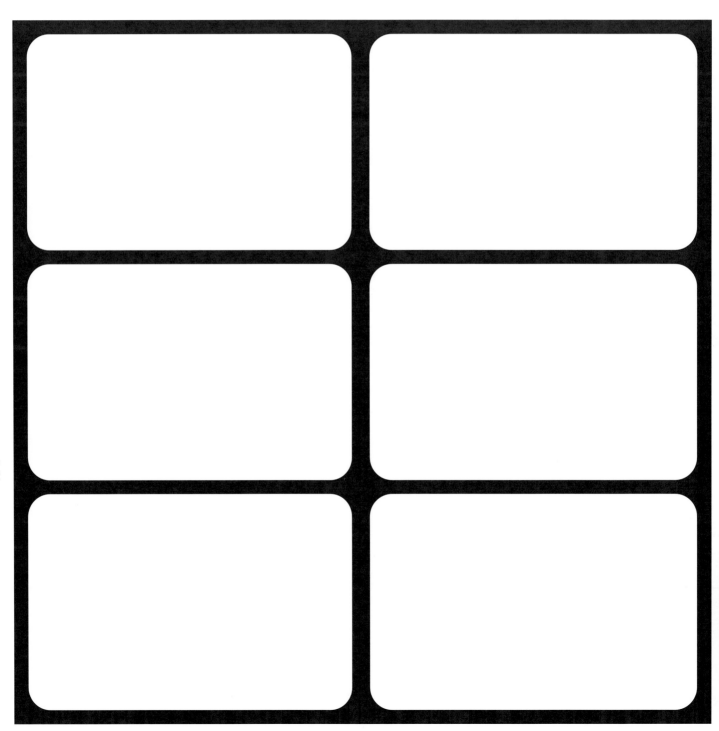

Copyright © Scholastic Inc.

Name

Story Map

Story Title ______________________________

Characters

Setting

Problem

Important Events

Solution

Copyright © Scholastic Inc.

Name

CHARACTER OF THE WEEK

Story Title ____________________

Draw a cartoon strip about your favorite character in the story. You can illustrate what you've read or make up a new story.

LITERACY PLACE

Copyright © Scholastic Inc.

Name

Mama, Do You Love Me?

Copyright © Scholastic Inc.

Name

CHARACTER OUTLINE

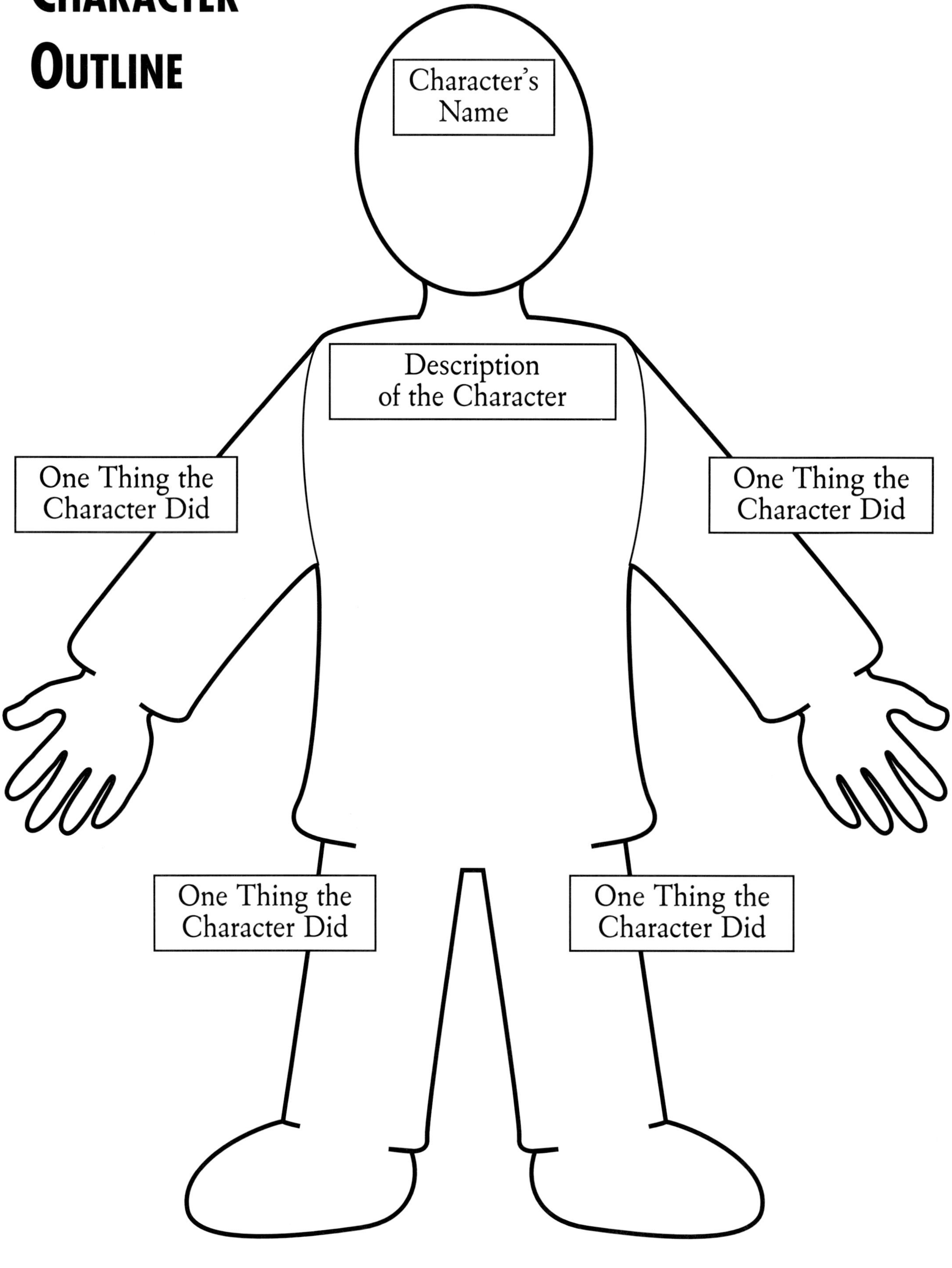
Character's Name
Description of the Character
One Thing the Character Did
One Thing the Character Did
One Thing the Character Did
One Thing the Character Did

Copyright © Scholastic Inc.

Name

Sound Bingo Game Board

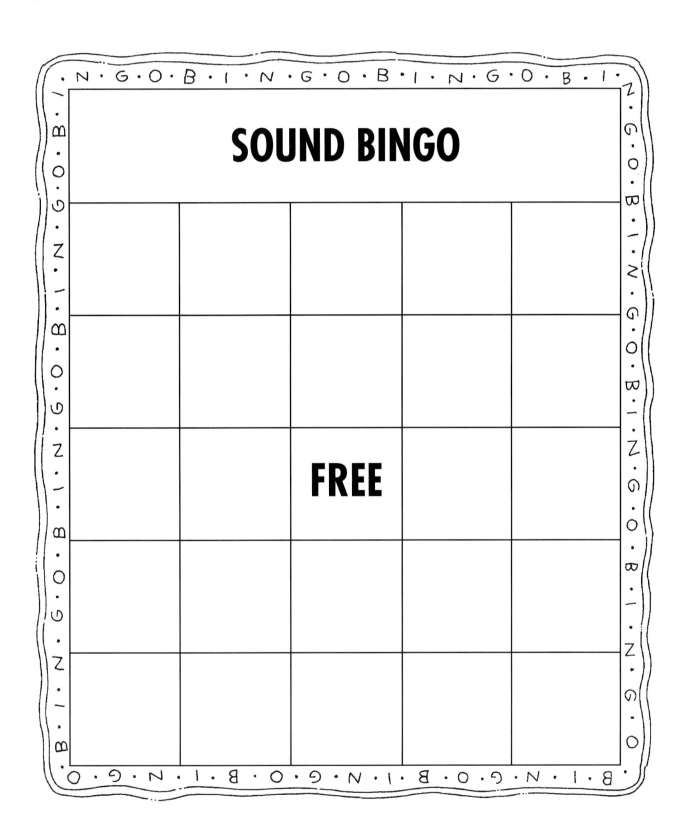

SOUND BINGO

		FREE		

Copyright © Scholastic Inc.

Name

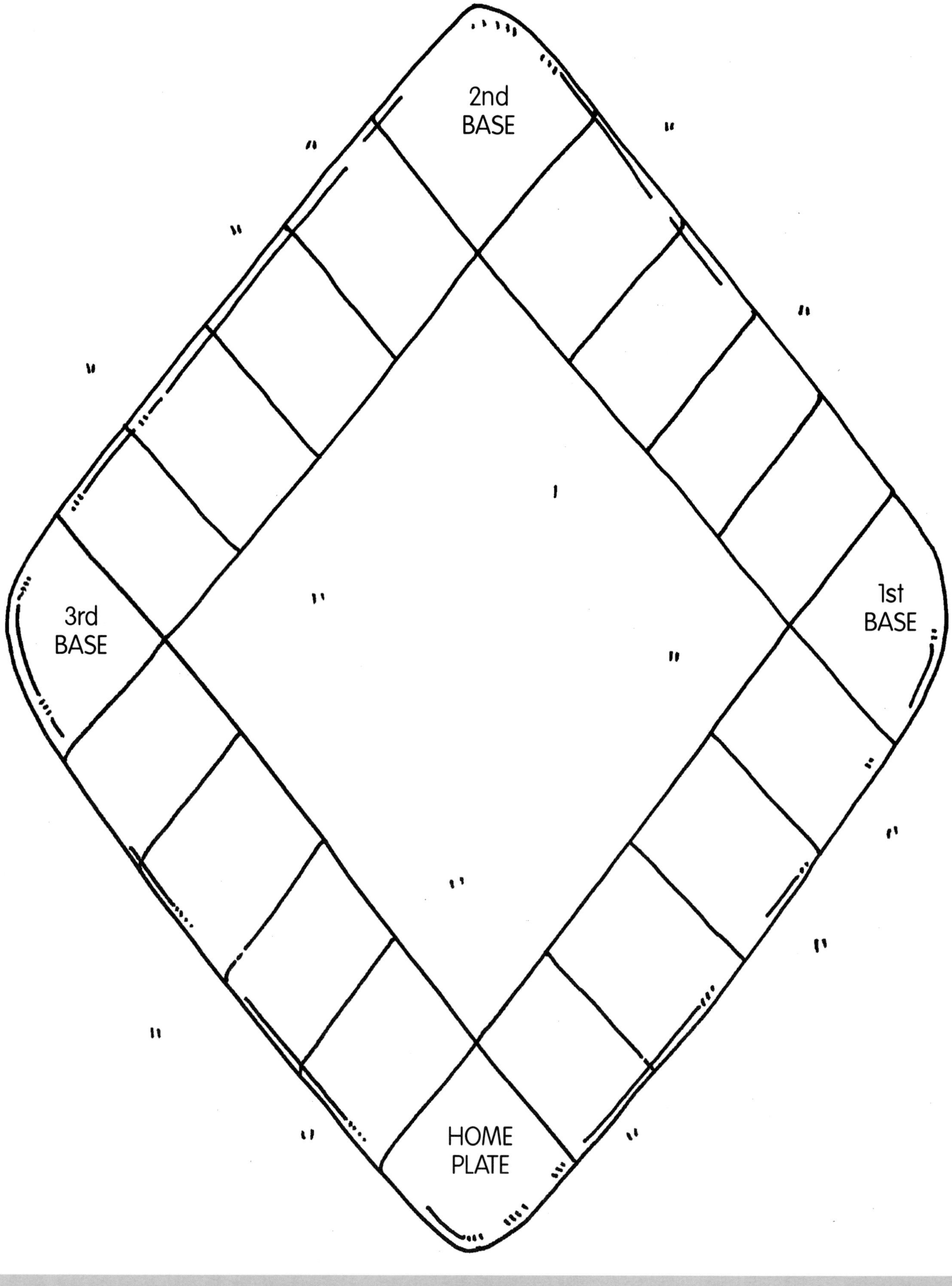
2nd
BASE
3rd
BASE
1st
BASE
HOME
PLATE

Copyright © Scholastic Inc.

Phonics Scope and Sequence

		Student Name										
UNIT 1												
Kindergarten Transition												
WEEK 1	Phonograms *-at, -an*											
	Review Consonants in Initial Position											
WEEK 2	Phonograms *-ot, -op*											
	Review Consonants in Initial Position											
Beginning with week 3, all consonants are taught in initial, medial, and final positions.												
WEEK 3	Consonant /m/*m*											
	Vowel /a/*a*											
WEEK 4	Consonant /l/*l*											
	Consonant /t/*t*											
WEEK 5	Consonant /s/*s*											
	Vowel /o/*o*											
UNIT 2												
WEEK 1	Consonant /h/*h*											
	Vowel /i/*i*											
WEEK 2	Consonant /p/*p*											
	Consonant /f/*f*											
	Consonant /n/*n*											
WEEK 3	Consonant /k/*c*											
	Consonant /b/*b*											
WEEK 4	Consonant /w/*w*											
	Consonant /j/*j*											
	Consonant /z/*z*											
WEEK 5	Consonant /d/*d*											
	Consonant /r/*r*											
UNIT 3												
WEEK 1	Vowel /e/*e*											
	Consonant /g/*g*											
	Consonant /ks/*x*											
WEEK 2	Consonant /k/*k, ck*											
	Vowel /u/*u*											
WEEK 3	Digraph /th/*th*											
	Consonant /z/*s*											
	Consonant /y/*y*											
WEEK 4	Consonant /v/*v*											
	Consonant /kw/*qu*											
WEEK 5	Digraph /sh/*sh*											
	Mid-Year Review											

Phonics Scope and Sequence

		Student Name										
UNIT 4												
WEEK 1	Final *e* (*a-e*)											
	Inflectional Ending *-ing*											
WEEK 2	Final *e* (*e-e, i-e, o-e, u-e*)											
	Vowel /ē/*ea, ee*											
WEEK 3	*l*-Blends											
	r-Blends											
WEEK 4	*s*-Blends											
	Digraph /ch/*ch*											
	Digraph /hw/*wh*											
WEEK 5	Contractions											
	Plurals											
UNIT 5												
WEEK 1	Homophones											
WEEK 2	Words With /ô/*all, aw*											
	Vowel /ā/*ai, ay*											
WEEK 3	Vowel /ō/*oa*											
	Inflectional Ending *-ed* /t/, /d/											
WEEK 4	Vowel /ē/*ey, y*											
	Compound Words											
WEEK 5	Vowel /ō/*o, ow*											
	r-Controlled Vowel /är/*ar*											
UNIT 6												
WEEK 1	Inflectional Ending -ed /ed/, /t/, /d/											
	Vowel /ī/*-ild, -ind*											
WEEK 2	Diphthong /ou/*ou, ow*											
WEEK 3	Vowel /ī/*igh, y*											
WEEK 4	r-Controlled Vowel /ûr/*ir*											
	r-Controlled Vowel /ôr/*or*											
	Words With /o͞o/*oo*, /o͝o/*oo*											
WEEK 5	r-Controlled Vowel /ûr/*er, ur*											

Grade	K	1	2	3	4	5
Reading						
Print Awareness						
recognize that print messages represent spoken language and convey meaning	•	•				
knows print moves left-right, top-bottom	•	•				
understands that written words are separated by spaces	•	•				
know the difference between individual letters and words	•	•				
know the difference between capital and lowercase letters	•	•				
know the order of the alphabet	•	•				
recognize conventions of capitalization and punctuation	•	•				
understand that spoken words are represented in written language by specific sequences of letters	•	•				
recognize parts of a book	•	•	•	•	•	•
recognize that there are correct spellings	•	•	•	•	•	•
recognize distinguishing features of paragraphs			•	•	•	•
Phonological Awareness						
divide sentences into individual words	•	•	•			
identify, segment, and combine syllables	•	•	•	•		
produce and distinguish rhyming words from non-rhyming	•	•	•	•		
identify and isolate initial and final sounds	•	•	•	•		
blend sounds	•	•	•	•		
segment one-syllable words into individual phonemes clearly producing beginning, medial, and final sounds	•	•	•	•		
Letter-Sound Relationships						
name and identify each letter of the alphabet	•	•				
understand that written words are composed of letters that represent sounds	•	•				
learn and apply letter-sound correspondences of:						
consonants (beginning, middle, end)	•	•	•			
short vowel sounds	•	•	•			
phonograms/word families/patterns	•	•	•			
digraphs		•	•	•	•	•
blends		•	•	•	•	•
long vowel sounds		•	•	•	•	•
diphthongs		•	•	•	•	•
variant vowels		•	•	•	•	•
blend initial letter-sounds with common vowel spelling patterns to read words	•	•	•	•		
decode by using all letter-sound correspondences within regularly spelled words	•	•	•	•	•	•
use letter-sound knowledge to read decodable texts	•	•	•	•		

Scope and Sequence

GRADE	K	1	2	3	4	5
Word Identification						
decode by using all letter-sound correspondences within a word	•	•	•	•	•	•
use common spelling patterns to read words	•	•	•	•	•	•
use structural cues to recognize compounds, base words, and inflectional endings		•	•	•	•	•
use structural cues to recognize prefixes and suffixes			•	•	•	•
use root words and other structural cues to recognize derivational endings			•	•	•	•
identify multisyllabic words by using common syllable patterns			•	•	•	•
recognize high-frequency irregular words	•	•	•	•	•	•
use knowledge or syntax and context to support word identification and confirm meaning	•	•	•	•	•	•
read regular and irregular words automatically		•	•	•	•	•
locate meanings, pronunciations, and derivations of unfamiliar words using dictionaries, glossaries, and other sources		•	•	•	•	•
Fluency						
read regularly in independent-level materials		•	•	•	•	•
read regularly in instructional-level materials		•	•	•	•	•
read orally from familiar texts		•	•	•	•	•
self-select independent-level materials		•	•	•	•	•
read silently for increasing amounts of time		•	•	•	•	•
demonstrate characteristics of fluent and effective reading		•	•	•	•	•
adjust reading rate based on purpose		•	•	•	•	•
read aloud		•	•	•	•	•
Text Structures/Literary Concepts						
distinguish different forms of texts	•	•	•	•	•	•
understand simple story structure	•	•	•	•	•	•
distinguish fiction from nonfiction	•	•	•	•	•	•
distinguish fact from fantasy	•	•	•	•	•	•
distinguish among types of text	•	•	•	•	•	•
distinguish between roles of the author and illustrator	•	•	•	•	•	•
identify text as narrative or expository			•	•	•	•
compare communication in different forms	•	•	•	•	•	•
understand and identify literary terms	•	•	•	•	•	•
analyze characters	•	•	•	•	•	•
identify importance of setting	•	•	•	•	•	•
recognize and analyze story problem/plot and resolution	•	•	•	•	•	•
judge internal consistency or logic of stories and texts		•	•	•	•	•
recognize that authors organize information in specific ways		•	•	•	•	•

• = direct instruction   = mastery

GRADE	K	1	2	3	4	5
identify purposes of different types of texts	•	•	•	•	•	•
recognize the distinguishing features of genres		•	•	•	•	•
describe the author's perspective or point of view			•	•	•	•
Variety of Texts						
read fiction, nonfiction, and poetry for pleasure and information	•	•	•	•	•	•
use graphs, charts, signs, captions and other informational texts to acquire information	•	•	•	•	•	•
read classic and contemporary works	•	•	•	•	•	•
read from print a variety of genres for pleasure and information	•	•	•	•	•	•
read from electronic sources a variety of genres for pleasure and information	•	•	•	•	•	•
read to accomplish various purposes		•	•	•	•	•
select varied sources, i.e., nonfiction, novels, textbooks, newspapers and magazines for information and pleasure		•	•	•	•	•
read for varied purposes, i.e., to be informed, entertained, appreciate writer's craft, and discover models for writing		•	•	•	•	•
Vocabulary Development						
discuss meanings and develop vocabulary through meaningful/concrete experiences	•	•	•	•	•	•
develop vocabulary by listening and discussing selections read aloud	•	•	•	•	•	•
identify words that name persons, places or things, and actions	•	•	•	•	•	•
use dictionaries, glossaries, technology, and context to build word meanings and confirm pronunciation		•	•	•	•	•
demonstrate knowledge of synonyms, antonyms and multiple-meaning words		•	•	•	•	•
draw on experiences to bring meanings to words in context		•	•	•	•	•
use thesaurus, synonym finder, dictionary and software to clarify meanings and usage				•	•	•
determining meanings of derivatives by applying knowledge of root words and affixes			•	•	•	•
use curricular content areas and current events to study words			•	•	•	•
Comprehension						
use prior knowledge and experiences	•	•	•	•	•	•
establish purposes for reading	•	•	•	•	•	•
retell or act out the order of events in stories	•	•	•	•	•	•
monitor own comprehension		•	•	•	•	•
draw, discuss, and describe visual and mental images		•	•	•	•	•
make and explain inferences, i.e., determining important ideas, causes and effects, making predictions, and drawing conclusions		•	•	•	•	•
identify similarities and differences in topics, characters, problems, and themes	•	•	•	•	•	•
produce summaries of text selections		•	•	•	•	•
represent text information through story maps, graphs, charts, outline, time line, or graphic organizer	•	•	•	•	•	•

Scope and Sequence

Grade	K	1	2	3	4	5
distinguish fact from opinion			•	•	•	•
practice different kinds of questions and tasks, including test-like questions		•	•	•	•	•
use cause and effect, or chronology to locate and recall information		•	•	•	•	•
determine main idea and supporting details	•	•	•	•	•	•
paraphrase and summarize text	•	•	•	•	•	•
draw inferences and support with text evidence and experience		•	•	•	•	•
find similarities and differences across texts in treatment, scope, organization		•	•	•	•	•
answer different types and levels of questions, i.e., open-ended, literal, and interpretative; multiple-choice, true-false, and short-answer	•	•	•	•	•	•
Literary Response						
listen to stories read aloud	•	•	•	•	•	•
participate actively during a read aloud of predictable and patterned selections	•	•	•	•		
respond through talk, movement, music, art, drama, and writing	•	•	•	•	•	•
describe how illustrations contribute to text	•	•	•	•	•	•
connect, compare, and contrast ideas, themes, and issues across texts	•	•	•	•	•	•
demonstrate understanding of informational texts through writing, illustrating, demonstrations	•	•	•	•	•	•
support interpretations or conclusions with examples from text		•	•	•	•	•
offer observations, make connections, react, speculate, interpret, and raise questions in response to text	•	•	•	•	•	•
interpret texts through journal writing, discussion, enactment, and media	•	•	•	•	•	•
support responses by referring to relevant aspects of the text and own experiences	•	•	•	•	•	•
Inquiry/Research						
identify and form relevant questions for research	•	•	•	•	•	•
use pictures, print, and people to gather and answer questions	•	•	•	•	•	•
draw conclusions from information gathered	•	•	•	•	•	•
locate and use important areas of the library/media center	•	•	•	•	•	•
use alphabetical order to locate information		•	•	•	•	•
recognize and use parts of a book to locate information	•	•	•	•	•	•
use multiple sources to locate information that addresses questions			•	•	•	•
interpret and use graphic sources of information, i.e., charts, graphs, and diagrams	•	•	•	•	•	•
demonstrate learning through productions and displays	•	•	•	•	•	•
organize information in systematic ways		•	•	•	•	•
use compiled information and knowledge to raise additional unanswered questions				•	•	•
use text organizers to locate and organize information			•	•	•	•
summarize and organize information from multiple sources by taking notes, outlining ideas, or making charts			•	•	•	•

• = direct instruction

(shaded) = mastery

GRADE	K	1	2	3	4	5
Culture						
connect own experiences with life experiences, language, customs, and cultures of others	•	•	•	•	•	•
compare experiences of characters across cultures	•	•	•	•	•	•
compare text events with own and other readers' experiences	•	•	•	•	•	•
determine distinctive and common characteristics of cultures through wide reading	•	•	•	•	•	•
articulate and discuss themes and connections that cross cultures	•	•	•	•	•	•
LISTENING/SPEAKING						
determine purposes	•	•	•	•	•	•
respond to directions and questions	•	•	•	•	•	•
participate in rhymes, songs, conversations and discussions	•	•	•	•	•	•
listen critically to interpret and evaluate	•	•	•	•	•	•
listen to stories and other texts read aloud	•	•	•	•	•	•
identify musical elements of literary language	•	•	•	•	•	•
connect experiences and ideas with those of others	•	•	•	•	•	•
compare language and oral traditions that reflect customs, regions, and cultures	•	•	•	•	•	•
choose appropriate language for audience, purpose, and occasion	•	•	•	•	•	•
use verbal and nonverbal communication when making announcements, directions, introductions	•	•	•	•	•	•
ask and answer relevant questions, and contribute	•	•	•	•	•	•
present dramatics	•	•	•	•	•	•
gain control of grammar	•	•	•	•	•	•
learn vocabulary of school	•	•	•	•		
use vocabulary to describe ideas, feelings, and experiences	•	•	•	•	•	•
support spoken language using props	•	•	•	•	•	•
retell by summarizing or clarifying	•	•	•	•	•	•
eliminate barriers to effective listening	•	•	•	•	•	•
understand major ideas and supporting evidence	•	•	•	•	•	•
interpret messages, purposes, and perspectives	•	•	•	•	•	•
identify and analyze persuasive techniques			•	•	•	•
distinguish between opinion and fact				•	•	•
monitor own understanding		•	•	•	•	•
listen to proficient models of oral reading	•	•	•	•	•	•
describe how language of literature affects listener	•	•	•	•	•	•
assess language choice and delivery				•	•	•
identify how regional labels/sayings reflect regions and cultures				•	•	•
demonstrate skills that reflect interviewing, reporting, requesting and providing information		•	•	•	•	•

Scope and Sequence

Grade	K	1	2	3	4	5
use effective rate, volume, pitch, tone	•	•	•	•	•	•
give precise directions and instructions in games and tasks	•	•	•	•	•	•
clarify and support with evidence, elaborations and examples		•	•	•	•	•
Writing						
Penmanship/Capitalization/Punctuation						
write own name and other important words	•	•				
write each letter of alphabet, capital and lowercase	•	•				
use phonological knowledge to map sounds to letters, in order to write messages	•	•	•	•	•	•
write messages left to right, top to bottom	•	•	•	•		
gain control of pencil grip, paper position, beginning strokes, posture, letter formation, appropriate size, and spacing	•	•				
use word and letter spacing and margins		•	•			
use capitalization and punctuation, i.e., names, first letters in sentences, periods, question marks, exclamation marks, proper nouns, abbreviations, commas, apostrophes, quotation marks, contractions, possessives	•	•	•	•	•	•
write legibly by selecting cursive or manuscript, as appropriate		•	•	•	•	•
Spelling						
write with proficient spelling of: CVC, CVC silent e, one syllable with blends		•	•	•	•	•
inflectional endings: plurals, verb tenses, drop final e when endings are added			•	•	•	•
single-syllable words with r-controlled vowels, final consonants		•	•	•	•	•
orthographic patterns, i.e., consonant doubling, dropping e, changing y to i			•	•	•	•
use resources to find correct spellings, synonyms, and replacements			•	•	•	•
use conventional spelling of familiar words in final drafts		•	•	•	•	•
spell multisyllabic words using regularly spelled phonogram patterns			•	•	•	•
write with more proficient spelling of contractions, compounds, and homonyms		•	•	•	•	•
open and closed syllables, consonant before -le, and syllable boundary patterns			•	•	•	•
spell words ending in -tion and -sion				•	•	•
spell accurately in final drafts		•	•	•	•	•
Composition/Process						
dictate messages	•	•	•			
write labels, notes, and captions for illustrations, possessions, charts, and centers	•	•	•	•	•	•
write to record ideas and reflections	•	•	•	•	•	•
generate ideas before writing on self-selected topics	•	•	•	•	•	•
generate ideas before writing on assigned topics	•	•	•	•	•	•
develop drafts		•	•	•	•	•
use available technology to compose text	•	•	•	•	•	•
revise selected drafts for varied purposes		•	•	•	•	•
revise drafts for coherence, progression, and logical support of ideas		•	•	•	•	•

• = direct instruction   ▢ = mastery

Grade	K	1	2	3	4	5
edit for appropriate grammar, spelling, punctuation, and features of polished writings		•	•	•	•	•
demonstrate understanding of language use and spelling by bringing pieces to final form and "publishing"		•	•	•	•	•
proofread own writing and that of others		•	•	•	•	•
select and use reference materials and resources for writing		•	•	•	•	•
Purposes						
dictate messages	•	•	•			
write labels, notes, and captions for illustrations, possessions, charts, and centers	•	•	•	•	•	•
write to record ideas and reflections	•	•	•	•	•	•
write to express, discover, record, develop, reflect, and refine ideas, and to problem solve	•	•	•	•	•	•
write to communicate with a variety of audiences	•	•	•	•	•	•
write in different forms for different purposes	•	•	•	•	•	•
write to influence			•	•	•	•
write to inform	•	•	•	•	•	•
write to entertain	•	•	•	•	•	•
exhibit an identifiable voice in personal narratives and stories			•	•	•	•
choose the appropriate form for own purpose for writing				•	•	•
use literary devices, i.e., suspense, dialogue, figurative language			•	•	•	•
Grammar/Usage/Mechanics						
use nouns and verbs in sentences	•	•	•	•	•	•
compose complete sentences and use appropriate punctuation	•	•	•	•	•	•
use singular and plural forms of regular nouns		•	•	•	•	•
compose sentences with interesting elaborated subjects				•	•	•
edit writing toward standard grammar and usage		•	•	•	•	•
use correct irregular plurals			•	•	•	•
use singular and plural forms of regular nouns, and adjust verbs for agreement		•	•	•	•	•
compose elaborated sentences and use appropriate punctuation				•	•	•
use regular and irregular plurals correctly			•	•	•	•
write in complete sentences, varying the types			•	•	•	•
employ standard English usage, subject-verb agreement, pronoun referents, and parts of speech		•	•	•	•	•
use adjectives and adverbs		•	•	•	•	•
use prepositional phrases to elaborate written ideas				•	•	•
use conjunctions to connect ideas				•	•	•
use apostrophes in contractions and possessives		•	•	•	•	•
use objective-case pronouns accurately			•	•	•	•

Scope and Sequence

GRADE	K	1	2	3	4	5
Evaluation						
identify the most effective features of a piece by using student and teacher criteria		●	●	●	●	●
respond constructively to others' writing	●	●	●	●	●	●
determine how own writing achieves its purposes		●	●	●	●	●
use published pieces as models	●	●	●	●	●	●
review collection of own work to monitor growth		●	●	●	●	●
apply criteria to evaluate writing		●	●	●	●	●
review a collection of written works to determining its strengths and weaknesses, and to set goals		●	●	●	●	●
Inquiry/Research						
record/dictate questions for investigating	●	●	●	●	●	●
record/dictate own knowledge	●	●	●	●	●	●
take simple notes from sources		●	●	●	●	●
compile notes into outlines, reports, summaries			●	●	●	●
frame questions, to direct research		●	●	●	●	●
organize prior knowledge with graphic organizer	●	●	●	●	●	●
take notes from various sources			●	●	●	●
summarize and organize ideas		●	●	●	●	●
present information in various forms	●	●	●	●	●	●
evaluate own research and raise new questions				●	●	●
Connections						
collaborate with other writers		●	●	●	●	●
correspond with peers or others by e-mail or conventional mail				●	●	●
VIEWING						
Representing/Interpretation						
describe illustrator's choice of style, elements, and media	●	●	●	●	●	●
interpret events and ideas from maps, charts, graphics, video segments, and technology presentations	●	●	●	●	●	●
Representing/Analysis						
interpret and evaluate visual image makers	●	●	●	●	●	●
compare-contrast print, visual, and electronic media	●	●	●	●	●	●
Representing/Production						
select, organize, and produce visuals to complement and extend meanings	●	●	●	●	●	●
produce communications using technology	●	●	●	●	●	●

● = direct instruction   = mastery

Skills and Strategies

Reading Skills and Strategies*

Emergent Literacy

Comprehension/Thinking Strategies

References to the book you're in are in blue. Each unit in Grade 1 is identified by the initials of its theme.

PV	·	Personal Voice: Hello!
PS	·	Problem Solving: Problem Patrol
TW	·	Teamwork: Team Spirit
CE	·	Creative Expression: Imagine That!
MI	·	Managing Information: Information Finders
CI	·	Community Involvement: Hometowns

* Boldface page references indicate full skill lesson.

Index

Index

Phonological Awareness

Cueing Systems

Enrichment

Literary Appreciation

Index

Writing and Language Arts Skills and Strategies

Conventions of Language

Daily Language Practice

Index

Instruction in Oral Language/Listening, Speaking, Viewing

Listening

Speaking

Viewing

Integrated Language Arts

Research and Study Skills

Index

Integrated Curriculum Activities

The Arts

Math

Science

Social Studies

Index

INSTRUCTIONAL ISSUES

Assessment

Portfolio

Tested Skills

Cultural Connections

Index

Grouping Strategies

Classroom Management

Cooperative/Small Groups

Individuals

Partners

Whole Class

Modify Instructions

ESL/ELD

Extra Help

Gifted & Talented

Real-life Connections

Journal

Mentors

Index

LITERATURE

Genre

Drama

Fiction

Myths, Legends, Fables, and Tales

Nonfiction

Poetry

Sources and Text Types

Titles, Authors, and Illustrators

Credits and Acknowledgments

Teacher's Edition

Acknowledgments

Grateful acknowledgment is made to the following sources for permission to reprint from previously published material. The publisher has made diligent efforts to trace the ownership of all copyrighted material in this volume and believes that all necessary permissions have been secured. If any errors or omissions have inadvertently been made, proper corrections will gladly be made in future editions.

Cover: Vince Andriani for Scholastic Inc.

Book Cover Credits: Cover from CURIOUS GEORGE RIDES A BIKE by H.A. Rey. Copyright © 1952 by H.A. Rey. Published by Scholastic Inc., by arrangement with Houghton Mifflin Company. Cover from GOING HOME by Margaret Wild, illustrated by Wayne Harris. Illustrations copyright © 1993 by Wayne Harris. Published by Scholastic Inc. Cover from JENNY'S JOURNEY by Sheila White Samton. Illustrations copyright © 1991 by Sheila Samton. Published by Scholastic Inc., by arrangement with Penguin Putnam Inc. Cover from MAMA, DO YOU LOVE ME? by Barbara M. Joosse, illustrated by Barbara Lavallee. Illustrations copyright © 1991 by Barbara Lavallee. Published by Scholastic Inc., by arrangement with Chronicle Books. Cover from PIERRE: A CAUTIONARY TALE IN FIVE CHAPTERS AND A PROLOGUE by Maurice Sendak. Illustrations copyright © 1962 by Maurice Sendak. Published by Scholastic Inc., by arrangement with HarperCollins Children's Books, a division of HarperCollins Publishers. Cover from THE THREE BILLY-GOATS GRUFF illustrated by Ellen Appleby. Illustrations copyright © 1984 by Ellen Appleby. Published by Scholastic Inc.

Sentence Strips: Text for sentence strips adapted from MAMA, DO YOU LOVE ME? by Barbara M. Joosse. Text copyright © 1991 by Barbara M. Joosse. Published by Scholastic Inc., by arrangement with Chronicle Books. All rights reserved.

Workshop and Project Cards: Workshop 1: Back of card: Photos: c: Francis Clark Westfield for Scholastic Inc.; br: Merry Alpern for Scholastic Inc. Illustrations: John Holm. **Workshop 2:** CLIFFORD and CLIFFORD THE BIG RED DOG are registered trademarks of Norman Bridwell. Published by Scholastic Inc. All rights reserved. Back of card: Photos: c: Francis Clark Westfield for Scholastic Inc.; br: Merry Alpern for Scholastic Inc. Illustrations: John Holm. **Project:** Front of card: Photos: bc: Merry Alpern for Scholastic Inc. Back of card: Photos: tc: Francis Clark Westfield for Scholastic Inc.; br: Merry Alpern for Scholastic Inc. Illustrations: John Holm.

Photography and Illustration Credits

Photos: Photo Stylists: Gayna Hoffman, Shawna Johnston. p. T51: Clara Von Aich for Scholastic Inc. p. T52: Ken O'Donoghue for Scholastic Inc. p. T59: Ken O'Donoghue for Scholastic Inc. p. T61: Lea Desiminis for Scholastic Inc. p. T95: Clara Von Aich for Scholastic Inc. : John Shefelbine for Scholastic Inc. p. T97: Clara Von Aich for Scholastic Inc. p. T110: Clara Von Aich for Scholastic Inc. p. T111: Satoshi Kitamura for Scholastic Inc. p. T125: Ken O'Donoghue for Scholastic Inc. p. T141: © Ken Cole/Animals, Animals. p. T155: Delores Stubblefield Seamster for Scholastic Inc. p. T157: Ken O'Donoghue for Scholastic Inc. p. T167: Miriam Cohen for Scholastic Inc. p. T177: Ken O'Donoghue for Scholastic Inc. p. T183: William Walsh for Scholastic Inc. p. T213: Ken O'Donoghue for Scholastic Inc. p. T215: Clara Von Aich for Scholastic Inc.: Gay Su Pinnell for Scholastic Inc. p. T216: Clara Von Aich for Scholastic Inc. p. T217: Clara Von Aich/Mary Alpern for Scholastic Inc. p. T220: © T. Rosenthal/ Superstock Inc. p. T221: Clara Von Aich for Scholastic Inc. p. T222: Clara Von Aich for Scholastic Inc. p. T226: Clara Von Aich for Scholastic Inc. p. T231: Mike Thaler for Scholastic Inc. p. T265: John Shefelbine for Scholastic Inc. p. T270: Clara Von Aich for Scholastic Inc. p. T275: © Michael Krasowitz/FPG International Corp. p. T285: Clara Von Aich for Scholastic Inc. p. R2: Gay Su Pinnell for Scholastic Inc. p. R3: Clara Von Aich for Scholastic Inc. p. R8: Ken O'Donoghue for Scholastic Inc. p. R9: Clara Von Aich for Scholastic Inc. p. R10: Gay Su Pinnell for Scholastic Inc. p. R11: Ken O'Donoghue for Scholastic Inc. p. R15: © Charlie Palek/Animals, Animals. p. R17: © Charlie Palek/Animals, Animals. p. R18: Gay Su Pinnell for Scholastic Inc. p. R19: Ken O'Donoghue for Scholastic Inc. p. R24: © Breck P. Kent/Animals, Animals. p. R25: © Stephen Dalton/ Animals, Animals. © Zig Leszczysnki/Animals, Animals. p. R26: Gay Su Pinnell for Scholastic Inc. p. R33: © Michael Krassowitz/FPG International.: © T. Rosenthal/Super Stock, Inc. p. R35: Clara Von Aich for Scholastic Inc. p. R40: © Fran Allen/Animals, Animals.

Upfront pages: All reduced facsimiles of Student Anthologies, Teacher Editions, ancillary components, and interior pages are credited, if necessary, in their original publication format.

Illustrations: p. T23: Ari Johnston for Scholastic Inc. p. T47: Shawna Johnston for Scholastic Inc. p. T59: Shawna Johnston for Scholastic Inc. p. T60: Gayna Hoffman for Scholastic Inc. p. T71: Garrett Johnson for Scholastic Inc. p. T84: Michelle Batho for Scholastic Inc. Garrett Johnson for Scholastic Inc. p. T93: Shawna Johnston for Scholastic Inc. p. T105: Emily Wiederhold for Scholastic Inc. p. T106: Shawna Johnston for Scholastic Inc. p. T119: Ben Lloyd for Scholastic Inc.: Rebecca Lloyd for Scholastic Inc. p. T121: Deborah Drummond for Scholastic Inc. p. T153: Gayna Hoffman for Scholastic Inc. p. T165: Gayna Hoffman for Scholastic Inc. Sam Crocker for Scholastic Inc. p. T175: Camille Venti for Scholastic Inc. John Walsh for Scholastic Inc. p. T218: Emily Wiederhold for Scholastic Inc. p. T225: Danny D'Amelio for Scholastic Inc. p. T239: Shawna Johnston for Scholastic Inc. Sam Crocker for Scholastic Inc. p. T263: Deborah Drummond for Scholastic Inc. p. R8: Hope Rathnam for Scholastic Inc. p. R27: Liz Carr for Scholastic Inc. p. R28: Deborah Drummond for Scholastic Inc. p. R91: Rusty Fletcher for Scholastic Inc. p. R92: Rusty Fletcher for Scholastic Inc.

Reduced Student Pages

Acknowledgments

Grateful acknowledgment is made to the following sources for permission to reprint from previously published material. The publisher has made diligent efforts to trace the ownership of all copyrighted material in this volume and believes that all necessary permissions have been secured. If any errors or omissions have inadvertently been made, proper corrections will gladly be made in future editions.

Unit Opener: From IN THE ATTIC by Hiawyn Oram, illustrated by Satoshi Kitamura. Illustrations copyright © 1984 by Satoshi Kitamura. Reprinted by arrangement with Henry Holt & Co. "The Night Sky" from THE NIGHT SKY by Alice Pernick, illustrated by Lisa Desimini. Copyright © 1994 by Scholastic Inc. "In the Attic" from IN THE ATTIC by Hiawyn Oram, illustrated by Satoshi Kitamura. Text copyright © 1984 by Hiawyn Oram. Illustrations copyright © 1984 by Satoshi Kitamura. Reprinted by arrangement with Henry Holt & Co. "By Myself" from HONEY, I LOVE by Eloise Greenfield. Text copyright © 1978 by Eloise Greenfield. Reprinted by permission of HarperCollins Publishers. "Starring First Grade" from STARRING FIRST GRADE by Miriam Cohen, illustrated by Lillian Hoban. Text copyright © 1985 by Miriam Cohen. Illustrations copyright © 1985 by Lillian Hoban. Reprinted by permission of Greenwillow Books, a division of William Morrow & Company, Inc. THE THREE BILLY GOATS GRUFF by Mike Thaler, illustrated by Vincent Andriani. Copyright © 1996 by Scholastic Inc.

Photography and Illustration Credits

Photos: pp. 2br, 2br, 2ml, 6br, 102 bl, 103c: Merry Alpern for Scholastic Inc.; p. 27, Courtesy Alma Flor Ada; p. 45, Moya McAllister for Scholastic Inc.; p. 73, Farrar, Strauss & Giroux; p. 105, Donna F. Aceto for Scholastic Inc.; p. 123, Courtesy Mike Thaler.

Cover: Vince Andriani for Scholastic Inc.

Illustrations: pp.2–3, 22–23:Vince Andriani for Scholastic Inc. pp.6–7: Jackie Snider for Scholastic Inc. pp.8–23:Loretta Lopez for Scholastic Inc. p.42:Eileen Gilbride for Scholastic Inc.

Illustrated Author Photos: pp.105, 27, 123, 73, 45: Gabe DiFiore for Scholastic Inc.